Study Guide
Tony L. Henthorne
University of Southern Mississippi

Principles of Marketing
Twelfth Edition

Philip Kotler
Gary Armstrong

PEARSON

Prentice
Hall

Upper Saddle River, New Jersey 07458

Project Manager: Melissa Pellerano
Production Editor: Carol O'Rourke
Buyer: Carol O'Rourke
Printer/Binder: Bind-Rite Graphics Robbinsville

Pearson Prentice Hall™ is a trademark of Pearson Education, Inc.

10 9 8 7 6 5 4 3 2 1

ISBN-13: 978-0-13-238987-7
ISBN-10:   0-13-238987-8

Table of Contents

Part 4: Extending Marketing

Preface

Congratulations! You have chosen to experience a journey of creativity; critical thinking, strategic challenges, and most importantly, fun! This journey is called the world of marketing and the discipline of marketing is an amazing combination of the best of the business disciplines, a melting pot of finance, advertising, business administration, management, leadership and even a dash of psychology.

This Study Guide has been specifically designed for students using Kotler/Armstrong's *Principles of Marketing*, 12th edition text. Covering all twenty chapters, this Study Guide provides you with an in-depth review of chapter material and the ability to apply the concepts you are learning to the "real world." Use this Study Guide as a valuable resource to support your marketing learning experience. The features of the Guide are described below.

LEARNING OBJECTIVES

Each chapter of the Study Guide contains a list of important learning objectives. Starting off each chapter, these objectives introduce the material to you and provide a checklist of all concepts that will be covered, the fundamental understanding of marketing begins with the real comprehension of terms, and there are many of them.

CHAPTER OVERVIEW

The Chapter Overview summarizes the information contained in each chapter. It will reinforce the main concepts of the chapter and will be helpful when you review the material. It often helps to read the Chapter Overview first.

CHAPTER OUTLINE

This is a thorough outline of the text material, using actual phrases and definitions from the textbook. You may find it helpful to peruse this outline prior to class discussions in order to strengthen your familiarity with the material. After reading the textbook chapter, you may find it useful to again refer to this outline, reviewing important concepts and reflecting on the material. Use a highlighter to reinforce the key concepts and terms.

STUDENT EXERCISES

The nature of marketing is very similar to the role of film director. The marketplace is a fluid stage and you, the marking manager, must respond, choreograph and give stage directions for a successful "show." Each exercise is based on a key term from the chapter and a specific scenario, industry trend or competitive fact that you, as a marketing manager, would react to as the situation arises. Suggested answers can be found at the end of the Study Guide.

MARKETING ADVENTURE EXERCISES

This section of the Study Guide provides a number of specific challenges in the form of exercises to use in conjunction with a bank of advertisements that are available at www.prenhall.com/adventure. For all of the exercises, the category is provided and specific ads noted, around which to develop your response. Suggested answers can be found at the end of the Study Guide.

SUGGESTED ANSWERS

This section offers suggested answers to the STUDENT EXERCISES and MARKETING ADVENTURE EXERCISES offered in each chapter of the Study Guide.

Chapter 1
Marketing: Managing Profitable Customer Relationships

Learning Objectives

1. Define marketing and outline the steps in the marketing process.
2. Explain the importance of understanding customers and the marketplace, and identify the five core marketplace concepts.
3. Identify the key elements of a customer-driven marketing strategy and discuss the marketing management orientations that guide marketing strategy.
4. Discuss customer relationship management, and identify strategies for creating value *for* customers and capturing value *from* customers in return.
5. Describe the major trends and forces that are changing the marketing landscape in this age of relationships.

Chapter Overview

Marketing is part of all of our lives and touches us in some way every day. To be successful, each company that deals with customers on a daily basis must not only be customer-driven, but customer-obsessed. The best way to achieve this objective is to develop a sound marketing function within the organization.

Marketing is defined as "a social and managerial process by which individuals and groups obtain what they need and want through creating and exchanging products and value with others." Marketing is a key factor in business success. The marketing function not only deals with the production and distribution of products and services, but it is also concerned with the ethical and social responsibility functions found in the domestic and global environment.

Marketers must be aware of customer value and customer satisfaction and make these concepts a central part of the firm's strategic plan. Marketing must also be aware of and respond to change. Four of the greatest changes that have had an impact on the way companies bring value to their customers are the explosive growth of the computer, the Internet, telecommunications, and information technology. Marketing and its core concepts, the exchange relationship, the major philosophies of marketing thought and practice, customer relationship management, and marketing challenges in the new "connected" millennium are the major topics presented in this introductory chapter. There is a special emphasis on *connectedness* and the technologies for accomplishing connections.

Chapter Outline

1. Introduction
    a. NASCAR is a great marketing organization. It is the second-highest rated regular season sport on television.
    b. It has a single-minded focus: creating lasting customer relationships.
    c. NASCAR's fans are more loyal to the sport's sponsors than fans of any other sport. Because of this, NASCAR has attracted more than 250 big-name sponsors.
    d. Today's successful companies have one thing in common: they are strongly customer focused and heavily committed to marketing.

2. What Is Marketing?
    a. Marketing, more than any other function, deals with customers.
    b. A simple definition of marketing is managing profitable customer relationships.
    c. Marketing is all around you.

    Marketing Defined
    d. Marketing must be understood in the new sense of satisfying customer needs.
    e. We define marketing as the process by which companies create value for customers and build strong customer relationships in order to capture value from customers in return.

    The Marketing Process
    f. Figure 1.1 presents a simple five-step model of the marketing process.
        i. In the first four steps, companies work to understand consumers, create customer value, and build strong customer relationships.
        ii. In the final step, companies reap the rewards of creating superior customer value.
        iii. By creating value for consumers, they in turn capture value from consumers in the form of sales, profits, and long-term customer equity.

3. Understanding the Marketplace and Consumer Needs
    a. There are five core customer and marketplace concepts.

    Customer Needs, Wants, and Demands
    b. Human needs are states of felt deprivation. They include basic physical needs, social needs, and individual needs.
    c. Wants are the form human needs take as they are shaped by culture and individual personality.
    d. When backed by buying power, wants become demands. Given their wants and resources, people demand products with benefits that add up to the most value and satisfaction.

e. Outstanding companies go to great lengths to learn about and understand customers' needs, wants, and demands. They conduct consumer research and analyze mountains of customer data.

Marketing Offerings—Products, Services, and Experiences

f. Consumers' needs and wants are fulfilled through marketing offerings—some combination of products, services, information, or experiences offered to a market to satisfy a need or want.

g. Marketing offerings are not limited to physical products. They also include services and other entities, such as persons, places, organizations, information, and ideas.

h. Sellers who are so taken with their products that they focus only on existing wants and lose sight of underlying customer needs suffer from "marketing myopia."

i. By orchestrating several services and products, companies create brand experiences for consumers.

Customer Value and Satisfaction

j. Customers form expectations about the value and satisfaction that various marketing offers will deliver and buy accordingly.

k. Marketers must be careful to set the right level of expectations. If they set expectations too low, they may satisfy those who buy but fail to attract enough buyers. If they raise expectations too high, buyers will be disappointed.

l. Customer value and satisfaction are key building blocks for developing and managing customer relationships.

Exchanges and Relationships

m. Marketing occurs when people decide to satisfy needs and wants through exchange relationships.

n. Exchange is the act of obtaining a desired object from someone by offering something in return.

o. Marketing consists of actions taken to build and maintain desirable exchange relationships with target audiences. The goal is to retain customers and grow their business.

Markets

p. A market is the set of actual and potential buyers of a product.

q. Marketing means managing markets to bring about profitable customer relationships.

r. Buyers also carry on marketing. Consumers do marketing when they search for the goods they need at prices they can afford. Company purchasing agents do marketing when they track down sellers and bargain for good terms.

s. Figure 1.2 shows the main elements in a modern marketing system. The company and the competitors send their respective offers and messages to consumers. Major environmental forces affect all of the actors in the system.

t. Each party in the system adds value for the next level.

4.   Designing a Customer-Driven Marketing Strategy

    a. We define marketing management as the art and science of choosing target markets and building profitable customer relationships with them.

    b. The marketing manager's aim is to find, attract, keep, and grow target customers by creating, delivering, and communicating superior customer value.

<u>Selecting Customers to Serve</u>

    c. The company must first decide whom it will serve. It does this by dividing the market into segments of customers (market segmentation) and selecting which segments it will go after (target marketing).

    d. Some companies may seek fewer customers and reduced demand. In cases of excess demand, companies may practice demarketing to reduce the number of customers or to shift their demand temporarily or permanently.

    e. Marketing management is customer management and demand management.

<u>Choosing a Value Proposition</u>

    f. The company must also decide how it will serve targeted customers—how it will differentiate and position itself in the marketplace.

    g. A company's value proposition is the set of benefits or values it promises to deliver to consumers to satisfy their needs.

    h. Value propositions differentiate one brand from another.

<u>Marketing Management Orientations</u>

    i. There are five alternative concepts under which organizations design and carry out their marketing strategies.

    j. The production concept holds that consumers will favor products that are available and highly affordable. Management focuses on improving production and distribution efficiency. The production concept can lead to marketing myopia.

    k. The product concept holds that consumers will favor products that offer the most in quality, performance, and innovative features. Marketing strategy focuses on making continuous product improvements. The product concept can also lead to marketing myopia.

    l. The selling concept holds that consumers will not buy enough of the firm's products unless it undertakes a large-scale selling and promotion effort. This concept is typically practiced with unsought goods—those that buyers normally do not think of buying. Most firms practice the selling concept when they face overcapacity.

m. The marketing concept holds that achieving organizational goals depends on knowing the needs and wants of target markets and delivering the desired satisfactions better than competitors do. This concept is customer centered. Figure 1.3 contrasts the selling concept and the marketing concept.

n. The societal marketing concept holds that the marketing strategy should deliver value to customers in a way that maintains or improves both the consumer's and the society's well-being.

o. Figure 1.4 shows that companies should balance three considerations in setting their marketing strategies: company profits, consumer wants, and society's needs.

5. Preparing a Marketing Plan and Program
   a. The company's marketing strategy outlines which customers the company will serve and how it will create value for these customers.
   b. Next, the marketer constructs a marketing program that will actually deliver the intended value to target customers.
   c. It consists of the firm's marketing mix, the set of marketing tools the firm uses to implement its marketing strategy.
   d. The major marketing mix tools are classified into four broad groups, called the 4 Ps of marketing: product, price, place, and promotion.

6. Building Customer Relationships
   a. The fourth and most important step in the marketing process is building profitable customer relationships.

   Customer Relationship Management
   b. Customer Relationship Management (CRM) is perhaps the most important concept of modern marketing.
   c. It is the overall process of building and maintaining profitable customer relationships by delivering superior customer value and satisfaction.
   d. Customer perceived value is the customer's evaluation of the difference between all the benefits and all the costs of a marketing offer relative to those of competing offers.
   e. Customers often do not judge product values and costs accurately or objectively. They act on perceived value.
   f. Customer satisfaction depends on the product's perceived performance relative to a buyer's expectations.
   g. Highly satisfied customers make repeat purchases and tell others about their good experiences with the product. The key is to match customer expectations with company performance.
   h. The purpose of marketing is to generate customer value profitably.
   i. At one extreme, a company with many low-margin customers may seek to develop basic relationships with them. At the other extreme, in markets with few customers and high margins, sellers want to create full partnerships with key customers.

j. Most leading companies are developing customer loyalty and retention programs. They offer frequency-marketing programs that reward customers who buy frequently or in large amounts.

The Changing Nature of Customer Relationships

k. Companies are targeting fewer, more profitable customers. They are beginning to assess carefully the value of customers to the firm. Called selective relationship management, many companies now use customer profitability analysis to weed out losing customers and target winning ones for pampering.

l. Today's companies are using customer relationship management to retain current customers and build profitable, long-term relationships with them.

m. On average, it costs five to ten times as much to attract a new customer as it does to keep a current customer satisfied.

n. Companies are also connecting more directly. Direct marketing is booming.

Partner Relationship Management

o. Companies must work directly with a variety of marketing partners; they must be good at partner relationship management.

p. Every functional area inside a company can interact with customers, especially electronically. Firms are linking all their departments in the cause of creating customer value.

q. Most companies today are networked, relying heavily on partnerships with other firms.

r. The supply chain describes a long channel, stretching from raw materials to components to final products that are carried to final buyers. Through supply chain management, many companies today are strengthening their connections with partners all along the supply chain.

7. Capturing Value from Customers

a. The final step in the marketing process involves capturing value from the customer, in the form of current and future sales, market share, and profits.

Creating Customer Loyalty and Retention

b. The aim of customer relationship management is to create not just customer satisfaction, but customer delight.

c. Companies are realizing that losing a customer means losing more than a single sale. It means losing the entire stream of purchases that the customer would make over a lifetime of patronage. This is called customer lifetime value.

d. Customer delight creates an emotional relationship with a product or service, not just a rational preference.

Growing Share of Customer

e. Customer relationship management can help marketers to increase their share of customer—the share they get of the customer's purchasing in their product categories.

f. To increase the share of customer, firms can leverage customer relationships by offering greater variety to current customers. Or they can train employees to cross-sell and up-sell in order to market more products and services to existing customers.

Building Customer Equity

g. Customer equity is the combined discounted customer lifetime values of all the company's current and potential customers.

h. The company can classify customers according to their potential profitability and manage its relationships with them accordingly.

i. Figure 1.5 classifies customers into one of four relationship groups, according to their profitability and projected loyalty. Each group requires a different relationship management strategy.

    i. Strangers show low profitability and little projected loyalty.

    ii. Butterflies are profitable but not loyal.

    iii. True friends are both profitable and loyal.

    iv. Barnacles are highly loyal but not very profitable.

8. The New Marketing Landscape

a. Dramatic changes are occurring in the marketplace; there are five major developments.

The New Digital Age

b. The technology boom has created exciting new ways to learn about and track customers, and to create products and services tailored to individual customer needs.

c. Technology is also helping companies to distribute products more efficiently and effectively.

d. It's helping them to communicate with customers in large groups or one-to-one.

e. Perhaps the most dramatic new technology is the Internet.

f. Internet penetration in the United States has reached 63 percent, with more than 186 million people accessing the Web in any given month.

g. The number of Internet users worldwide reached 719 million last year and is expected to approach 1.5 billion by 2007.

Rapid Globalization

h. Many marketers are now connected globally with their customers and marketing partners.

i. Almost every company, large or small, is touched in some way by global competition.

j. Companies are not only trying to sell more of their locally produced goods in international markets, they are also buying more supplies and components abroad.

The Call for More Ethics and Social Responsibility

k. Marketers are re-examining their relationships with social values and responsibilities and with the very earth that sustains us.

l. Today's marketers are being called upon to take greater responsibility for the social and environmental impact of their actions.

The Growth of Not-for-Profit Marketing

m. Marketing has become a major part of the strategies of many not-for-profit organizations.

n. Government agencies have also shown an increased interest in marketing.

The New World of Marketing Relationships

o. Table 1.1 compares the old marketing thinking to the new.

p. Modern marketing companies are improving their customer knowledge and customer relationships.

9. So, What Is Marketing? Pulling It All Together

    a. Figure 1.6 presents an expanded model that will help pull it all together.

    b. The first question a company needs to ask is, "What consumers will we serve?" This is market segmentation and targeting.

    c. The second marketing strategy question is, "How can we best serve targeted customers?" This is differentiation and positioning.

    d. With its marketing strategy decided, the company now constructs a marketing program—consisting of the four marketing mix elements, the 4 Ps.

    e. Perhaps the most important step in the marketing process involves building value-laden, profitable relationships with target customers.

Student Exercises

1. Key Term: Marketing

The two-fold goal of marketing is to attract new customers by promising superior value and keep and grow current customers by keeping them happy. Take a look at Apple Computers (www.apple.com), Cingular (www.cingular.com), and the American Cancer Society (www.cancer.org). How would you say these companies use marketing?

2.   Key Term: Market Offering

According to the chapter, a market offering is some combination of products, services, information, or experiences offered to a market to satisfy a need or want. LaSalle Bank (www.lasallebank.com) recently sponsored an open forum concerned with identifying the challenges and opportunities in providing residents of communities with healthy food options that traditionally have little or no access to grocery stores and quality, nutritious food choices. What is the market offering of LaSalle Bank, in this instance?

3.   Key Term: Marketing Myopia

Paying undue attention to the specific products offered and not enough attention to the benefits and experiences created by those products is classic marketing myopia. Examine the current battle between Blu-ray DVD technology (http://www.blu-ray.com/) and HD-DVD technology (http://www.thelookandsoundofperfect.com) in the race to replace the current DVD format. Point out possible instances of marketing myopia based on their promotional materials.

4.   Key Term: Market Segmentation

Firms decide who to serve (partly) through the process of market segmentation. Visit the websites of Starbucks coffee (www.starbucks.com) and Caribou Coffee (www.cariboucoffee.com). What major market segments are being targeted by each of these coffee companies?

5.   Key Term: Societal Marketing Concept

The societal marketing concept is concerned with the long-term welfare of the consumer and society. However, at times this viewpoint may be seen as contradictory with the products a company may offer. How do you believe (or, do you believe) tobacco makers are employing this concept in the marketing of cigarettes? You may want to visit the websites of Phillip Morris (www.philipmorrisusa.com), R.J. Reynolds (www.rjrt.com), and Lorillard (http://www.lorillard.com).

6.   Key Term: Customer Relationship Management

The overall process of building and maintaining profitable customer relationships—the acquiring, keeping, and growing of customers is known as Customer Relationship Management (CRM). Examine your college/university. How are they implementing CRM?

7.   Key Term: Partner Relationship Management

Sometimes, to bring greater value to customers, even competitors have been known to work together and/or join forces. Time Warner and CBS, highlighted in the chapter, is one good example. What are some other high profile examples of competitors joining forces for the overall good of the consumer?

8.   Key Term: Customer Equity

Maintaining loyal, profitable customers is the key to high customer equity. Dell Computers (www.dell.com), L.L. Bean (www.llbean.com), and Lexus (www.lexus.com) are all great examples. Look for examples in your local community of companies you consider holding high levels of customer equity. Why?

9.   Key Term: Globalization

Even the smallest company today is impacted by the global community, whether it is sparing with competitors halfway across the globe or receiving internet orders for products to ship to another country. How has this globalization impacted you directly? Do you believe this globalization has benefited you or do you think it has created more headaches than good?

10.   Key Term: Social Responsibility

The social responsibility movement will place ever-stricter demands on companies in the future. Some companies resist this movement, adapting only when forced. Others, however, embrace their social responsibility to their customers and the world around them. What are some examples of companies you believe have this forward-looking view of social responsibility? Also, what are some examples of companies you do not believe place much emphasis on this view?

Marketing ADventure Exercises

1.   Ad Interpretation Challenge: New Marketing Frontiers
        Ad: Apparel—Levis New Collection

Market offerings change over time. For a company to remain current and relevant, they must. What is this ad saying about the Levi Jean Company and it current market offering?

2.   Ad Interpretation Challenge: Insightful Segmentation
        Ad: Electronics—Compaq

Careful segmentation of the markets to serve is one of the challenges facing every marketer. Consider the featured ad. What market segment do you believe Compaq is attempting to reach with this ad? Do you believe this ad effectively reaches this segment?

3.   Ad Interpretation Challenge: The Production Concept
        Ad: Student Choice

One of the oldest marketing management orientations is the production concept, which states that consumers favor products that are available and highly affordable.

4.   Ad Interpretation Challenge: The Marketing Concept
        Ad: Travel and Tourism—Leisure Entertainment—Bali

The "outside-in" perspective is the key to the marketing concept. This concept focuses on what the consumer wants and needs and then seeks to develop a market offering to satisfy those needs and wants. Take a look at this ad. How is this ad employing the marketing concept?

5.   Ad Interpretation Challenge: The Marketing Concept
        Ad: Student Choice

Based on your work in the previous ADventure, find another ad of your selection that prominently displays the marketing concept and explain it. Remember, the marketing concept is a *customer*-driven concept.

6.   Ad Interpretation Challenge: What's Good for Society
        Ad: Auto—Hyundai Avante

The social marketing concept is a principle of enlightened marketing that considers, among other things, what is in the long-run best interest of society. However, nothing says that this has to be contradictory to what is good for the marketer. How does this particular ad fulfill both requirements—doing what is best for society AND what is best for the company?

7.   Ad Interpretation Challenge: Value
        Ad: General Retail—World's Biggest

The customer will buy from the firm that offers the highest perceived value. Perceived value is the difference between all of the benefits and all of the costs of a market offering relative to those of competing offers. How does this ad for World's Biggest Bookstore show value for the customer?

8.   Ad Interpretation Challenge: Making the Customer Happy
        Ad: Auto—Volvo S60

Providing superior customer satisfaction is the ultimate goal of all customer-oriented companies. Higher levels of customer satisfaction lead to greater customer loyalty that leads to greater company performance. How does this ad show customer loyalty? Select another ad of your choice, which also overtly displays customer loyalty.

9.   Ad Interpretation Challenge: Club Marketing Program
        Ad: Student Choice

One of the great ways to build customer loyalty is for the marketer to create programs that offer members special benefits and create member communities. Such programs have the potential to assist in long-term customer retention. For the ADventure, select an ad that you believe displays this concept of club marketing.

10.   Ad Interpretation Challenge: Increasing Lifetime Value and Customer
        Equity
        Ad: Auto—Jaguar

Whereas sales and market share reflect the past, customer equity suggests the future. Building that long-term relationship with the customer is the key to creating customer equity. Clearly, the more loyal a firm's profitable customers, the greater the firm's customer equity. How do the two ads for Jaguar relate to lifetime value and customer equity?

Chapter 2
Company and Marketing Strategy:
Partnering to Build Customer Relationships

Learning Objectives

1. Explain companywide strategic planning and its four steps.
2. Discuss how to design business portfolios and develop growth strategies.
3. Explain marketing's role under strategic planning and how marketing works with its partners to create and deliver customer value.
4. Describe the elements of a customer-driven marketing strategy and mix, and the forces that influence it.
5. List the marketing management functions, including the elements of a marketing plan, and discuss the importance of measuring and managing return on marketing.

Chapter Overview

To meet changing conditions in their industries, companies need to look ahead and develop long-term strategies. Strategic planning involves developing a strategy to meet competition and ensure long-term survival and growth. The marketing function plays an important role in this process in that it provides information and other inputs to help in the preparation of the organization's strategic plan.

Strategic planning is described as the process of developing and maintaining a strategic fit between the organization's goals and capabilities and its changing marketing opportunities. Strategic planning sets the stage for the rest of the planning in the firm. Formally, strategic planning consists of developing a company mission (to give it direction), objectives and goals (to give it means and methods for accomplishing its mission), a business portfolio (to allow management to utilize all facets of the organization), and functional plans (to carry out daily operations from the different functional disciplines). Because most companies are interested in growth, this chapter explores several growth alternatives within the context of strategic planning and portfolio analysis. The product/market expansion grid shows four avenues for growth: market penetration, market development, product development, and diversification.

No matter how well the strategic planning process has been designed and implemented, success depends on how well each department performs its customer-value-adding activities and how well the departments work together to serve the customer. Value chains and value delivery networks have become popular with organizations that are sensitive to the wants and needs of consumers. The marketing department (because of its ability to stress the customer's view) has become central in the implementation of most strategic plans. Connecting to customers is central to this process.

13

As a means of discussing the marketing process, this chapter carefully outlines and discusses the steps in the process, the marketing plan and its component parts, the marketing mix variables and their relationship to planning, the management of the planning process, how marketing departments are organized, how plans are implemented, and how marketing managers attempt to control the process. One of the secrets to success within the context of the marketing process is how the company watches and adapts to the changing marketing and competitive environment.

Chapter Outline

1. Introduction
    a. Now one of the best-known brand symbols, Nike is far different today from the brash young start-up company of 40 years ago.
    b. In its earlier days, Nike's image relied on passion, performance, and an anti-establishment rebelliousness.
    c. By the 1990s, Nike became so big that it *was* the establishment. With the critical cool factor gone, Nike's growth suffered.
    d. Nike's marketing strategy has matured. Marketing dollars are spent much more carefully to balance the creative and business sides.
    e. Additionally, Nike has overhauled its supply chain, focused on international growth, and allowed acquired brands to flourish independently.

2. Companywide Strategic Planning: Defining Marketing's Role
    a. The hard task of selecting an overall company strategy for long-run survival and growth is called strategic planning.
    b. Strategic planning is the process of developing and maintaining a strategic fit between the organization's goals and capabilities and its changing market opportunities.
    c. Strategic planning sets the stage for the rest of the planning in the firm. Companies usually prepare annual plans, long-range plans, and strategic plans.
    d. Figure 2.1 shows the steps in the strategic planning process.

    Defining a Market-Oriented Mission
    e. Many organizations develop formal mission statements. A mission statement is a statement of the organization's purpose—what it wants to accomplish in the larger environment.
    f. A clear mission statement acts as an "invisible hand" that guides people in the organization.
    g. A market-oriented mission statement defines the business in terms of satisfying basic customer needs.
    h. Table 2.1 provides several examples of product-oriented versus market-oriented business definitions.

i. Management should avoid making its mission too narrow or too broad. Missions should be realistic, be specific, fit the market environment, be based on the company's distinctive competencies, and be motivating.

Setting Company Objectives and Goals

j. The company's mission needs to be turned into detailed supporting objectives for each level of management.

k. The mission leads to a hierarchy of objectives, including business objectives and marketing objectives.

l. Marketing strategies and programs must be developed to support these marketing objectives.

Designing the Business Portfolio

m. A business portfolio is the collection of businesses and products that make up the company. The best portfolio is the one that best fits the company's strengths and weaknesses to opportunities in the environment.

n. The major activity in strategic planning is business portfolio analysis, whereby management evaluates the products and businesses making up the company.

o. A strategic business unit (SBU) is a unit of the company that has a separate mission and objectives and that can be planned independently from other company businesses.

p. The next step in business portfolio analysis calls for management to assess the attractiveness of its various SBUs and decide how much support each deserves.

q. Most standard portfolio-analysis methods evaluate SBUs on two important dimensions—the attractiveness of the SBU's market or industry and the strength of the SBU's position in that market or industry.

   i. The best-known portfolio-planning method was developed by the Boston Consulting Group.

  ii. Figure 2.2 shows the BCG growth-share matrix approach. This matrix defines four types of SBUs: stars, cash cows, question marks, and dogs.

 iii. Once it has classified its SBUs, the company must determine what role each will play in the future. The company can invest more in the business unit in order to grow its share. It can invest just enough to hold the SBU's share at the current level. It can harvest the SBU, milking its short-term cash flow regardless of the long-term effect. Or it can divest the SBU by selling it or phasing it out and using resources elsewhere.

r. Portfolio-analysis approaches have limitations.
    i. They can be difficult, time-consuming, and costly to implement.
    ii. Management may find it difficult to define SBUs and measure market share and growth.
    iii. These approaches focus on classifying current businesses but provide little advice for future planning.

s. Because of such problems, many companies have dropped formal matrix methods in favor of more customized approaches that are better suited to their specific situations.

t. Designing the business portfolio involves finding businesses and products the company should consider in the future.

u. Marketing has the main responsibility for achieving profitable growth for the company. Marketing must identify, evaluate, and select market opportunities and lay down strategies for capturing them. The product/market expansion grid is shown in Figure 2.3.
    i. Market penetration involves making more sales to current customers without changing its products.
    ii. Market development involves identifying and developing new markets for its current products.
    iii. Product development is offering modified or new products to current markets.
    iv. Diversification is where a company starts up or buys businesses outside of its current products and markets.

v. Companies must also develop strategies for downsizing their businesses.

3. Planning Marketing: Partnering to Build Customer Relationships
    w. Within each business unit, more detailed planning takes place. The major functional departments in each unit must work together to accomplish strategic objectives.
    x. Marketing provides a guiding philosophy—the marketing concept—that suggests that company strategy should revolve around building profitable relationships with important customer groups.
    y. Marketing provides inputs to strategic planners by helping to identify attractive market opportunities and by assessing the firm's potential to take advantage of them.
    z. Marketing designs strategies for reaching the unit's objectives.

Partnering with Other Company Departments
    aa. Each company department can be thought of as a link in the company's value chain. Each department carries out value-creating activities to design, produce, market, deliver, and support the firm's products.
    bb. A company's value chain is only as strong as its weakest link. Success depends on how well each department performs its work of adding customer value and on how well the activities of various departments are coordinated.

cc. In practice, departmental relations are full of conflicts and misunderstandings.

Partnering with Others in the Marketing System

dd. The firm needs to look beyond its own value chain and into the value chains of its suppliers, distributors, and ultimately, customers.

ee. More companies today are partnering with other members of the supply chain to improve the performance of the customer value-delivery network.

ff. Increasingly, today's competition no longer takes place between individual competitors. Rather, it takes place between the entire value-delivery networks created by these competitors.

4. Marketing Strategy and the Marketing Mix

gg. Marketing's role and activities are shown in Figure 2.4; it summarizes the major activities involved in managing marketing strategy and the marketing mix.

hh. Marketing strategy is the marketing logic by which the company hopes to achieve these profitable relationships.

Customer-Driven Marketing Strategy

ii. Companies know that they cannot profitably serve all consumers in a given market—at least not all consumers in the same way.

jj. The process of dividing a market into distinct groups of buyers with different needs, characteristics, or behavior who might require separate products or marketing programs is called market segmentation.

kk. A market segment consists of consumers who respond in a similar way to a given set of marketing efforts.

ll. Market targeting involves evaluating each market segment's attractiveness and selecting one or more segments to enter. A company should target segments in which it can profitably generate the greatest customer value and sustain it over time.

mm. A product's position is the place the product occupies relative to competitors in consumers' minds. Marketers want to develop unique market positions for their products.

nn. Market positioning is arranging for a product to occupy a clear, distinctive, and desirable place relative to competing products in the minds of target customers. Positioning thus establishes differentiation.

oo. In positioning its product, the company first identifies possible competitive advantages upon which to build the position. To gain competitive advantage, the company must offer value to target consumers.

Developing an Integrated Marketing Mix

pp. The marketing mix is the set of controllable, tactical marketing tools that the firm blends to produce the response it wants in the target market. This is described in Figure 2.5.

qq. Product means the goods-and-services combination the company offers to the target market.

rr. Price is the amount of money customers have to pay to obtain the product.

ss. Place includes company activities that make the product available to target consumers.

tt. Promotion means activities that communicate the merits of the product and persuade target customers to buy it.

uu. An effective marketing program blends all of the marketing mix elements into a coordinated program designed to achieve the company's marketing objectives by delivering value to consumers.

vv. Some critics feel that the 4 Ps may omit or underemphasize certain important activities.

ww. From the buyer's viewpoint, in this age of customer relationships, the 4 Ps might be better described as the 4 Cs: customer solution, customer cost, convenience, and communication.

5. Managing the Marketing Effort

xx. Managing the marketing process requires the four marketing management functions shown in Figure 2.6.

Marketing Analysis

yy. Managing the marketing function begins with a complete analysis of the company's situation.

zz. The company must analyze its markets and marketing environment to find attractive opportunities and avoid environmental threats.

aaa. Marketers should conduct a SWOT analysis; it must analyze company strengths and weaknesses as well as current and possible marketing actions to determine which opportunities it can best pursue and threats it can confront.

Marketing Planning

bbb. Marketing planning involves deciding on marketing strategies that will help the company attain its overall strategic objectives.

ccc. A detailed marketing plan is needed for each business, product, or brand.

ddd. Table 2.2 outlines the major sections of a typical product or brand plan.

eee. A marketing strategy consists of specific strategies: target markets, positioning, the marketing mix, and marketing expenditure levels.

Marketing Implementation

fff. Marketing implementation is the process that turns marketing plans into marketing actions in order to accomplish strategic marketing objectives. Implementation involves day-to-day, month-to-month activities that effectively put the marketing plan to work.

ggg. In an increasingly connected world, people at all levels of the marketing system must work together to implement marketing strategies and plans.

hhh. Successful marketing implementation depends on how well the company blends its people, organizational structure, decision and reward systems, and company culture into a cohesive action program that supports its strategies.

iii. Finally, to be successfully implemented, the firm's marketing strategies must fit with its company culture—the system of values and beliefs shared by people in the organization.

Marketing Department Organization

jjj. The company must design a marketing organization that can carry out marketing strategies and plans.

kkk. The most common form of marketing organization is the functional organization. Under this organization, a functional specialist heads different marketing activities.

lll. A company that sells across the country or internationally often uses a geographic organization.

mmm. Companies with many very different products or brands often create a product management organization. A product manager develops and implements a complete strategy and marketing program for a specific product or brand.

nnn. For companies that sell one product line to many different types of markets and customers that have different needs and preferences, a market or customer management organization might be best. A market management organization is similar to the product management organization. Market managers are responsible for developing marketing strategies and plans for their specific markets or customers.

ooo. Large companies that produce many different products flowing into many different geographic and customer markets usually employ some combination of the functional, geographic, product, and market organization forms.

ppp. Many companies are finding that today's marketing environment calls for less focus on products, brands, and territories and more focus on customers and customer relationships. More and more companies are shifting their brand management focus toward customer management.

Marketing Control

qqq. Marketing control involves evaluating the results of marketing strategies and plans and taking corrective action to ensure that objectives are attained.

rrr. Operating control involves checking ongoing performance against the annual plan and taking corrective action when necessary. Its purpose is to ensure that the company achieves the sales, profits, and other goals set out in its annual plan.

sss. Strategic control involves looking at whether the company's basic strategies are well matched to its opportunities. A major tool for such strategic control is a marketing audit. This is a comprehensive, systematic, independent, and periodic examination of a company's environment, objectives, strategies, and activities to determine problem areas and opportunities.

6. Measuring and Managing Return on Marketing Investment

ttt. Marketing managers must ensure that their marketing dollars are being well spent.

uuu. Many companies now view marketing as an investment rather than an expense.

vvv. Marketers are developing better measures of return on marketing investment; that is, the net return from a marketing investment divided by the costs of the marketing environment. It measures the profits generated by investments in marketing activities.

www. A company can assess return on marketing in terms of standard marketing performance measures, such as brand awareness, sales, or market share.

xxx. Increasingly, though, marketers are using customer-centered measures of marketing impact, such as customer acquisition, customer retention, and customer lifetime value.

yyy. Figure 2.7 views marketing expenditures as investments that produce returns in the form of more profitable customer relationships.

Student Exercises

1. Key Term: Strategic Planning

For long-term survival, every company must engage in effective strategic planning—the process of developing and maintaining a strategic fit between the organization's goals and capabilities and its marketing opportunities. Consider the competitive U.S. automobile market. How would you describe the strategic planning of Ford Motor Company (www.ford.com)?

2. Key Term: Mission Statement

A mission statement is a statement of the organization's purpose—what it wants to accomplish in the larger environment. Take a look at the mission statements of Starbucks coffee (www.starbucks.com), IBM (www.ibm.com), and John Deere (www.deere.com). Look for similarities and differences. Are any better than others?

3.   Key Term: Business Portfolio

The collection of businesses and products that make up a company is known as its *business portfolio*. Visit the home page of Ford Motor Company (www.ford.com) and make a list of the products and/or businesses that comprise this company.

4.   Key Term: Market Penetration

Market penetration—a strategy for company growth by increasing sales of current products to current market segments without changing the product—is only one possible strategy for growth. Find a company whose strategy you believe follows market penetration.

5.   Key Term: Diversification

Another strategy for company growth is diversification, which is growing through the acquisition or starting of businesses outside of a company's current products and markets. Find a company whose strategy you believe typifies diversification.

6.   Key Term: Downsizing

Business unit growth is not always the desirable or achievable option. Downsizing involves reducing the business portfolio by eliminating products or business units that are not profitable or no longer fit the company's overall corporate strategy. What are two companies you believe have employed downsizing in past few years?

7.   Key Term: Market Segment

A market segment is a group of consumers who respond in a similar way to a given set of marketing efforts. Take a look at Rolls Royce (www.rolls-roycemotorcars.com) and Chery Automobile Company (www.cheryglobal.com). Describe the basic market segments these two companies are attempting to reach.

8.   Key Term: Positioning

Positioning is arranging for a product to occupy a clear, distinctive, and desirable place relative to competing products in the minds of target consumers. How is your favorite local restaurant attempting to position itself, relative to its competition? Is it working?

9.   Key Term: Marketing Mix

The marketing mix is the set of controllable, tactical marketing tools the firm blends to product the responses it wants from the target market. These marketing tools can all be collected into four sets of variables known as the "4 Ps." Consider Southwest Airlines (www.southwest.com). Briefly describe the "4 Ps" employed by Southwest.

10.   Key Term: SWOT Analysis

A complete analysis of the company situation is a key component in managing the marketing function. A SWOT analysis is central to this evaluation process. Think about your school. What do you consider to be the primary strengths, weaknesses, opportunities, and threats it is facing?

Marketing ADventure Exercises

1.   Ad Interpretation Challenge: The Mission Statement
       Ad: Apparel—Polartec

The mission statement is the core of what a company is all about. Take a look at this Polartec ad. How would you interpret the company's mission statement, based on this ad?

2.   Ad Interpretation Challenge: Distinctive Competencies
       Ad: Apparel—Umbro

A company should base its mission statement on its distinctive competencies—those things it does extremely well. What distinctive competency is being displayed by these two Umbro ads?

3.   Ad Interpretation Challenge: Business Portfolio
       Ad: Food and Beverage—Pizza World

A business portfolio is the collection of businesses or products that make up the company. How does this Pizza World ad give the consumer insight into the products of the company?

4.   Ad Interpretation Challenge: Stars
       Ad: Student Choice

"Stars" are defined as being high-growth, high-share businesses or products. Find an ad that you believe is promoting a "star."

5.   Ad Interpretation Challenge: Market Penetration
       Ad: General Retail—Drugmart

The idea of market penetration is to increase sales of your current products to your current market segments. How does this ad for Drugmart seek to accomplish this?

6.   Ad Interpretation Challenge: Market Development
        Ad: Travel and Tourism—Turkish Airlines

A company undertakes a strategy of product development when it decides to offer new or modified products to its current market segments. Examine this ad for Turkish Airlines. How does it epitomize the strategy of product development?

7.   Ad Interpretation Challenge: Value Chain
        Ad: Exhibits and Entertainment—D-Day (Melting Pot)

A firm's success depends not only on how well each department performs its work but also on how well the activities of various departments are coordinated. Consider this advertisement for the National D-Day Museum in New Orleans. What does this ad say about value chains?

8.   Ad Interpretation Challenge: The Value-Delivery Network
        Ad: Internet—Shopnow

A value-delivery network is a network made up of the company, suppliers, distributors, and the customer who "partner" with each other to improve the performance of the system and, therefore, provide greater value to the customer. How does Shopnow accomplish this?

9.   Ad Interpretation Challenge: Product Positioning
        Ad: Auto—Lincoln

Successfully positioning a product involves clearly and distinctively placing the product as superior to competing products in the mind of the consumer. How has Lincoln achieved this in the featured ad?

10.   Ad Interpretation Challenge: The Product
        Ad: Student Choice

All successful ads make certain you know what the product is they are highlighting, otherwise they have accomplished nothing. Sometimes, however, they may do this very subtly. Find an ad when the product is evident, but not "in your face."

Chapter 3
The Marketing Environment

Learning Objectives

1. Describe the environmental forces that affect the company's ability to serve its customers.
2. Explain how changes in the demographic and economic environments affect marketing decisions.
3. Identify the major trends in the firm's natural and technological environments.
4. Explain the key changes in the political and cultural environments.
5. Discuss how companies can react to the marketing environment.

Chapter Overview

In order to correctly identify opportunities and monitor threats, the company must begin with a thorough understanding of the marketing environment in which the firm operates. The marketing environment consists of all the factors and forces outside marketing that affect the marketing management's ability to develop and maintain successful relationships with its target customers. Though these factors and forces may vary depending on the specific company and industrial group, they can generally be divided into broad microenvironmental and macroenvironmental components. For most companies, the microenvironmental components are: the company, suppliers, marketing channel firms (intermediaries), customer markets, competitors, and publics. The macroenvironmental components are thought to be: demographic, economic, natural, technological, political, and cultural forces. The wise marketing manager knows that he or she cannot always affect environmental forces. Smart managers can take a proactive, rather than reactive, approach to the marketing environment.

As a company's marketing management collects and processes data on these environments, it must be ever vigilant in its efforts to apply what it learns to developing opportunities and dealing with threats. Studies have shown that excellent companies not only have a keen sense of customer but an appreciation of the environmental forces swirling around them. By constantly looking at the dynamic changes that are occurring in the aforementioned environments, companies are better prepared to adapt to change, prepare long-range strategy, meet the needs of today's and tomorrow's customers, and compete with the intense competition present in the global marketplace.

Chapter Outline

1.   **Introduction**
     a. McDonald's has been losing share to what the industry calls "fast-casual" restaurants because consumers today want more choices.
     b. Americans are seeking healthier eating options. As the market leader, McDonald's often bears the brunt of criticism.
     c. McDonald's has strived to realign itself with the changing marketing environment, and it appears to be paying off.
     d. Marketers need to be good at building relationships with customers, others in the company, and external partners.
     e. A company's marketing environment consists of the factors and forces outside marketing that affect marketing management's ability to build and maintain successful relationships with target customers.
     f. More than any other group in the company, marketers must be the trend trackers and opportunity seekers. They have disciplined methods—marketing intelligence and marketing research—for collecting information about the marketing environment. They also spend more time in the customer and competitor environments.

2.   **The Company's Microenvironment**
     a. Figure 3.1 shows the major factors in the marketer's environment.

     The Company
     b. In designing marketing plans, marketing management takes other company groups into account. These interrelated groups form the internal environment.
     c. Marketing managers must work closely with other company departments.

     Suppliers
     d. Suppliers form an important link in the company's overall customer value delivery system.
     e. Marketing managers must watch supply availability. They also monitor the price trends of their key inputs.
     f. Most marketers today treat their suppliers as partners in creating and delivering customer value.

     Marketing Intermediaries
     g. Marketing intermediaries help the company to promote, sell, and distribute its goods to final buyers.
         i.   Resellers are distribution channel firms that help the company find customers or make sales to them.
         ii. Physical distribution firms help the company to stock and move goods from their points of origin to their destinations.

        iii. Marketing services agencies are the marketing research firms, advertising agencies, media firms, and marketing consulting firms that help the company target and promote its products to the right markets.

        iv. Financial intermediaries help finance transactions or insure against the risks associated with the buying and selling of goods.

    h. Marketing intermediaries form an important component of the company's overall value delivery system.

    i. Today's marketers recognize the importance of working with their intermediaries as partners rather than simply as channels through which they sell their products.

Customers

    j. The company needs to study five types of customer markets closely.

        i. Consumer markets consist of individuals and households that buy goods and services for personal consumption.

        ii. Business markets buy goods and services for further processing or for use in their production process.

        iii. Reseller markets buy goods and services to resell at a profit.

        iv. Government markets are made up of government agencies that buy goods and services to produce public services or transfer the goods and services to others who need them.

        v. International markets consist of buyers in other countries, including consumers, producers, resellers, and governments.

Competitors

    k. Marketers must gain strategic advantage by positioning their offers strongly against competitors' offerings in the minds of consumers.

    l. No single competitive marketing strategy is best for all companies. Each firm should consider its own size and industry position compared to those of its competitors.

Publics

    m. A public is any group that has an actual or potential interest in or impact on an organization's ability to achieve its objectives.

        i. Financial publics influence the company's ability to obtain funds.

        ii. Media publics carry news, features, and editorial opinion.

        iii. Government publics regulate public safety, truth in advertising, and other matters.

        iv. Citizen-action publics include consumer organizations, environmental groups, minority groups, and others.

        v. Local publics include neighborhood residents and community organizations.

        vi. The general public may be concerned about the company's products and activities.

> vii. Internal publics include workers, managers, volunteers, and the board of directors.

3. **The Company's Macroenvironment**
   a. Figure 3.2 shows the six major forces in the company's macroenvironment.

Demographic Environment
   b. Demography is the study of human populations in terms of size, density, location, age, gender, race, occupation, and other statistics. It involves people, and people make up markets.
   c. Changes in the world demographic environment have major implications for business.
   d. The single most important demographic trend in the United States is the changing age structure of the population.
   e. Figure 3.3 shows the seven generational groups in the United States.
   > **i.** The post–World War II baby boom produced 78 million baby boomers, born between 1946 and 1964.
   > > **a.** The baby boomers have become one of the most powerful forces shaping the marketing environment.
   > > **b.** Today's baby boomers account for about 28 percent of the population, but earn more than half of all personal income.
   > > **c.** Baby boomers cross all walks of life, creating a diverse set of target segments for businesses.
   > > **d.** Boomers span a 20-year age range, and almost 25 percent of boomers belong to a racial or ethnic minority.
   >
   > **ii.** The baby boom was followed by a "birth dearth," creating another generation of 49 million people born between 1964 and 1976. They are called Generation X, because they lie in the shadow of the boomers and lack obvious distinguishing characteristics.
   > > **a.** They are defined as much by their shared experiences as by their age. Increasing divorce rates and higher employment for their mothers made them the first generation of latchkey kids.
   > > **b.** They have developed a more cautious economic outlook. They care about the environment and respond favorably to socially responsible companies.
   > > **c.** The GenXers are a skeptical bunch, cynical of frivolous marketing pitches that promise easy success.
   > **iii.** Generation Y is also called *echo boomers.* Born between 1977 and 1994, these children of the baby boomers now number 72 million, dwarfing the GenXers and almost equal in size to the baby boomer segment.

      a. The echo boom has created a large teen and young adult market. The nation's teens spend \$175 billion a year and influence another \$30 billion in family spending.

      iv. Do marketers have to create separate products and marketing programs for each generation? Some experts caution that each generation spans decades of time and many socioeconomic levels. Others warn that marketers have to be careful about turning off one generation each time they craft a product or message that appeals effectively to another.

f. The "traditional household" consists of a husband, wife, and children (and sometimes grandparents).

      i. In the United States today, married couples with children now make up only about 34 percent of the nation's 105 million households, and this percentage is falling.

      ii. The number of working women has increased greatly, growing from under 30 percent of the U.S. workforce in 1950 to just over 60 percent today.

g. This is a period of great migratory movements between and within countries.

      i. Over the past two decades, the U.S. population has shifted toward the Sunbelt states. The West and South have grown, while the Midwest and Northeast states have lost population.

      ii. For more than a century, Americans have been moving from rural to metropolitan areas.

      iii. The shift in where people live has also caused a shift in where they work. One in five Americans is now working out of the home with the help of electronic conveniences.

h. The U.S. population is becoming better educated.

      i. In 2002, 84 percent of the U.S. population over the age of 25 had completed high school and 27 percent had completed college, compared with 69 percent and 17 percent in 1980.

      ii. The workforce is also becoming more white collar. Between 1950 and 1985, the proportion of white-collar workers rose from 42 percent to 54 percent, that of blue-collar workers declined from 47 percent to 33 percent, and that of service workers increased from 12 percent to 14 percent.

i. The United States is called a melting pot—diverse groups from many nations and cultures have melted into a single, more homogenous whole. Instead, though, the United States seems to have become more of a "salad bowl" in which various groups have mixed together but maintained their diversity by retaining and valuing important ethnic and cultural differences.

      i. Marketers are facing increasingly diverse markets, both at home and abroad.

ii. Most large companies now target specially designed products and promotions to one or more ethnic groups.

iii. Diversity goes beyond ethnic heritage. For example, many major companies have recently begun to explicitly target gay and lesbian customers.

iv. Another attractive segment is the more than 54 million people with disabilities in the United States; they represent almost $1 trillion in annual spending power.

v. Marketers should pay attention to income distribution as well as average income.

Economic Environment

j. The economic environment consists of factors that affect consumer purchasing power and spending patterns.

k. Nations vary greatly in their levels of distribution of income.

i. Subsistence economies are ones in which the population consumes most of their own agricultural and industrial output.

ii. Industrial economies are those with rich markets for many different kinds of goods.

l. Value marketing has become the watchword for many marketers. They are looking for ways to offer today's more financially cautious buyers greater value.

m. Marketers should pay attention to income distribution as well as average income.

i. In the United States, the top is populated by upper-class consumers, whose spending patterns are not affected by current economic events.

ii. The middle class is somewhat careful about its spending, but can still afford the good life some of the time.

iii. The working class must stick close to the basics of food, clothing, and shelter.

iv. The underclass must count their pennies when making even the most basic purchases.

n. Consumers at different income levels have different spending patterns. Some of these differences were noted over a century ago by Ernst Engel, who studied how people shifted their spending as their income rose. Engel's laws generally have been supported by later studies.

Natural Environment

o. The natural environment involves the natural resources that are needed as inputs by marketers or that are affected by marketing activities.

p. Environmental concerns have grown steadily during the past three decades.

q. Marketers should be aware of several trends in the natural environment.

     i. The first involves growing shortages of raw materials. Air and water may seem to be infinite resources, but some groups see long-run dangers.

     ii. A second environmental trend is increased pollution. Industry will almost always damage the quality of the natural environment.

     iii. A third trend is increased government intervention in natural resource management. The governments of different countries vary in their concern and efforts to promote a clean environment.

r. Concern for the natural environment has spawned the so-called green movement. Enlightened companies are developing environmentally sustainable strategies and practices in an effort to create a world economy that the planet can support indefinitely.

Technological Environment

s. The technological environment is perhaps the most dramatic force now shaping our destiny.

t. New technologies create new markets and opportunities. However, every new technology replaces on older technology. Marketers should watch the technological environment closely.

Political Environment

u. The political environment consists of laws, government agencies, and pressure groups that influence or limit various organizations and individuals in a given society.

v. Well-conceived legislation can encourage competition and ensure fair markets for goods and services. Governments develop public policy to guide commerce.

w. Legislation affecting business around the world has increased steadily over the years. The United States has many laws covering these issues; see Table 3.1.

x. Understanding the public policy implications of a particular marketing activity is not a simple matter. Marketers must work hard to keep up with changes in regulations and their interpretations.

y. Business legislation has been enacted for a number of reasons.

     i. The first is to protect companies from each other.

     ii. The second purpose of government regulation is to protect consumers from unfair business practices.

     iii. The third is to protect the interests of society against unrestrained business behavior.

     iv. International marketers will encounter dozens, or even hundreds, of agencies set up to enforce trade policies and regulations.

z. Business is also governed by social codes and rules of professional ethics.

     i. Enlightened companies encourage their managers to look beyond what the regulatory system allows and simply "do the right thing." These socially responsible firms actively seek out ways to protect the long-run interests of their consumers and the environment.

      ii. The recent rash of business scandals and increased concerns about the environment have created fresh interest in the issues of ethics and social responsibility.

      iii. The boom in e-commerce and Internet marketing has created a new set of social and ethical issues. Online privacy issues are the primary concern.

aa. To exercise their social responsibility and build more positive images, companies are now linking themselves to worthwhile causes.

      i. Cause-related marketing has become a primary form of corporate giving.

      ii. Cause-related marketing has stirred some controversy. Critics worry that cause-related marketing is more a strategy for selling than a strategy for giving.

      iii. If handled well, cause-related marketing can greatly benefit both the company and the cause.

Cultural Environment

bb. The cultural environment is made up of institutions and other forces that affect a society's basic values, perceptions, preferences, and behaviors. People grow up in a particular society that shapes their basic beliefs and values.

      i. Core beliefs and values are passed on from parents to children and are reinforced by schools, churches, business, and government.

      ii. Secondary beliefs and values are more open to change.

cc. Although core values are fairly persistent, cultural swings do take place. Marketers want to predict cultural shifts in order to spot new opportunities or threats.

dd. The major cultural values of a society are expressed in people's views.

      i. People vary in their emphasis on serving themselves versus serving others.

      ii. Recently, observers have noted a shift from a "me society" to a "we society" in which more people want to be with and serve others.

      iii. People vary in their attitudes toward corporations, government agencies, trade unions, universities, and other organizations. By and large, people are willing to work for major organizations and expect them, in turn, to carry out society's work.

      iv. People vary in their attitudes toward their society.

      v. People vary in their attitudes toward the natural world.

      vi. People vary in their beliefs about the origin of the universe and their place in it.

4. **Responding to the Marketing Environment**

a. Many companies view the marketing environment as an uncontrollable element in which they must react and adapt. They passively accept the marketing environment and do not try to change it.

      b. Other companies take a proactive stance toward the marketing environment.

          i. Rather than simply watching and reacting, these firms take aggressive actions to affect the publics and forces in their marketing environment.

          ii. Such companies hire lobbyists to influence legislation affecting their industries and stage media events to gain favorable press coverage. They press lawsuits and file complaints with regulators to keep competitors in line, and they form contractual agreements to better control their distribution channels.

Student Exercises

1.   Key Term: Microenvironment

The marketing environment is made up of both a macroenvironment and a microenvironment. The microenvironment consists of the actors close to a company that affect its ability to serve its customers. Take a look at your school. What elements comprise its microenvironment?

2.   Key Term: Marketing Intermediaries

Marketing intermediaries are firms that help the company promote, sell, and distribute its goods to the final buyers. Take a look at the websites for Amazon.com (www.amazon.com) and Bebe (www.bebe.com). From an examination of their websites and other materials, what marketing intermediaries are assisting either of these two very different companies?

3.   Key Term: Publics

A "public" is any group that has an actual or potential interest in or impact on an organization's ability to achieve its objectives. Once again, consider your university. What are the publics that your college administrators must be cognizant of?

4.   Key Term: Baby Boomers

The Baby Boomers are those individuals born during the post-World War II euphoria of 1946 to 1964. They number almost 78 million Americans and account for over 27 percent of the U.S. population. The aging of this group has opened numerous opportunities for marketers. Find two companies that appear to be targeting this group.

5.   Key Term: Generation Y

If you were born between the years 1977 and 2000, you are a member of Generation Y. This "echo boom" amounts to over 75 million people—much larger than Generation X and almost as large as the Baby Boomers. Take a look at Scion (www.scion.com), the new brand that Toyota created strictly to appeal to this group. Do you think the Scion holds attraction to members of Generation Y?

6.   Key Term: Traditional Family

The "traditional American household" typically consists of a husband, wife, and kids. However, today, that once idealistic view of the American family seems to be covering a smaller and smaller portion of the American population. Currently, only about 23 percent of households are made up of mom, dad, and kids. Find two companies that seem to be targeting this group.

7.   Key Term: Diversity

Countries vary in their ethnic and racial makeup. According to your text, we find Japan at one extreme, where pretty much everyone is Japanese. At the other end, we have the United States, where we have people from everywhere. Companies have to be careful in their promotions to faithfully and responsibly depict their customer markets as they really are. Take a look at Abercrombie and Fitch (www.abercrombie.com). Do you believe they have reasonably represented their target markets?

8.   Key Term: Engel's Law

According to Engel's Law, consumers at different income levels have different spending patterns. Percent of spending on transportation remains relatively flat across all income categories. How can you explain Jaguar and BMW's decisions to offer lower-priced luxury models to appeal to a new group of consumers?

9.   Key Term: Technological Environment

Technology continues to evolve at an astounding pace. It is difficult to predict where technology will lead us next. The technological environment is perhaps the most dramatic force now shaping the future. Impressive technological achievements continue to occur with remarkable speed. Make a list of four new accomplishments that would not have been possible without technology.

10.   Key Term: Political Environment

Every company must operate within the existing political environment and be able to anticipate changes to that environment. Mounting legislation has increasing impacted many U.S. businesses over the years. One of the most controversial, yet increasingly invoked pieces of legislation has been the implementation of smoking bans in public facilities, including outdoor sporting arenas, and indoor restaurants and bars. What do you feel about this? Is this serving the public good or is it unfairly targeting a legal product (tobacco)?

Marketing ADventure Exercises

1.   Ad Interpretation Challenge: The Macroenvironment
       Ad: Auto—Hyundai Avante

The macroenvironment is composed of the larger societal forces that impact a company, such as demographic, economic, natural, environmental, political, and cultural forces. Take a look at this ad. How is this ad appealing to the larger macroenvironment?

2.   Ad Interpretation Challenge: The Macroenvironment
       Ad: Food and Beverage—McDonald's

Again, consider what makes up the macroenvironment in which a company must operate. Consider the McDonald's ads pertaining to the Sydney Olympics. What factor(s) of the macroenvironment is(are) these ads targeting?

3.   Ad Interpretation Challenge: Marketing Intermediaries
       Ad: Student Choice

Marketing intermediaries are firms that help the company promote, sell, or distribute its goods or services to the final users. Many types of companies are included here, such as physical distribution firms, financial intermediaries, and resellers. Find an ad that highlights a marketing intermediary.

4.   Ad Interpretation Challenge: Competition
       Ad: Student Choice

Everybody has competitors. To be successful, a company must provide greater customer value and satisfaction than its competitors. Locate an ad that is attempting to show consumers that the company provides better value than does its competitors.

5. Ad Interpretation Challenge: Publics
    Ad: Auto—Cadillac Escalade

A company's marketing environment also includes various publics. Publics are any group that has an interest or impact (actual or potential) on an organization. What potential publics might Cadillac want to consider due to this ad?

6. Ad Interpretation Challenge: Demography
    Ad: Travel and Tourism—Leisure Entertainment

Demography is the study of human populations in terms of size, density, location, age, occupation, and other statistics. How does the featured ad show a foundation in the study of demography?

7. Ad Interpretation Challenge: Baby Boomers
    Ad: Student Choice

Baby boomers spend over $2 trillion annually and will soon control over 40 percent of this nation's disposable income. Baby boomers are those 78 million people born after World War II and up until 1964. Find an ad that is clearly targeted to this generation of people.

8. Ad Interpretation Challenge: Generation Y
    Ad: Apparel—Levis New Collection

Levi's is an apparel company that was late in joining the newest fashion craze touting $100 jeans. But they are attempting to rapidly catch up with the Levi's New Collection of jeans. Why would this ad appeal to those of Generation Y?

9. Ad Interpretation Challenge: The "Traditional Family"
    Ad: Auto—Toyota

The traditional American family (mom, dad, and children) seems to have lost a bit of its luster as a smaller and smaller percentage of households are comprised of this once American ideal. Today, only around 23 percent of households are made up of married couples with children. How would you say this Toyota ad appeals to this group?

10. Ad Interpretation Challenge: Diversity
    Ad: Nonprofit Corporate Images—Nike

Increasing diversity in the American landscape is an everyday fact of life. As Americans, we are not all alike. Diversity is not just ethnic heritage, but also includes the 60 million people with disabilities in the United States. How is Nike seeking to recognize this group and bring them more into the mainstream?

Chapter 4
Managing Marketing Information

Learning Objectives

1. Explain the importance of information to the company and its understanding of the marketplace.
2. Define the marketing information system and discuss its parts.
3. Outline the steps in the marketing research process.
4. Explain how companies analyze and distribute marketing information.
5. Discuss the special issues some marketing researchers face, including public policy and ethics issues.

Chapter Overview

In carrying out their marketing responsibilities, marketing managers need a great deal of information. "Information is power" is a legitimate statement. Despite the importance and growing supply of information, managers often lack enough information of the right kind or have too much of the wrong kind to make the critical decisions necessary to be successful in our highly competitive global marketplace. Most marketing managers don't need *more* information, they need *better* information. To overcome these problems, many companies are taking steps to improve their marketing information systems. A commitment to an information system is not just a technological commitment but a corporate culture commitment as well.

A well-designed marketing information system (MIS) first *assesses information needs*. The MIS next *develops needed information* (generally from internal company data, marketing intelligence activities, marketing research, and information analysis procedures and sources). Finally, the MIS *distributes information* to managers in the right form at the right time to help them make better marketing decisions. Once the system is in place and functioning, decision making becomes easier and better. Few firms with efficient information systems fail in the marketplace.

Marketing research, which is one of the components of an information system, involves collecting information relevant to a specific marketing problem facing the company. The marketing research process consists of four steps: defining the problem and research objectives, developing the research plan, implementing the research plan, and interpreting and reporting the findings. In addition to traditional sources of information that can now be used for marketing research, online databases and Internet data sources are becoming more important to the marketing research process.

In recent years, many companies have acquired or developed special software and analysis techniques—called *customer relationship management (CRM)*—for integrating and applying the mountains of individual customer data contained in their databases.

Where does this lead the organization? Business history, like military history, has shown that the organization that has superior information (and the ability to act on it) has a significant advantage over competition. Acquisition of information and development of information systems will be one of the challenges and necessities of the twenty-first century. Companies must be careful, however, to respect the privacy of the consumers that are being studied. Intrusions into the lives of consumers and the misuse of data about consumers are growing problems. Solving this problem in the rapidly changing information age will be a challenge for marketers and researchers alike.

Chapter Outline

1. **Introduction**
   a. Founded in 1941, Coach operated successfully for 50 years as a manufacturer of classically styled, high-quality leather handbags and accessories.
   b. By the 1990s, the market for handbags had changed dramatically with a strong shift toward stylish, colorful, designer brands that only affluent women could afford. Coach sales suffered.
   c. For the first time, Coach engaged in a strategic marketing research program and started to think like a consumer-products company.
   d. Coach launched into a makeover based on the strategy of "accessible luxury," creating high-end handbags that the average woman could afford.
   e. In doing so, Coach focused on identifying "usage voids." These results led to the following lines: stylish colorful bags, small bags to hold essentials, non-leather summer bags, and daytime formal bags. All of these lines have contributed to soaring sales and profits.
   f. Marketing research is far from an exact science. Consumers are full of surprises, and figuring them out can be tough.
   g. Good products and marketing programs begin with solid information on consumer needs and wants. Companies also need an abundance of information on competitors, resellers, and other factors and forces in the marketplace.
   h. But today's managers often receive too much information. Running out of information is not a problem, but seeing through the "data smog" is.
   i. Marketers frequently complain that they lack enough information of the right kind.
   j. A marketing information system (MIS) consists of people, equipment, and procedures to gather, sort, analyze, evaluate, and distribute needed, timely, and accurate information to marketing decision makers.
   k. Figure 4.1 shows that the MIS begins and ends with information users.

2. Assessing Marketing Information Needs

    a. A good marketing information system balances the information users would like to have against what they really need and what is feasible to offer.

    b. The company begins by interviewing managers to find out what information they would like to have.

    c. Sometimes the company cannot provide the needed information, either because it is not available or because of MIS limitations.

    d. The costs of obtaining, processing, storing, and delivering information can mount quickly. The company must decide whether the benefits of having additional information are worth the costs of providing it, and both value and cost are often hard to assess.

3. Developing Marketing Information

    a. There are several ways to obtain needed information.

Internal Data

    b. Many companies build extensive internal databases, electronic collections of information obtained from data sources within the company. Marketing managers can readily access and work with information in the database to identify marketing opportunities and problems, plan programs, and evaluate performance.

    c. Information in the database can come from many sources.

        i. The accounting department prepares financial statements and keeps detailed records of sales, costs, and cash flows.

        ii. Operations reports on production schedules, shipments, and inventories.

        iii. Sales force reports on reseller reactions and competitor activities.

        iv. The marketing department furnishes information on customer demographics, psychographics, and buying behavior.

        v. The customer service department keeps records of customer satisfaction or service problems.

        vi. Research studies done for one department may provide useful information for several others.

    d. Internal databases can be accessed more quickly and cheaply than other information sources, but they also present some problems.

        i. Because internal information was collected for other purposes, it may be incomplete or in the wrong form for making marketing decisions.

        ii. Data ages quickly.

Marketing Intelligence

    e. Marketing intelligence is systematic collection and analysis of publicly available information about competitors and developments in the marketplace.

f. The goal of marketing intelligence is to improve strategic decision making, assess and track competitors' actions, and provide early warning of opportunities and threats.

g. Much intelligence can be collected from people inside the company.

h. The company can also obtain important intelligence information from suppliers, resellers, and key customers.

i. It can get good information by observing competitors.

    i. It can buy and analyze competitors' products, monitor their sales, check for new patents, and examine various types of physical evidence.

    ii. Competitors may reveal intelligence information through their annual reports, business publications, trade show exhibits, press releases, advertisements, and Web pages.

    iii. The Internet is proving to be a vast new source of competitor-supplied information.

4. **Marketing Research**

a. Marketers often need formal studies of specific situations.

b. Marketing research is the systematic design, collection, analysis, and reporting of data relevant to a specific marketing situation facing an organization.

c. Companies use marketing research in a wide variety of situations.

    i. It can help marketers understand customer satisfaction and purchase behavior.

    ii. It can help them assess market potential and market share.

    iii. It can measure the effectiveness of pricing, product, distribution, and promotion activities.

d. Some large companies have their own research departments that work with marketing managers on marketing research projects.

    i. But companies frequently hire outside research specialists to consult with management on specific marketing problems and conduct marketing research studies.

    ii. Sometimes firms simply purchase data collected by outside firms to aid in their decision making.

e. Figure 4.2 shows the four steps of marketing research.

Defining the Problem and Research Objectives

f. Marketing managers and researchers must work closely together to define the problem and agree on research objectives.

g. Defining the problem and research objectives is often the hardest step in the research process.

h. The manager and researcher must set the research objectives. There are three types.

    i. The objective of exploratory research is to gather preliminary information that will help define the problem and suggest hypotheses.

        ii. The objective of descriptive research is to describe things, such as the market potential for a product or the demographics and attitudes of consumers who buy the product.

       iii. The objective of causal research is to test hypotheses about cause-and-effect relationships.

i. The statement of the problem and research objectives guides the entire research process.

Developing the Research Plan

j. Once the research problems and objectives have been defined, researchers must determine the exact information needed, develop a plan for gathering it efficiently, and present the plan to management.

k. The research plan outlines sources of existing data and spells out the specific research approaches, contact methods, sampling plans, and instruments that researchers will use to gather new data.

l. Research objectives must be translated into specific information needs.

m. To meet the manager's information needs, the research plan can call for gathering secondary data, primary data, or both.

       i. Secondary data consists of information that already exists somewhere, having been collected for another purpose.

       ii. Primary data consists of information collected for the specific purpose at hand.

Gathering Secondary Data

n. Researchers usually start gathering secondary data. Table 4.1 shows various sources of data.

o. Companies can buy secondary data reports from outside suppliers.

       i. Using commercial online databases, marketing researchers can conduct their own searches of secondary data sources.

       ii. Almost every industry association, government agency, business publication, and news medium offers free information to those tenacious enough to find their Web sites.

p. Secondary data can usually be obtained more quickly and at a lower cost than primary data. Also, secondary sources can sometimes provide data an individual company cannot collect on its own—information that is either not directly available or would be too expensive to collect.

q. Secondary data can also present problems.

       i. The needed information may not exist—researchers can rarely obtain all the data they need from secondary sources.

       ii. Even when data can be found, they might not be very usable. The researcher must evaluate secondary information carefully to make certain it is relevant, accurate, current, and impartial.

Primary Data Collection

r. Table 4.2 shows that designing a plan for primary data collections calls for a number of decisions.

i. There are several research approaches.
- **a.** Observational research involves gathering primary data by observing relevant people, actions, and situations. In some cases, observation may be the only way to obtain the needed information. In ethnographic research, trained observers watch people. This often yields the kinds of intimate details that just don't emerge from traditional focus groups.
- **b.** Survey research, the most widely used method for primary data collection, is the approach best suited for gathering descriptive information.
- **c.** Experimental research is best suited for gathering causal information. Experiments involve selecting matched groups of subjects, giving them different treatments, controlling unrelated factors, and checking for differences in group responses.

ii. Table 4.3 shows the strengths and weaknesses of various contact methods.
- **a.** Mail questionnaires can be used to collect large amounts of information at a low cost per respondent. Respondents may give more honest answers to more personal questions on a mail questionnaire than to an unknown interviewer in person or over the phone. There is no interviewer bias here. Mail questionnaires are not flexible.
- **b.** Telephone interviewing is one of the best methods of gathering information quickly, and it provides greater flexibility than mail questionnaires. Interviewers can explain difficult questions, and depending on the answers they receive, skip some questions or probe on others. The cost per respondent is higher than with mail questionnaires. People may not want to discuss personal questions with an interviewer. Interviewer bias may be present.
- **c.** Personal interviewing can be done individually or in groups. Individual interviewing is flexible. Interviewers can guide interviews, explain difficult questions, and explore issues as the situation requires. Group interviewing consists of inviting six to 10 people to talk with a trained moderator. This is called a focus group. The discussion is free and easy, but the moderator "focuses" the discussion. This has become one of the major marketing research tools for gaining insight into consumer thoughts and feelings.
- **d.** Some researchers today are using videoconferencing technology to connect marketers in distant locations with live focus group action.

iii. Advances in communications have resulted in a number of high-tech contact methods.

41

     a. Computer assisted telephone interviewing (CATI) is where interviewers sit at computers, read questions on the screen, and type in respondents' answers.

     b. Completely automated telephone surveys (CATS) enable respondents to be dialed by computer and asked prerecorded questions.

     c. Online (Internet) marketing research includes Internet surveys, experiments, and online focus groups.

s. A sample is a segment of the population selected to represent the population as a whole. Ideally, the sample should be representative so that the researcher can make accurate estimates of the thoughts and behaviors of the larger population.

    i. Designing the sample requires three decisions:

      a. Who is to be surveyed (the sampling unit)?

      b. How many people should be surveyed (the sample size)?

      c. How should people in the sample be chosen (the sampling procedure)?

    ii. Table 4.4 describes different kinds of samples.

      a. Probability samples ensure that each population's member has a known chance of being included in the sample, and researchers can calculate confidence limits for sampling error.

      b. Marketing researchers often take nonprobability samples, even though their sampling error cannot be measured.

t. In collecting primary data, marketing researchers have a choice of two main research instruments.

    i. The questionnaire is by far the most common instrument, whether administered in person, by phone, or online.

      a. They are very flexible—there are many ways to ask questions.

      b. Closed-ended questions include all the possible answers, and subjects make choices among them.

      c. Open-ended questions allow respondents to answer in their own words.

      d. Researchers should use care in the wording and ordering of questions.

      e. Table 4.5 shows some poorly worded questions and points out their problems.

    ii. Mechanical devices can also monitor consumer behavior.

      a. Nielsen Media Research attaches people meters to television sets in selected homes to record who watches which programs.

      b. Retailers use checkout scanners to record shoppers' purchases.

      c. Other mechanical devices measure subjects' physical responses.

Implementing the Research Plan

u. The researcher next puts the marketing research plan into action. The data collection phase of marketing research process is generally the most expensive and the most subject to error.

v. Researchers must process and analyze the collected data to isolate important information and findings. They need to check data for accuracy and completeness and code it for analysis. The researchers then tabulate the results and compute averages and other statistical measures.

Interpreting and Reporting of the Findings

w. The market researcher must now interpret the findings, draw conclusions, and report them to management. The researcher should present important findings that are useful in the major decisions faced by management.

x. Interpretation should not be left only to the researchers. The marketing manager knows more about the problem and the decisions that must be made.

y. In many cases, findings can be interpreted in different ways, and discussions between researchers and managers will help point to the best interpretations.

5. Analyzing Marketing Information

a. Information analysis might involve a collection of analytical models that will help marketers make better decisions. Marketing scientists have developed numerous models to help marketing managers make better marketing mix decisions, design sales territories and sales call plans, select sites for retail outlets, develop optimal advertising mixes, and forecast new-product sales.

Customer Relationship Management

b. Smart companies capture information at every possible customer touch-point. These touchpoints include customer purchases, sales force contacts, service and support calls, Web site visits, satisfaction surveys, and every contact between the customer and the company.

c. This information is usually scattered widely across the organization.

d. Many companies are now turning to customer relationship management (CRM) to manage detailed information about individual customers and carefully manage customer touchpoints in order to maximize customer loyalty.

    i. CRM consists of sophisticated software and analytical tools that integrate information from all sources, analyze it in depth, and apply the results to build stronger customer relationships.

    ii. CRM analysts develop data warehouses. A data warehouse is a companywide electronic database of finely detailed customer information that needs to be sifted through for gems.

43

      iii. Once the data warehouse brings the data together, the company uses high-powered data mining techniques to sift through the mounds of data and dig out interesting findings about customers.

      iv. By using CRM to understand customers better, companies can provide the higher levels of customer service and develop deeper customer relationships.

      v. An estimated half of all CRM efforts fail to meet their objectives. The most common cause of CRM failures is that companies mistakenly view CRM only as a technology and software solution.

      vi. When it works, the benefits of CRM can far outweigh the costs and risk.

6.   **Distributing and Using Marketing Information**
    a. Marketing information has no value until it is used to make better marketing decisions.
    b. Many firms use a company intranet to facilitate this process. The intranet provides ready access to research information, stored reports, shared work documents, contact information for employees and other stakeholders, and more.
    c. Companies are also increasingly allowing key customers and value-network members to access account, product, and other data on demand through extranets.

7.   **Other Marketing Information Considerations**
    a. There are several other considerations that must be taken into account when collecting marketing information.

Marketing Research in Small Businesses and Nonprofit Organizations
    b. Managers of small businesses and nonprofit organizations can obtain good marketing information simply by observing things around them.
    c. Managers can conduct informal surveys using small convenience samples.
    d. Managers can also conduct their own experiments.
    e. Small organizations can obtain most of the secondary data available to large businesses.
    f. The business sections of local libraries can also be a good source of information.

International Marketing Research
    g. International marketing researchers follow the same steps as domestic researchers. However, these researchers often face more and different problems.
      i. In many foreign markets, the international researcher sometimes has a difficult time finding good secondary data. Many countries have almost no research services at all.
      ii. International researchers often must collect their own primary data. They may find it difficult simply to develop good samples.
      iii. Reaching respondents in other parts of the world is often not easy.

      iv. Translating a questionnaire from one language to another is anything but easy.

      v. Even when respondents are willing to respond, they may not be able to because of high functional illiteracy rates.

Public Policy and Ethics in Marketing Research

h. The misuse of marketing research can harm or annoy consumers.

i. Privacy is a concern.

      i. A few consumers fear that researchers might use sophisticated techniques to probe their deepest feelings and then use this knowledge to manipulate their buying.

      ii. They worry that marketers are building huge databases of personal information about customers.

      iii. Some consumers have been taken in by "research surveys" that actually turned out to be attempts to sell them something.

j. The research industry is considering several options for responding to this problem.

k. If researchers provide value in exchange for information, customers will gladly provide it.

l. Research studies can be powerful persuasion tools; companies often use study results as claims in their advertising and promotion.

Student Exercises

1.   Key Term: Internal Database

Internal databases are electronic collections of consumer and market information obtained from data sources within the company. In today's highly competitive environment, colleges and universities are continually striving to provide better service and be more responsive to the various publics it serves. How does your school use internal databases in its effort to provide better quality customer service to students?

2.   Key Term: Marketing Research

Take a look at Domino's Pizza (www.dominos.com). If you were in charge of marketing research for this company, what are the two types of information you would be interested in having available to you? Remember that marketing research is the systematic design, collection, analysis, and reporting of data relevant to a specific marketing situation facing an organization.

3.   Key Term: Secondary Data

Secondary data is information that already exists somewhere, having been collected for another purpose. Review the website media kit for the new magazine, *Beach Blvd* (www.beachblvd.bz). What secondary data do you see displayed?

4.   Key Term: Secondary Data—External Information Sources

You know what secondary data is now. Many possible sources exist that a company can turn to in an effort to secure needed secondary information. Among government data sources available for use are the U.S. Census (www.census.gov). Take a look. What types of information can you find from an examination of the U.S. Census?

5.   Key Term: Survey

Survey research is the most popular method for primary data collection. It is the approach best suited for gathering descriptive information. Many online data collection company now exist to facilitate the gathering of survey research. One of the most popular is called Zoomerang (www.zoomerang.com). Log on to Zoomerang, take the self guided tour of its capabilities, and then design your own survey.

6.   Key Term: Focus Groups

Group interviewing consists of inviting a small number of people (usually six to ten) to meet with a trained moderator to talk about a product, service, or organization. It is the moderator's job to keep the conversation "focused" on the relevant issues. Focus groups allow marketers access and insights into consumer thoughts and feelings. If you were in charge of marketing for CiCi's Pizza (www.cicispizza.com), how might you employ a focus group to learn more about your market?

7.   Key Term: The Sample

You can't survey everyone. Due to this, marketers typically draw conclusions about the market as a whole by studying a small sample of the total consumer population. A sample is a segment of the population selected to represent the population as a whole. Imagine that your school is contemplating becoming an only online provider of education. You have been asked to design a plan to sample the relevant individuals about there feelings regarding this. What factors must you consider as you determine who to sample, how many people to sample, and how you would choose the sample?

8.   Key Term: The Questionnaire

The questionnaire is by far the most popular data collection instrument—whether administered in person, online, or by phone. Find two examples of online questionnaires.

9.   Key Term: Data Mining

Data mining is the process of sifting through mounds of data to dig out interesting findings about customers. These findings can then be used as the basis of future marketing endeavors. How might Harrah's Entertainment (www.harrahs.com), the world's largest casino operator, use data mining?

10.   Key Term: Small Business Marketing Research

Even small businesses need the benefits of marketing research. To make long-term strategic decisions without the benefits of research is potentially disastrous. However, small businesses many times can not afford the large formalized marketing research programs of the larger organizations. A friend of yours is contemplating opening a new coffee shop close to school and has turned to you for insight on conducting marketing research. How would you advise your friend?

Marketing ADventure Exercises

1.   Ad Interpretation Challenge: Marketing Information System
       Ad: Services and B2B—24 Hour Fitness

A marketing information system is the people, equipment, and procedures used to gather, sort, analyze, evaluate, and distribute needed, timely, and accurate information to marketing decision makers. The effective use of a marketing information system can provide the marketer with a wealth of competitively useful information. Consider 24 Hour Fitness. How could the effective use of a marketing information system have led to the creation of this company?

2.   Ad Interpretation Challenge: Internal Data
       Ad: Apparel—Puma

Internal data is that information obtained from data sources within a company's network. It is information based on current customers. This information may include anything from their purchases over the past year to attitudinal data on likes and dislikes. Look at this ad for Puma. How might a review of Puma's internal data have led to the creation of this ad?

3.   Ad Interpretation Challenge: Internal Data
       Ad: Services and B2B—University of Toronto

Internal data can provide a company with incredibly valuable information about its current (or past) customers. Skillfully used, this information may be used as the basis of a campaign designed to bring more customers into the company fold. Review the ads for the University of Toronto. How do you believe these ads could be the product of the artful use of internal data?

4.   Ad Interpretation Challenge: Causal Research
        Ad: Student Choice

The basic objective of causal research is to test hypotheses about cause-and-effect. For example, if I were to raise my prices by 10 percent, what would happen to sales? Find an ad that highlights the basic premise of cause-and-effect.

5.   Ad Interpretation Challenge: Secondary Data
        Ad: Auto—Cadillac Escalade

Take a look at this ad for the Cadillac Escalade. The information presented in this ad is based on secondary data sources. Secondary data is information that already exists somewhere. You did not create this information. What information is this ad presenting from a secondary data source?

6.   Ad Interpretation Challenge: Primary Data
        Ad: Autos—Dunlop

Primary data is data that is collected specifically for the purpose at hand. Review this ad for Dunlop tires. What is the primary data finding this ad is presenting?

7.   Ad Interpretation Challenge: Ethnographic Research
        Ad: Student Choice

Ethnographic research is a form of observational research that involves sending trained observers to watch and interact with consumers in their "natural habitat." Find an ad that you believe may have been based on ethnographic research.

8.   Ad Interpretation Challenge: Contact Methods—Personal
        Ad: Financial—Alliance

There are many different ways to collect information—by mail, telephone, online, and personal interview. Each method has its own advantages and disadvantages. How does this ad for Alliance Financial Services make use of the personal interview method to get its informational point across?

9.   Ad Interpretation Challenge: Data Mining
        Ad: Internet—EPage

Data mining is a great technique to sift through the mounds of data and dig out interesting and useful bits of information about your customers. Look at the EPage ad. How does this company propose to use data mining to the benefit of its customers?

10.   Ad Interpretation Challenge: Public Policy
       Ad: Nonprofit Corporate Images—Labatt

Companies must always be cognizant of the publics within which they operate and must at all times be good corporate citizens. Public policy issues that have an impact on the company should be addressed and incorporated into the company framework. Labatt, a well-known Canadian brewery, is acknowledging a public policy issue in this ad. What is it?

Chapter 5
Consumer Markets and Consumer Buyer Behavior

Learning Objectives

1. Define the consumer market and construct a simple model of consumer buyer behavior.
2. Name the four major factors that influence consumer buyer behavior.
3. List and understand the major types of buying decision behavior and the stages in the buyer decision process.
4. Describe the adoption and diffusion process for new products.

Chapter Overview

This chapter explores the dynamics of consumer buying behavior and consumer markets. Markets (and those which they serve) have to be understood before marketing strategies can be developed. The consumer market buys goods and services for personal consumption. At present, the world consumer market consists of 6.2 billion people. As will be shown in the next chapter, the consumer market differs from the business market.

With respect to the individuals in the consumer market, the behavior of the consumer is influenced by the buyer's decision process. Buyer characteristics include four major factors: cultural, social, personal, and psychological. Each of these factors is explored in detail. Relationships are drawn between the factors (and factor subparts) and the consumption purchases made by consumers. Because many of these factors are deep and long lasting in their effect, the marketing manager should pay special attention to acquiring information about them with respect to the organization's target markets. Several examples are presented to illustrate how this might be done.

After the chapter examines the influences that affect buyers, a discussion is presented which examines how consumers make actual buying decisions. Decisions vary based on the degree of buyer involvement and the degree of differences among brands. A summary discussion is presented that outlines complex buying behavior, dissonance-reducing buying behavior, habitual buying behavior, and variety-seeking buying behavior. Special focus is directed toward a simple model of buying behavior that explains most of the terms pertinent to the study of buying behavior. The simple model (consisting of five stages—*need recognition, information search, evaluation of alternatives, purchase decision,* and *postpurchase behavior*) ties together material about the buying decision process.

For new products, special situations affect the consumer choice decision. It has been found that consumers respond at different rates (depending on consumer and product characteristics), gain knowledge about the products in different ways, and become aware of "newness" with varying rates of consideration. Factors that speed the rate of adoption of new products are covered and explained.

Understanding consumer behavior is difficult enough for companies marketing within the borders of a single country. The problem is compounded when a firm attempts to market in the global environment. The chapter briefly discloses differences between global and local consumer markets. Lastly, marketers must decide whether to adapt their products to match the demands of the global marketplace or not. The question of adaptation or standardization will be a topic for debate for several years to come.

Chapter Outline

1. **Introduction**
   a. Few brands engender such intense loyalty as that found in the hearts of Harley-Davidson owners.
   b. Harley-Davidson's marketers spend a great deal of time thinking about customers and their buying behavior.
   c. The Harley-Davidson example shows that many factors affect consumer buying behavior.
   d. Consumer buyer behavior refers to the buying behavior of final consumers—individuals and households who buy goods and services for personal consumption.
   e. All of these final consumers combine to make up the consumer market.

2. **Model of Consumer Behavior**
   a. Most large companies research consumer buying decisions in great detail to answer questions about what consumers buy, where they buy, how and how much they buy, when they buy, and why they buy.
   b. Learning about the whys of consumer buying behavior is not so easy—the answers are often locked deep within the consumer's head.
   c. How do consumers respond to various marketing efforts? The starting point is the stimulus-response model of buyer behavior shown in Figure 5.1.
      i. Marketing and other stimuli enter the consumer's "black box" and produce certain responses.
      ii. Marketers must figure out what is in the buyer's black box.
      iii. Marketing stimuli consist of the 4 Ps: product, price, place, and promotion.
      iv. Other stimuli include major forces and events in the buyer's environment.

        v. The buyer's characteristics influence how he or she perceives and reacts to the stimuli.

       vi. The buyer's decision process itself affects the buyer's behavior.

3.   **Characteristics Affecting Consumer Behavior**

   a. Consumer purchases are influenced strongly by several characteristics, shown in figure 5.2.

Cultural Factors

   b. Cultural factors exert a broad and deep influence on consumer behavior.

   c. Culture is the most basic cause of a person's wants and behavior.

       i. Human behavior is largely learned. Growing up in a society, a child learns basic values, perceptions, wants, and behaviors from the family and other important institutions.

      ii. Marketers are always trying to spot cultural shifts in order to discover new products that might be wanted.

   d. Each culture contains smaller subcultures, or groups of people with shared value systems based on common life experiences and situations. Subcultures include nationalities, religions, racial groups, and geographic regions.

       i. The U.S. Hispanic market consists of almost 39 million consumers. Last year, Hispanic consumers bought more than $580 billion worth of goods and services, up 25 percent from just two years earlier. Expected to double in the next 25 years, this group will make up more than 20 percent of the total U.S. population by 2030. Hispanic consumers tend to buy more branded, higher-quality products. Generics do not sell well to this group.

      ii. If the U.S. population of 39 million African Americas were a separate nation, its buyer power of $630 billion annually would rank among the top 15 in the world. The black population in the United States is growing in affluence and sophistication. Although more price conscious than other segments, blacks are also strongly motivated by quality and selection. Brands are important.

     iii. Asian Americans, the fastest-growing and most affluent U.S. demographic segment, now number more than 12 million, with disposable income of $296 billion annually. The U.S. Asian American population is expected to more than double by 2050, when it will make up more than 9 percent of the U.S. population. Asian consumers may be the most tech savvy segment. As a group, Asian consumers shop frequently and are the most brand-conscious of all the ethnic groups. Interestingly, they are also the least brand loyal.

    iv. As the U.S. population ages, mature consumers are becoming a very attractive market. Now 75 million strong, the population of U.S. seniors will more than double during the next 25 years. The 65-and-over crowd alone numbers 36 million, more than 12 percent of the population. Mature consumers are better off financially than are younger consumer groups.

e. Almost every society has some form of social class structure. Social classes are society's relatively permanent and ordered divisions whose members share similar values, interests, and behaviors.

f. Social scientists have identified the seven American social classes shown in Figure 5.3.

g. Social class is not determined by a single factor, such as income, but is measured as a combination of occupation, income, education, wealth, and other variables.

Social Factors

h. A consumer's behavior is also influenced by social factors.

i. A person's behavior is influenced by many small groups.

    i. Groups that have a direct influence and to which a person belongs are called membership groups.

    ii. In contrast, reference groups serve as direct or indirect points of comparison or reference in forming a person's attitudes or behavior. An aspirational group is one to which the individual wishes to belong.

    iii. Manufacturers of products and brands subjected to strong group influence must figure out how to reach opinion leaders—people within a reference group who, because of special skills, knowledge, personality, or other characteristics, exert influence on others. Many marketers use buzz marketing by enlisting or even creating opinion leaders to spread the word about their brands.

j. Family members can strongly influence buyer behavior.

    i. The family is the most important consumer buying organization in society, and it has been researched extensively. Marketers are interested in the roles and influence of the husband, wife, and children on the purchase of different products and services.

    ii. Husband-wife involvement varies widely by product category and by stage in the buying process.

    iii. Children may also have a strong influence on family buying decisions.

k. A person belongs to many groups—family, clubs, and organizations. The person's position in each group can be defined in terms of both role and status.

    i. A role consists of the activities people are expected to perform according to the persons around them.

        ii. Each role carries a status reflecting the general esteem given to it by society.

        iii. People usually choose products appropriate to their roles and status.

<u>Personal Factors</u>

l. A buyer's decisions also are influenced by personal characteristics.

        i. People change the goods and services they buy over their lifetimes.

        ii. Buying is also shaped by the stage of the family life cycle—the stages through which families might pass as they mature over time.

        iii. Traditional family life-cycle stages include young singles and married couples with children.

        iv. Marketers are increasingly catering to a growing number of alternative, nontraditional stages such as unmarried couples, singles marrying later in life, childless couples, same-sex couples, single parents, extended parents (those with young children returning home), and others.

m. A person's occupation affects the goods and services bought.

n. A person's economic situation will affect product choice.

o. People coming from the same subculture, social class, and occupation may have quite different lifestyles.

        i. Lifestyle is a person's pattern of living as expressed in his or her psychographics.

        ii. It involves measuring consumers' major AIO dimensions.

            a. Activities—work, hobbies, shopping sports, social events

            b. Interests—food, fashion, family, recreation

            c. Opinions—about themselves, social issues, business, products

        iii. Several research firms have developed lifestyle classifications. The most widely used is the SRI Consulting's Values and Lifestyles (VALS) typology shown in Figure 5.4.

            a. VALS classifies people according to how they spend their time and money.

            b. It divides consumers into eight groups based on two major dimensions: primary motivation and resources.

            c. Primary motivations include ideals, achievement, and self-expression.

            d. Consumers within each orientation are further classified into those with high resources and those with low resources.

        iv. Lifestyle segmentation can also be used to understand how consumers use the Internet, computers, and other technology.

            a. Forrester developed its "technographics" scheme, which segments consumers according to motivation, desire, and ability to invest in technology.

p. Each person's distinct personality influences his or her buying behavior.

      i. *Personality* refers to the unique psychological characteristics that lead to relatively consistent and lasting responses to one's own environment.

      ii. The idea is that brands also have personalities, and that consumers are likely to choose brands whose personalities match their own.

q. Related to personality is a person's self-concept. The basic self-concept premise is that people's possessions contribute to and reflect their identities.

Psychological Factors

r. A person's buying choices are further influenced by four major psychological factors.

      i. A person has many needs at any given time. Some are biological, others psychological.

      ii. A need becomes a motive when it is aroused to a sufficient level of intensity.

      iii. A motive or drive is a need that is sufficiently pressing to direct the person to seek satisfaction.

      iv. Sigmund Freud assumed that people are largely unconscious about the real psychological forces shaping their behavior.

            a. He saw the person as growing up and repressing many urges.

            b. Freud's theory suggests that a person's buying decisions are affected by subconscious motives that even the buyer may not fully understand.

            c. The term *motivation research* refers to qualitative research designed to probe consumers' hidden, subconscious motivations.

            d. Many companies employ teams of psychologists, anthropologists, and other social scientists to carry out motivation research.

      v. Abraham Maslow sought to explain why people are driven by particular needs at particular times.

            a. Human needs are arranged in a hierarchy, as shown in Figure 5.5, from the most pressing at the bottom to the least pressing at the top.

            b. They include physiological needs, safety needs, social needs, esteem needs, and self-actualization needs.

            c. A person tries to satisfy the most important need first. When that need is satisfied, it will stop being a motivator and the person will then try to satisfy the next most important need.

s. A motivated person is ready to act. How that person acts is influenced by his or her own perception of the situation.

    i. Perception is the process by which people select, organize, and interpret information to form a meaningful picture of the world.

    ii. People can form different perceptions of the same stimulus because of three perceptual processes.

        a. Selective attention is the tendency for people to screen out most of the information to which they are exposed.

        b. Selective distortion describes the tendency of people to interpret information in a way that will support what they already believe.

        c. Because of selective retention, consumers are likely to remember good points about a brand they favor and to forget good points made about competing brands.

t. Learning describes changes in an individual's behavior arising from experience.

    i. Learning theorists say that most human behavior is learned. Learning occurs through the interplay of drives, stimuli, cues, responses, and reinforcement.

        a. A drive is a strong internal stimulus that calls for action.

        b. A drive becomes a motive when it is directed toward a particular stimulus object.

        c. Cues are minor stimuli that determine when, where, and how the person responds.

    ii. The practical significance of learning theory for marketers is that they can build up demand for a product by associating it with strong drives, using motivating cues, and providing positive reinforcement.

u. A belief is a descriptive thought that a person has about something. An attitude describes a person's relatively consistent evaluations, feelings, and tendencies toward an object or idea.

    i. Attitudes are difficult to change. A person's attitude fits into a pattern, and to change one attitude may require difficult adjustments in many others.

4.   **Types of Buying Decision Behavior**

    a. Figure 5.6 shows types of consumer buying behavior based on the degree of buyer involvement and the degree of differences among brands.

Complex Buying Behavior

    b. Consumers undertake complex buying behavior when they are highly involved in a purchase and perceive significant differences among brands.

        i. Consumers may be highly involved when the product is expensive, risky, purchased infrequently, and highly self-expressive.

        ii. Typically, the consumer has much to learn about the product category.

    c. Marketers of high-involvement products must understand the information-gathering and evaluation behavior of high-involvement consumers.

Dissonance-Reducing Buying Behavior

d. Dissonance-reducing buying behavior occurs when consumers are highly involved with an expensive, infrequent, or risky purchase, but see little difference among brands.

e. After the purchase, consumers might experience postpurchase dissonance (after-sale discomfort) when they notice certain disadvantages of the purchased brand or hear favorable things about brands not purchased.

f. To counter such dissonance, the marketer's after-sale communications should provide evidence and support to help consumers feel good about their brand choices.

Habitual Buying Behavior

g. Habitual buying behavior occurs under conditions of low consumer involvement and little significant brand difference.

h. Consumer behavior does not pass through the usual belief-attitude-behavior sequence.

    i. Consumers do not search extensively for information about the brands, evaluate brand characteristics, and make weighty decisions about which brands to buy.

    ii. They passively receive information as they watch television or read magazines.

i. Because buyers are not highly committed to any brands, marketers of low-involvement products with few brand differences often use price and sales promotions to stimulate product trial.

Variety-Seeking Buying Behavior

j. Consumers undertake variety-seeking buying behavior in situations characterized by low consumer involvement but significant perceived brand differences.

k. In such cases, consumers often do a lot of brand switching.

5. The Buyer Decision Process

a. Figure 5.7 shows that the buyer decision process consists of five stages.

b. The buying process begins long before actual purchase and continues long after. Marketers need to focus on the entire buying process rather than just on the purchase decision.

Need Recognition

c. The buying process starts with need recognition—the buyer recognizes a problem or need.

d. The need can be triggered by internal stimuli when one of the person's normal needs—hunger, thirst, or sex—rises to a level high enough to become a drive.

e. A need can also be triggered by external stimuli, e.g., an advertisement or a discussion with a friend.

Information Search

f. An interested consumer may or may not search for more information.

g. If so, a consumer will undertake an information search related to the need.

h. The amount of searching you will do depends on the strength of your drive, the amount of information you start with, the ease of obtaining more information, the value you place on additional information, and the satisfaction you get from searching.

i. Consumers can obtain information from several sources.

    i. Personal sources.

    ii. Commercial sources.

    iii. Public sources.

    iv. Experiential sources.

    v. The relative influence of these information sources varies with the product and the buyer.

j. As more information is obtained, the consumer's awareness and knowledge of the available brands and features increase.

Evaluation of Alternatives

k. The marketer needs to know about alternative evaluation—that is, how the consumer processes information to arrive at brand choices.

l. Consumers do not use a simple and single evaluation process in all buying situations. Instead, several evaluation processes are at work.

m. How consumers go about evaluating purchase alternatives depends on the individual consumer and the specific buying situation.

Purchase Decision

n. In the evaluation stage, the consumer ranks brands and forms purchase intentions.

o. Generally, the consumer's purchase decision will be to buy the most preferred brand, but two factors can come between the purchase intention and the purchase decision.

    i. The first factor is the attitudes of others.

    ii. The second factor is unexpected situational factors.

Postpurchase Behavior

p. After purchasing the product, the consumer will be satisfied or dissatisfied and will engage in postpurchase behavior of interest to the marketer.

q. Determining if the consumer is satisfied or not is the relationship between the consumer's expectations and the product's perceived performance.

r. The larger the gap between expectations and performance, the greater the consumer's dissatisfaction.

s. Almost all major purchases result in cognitive dissonance, or discomfort caused by postpurchase conflict.

6. **The Buyer Decision Process for New Products**
  a. A new product is a good, service, or idea that is perceived by some potential customers as new. It may have been around for a while, but our interest is in how consumers learn about products for the first time and make decisions on whether to adopt them.
  b. The *adoption process* is defined as the mental process through which an individual passes from first learning about an innovation to final adoption.
  c. *Adoption* is defined as the decision by an individual to become a regular user of the product.

Stages in the Adoption Process
  d. Consumers go through five stages in the process of adopting a new product.
      i. Awareness
      ii. Interest
      iii. Evaluation
      iv. Trial
      v. Adoption
  e. This model suggests that the new-product marketer should think about how to help consumers move through these stages.

Individual Differences in Innovativeness
  f. People differ greatly in their readiness to try new products.
  g. People can be classified into the major adopter categories shown in Figure 5.8.
  h. This adopter classification suggests that an innovating firm should research the characteristics of innovators and early adopters and should direct marketing efforts towards them.

Influence of Product Characteristics on Rate of Adoption
  i. The characteristics of the new product affect its rate of adoption.
      i. Relative advantage—the degree to which the innovation appears superior to existing products
      ii. Compatibility—the degree to which the innovation fits the values and experiences of potential consumers
      iii. Complexity—the degree to which the innovation is difficult to understand or use
      iv. Divisibility—the degree to which the innovation may be tried on a limited basis
      v. Communicability—the degree to which the results of using the innovation can be observed or described by others

Consumer Behavior Across International Borders
  j. For companies operating in many countries, understanding and serving the needs of consumers can be daunting.

    k. Although consumers in different countries may have some things in common, their values, attitudes, and behaviors often vary greatly.

    l. Sometimes the differences are obvious. But often they are subtle.

    m. There may be physical differences in consumers and their environments. Other differences result from varying customs.

    n. Marketers must decide on the degree to which they will adapt their products and marketing programs to meet the unique cultures and needs of consumers in various markets.

    o. On the one hand, they want to standardize their offerings in order to simplify operations and take advantage of cost economies. On the other hand, adapting marketing efforts within each country results in products and programs that better satisfy the needs of local consumers.

Student Exercises

1.   Key Term: Cultural Shifts

Culture is not a static phenomenon. It is constantly changing and evolving. This results in cultural shifts—the shifting of culture to incorporate these changes. Companies have to pay attention and adapt to these shifts if they are to remain viable businesses. The cigarette industry is a great example. Take a look at RJR Tobacco Company (www.rjrt.com). How are they adapting as the U.S. culture shifts towards non-smoking?

2.   Key Term: Subculture

Every culture contains subcultures. Subcultures are groups of people with shared value systems based on common life experiences and situations. Many subcultures make up important markets and marketers design products and programs tailored to their specific needs. Think about how your school is attempting to reach important subcultures.

3.   Key Term: Hispanic Market

The Hispanic market now contains more than 41 million consumers. It is the fastest growing U.S. subsegment. Hispanic consumers tend to buy more branded, higher-quality products. They tend to make shopping a family affair. How is Chevrolet (www.chevrolet.com) catering to this important subsegment of the U.S. population?

4.   Key Term: Mature Consumers

The U.S. population is getting older. Due to this, mature consumers are becoming a very attractive market segment. Currently, over 37 million Americans are over the age of 65, and the number is growing rapidly. Mature consumers are typically better off financially than their under counterparts. What is one company that caters exclusively to this market?

5.   Key Term: Social Groups

Pretty much every society has some form of social class structure. Social classes are a society's relatively permanent and ordered divisions whose members share similar values, interests, and behaviors. Go to Bentley Motorcars (www.bentley.com). To what social class do you believe this company caters?

6.   Key Term: Opinion Leader

People within a reference group who, because of special skills, knowledge, personality, or other characteristic, exert social influence on others are known as opinion leaders. These people are also called the "influentials" or "leading adopters." They are a very important group to marketers as they influence those who adopt a product after them. Take a look at the homepage for Scion (a marquee of Toyota Motors) (www.scion.com). How would you say Scion has used opinion leaders to get the word out about their cars?

7.   Key Term: Family

The American family isn't what it used to be. Cultural shifts have caused changes in family structure and functions. Undoubtedly, the family is the most important consumer buying organization in our society. Many companies focus on the family with their products and promotions. In many cases, children also have a strong influence on family buying decisions. Find examples of companies that promote to children in hopes of reaching the parents.

8.   Key Term: Lifestyle

A lifestyle is a person's pattern of living as expressed in his/her psychographics. It is based around their AIO dimensions—activities (work, school, hobbies, shopping, etc.), interests (fashion, recreation, food, etc.), and opinions (about themselves, the community, business, anything). What is your lifestyle and what does it say about you?

9.   Key Term: Motive

A motive (or a drive) is a need that is sufficiently pressing to direct the person to seek satisfaction. It is believed that motivation drives us to satisfy lower level needs before we can reach attempt to satisfy higher level need. (You may want to review Maslow's hierarchy of needs.) Find a company whose purpose it is to satisfy our lower level needs.

10.   Key Term: Cognitive Dissonance

Almost all major purchases result in some form of cognitive dissonance. Cognitive dissonance is buyer discomfort caused by post-purchase conflict. There is a tendency for consumers to feel some level of post-purchase dissonance (or discomfort) for every purchase. Companies want to do what they can to help lessen this post-purchase anxiety. Take a look at L.L. Bean (www.llbean.com). What does this company do to help its customers do away with cognitive dissonance and remain happy, satisfied customers?

Marketing ADventure Exercises

1.   Ad Interpretation Challenge: Cultural Shifts
      Ad: Apparel—Levi's New Collection

Culture is constantly changing and evolving. It is not a static phenomenon. This results in cultural shifts—the shifting of culture to incorporate these changes. Companies have to pay attention and adapt to these shifts if they are to remain viable businesses. Often, companies miss out on these shifts and face the real risk of becoming marginalized by their competition. Take a look at this ad for Levi's New Collection. What does this ad say about their response to this phenomenon?

2.   Ad Interpretation Challenge: Subcultures
      Ad: Autos—Chevy S10 Truck

Each culture contains multiple subcultures—those groups of people with shared value systems based on common life experiences and situations. The U.S. Hispanic market is one such subculture. The Hispanic market is the fastest growing submarket in the United States today. Soon, this group will make up almost 25 percent of the U.S. population. No wonder businesses are starting to pay attention. How does this ad for the S10 truck appeal to this important subculture?

3.   Ad Interpretation Challenge: Mature Consumers
      Ad: Student Choice

Mature consumers are becoming increasingly important to American business. Currently, more than 68 million consumers are considered part of this market. Generally, mature consumers have more time and money than other age groups. Find an ad for a product that you believe appeals to this market segment.

4.   Ad Interpretation Challenge: Social Class
        Ad: Autos—Jaguar

Social classes are society's relatively permanent and ordered divisions whose members share similar values, interests, and behaviors. Products are designed to appeal to members of particular social classes. Look at the Jaguar ads. To which social class would you say Jaguar is attempting to appeal?

5.   Ad Interpretation Challenge: Opinion Leader
        Ad: Internet—Leaping Salmon

Manufacturers of products or services subjected to strong group influence must figure out how to reach the opinion leaders. Opinion leaders are those people within a particular reference group who exert social influence on others within the group. How might Leaping Salmon use opinion leaders to encourage adoption of its products?

6.   Ad Interpretation Challenge: Family
        Ad: Food and Beverage—McDonald's Happy Meal

Family is the most important consumer buying organization in society. All family members can have a strong influence on buyer behavior. Recognizing the importance of family, many companies target this group. Look at this ad for McDonald's. Who, within the family, does this ad target?

7.   Ad Interpretation Challenge: Life-Cycle
        Ad: Financial—MasterCard Home Alone

People change the products and services they buy over the course of their lifetimes. Tastes in food, clothes, transportation, and recreation are often age related. Find an ad that is targeted to a specific stage of the life-cycle. To whom do you believe this ad it targeted? How might this ad be changed to target a different stage?

8.   Ad Interpretation Challenge: Brand Personality
        Ad: Student Choice

Brand personality is the specific mix of human traits that may be attributed to a particular brand. Researchers have identified five brand personality traits. Find an ad that personifies the brand personality trait of "sophistication."

9.   Ad Interpretation Challenge: Selective Attention
       Ad: Cosmetics and Pharmaceuticals—Schick

Selective attention is the tendency for people to screen out most of the information to which they are exposed. Because of this, marketers have to work especially hard to attract the consumer's attention to where they really want it. Look quickly at this ad for Lady Schick. What features within this ad did you initially notice? Now, go back and review this ad again in detail. What other information do you notice? This exemplifies the issues facing marketers—to get you to notice all the information contained in an ad in the initial review.

10.   Ad Interpretation Challenge: Information Search
       Ad: Student Choice

Information search is the stage of the buyer decision process in which the consumer is aroused to search for more information. At this time, the person may simply have heightened attention or may go into an active information search. Find an ad that provides the reader with a quantity of information with which to make comparisons between alternatives.

Chapter 6
Business Markets and Business Buyer Behavior

Learning Objectives

1. Define the business market and explain how business markets differ from consumer markets.
2. Identify the major factors that influence business buyer behavior.
3. List and define the steps in the business buying-decision process.
4. Compare the institutional and government markets and explain how institutional and government buyers make their buying decisions.

Chapter Overview

The business market is huge. In the United States alone, it consists of millions of organizations that buy trillions of dollars worth of goods and services each year. In many ways business markets are like consumer markets, but in many other ways they are much different. Points of comparison can be in areas of market structure and demand, the nature of the buying unit, the types of decisions, and the decision process involved.

It can be observed that business markets usually have fewer but larger (volume) buyers who are more geographically concentrated and use more rational methods for making their purchasing decisions. In addition, there are usually more individuals involved in the business buying decision (for example, purchasing by committee). These professional buyers are also usually better trained and skilled at negotiation than their counterpart consumer buyers. Difficulties arise because business buying decisions are often very complex, lengthier, and more formal in nature. The seller must accommodate and adjust to these characteristics if success in this market is to be obtained.

The chapter explores a variety of models that explain the business buying process. These models are excellent ways to show the main points of the business buying process as compared to those of the consumer buying process mentioned above. It should be remembered that four key questions must be answered before the business market is pursued by the firm's marketing efforts. What buying decisions do business buyers make? Who participates in the buying process? What are the major influences on buyers? How do business buyers make their buying decisions?

During the past few years, incredible advances in information technology have changed the face of the business-to-business marketing process. Increasingly, business buyers are purchasing all kinds of products and services electronically, either through electronic data interchange links or on the Internet. The chapter discusses how the "e-purchasing" process works for the business-to-business market and details the benefits shared by exchange partners. The process is, however, not without drawbacks. A challenge for managers will be to increase the benefits and decrease the drawbacks, to link their organizations to cyber-networks, and to create new models that will work in the new Internet age.

The chapter concludes with an examination of two unique non-business markets—institutional and government markets. These markets have additional characteristics and needs. The special features of each are examined.

Chapter Outline

1. **Introduction**
   a. Most of UPS' revenues come not from the residential customers who receive packages, but from the business customers who send them.
   b. Over the years, UPS has grown to become much more than a neighborhood small package delivery service. It is now a $35 billion corporate giant providing a broad range of logistics solutions. UPS handles the logistics, allowing customers to focus on what they do best.
   c. In one way or another, most large companies sell to other organizations.
   d. Business buyer behavior refers to the buying behavior of the organizations that buy goods and services for use in the production of other products and services that are sold, rented, or supplied to others. It also includes the behavior of retailing and wholesaling firms that acquire goods for the purpose of reselling or renting them to others at a profit.
   e. In the business buying process, business buyers determine which products and services their organizations need to purchase, and then find, evaluate, and choose among alternative suppliers and brands.
   f. Business-to-business marketers must do their best to understand business markets and business buyer behavior.

2. **Business Markets**
   a. The business market is huge. In fact, business markets involve far more dollars and items than do consumer markets.

   Market Structure and Demand
   b. The main differences between business and consumer markets are shown in Table 6.1
   c. The business marketer normally deals with far fewer but far larger buyers than the consumer marketer does.

      i. Even in large business markets, a few buyers often account for most of the purchasing.

      ii. Business markets are more geographically concentrated. More than half the business buyers are concentrated in eight states.

      iii. Business demand is derived demand—it ultimately derives from the demand of consumer goods. B2B marketers sometimes promote their products directly to final consumers to increase business demand.

      iv. Many business markets have inelastic demand; that is, total demand for many business products is not affected much by price changes, especially in the short run.

      v. Business markets have more fluctuating demand. The demand for many business goods and services tends to change more—and more quickly—than the demand for consumer goods and services does.

Nature of the Buying Unit

d. Compared with consumer purchases, a business purchase usually involves more decision participants and a more professional purchasing effort.

      i. Often, business buying is done by trained purchasing agents who spend their working lives learning how to buy better.

      ii. The more complex the purchase, the more likely that several people will participate in the decision-making process.

      iii. Many companies are now upgrading their purchasing functions to "supply management" or "supplier development" functions.

Types of Decisions and the Decision Process

e. Business buyers usually face more complex buying decisions than do consumer buyers.

      i. Purchases often involve large sums of money, complex technical and economic considerations, and interactions among many people at many levels of the buyer's organization.

      ii. The business buying process also tends to be more formalized than the consumer buying process.

      iii. In the business buying process, buyer and seller are often much more dependent on each other.

      iv. Many customer companies are now practicing supplier development, systematically developing networks of supplier-partners to ensure an appropriate and dependable supply of products and materials that they will use in making their own products or reselling to others.

3. **Business Buyer Behavior**

    a. There are four major areas that must be studied to understand business buyer behavior.

    b. Figure 6.1 shows a model business buyer behavior.

   c. Marketing and other stimuli affect the buying organization and produce certain buyer responses.

   d. As with consumer buying, the marketing stimuli for business buying consist of the 4 Ps.

   e. Other stimuli include major forces in the environment: economic, technological, political, cultural, and competitive.

   f. In order to design good marketing mix strategies, the marketer must understand what happens within the organization to turn stimuli into purchase responses.

Major Types of Buying Situations

   g. There are three major types of buying situations.

      i. In a straight rebuy, the buyer reorders something without any modifications. It is usually handled on a routine basis by the purchasing department.

      ii. In a modified rebuy, the buyer wants to modify the product specifications, prices, terms, or suppliers. The modified rebuy usually involves more decision participants than does the straight rebuy.

      iii. A company buying a product or service for the first time faces a new-task situation. In such cases, the greater the cost or risk, the larger the number of decision participants and the greater their efforts to collect information will be.

   h. The buyer makes the fewest decisions in the straight rebuy and the most in the new-task process.

   i. Many business buyers prefer to buy a packaged solution to a problem from a single seller. Instead of buying and putting all the components together, the buyer may ask sellers to supply the components and assemble the package or system. Thus, systems selling is often a key business marketing strategy for winning and holding accounts.

Participants in the Business Buying Process

   j. The decision-making unit of a buying organization is called its buying center: all the individuals and units that participate in the business decision-making process.

   k. The buying center includes all members of the organization who play any of five roles in the purchase decision process.

      i. Users are members of the organization who will use the product or service.

      ii. Influencers often help define specifications and also provide information for evaluating alternatives.

      iii. Buyers have formal authority to select the supplier and arrange terms of purchase.

      iv. Deciders have formal or informal power to select or approve the final suppliers.

      v. Gatekeepers control the flow of information to others.

l. The buying center is not a fixed and formally identified unit within the buying organization. It is a set of buying roles assumed by different people for different purchases.

m. Within the organization, the size and makeup of the buying center will vary for different products and for different buying situations.

n. The buying center concept presents a major marketing challenge. The business marketer must learn who participates in the decision, each participant's relative influence, and what evaluation criteria each decision participant uses.

o. The buying center usually includes some obvious participants who are involved formally in the buying process. It may also involve less obvious, informal participants, some of whom may actually make or strongly affect the buying decision. Sometimes, even the people in the buying center are not aware of all the buying participants.

Major Influences on Business Buyers

p. Business buyers are subject to many influences when they make their buying decisions.

q. Business buyers respond to both economic and personal factors. They react to both reason and emotion.

    i. When suppliers' offers are very similar, business buyers have little basis for strictly rational choice. Because they can meet organizational goals with any supplier, buyers can allow personal factors to play a larger role in their decisions.

    ii. When competing products differ greatly, business buyers are more accountable for their choice and tend to pay more attention to economic factors.

r. Figure 6.2 lists various groups of influences on business buyers.

s. Business buyers are heavily influenced by factors in the current and expected economic environment, such as the level of primary demand, the economic outlook, and the cost of money.

    i. An increasingly important environmental factor is shortages in key materials. Many companies are now more willing to buy and hold larger inventories of scarce materials to ensure adequate supply.

    ii. Business buyers also are affected by technological, political, and competitive developments in the environment.

    iii. Culture and customs can strongly influence business buyer reactions to the marketer's behavior and strategies, especially in the international marketing environment.

t. Each buying organization has its own objectives, policies, procedures, structure, and systems, and the business marketer must understand those factors as well.

u. The buying center usually includes many participants who influence each other, so interpersonal factors also influence the business buying process. It is often difficult to assess such interpersonal factors and group dynamics.

v. Each participant in the business buying-decision process brings in personal motives, perceptions, and preferences. These individual factors are affected by personal characteristics such as age, income, education, professional identification, personality, and attitudes toward risk.

<u>The Business Buying Process</u>

w. Figure 6.3 lists the eight stages of the business buying process.

    i. Buyers who face a new-task buying situation usually go through all stages of the buying process.

    ii. Buyers making modified or straight rebuys may skip some of the stages.

    iii. Problem recognition can result from internal or external stimuli.

        a. Internally, the company may decide to launch a new product that requires new production equipment and materials.

        b. Externally, the buyer may get some new ideas at a trade show, see an ad, or receive a call from a salesperson who offers a better product or a lower price.

    iv. The buyer next prepares a general need description that describes the characteristics and quantity of the needed item.

        a. For standard items, this process presents few problems.

        b. For complex items, however, the buyer may have to work with others—engineers, users, consultants—to define the item.

    v. The buying organization next develops the item's technical product specifications, often with the help of a value analysis engineering team.

        a. Value analysis is an approach to cost reduction in which components are studied carefully to determine if they can be redesigned, standardized, or made by less costly methods of production.

        b. The team decides on the best product characteristics and specifies them accordingly.

    vi. The buyer now conducts a supplier search to find the best vendors.

        a. The buyer can compile a small list of qualified suppliers by reviewing trade directories, doing a computer search, or phoning other companies for recommendations.

        b. Today, more and more companies are turning to the Internet to find suppliers.

        c. The newer the buying task, the more complex and costly the item, and the greater the amount of time the buyer will spend searching for suppliers.

  vii. In the proposal solicitation stage of the business buying process, the buyer invites qualified suppliers to submit proposals.

    a. When the item is complex or expensive, the buyer will usually require detailed written proposals or formal presentations from each potential supplier.

 viii. During supplier selection, the buying center often will draw up a list of the desired supplier attributes and their relative importance.

    a. Buyers may attempt to negotiate with preferred suppliers for better prices and terms before making the final selections.

    b. In the end, they may select a single supplier or a few suppliers.

    c. Many buyers prefer multiple sources of suppliers to avoid being totally dependent on one supplier and to allow comparisons of prices and performance of several suppliers over time.

  ix. The buyer now prepares an order-routine specification.

    a. It includes the final order with the chosen supplier or suppliers and lists items such as technical specifications, quantity needed, expected time of delivery, return policies, and warranties.

    b. In the case of maintenance, repair, and operating items, buyers may use blanket contracts rather than periodic purchase orders. A blanket contract creates a long-term relationship in which the supplier promises to resupply the buyer as needed at agreed prices for a set time period.

  x. The performance review may lead the buyer to continue, modify, or drop the arrangement.

  xi. The eight-stage model provides a simple view of the business buying-decision process. The actual process is usually much more complex.

E-Procurement: Buying on the Internet

x. Online purchasing, often called e-procurement, is growing rapidly.

  i. In a recent survey, almost 75 percent of business buyers indicated that they use the Internet to make at least some of their purchases.

  ii. Much online purchasing takes place through online auctions and on public and private online trading exchanges (or e-market-places).

 iii. E-procurement gives buyers access to new suppliers and lower purchasing costs, and hastens order processing and delivery. In turn, business marketers can connect with customers online to share marketing information, sell products and services, provide customer support services, and maintain ongoing customer relationships.

y. So far, most products bought online are MRO materials—maintenance, repair, and operations.

    i. The actual dollar amount spent on these types of MRO materials pales in comparison to the amount spent for items such as airplane parts, computer systems, and steel tubing.

    ii. Yet MRO materials make up 80 percent of all business orders, and the transaction costs for order processing are high.

    iii. Thus, companies have much to gain by streamlining the MRO buying process on the Web.

z. Business-to-business e-procurement yields many benefits.

    i. It shaves transaction costs and results in more efficient purchasing for both buyers and suppliers.

    ii. A Web-powered purchasing program eliminates the paperwork associated with traditional requisition and ordering procedures. On average, companies can trim the costs of procured goods alone by 15 percent to 20 percent.

    iii. E-procurement reduces the time between order and delivery. Time savings are particularly dramatic for companies with many overseas suppliers.

    iv. Beyond the cost and time savings, e-procurement frees purchasing people to focus on more strategic issues.

aa. The use of e-purchasing also presents some problems.

    i. At the same time that the Web makes it possible for suppliers and customers to share business data and even collaborate on product design, it can also erode decades-old customer-supplier relationships.

    ii. E-procurement can create potential security disasters. More than 80 percent of companies say security is the leading barrier to expanding electronic links with customers and partners.

4. **Institutional and Government Markets**

    a. Much of this discussion also applies to the buying practices of institutional and government organizations. However, these two non-business markets have additional characteristics and needs.

Institutional Markets

    b. The institutional market consists of schools, hospitals, nursing homes, prisons, and other institutions that provide goods and services to people in their care. Institutions differ from one another in their sponsors and in their objectives.

    c. Many institutional markets are characterized by low budgets and captive patrons.

    d. Many marketers set up separate divisions to meet the special characteristics and needs of institutional buyers.

Government Markets

e. The government market offers large opportunities for many companies, both big and small.

f. In most countries, government organizations are major buyers of goods and services. In the United States alone, federal, state, and local governments contain more than 82,000 buying units.

g. Government organizations typically require suppliers to submit bids, and normally they award the contract to the lowest bidder.

    i. In some cases, the government unit will make allowance for the supplier's superior quality or reputation for completing contracts on time.

h. Government organizations tend to favor domestic suppliers over foreign suppliers.

i. Government buyers are affected by environmental, organizational, interpersonal, and individual factors.

    i. One unique thing about government buying is that it is carefully watched by outside publics, ranging from Congress to a variety of private groups interested in how the government spends taxpayers' money.

    ii. Because their spending decisions are subject to public review, government organizations require considerable paperwork from suppliers, who often complain about excessive paperwork, bureaucracy, regulations, decision-making delays, and frequent shifts in procurement personnel.

j. Most governments provide would-be suppliers with detailed guides describing how to sell to the government.

k. Non-economic criteria also play a growing role in government buying.

    i. Government buyers are asked to favor depressed business firms and areas; small business firms; minority-owned firms; and business firms that avoid race, gender, or age discrimination.

l. Many firms that sell to the government have not been marketing oriented.

    i. Total government spending is determined by elected officials rather than by any marketing effort to develop this market.

    ii. Government buying has emphasized price, making suppliers invest their effort in technology to bring costs down.

    iii. When the product's characteristics are specified carefully, product differentiation is not a marketing factor.

    iv. Nor do advertising or personal selling much matter in winning bids on an open-bid basis.

m. Several companies, however, have established separate government marketing departments.

i. These companies anticipate government needs and projects, participate in the product specification phase, gather competitive intelligence, prepare bids carefully, and produce stronger communications to describe and enhance their companies' reputations.

n. During the past decade, some of the government's buying has gone online.

Student Exercises

1.   Key Term: B2B Marketers

In essence, B2B marketers are those organizations that sell to other organizations. This includes companies as diverse as Boeing, Caterpillar, General Mills, and Procter and Gamble. Take a look at the Folgers Coffee (a product of PandG) website (www.folgers.com). From this review, why would you say Folgers (and PandG) operates as a B2B marketer?

2.   Key Term: Derived Demand

Derived demand is demand that originates from the consumer and their purchase of consumer goods. Your text uses the example of Intel. HP, Dell, and other computer manufacturers buy Intel chips because consumers buy PCs. If consumer demand for personal computers slows, so will the demand for computer chips. Log on to American Bolt and Screw's website (www.absfasteners.com) and take a look at the products they offer. How is their business a function of derived demand?

3.   Key Term: Supplier Development

The systematic development of networks of supplier-partners to ensure an organization appropriate and dependable supplies of products and materials that will be used in the making of their own products or in resell to others is known as supplier development. This is the result of shifts in the relationship between customers and suppliers from somewhat adversarial to close alliances. Find two companies that promote this supplier-partner relationship (other than listed in your chapter).

4.   Key Term: Straight Rebuy
There are only three major types of buying situations, one of which is the straight rebuy. A straight rebuy occurs when a buyer reorders something without any modification. Think about your favorite restaurant in town. What would be examples of a straight rebuy your restaurant might place?

5.   Key Term: Systems Selling

When a vendor provides a packaged solution to a problem, thus alleviating a company from having to make all of the separate decisions involved in a complex buying situation, they are engaging in "systems selling." Systems selling is a key marketing strategy for winning and holding accounts. Find a company that engages in systems selling.

6.   Key Term: The Buying Center

The buying center of an organization is made up of all the individuals and units that play a role in the purchase decision-making process. To bring the buying center to a more personal level, think about your family. Describe your family in "buying center" terms for the purchase of a new automobile.

7.   Key Term: Environmental Factors

Business buyers are heavily influenced by factors in the current and expected economic environment—factors such as supply conditions, technological change, and political and regulatory developments. Consider R.J. Reynolds (www.rjrt.com), the manufacturer of one out of three cigarettes sold in the U.S. How may have environmental factors impacted the buyers within this company?

8.   Key Term: Proposal Solicitation

The stage of the business buying process in which the buyer invites qualified suppliers to submit a proposal is known as the proposal solicitation stage. Locate a company that is currently seeking proposals from qualified suppliers.

9.   Key Term: E-Procurement

Online purchasing is growing at a very rapid pace, thanks to advances in information technology. B2B marketers help customers who wish to purchase online by providing them with easy-to-use websites. Take a look at e-procurement site for Office Depot (https://bsd.officedepot.com/). How are they making it easier for organization to take advantage of online purchasing?

10.   Key Term: Institutional Markets

Institutional markets are different from other markets. In many cases, the lowest price is not the primary objective. Take a look at your school's cafeterias. Why would you characterize them as an institutional market?

Marketing ADventure Exercises

1.   Ad Interpretation Challenge: Business Markets
     Ad: Service and B2B—SpeedStart

As your text points out, the business market is huge—far larger than the consumer market. The business market is made up of goods and services for use in the production of other products and services that are sold to others. This ad for SpeedStart is just one of many examples of advertisements directed to a business market. From this ad, what lets you know that SpeedStart is a B2B company?

2.   Ad Interpretation Challenge: Derived Demand
     Ad: Electronics—Axiom

Derived demand is business demand that ultimately comes from the demand for consumer goods or services. How does Axiom provide an example of derived demand?

3.   Ad Interpretation Challenge: Inelastic Demand
     Ad: Autos—Dunlop

Many business markets have inelastic demand—meaning that total demand for many business products is affected very little by price changes, at least in the short run. Think about this ad for Dunlop tires. What business products, used by Dunlop in the production of these tires, may display inelastic demand?

4.   Ad Interpretation Challenge: Straight Rebuy
     Ad: Services and B2B—EMS

A straight rebuy situation occurs when the business routinely reorders something without any modification. They use the same product or service over and over. Check out this ad for EMS. Think of a situation in which EMS services become a straight rebuy for a company.

5.   Ad Interpretation Challenge: Systems Selling
     Ad: Services and B2B—Springbow

Many business buyers prefer to buy a packaged solution to a problem from a single supplier. This keeps the company from having to buy the separate components and create the package solution themselves. This is systems selling. How is Springbow engaging in systems selling?

6.   Ad Interpretation Challenge: Environmental Factors
        Ad: Services and B2B—Posta

Business buyers are heavily influenced by factors in the current and anticipated economic environment. Business buyers are also impacted by technological, political, and competitive developments in the environment. Additionally, culture and customs can play a significant role in buyer behavior. What environmental factors may be at play in this ad for the Italian Postal System?

7.   Ad Interpretation Challenge: Problem Recognition
        Ad: Services and B2B—Varig

The first stage of the business buying process is when someone in the company recognizes a problem or need that can be met by acquiring a good or a service. Sometimes, marketers can facilitate this problem recognition by providing information to buying centers that may assist them is recognizing a problem. Think about this ad for Varig cargo services. How might this ad be useful in helping a member of the buying center realize a problem exists?

8.   Ad Interpretation Challenge: E-Procurement
        Ad: Student Choice

During the past several years, technology has made it much easier to accomplish online purchasing (e-procurement). This advance is changing the face of the B2B marketing process. Find an ad for a company that you believe could have their product or services purchased through an e-procurement system.

9.   Ad Interpretation Challenge: Institutional Markets
        Ad: Student Choice

The institutional market consists of schools, hospitals, prisons, and other institutions that provide goods and services to people in their care. Many institutional markets are characterized by captive patrons. Find an ad for an institutional marketer.

10.   Ad Interpretation Challenge: Government Markets
        Ad: Electronics—Energizer

In most countries, government organizations are major buyers of goods and services. Although government buying and business buying are alike in many ways, differences do exist. Government organizations typically award contracts to the lowest bidder, but not always. How could Energizer hope to persuade a government organization to accept their bid for batteries, even though it was not the lowest?

Chapter 7
Customer-Driven Marketing Strategy:
Creating Value for Target Customers

Learning Objectives

1. Define the four steps in designing a customer-driven market strategy: market segmentation, market targeting, differentiation, and market positioning.
2. List and discuss the major bases for segmenting consumer and business markets.
3. Explain how companies identify attractive market segments and choose a target marketing strategy.
4. Discuss how companies position their products for maximum competitive advantage in the marketplace.

Chapter Overview

The chapter emphasizes the key steps in designing a customer-driven market strategy: market segmentation, market targeting, differentiation, and market positioning. *Market segmentation* provides a method to divide or segment the market into narrow segments (using a variety of different meaningful variables—these variables or bases are discussed at length in the chapter) that can be better reached with the resources of the marketer. *Market targeting* examines each of the designated segment's attractiveness and chooses one or more that match the marketing desires and objectives of the organization. Various coverage strategies are explained and detailed. The concept of *market positioning* arranges for a product to occupy a clear, distinctive, and desirable place relative to competition. Various methods for achieving significant differentiation are explained and illustrated. The above three steps aid the marketer in effectively arranging the company's marketing mix so that the likelihood of consumer response and competitive advantage is maximized by the organization.

Chapter Outline

1. **Introduction**
   a. Dunkin' Donuts is riding the wave of a booming coffee market by moving its restaurants upscale and expanding the number of outlets.
   b. Dunkin' shows early signs of success based on a strategy that does not mimic Starbucks, but focuses on a different set of customers altogether. And what Dunkin' has found is that there are indeed two different kinds of coffee buying customers, and never the twain shall meet.

c. Companies today recognize that they cannot appeal to all buyers in the marketplace, or at least not to all buyers in the same way. Buyers are too numerous, too widely scattered, and too varied in their needs and buying practices.

d. A company must identify the parts of the market that it can serve best and most profitably. It needs to design strategies to build the right relationships with the right customers.

e. Most companies have moved away from mass marketing and toward market segmentation and targeting—identifying market segments, selecting one or more of them, and developing products and marketing programs tailored to each.

f. Figure 7.1 shows the three major steps in target marketing.

    i. The first is market segmentation—dividing a market into smaller groups of buyers with distinct needs, characteristics, or behaviors who might require separate products or marketing mixes. The company identifies different ways to segment the market and develops profiles of the resulting marketing segments.

    ii. The second step is target marketing—evaluating each market segment's attractiveness and selecting one or more of the market segments to enter.

    iii. The third step is differentiation—differentiating the firm's market offering to create superior customer value.

    iv. The fourth and final step is market positioning—setting the competitive positioning for the product and creating a detailed marketing mix.

2. **Market Segmentation**

a. Markets consist of buyers, and buyers differ in one or more ways.

    i. They may differ in their wants, resources, locations, buying attitudes, and buying practices.

    ii. Through market segmentation, companies divide large, heterogeneous markets into smaller segments that can be reached more efficiently and effectively with products and services that match their unique needs.

<u>Segmenting Consumer Markets</u>

b. There is no single way to segment a market. A marketer has to try different segmentation variables, alone and in combination, to find the best way to view the market structure.

c. Table 7.1 outlines the major variables that might be used in segmenting consumer markets.

i. Geographic segmentation calls for dividing the market into different geographical units such as nations, regions, states, counties, cities, or even neighborhoods. Many companies today are localizing their products, advertising, promotion, and sales efforts to fit the needs of individual regions, cities, and even neighborhoods.

ii. Demographic segmentation divides the market into groups based on variables such as age, gender, family size, family life cycle, income, occupation, education, religion, race, generation, and nationality.

    a. Demographic factors are the most popular basis for segmenting customer groups. One reason is that consumer needs, wants, and usage rates often vary closely with demographic variables. Another is that demographic variables are easier to measure than most other types of variables.

    b. Some companies use age and life-cycle segmentation, offering different products or using different marketing approaches for different age and life-cycle groups. Marketers must be careful to guard against stereotypes when using age and life-cycle segmentation. Age is often a poor predictor of a person's life cycle, health, work or family status, needs, and buying power.

    c. Gender segmentation has long been used in clothing, cosmetics, toiletries, and magazines.

    d. Income segmentation has long been used by the marketers of products and services such as automobiles, boats, clothing, cosmetics, financial services, and travel. Many companies target affluent consumers with luxury goods and convenience services. Many retailers successfully target lower income groups.

    e. Psychographic segmentation divides buyers into different groups based on social class, lifestyle, or personality characteristics. People in the same demographic group can have very different psychographic makeup. Marketers often segment their markets by consumer lifestyles.

    f. Marketers have also used personality variables to segment markets.

iii. Behavioral segmentation divides buyers into groups based on their knowledge, attitudes, uses, or responses to a product.

    a. Buyers can be grouped according to occasions when they get the idea to buy, actually make their purchase, or use the purchased item. Occasion segmentation can help firms build up product usage.

    b. A powerful form of segmentation is to group buyers according to the different benefits that they seek from the product. Benefit segmentation requires finding the major benefits people look for in their product class, the kinds of people who look for each benefit, and the major brands that deliver each benefit.

    c. Markets can be segmented into groups of nonusers, ex-users, potential users, first-time users, and regular users of a product.

    d. Markets can also be segmented into light, medium, and heavy product users.

    e. A market can additionally be segmented by consumer loyalty. Consumers can be loyal to brands, stores, and companies. Buyers can be divided into groups according to their degree of loyalty. By studying its less loyal buyers, the company can detect which brands are most competitive with its own.

d. Marketers rarely limit their segmentation analysis to only one or a few variables. They are increasingly using multiple segmentation bases in an effort to identify smaller, better defined target groups.

    i. One good example of multivariable segmentation is "geodemographic" segmentation. Several business information services have arisen to help marketing planners link U.S. census and consumer transaction data with consumer lifestyle patterns to better segment their markets down to zip codes, neighborhoods, and even city blocks.

    ii. One of the leading lifestyle segmentation systems is the PRIZM "You Are Where You Live" system by Claritas. The PRIZM system marries a host of demographic factors—such as age, educational level, income, occupation, family composition, ethnicity, and housing—with buying transaction data and lifestyle information taken from consumer surveys.

Segmenting Business Markets

e. Consumer and business marketers use many of the same variables to segment their markets.

    i. Business buyers can be segmented geographically, demographically (industry, company size), or by benefits sought, user status, usage rate, and loyalty status.

    ii. Yet business marketers also use some additional variables, such as customer operating characteristics, purchasing approaches, situational factors, and personal characteristics.

f. As in consumer segmentation, many marketers believe that buying behavior and benefits provide the best basis for segmenting business markets.

Segmenting International Markets

g. Few companies have either the resources or the will to operate in all, or even most, of the countries that dot the globe.

h. Different countries, even those that are close together, can vary greatly in their economic, cultural, and political makeup.

i. Companies can segment international markets using one or a combination of several variables.

   i. They can segment by geographic location, grouping countries by regions. Geographic segmentation assumes that nations close to one another will have many common traits and behaviors. Although this is often the case, there are many exceptions.

   ii. World markets can also be segmented on the basis of economic factors. Countries might be grouped by population income levels or by their overall level of economic development.

   iii. Countries can be segmented by political and legal factors such as the type and stability of government, receptivity to foreign firms, monetary regulations, and the amount of bureaucracy.

   iv. Cultural factors can also be used, grouping markets according to common languages, religions, values and attitudes, customs, and behavioral patterns.

   v. Many companies use an approach called intermarket segmentation. Using this approach, they form segments of consumers who have similar needs and buying behavior even though they are located in different countries.

Requirements for Effective Segmentation

j. Not all segmentations are effective. To be useful, market segments must be:

   i. Measurable: The size, purchasing power, and profiles of the segments can be measured.

   ii. Accessible: The market segments can be effectively reached and served.

   iii. Substantial: The market segments are large or profitable enough to serve.

   iv. Differentiable: The segments are conceptually distinguishable and respond differently to different marketing mix elements and programs.

   v. Actionable: Effective programs can be designed for attracting and serving the segments.

3. **Market Targeting**

   a. Market segmentation reveals the firm's market segment opportunities. The firm now has to evaluate the various segments and decide how many and which segments it can serve best.

Evaluating Market Segments

b. In evaluating different market segments, a firm must look at three factors: segment size and growth, segment structural attractiveness, and company objectives and resources.

  i. The company must first collect and analyze data on current segment sales, growth rates, and expected profitability for various segments.

  ii. It will be interested in segments that have the right size and growth characteristics. But "right size and growth" is a relative matter.

c. The company also needs to examine major structural factors that affect long-run segment attractiveness.

  i. A segment is less attractive if it already contains many strong and aggressive competitors.

  ii. The existence of many actual or potential substitute products may limit prices and the profits that can be earned in a segment.

  iii. The relative power of buyers also affects segment attractiveness.

  iv. A segment may be less attractive if it contains powerful suppliers who can control prices or reduce the quality or quantity of ordered goods and services.

d. Even if a segment has the right size and growth and is structurally attractive, the company must consider its own objectives and resources.

  i. Some attractive segments can be dismissed quickly because they do not mesh with the company's long-run objectives.

  ii. Or, the company may lack the skills and resources needed to succeed in an attractive segment.

Selecting Target Market Segments

e. A target market consists of a set of buyers who share common needs or characteristics that the company decides to serve.

f. Target marketing can be carried out at several different levels. Figure 7.2 shows that companies can target very broadly, very narrowly, or somewhere in between.

  i. Using an undifferentiated marketing (or mass-marketing) strategy, a firm might decide to ignore market segment differences and target the whole market with one offer. This mass-marketing strategy focuses on what is common in the needs of consumers rather than on what is different.

  ii. Using a differentiated marketing (or segmented marketing) strategy, a firm decides to target several market segments and designs separate offers for each.

    a. By offering product and marketing variations to segments, companies hope for higher sales and a stronger position within each market segment. Developing a stronger position within several segments creates more total sales than undifferentiated marketing across all segments.

    b. But differentiated marketing also increases the costs of doing business. Developing separate marketing plans for the separate segments requires extra marketing research, forecasting, sales analysis, promotion, planning, and channel management. And trying to reach different market segments with different advertising increases promotion costs. Thus, the company must weigh increased sales against increased costs when deciding on a differentiated marketing strategy.

  iii. A third market-coverage strategy, concentrated marketing (or niche marketing), is especially appealing when company resources are limited. Instead of going after a small share of a large market, the firm goes after a large share of one or a few segments or niches.

    a. Through concentrated marketing, the firm achieves a strong market position because of its greater knowledge of consumer needs in the niches it serves and the special reputation it acquires. It can market more effectively by fine-tuning its products, prices, and programs to the needs of carefully defined segments. It can also market more efficiently, targeting its products or services, channels, and communications programs toward only consumers that it can serve best and most profitably.

    b. Whereas segments are fairly large and normally attract several competitors, niches are smaller and may attract only one or a few competitors. Niching offers smaller companies an opportunity to compete by focusing their limited resources on serving niches that may be unimportant to or overlooked by larger competitors.

    c. Many companies start as nichers to get a foothold against larger, more resourceful competitors, then grow into broader competitors.

    d. The low cost of setting up shop on the Internet makes it even more profitable to serve seemingly minuscule niches.

    e. Concentrated marketing can be highly profitable. At the same time, it involves higher-than-normal risks. Companies that rely on one or a few segments for all of their business will suffer greatly if the segment turns sour. Or large competitors may decide to enter the same segment with greater resources.

  iv. Micromarketing is the practice of tailoring products and marketing programs to suit the tastes of specific individuals and locations. Rather than seeing a customer in every individual, micromarketers see the individual in every customer.

    a. Local marketing involves tailoring brands and promotions to the needs and wants of local customer groups—cities, neighborhoods, and even specific stores. Local marketing has some drawbacks. It can drive up manufacturing and marketing costs by reducing economies of scale. It can also create logistics problems as companies try to meet the varied requirements of different regional and local markets. The advantages of local marketing often outweigh the drawbacks.

    b. In the extreme, micromarketing becomes individual marketing—tailoring products and marketing programs to the needs and preferences of individual customers. Individual marketing has also been labeled one-to-one marketing, mass customization, and markets-of-one marketing.

    c. Business-to-business marketers are also finding new ways to customize their offerings.

    d. The move toward individual marketing mirrors the trend in consumer self-marketing. Increasingly, individual customers are taking more responsibility for determining which products and brands to buy.

v. Companies need to consider many factors when choosing a target-marketing strategy. Which strategy is best depends on company resources.

    a. When the firm's resources are limited, concentrated marketing makes the most sense.

    b. The best strategy also depends on the degree of product variability. Undifferentiated marketing is more suited for uniform products such as grapefruit or steel. Products that can vary in design, such as cameras and automobiles, are more suited to differentiation or concentration.

    c. The product's life-cycle stage also must be considered. When a firm introduces a new product, it may be practical to launch only one version, and undifferentiated marketing or concentrated marketing may make the most sense.

    d. Another factor is market variability. If most buyers have the same tastes, buy the same amounts, and react the same way to marketing efforts, undifferentiated marketing is appropriate.

    e. Finally, competitors' marketing strategies are important. When competitors use differentiated or concentrated marketing, undifferentiated marketing can be suicidal.

Socially Responsible Target Marketing

g. Smart targeting helps companies to be more efficient and effective by focusing on the segments that can satisfy best and most profitably. The biggest issues usually involve the targeting of vulnerable or disadvantaged consumers with controversial or potentially harmful products.

h. Problems arise when the marketing of adult products spills over into the kid segment—intentionally or unintentionally.

i. Cigarette, beer, and fast-food marketers have also generated much controversy in recent years by their attempts to target inner-city minority consumers.

j. The meteoric growth of the Internet and other carefully targeted direct media has raised fresh concerns about potential targeting abuses. The Internet allows increasing refinement of audiences and, in turn, more precise targeting. Unscrupulous marketers can now send tailor-made deceptive messages directly to the computers of millions of unsuspecting consumers.

k. Not all attempts to target children, minorities, or other special segments draw such criticism. In fact, most provide benefits to targeted consumers.

l. In target marketing, the issue is not really who is targeted by rather how and for what. Controversies arise when marketers attempt to profit at the expense of targeted segments.

m. Socially responsible marketing calls for segmentation and targeting that serve not just the interests of the company but also the interests of those targeted.

4. **Differentiation and Positioning**

a. A product's position is the way the product is defined by consumers on important attributes—the place the product occupies in consumers' minds relative to competing products. Positioning involves implanting the brand's unique benefits and differentiation in customers' minds.

b. To simplify the buying process, consumers organize products, services, and companies into categories and "position" them in their minds.

c. A product's position is the complex set of perceptions, impressions, and feelings that consumers have for the product compared with competing products.

Positioning Maps

d. Marketers often prepare perceptual positioning maps that show consumer perceptions of their brand versus competing products on important buying dimensions.

e. Figure 7.3 shows a positioning map. The position of each circle on the map indicates the brand's perceived positioning on two dimensions—price and orientation. The size of each circle indicates the brand's relative market share.

<u>Choosing a Differentiation and Positioning Strategy</u>

f. The positioning task consists of three steps.

    i. To build profitable relationships with target customers, marketers must understand customer needs better than competitors do and deliver more value. To the extent that a company can position itself as providing superior value, it gains competitive advantage.

        a. To find points of differentiation, marketers must think through the customer's entire experience with the company's product or service.

        b. Product differentiation takes place along a continuum. At one extreme we find physical products that allow little variation: chicken, steel, and aspirin. At the other extreme are products that can be highly differentiated, such as autos, clothing, and furniture. Such products are differentiated on features, performance, style, or design.

        c. Beyond differentiating its physical product, a firm can also differentiate the services that accompany the product. Some companies gain services differentiation through speedy, convenient, or careful delivery. Installation can also differentiate one company from another.

        d. Firms that practice channel differentiation gain competitive advantage through the way they design their channel's coverage, expertise, and performance.

        e. Companies can gain a strong competitive advantage through people differentiation—hiring and training better people than their competitors do.

        f. Even when competing offers look the same, buyers may perceive a difference based on company or brand image differentiation.

    ii. Suppose a company is fortunate enough to discover several potential competitive advantages. It now must choose the ones on which it will build its positioning strategy. It must decide how many differences to promote and which ones.

        a. Many marketers think that companies should aggressively promote only one benefit to the target market, a unique selling proposition. Other marketers think that companies should position themselves on more than one differentiator. This may be necessary if two or more firms are claiming to be best on the same attribute.

        b. Not all brand differences are meaningful or worthwhile; not every difference makes a good differentiator. A difference is worth establishing to the extent that it satisfies the following criteria:

            1. Important—the difference delivers a highly valued benefit to target buyers.

87

2. Distinctive—competitors do not offer the difference, or the company can offer it in a more distinctive way.

3. Superior—the difference is superior to other ways that customers might obtain the same benefit.

4. Communicable—the difference is communicable and visible to buyers.

5. Preemptive—competitors cannot easily copy the difference.

6. Affordable—buyers can afford to pay for the difference.

7. Profitable—the company can introduce the difference profitably.

iii. Consumers typically choose products and services that give them the greatest value. The full positioning of a brand is called the brand's value proposition—the full mix of benefits upon which the brand is positioned. Figure 7.4 shows possible value propositions upon which a company might position its products.

a. "More for more" positioning involves providing the most upscale product or service and charging a higher price to cover the higher costs. In general, companies should be on the lookout for opportunities to introduce a "much-more-for-much-more" brand in any underdeveloped product or service category. Yet "more-for-more" brands can be vulnerable. They often invite imitators who claim the same quality but at a lower price.

b. Companies can attack a competitor's more-for-more positioning by introducing a brand offering comparable quality but at a lower price. This is "more for the same."

c. Offering the "same for less" can be a powerful value proposition—everyone likes a good deal.

d. A market almost always exists for products that offer less and therefore cost less. Few people need, want, or can afford "the very best" in everything they buy. In many cases, consumers will gladly settle for less than optimal performance or give up some of the bells and whistles in exchange for a lower price. "Less-for-much-less" positioning involves meeting consumers' lower performance or quality requirements at a much lower price.

e. Of course, the winning value proposition would be to offer "more for less." Many companies claim to do this. Yet in the long run, companies will find it difficult to sustain such best-of-both positioning. Offering more usually costs more, making it difficult to deliver on the "for less" promise. Companies that try to deliver both may lose out to more focused competitors.

g. Each brand must adopt a positioning strategy designed to serve the needs and wants of its target market.

h. The important thing is that each company must develop its own winning positioning strategy, one that makes it special to its target consumers. Offering only "the same for the same" provides no competitive advantage, leaving the firm in the middle of the pack.

i. Company and brand positioning should be summed up in a positioning statement. The statement should follow the form: "To (target segment and need) our (brand) is (concept) that (point of difference)." For example: "To busy professionals who need to stay organized, Palm is an electronic organizer that allows you to backup files on your PC more easily and reliably than competitive products."

j. Note that the positioning first states the product's membership in a category, and then shows its point-of-difference from other members of the category.

Communicating and Delivering the Chosen Position

k. Once it has chosen a position, the company must take strong steps to deliver and communicate the desired position to target consumers.

l. Positioning the company calls for concrete action, not just talk. If the company decides to build a position on better quality and service, it must first deliver that position. Designing the marketing mix—product, price, place, and promotion—involves working out the tactical details of the positioning strategy.

m. Establishing a position or changing one usually takes a long time. In contrast, positions that have taken years to build can quickly be lost. Once a company has built the desired position, it must take care to maintain it through consistent performance and communication. It must closely monitor and adapt the position over time to match changes in consumer needs and competitors' strategies.

Student Exercises

1.   Key Term: Market Segmentation

In designing a customer-driven marketing strategy, the company must first decide which customers it will serve. Market segmentation is dividing a market into smaller groups with distinct needs, characteristics, or behaviors who might require separate products or marketing mixes. Take a look at Bebe (www.bebe.com). Bebe has done a nice job of segmenting the overall women's clothing market. They do not attempt to service everyone. How has Bebe segmented this market?

2.   Key Term: Geographic Segmentation

There are many ways to segment a consumer market. Geographic segmentation is but one. Geographic segmentation is dividing a market into different geographical units such as nations, regions of a country, states, or even neighborhoods. Go to Polaris Industries website (www.polarisindustries.com) and take a look at their product offering. Polaris is best known for two products: snowmobiles and all-terrain vehicles (ATVs). Talk about the geographic segmentation you would employ to reach customers most interested in both of these products.

3.   Key Term: Gender Segmentation

Gender segmentation has long been used to effectively market some product categories, such as clothing, cosmetics, and magazines. Your text talks about the efforts Nike has made to better service the female segment of its market, like overhauling its women's apparel line to make it more appealing. Take a look at Clinique cosmetics (www.clinique.com). What are they doing in an effort to reach male customers?

4.   Key Term: Psychographic Segmentation

Psychographic segmentation divides buyers into different groups based on social class, lifestyle, or personality characteristics. Just because you are in the same demographic group as someone else does not mean you share the same psychographic makeup. Pottery Barn (www.potterybarn.com), mentioned in your text, has done an excellent job of using psychographic segmentation to effectively segment the market it serves. Review the Pottery Barn website. How would you say they use psychographic segmentation?

5.   Key Term: Occasion Segmentation

Buyers can be segmented on the basis of when they get the idea to buy, actually buy, or consume a purchased product. For example, flowers are mostly commonly purchased for Mother's Day or Valentine's Day. Fruit juices are most likely consumed in the morning. There is always a spike in Champaign sales around New Year's. What are two other types of products whose increase in consumption can be predicted by the occasion?

6.   Key Term: Loyalty Status

A company's customers can be completely loyal, somewhat loyal, or not loyal at all. Obviously, companies would prefer their customers to be completely loyal customers. As such, they buy one brand all of the time. They do not generally take the time to consider the marketing efforts of competing companies. Companies spend considerable time, effort, and expense, in catering to these loyal customers, in an effort to keep them loyal and to keep them coming back time after time. Look at Wyndham Hotels (www.wyndham.com). What are they doing to keep loyal customers loyal?

7.   Key Term: International Markets

The world seems to be becoming a smaller and smaller place. As such, more and more companies are operating in the international arena, to one degree or the other. Few companies have the resources to operate in all corners of the globe. Different countries can vary greatly in their economic, cultural, and political makeup. Even countries that are located in close proximity with one another may be very different. Thus, international firms need to group their world markets into segments with distinct buying needs and behaviors. Go to the homepage for EBay (www.ebay.com) and take a look at some of their international sites (they are located at the bottom of the main page). How have the international sites been adapted to meet local markets?

8.   Key Term: Measurable

One of the requirements for effective market segmentation is that the segment must be measurable. This means that the size of the segment, its purchasing power, and profile must all be able to be measured. You may have what you believe would be a good market segment, but if you can not measure the segment, how would you know if it is viable to market to the segment? Visit Nielsen Media Research (www.neilsenmedia.com) and take a look at the variety of market reports that are available to subscribers. This will give you a feel of the type, quality, and quantity of segmentation data available from just one source.

9.   Key Term: Concentrated Marketing

Concentrated marketing (also called niche marketing) is a market coverage strategy that is particularly appropriate to use when company resources are limited. A company choosing to employ a niche marketing strategy is devoting its resources to go after a large share of a small segment (or niche), instead of going after a small share of a larger market. Find two companies that employ concentrated marketing strategies.

10.   Key Term: Individual Marketing

The ultimate example of micromarketing is individual marketing. Individual marketing is the tailoring of products and marketing programs to the needs and preferences of individual consumers. The advent of advanced web technology has made it easier for some companies to employ this version of micromarketing. Look at Audi's website (www.audiusa.com). How is Audi using technology to make use of individual marketing?

Marketing ADventure Exercises

1. Ad Interpretation Challenge: Market Segmentation
    Ad: Apparel—Levi's Diamond Jeans

The first thing a company must do, in the design of a customer-driven marketing strategy, is to decide which customers it will serve. Market segmentation is dividing a market into smaller groups with distinct needs, characteristics, or behaviors that might require separate products or marketing mixes. Take a look at this Levi's ad. Based on this ad, Levi's has done a nice job of segmenting the women's jean market. They are not attempting to service everyone. What market do you believe Levi's is targeting?

2. Ad Interpretation Challenge: Geographic Segmentation
    Ad: Student Choice

Geographic segmentation is one of many methods of market segmentation available to the marketer. Geographic segmentation is dividing a market into different geographical units such as nations, regions of a country, states, or even neighborhoods. Find an ad that is based on geographic segmentation.

3. Ad Interpretation Challenge: Demographic Segmentation
    Ad: Services and B2B—University of Toronto

The most popular and widely used form of market segmentation is demographic segmentation. Demographic segmentation is so popular, in part, due to the fact that demographics are easier to measure than other segmentation variables. Demographic segmentation is the dividing of a market into groups based on variables such as age, gender, income, education, or other easily observable characteristic. Look at the ads for the University of Toronto. What would you say is the demographic segmentation variable is use here?

4. Ad Interpretation Challenge: Gender Segmentation
    Ad: Student Choice

Gender segmentation is dividing the market into groups on the basis of gender. Gender segmentation has long been used in clothing, cosmetics, and magazines. Find an ad for a product that you believe is targeted to men. How could this product (or ad) be altered to be more appealing to women?

5.   Ad Interpretation Challenge: Income Segmentation
        Ad: Autos—Hyundai

Income segmentation is dividing the market into different groups on the basis of overall income. This form of segmentation has long been used by marketers of products and services such as automobiles, jewelry, travel, and financial services. Income segmentation is a valuable form of market segmentation at both the upper ends of the income categories and at the lower ends. Too frequently we think of using income segmentation at only the high end. Take a look at Hyundai. How might they position themselves to appeal more to lower income market segments?

6.   Ad Interpretation Challenge: Psychographic Segmentation
        Ad: Apparel—Umbro

People in the same demographic group may have very different likes and dislikes. They may possess very different psychographic profiles. Psychographic segmentation is dividing a market into different groups based on social class, lifestyle, or personality characteristics. How is Umbro using psychographic segmentation?

7.   Ad Interpretation Challenge: Occasions Based Segmentation
        Ad: Services and B2B: 24 Hour Fitness

Sometimes we can group buyers together on the basis of when they purchase or use a product (or service). Culture and habit many times dictate when we typically use some products. For example, the most popular nights for consumers to eat a meal out in a restaurant are Friday and Saturday. Most yogurts are consumed in the morning during the time we typically eat breakfast. How might occasions based segmentation have been behind the company 24 Hour Fitness?

8.   Ad Interpretation Challenge: Undifferentiated Marketing
        Ad: Student Choice

Undifferentiated (or mass) marketing is a market-coverage strategy in which a firm decides to ignore market segment differences and go after the whole market with one offer. This strategy focuses on what is common in the needs of consumers rather than what is unique or different about them. Look through the offered advertisements and try to locate one that is using an undifferentiated marketing approach.

9.   Ad Interpretation Challenge: Niche Marketing
        Ad: Newspapers and TV—Football Channel

Sometimes you do not want to be a player in the larger markets. Sometimes it makes more sense to use your limited resources to become a big player in a small market. Concentrated marketing (niche marketing) is just that. Instead of going after a small share of a large market, niche marketers go after a large share of a smaller market. Look at the Football Channel. Why would this company be considered playing in a niche market?

10.   Ad Interpretation Challenge: Individual Marketing
        Ad: Student Choice

Individual marketing is the tailoring of products and marketing programs to the needs and wants of individual customers. Individual marketing has also been called *one-to-one marketing* and *mass customization.* Find an ad that promotes this concept of individual marketing.

Chapter 8
Product, Services, and Branding Strategy

Learning Objectives

1. Define product and the major classifications of products and services.
2. Describe the decisions companies make regarding their individual products and services, product lines, and product mixes.
3. Discuss branding strategy—the decisions companies make in building and managing their brands.
4. Identify the four characteristics that affect the marketing of a service and the additional marketing considerations that services require.

Chapter Overview

Product is a complex concept that must be carefully defined. As the first of the four marketing mix variables, it is often where strategic planning begins. Product strategy calls for making coordinated decisions on individual products, product lines, and the product mix. Products and services can be thought of as occupying three levels: the core product, the actual product, and the augmented product. Consumer products are usually classified according to how consumers buy them (convenience, shopping, specialty, or unsought products). Industrial goods are classified according to whether materials and parts, capital items, and supplies and services are produced. The primary difference between industrial and consumer goods is the purpose for which the product is bought.

In addition to tangible products and services, in recent years marketers have broadened the concept of a product to include other "marketable entities"—namely, organizations, persons, places, and ideas. Whether an organization is classed as profit or nonprofit, marketing has a role to play in the entity. Political candidates and sports figures are perhaps the best examples of how important marketing is to person marketing. With the growth of tourism marketing, many states, nations, and attractions have learned how to market themselves effectively. Lastly, idea marketing (primarily social marketing issues) has gained in popularity in the latter part of this century. Those that study trends in marketing believe that all of the above areas will continue to grow and expand in the years ahead.

Companies have to develop strategies for the items in their product lines. They must decide on product attributes, branding, packaging, labeling, and product support services. Each of these areas is explained so that the individual product decision is seen as a sequence of planned events. Most companies produce a product line rather than a single product. Product line and product mix decisions are critical to the success of the product in a competitive environment. The product mix describes the set of product lines and items offered to customers by a particular seller. Product lines must be managed carefully. One way to do this is to examine how to *stretch* and *fill* lines. The product mix is described by its width, length, depth, and consistency. Each of these tools helps the planner to properly view the product so it can achieve competitive superiority and better product strategy.

The twenty-first century may well indeed be the century of the brand. There has been renewed interest in the concept of brand equity (the positive differential effect that knowing the brand name has on customer response to the product or service). Solid brands counter cynical consumers. The chapter discusses how to build strong brands through brand positioning, good brand name selection, positive brand sponsorship, and ongoing brand development. Managing brand is an art that must be mastered by the successful marketer. This art is increasingly difficult and complicated with the emergence of strong global brands and increasing competition for consumer dollars. In reality, a brand's position will not take hold fully unless everyone in the company lives the brand.

Services (although many times mentioned in the same breath as product) are different from products. Because the United States has become a service economy, it is very important that the marketer understand the strategies associated with the delivery of services. The characteristics of services (intangibility, inseparability, variability, and perishability) are examined and detailed. The ability to differentiate and produce high quality services is a must for the services marketer. Today, successful companies focus on the creation of service-profit chains. To make these chains work, a company may have to undertake internal and interactive marketing. Service productivity is as important as manufacturing productivity.

Chapter Outline

1. **Introduction**
   a. To a true believer, Fiji bottled water is not just water. It's an experience.
   b. Fiji has succeeded in branding its natural artesian water in such a way that restaurants charge up to $10 a bottle and chefs use it as a cooking ingredient.
   c. This chapter answers the question, *What is a product?* and then classifies the products and discusses the important issues around product decisions and managing brands.

2. **What Is a Product?**
    a. We define a product as anything that can be offered to a market for attention, acquisition, use, or consumption and that might satisfy a need or want.
    b. Broadly defined, products include physical objects, services, events, persons, places, organizations, ideas, or mixes of these entities.
    c. Services are a form of product that consists of activities, benefits, or satisfactions offered for sale that are essentially intangible and do not result in the ownership of anything.

    Products, Services, and Experiences
    d. Product is a key element in the market offering. Marketing-mix planning begins with formulating an offering that brings value to target customers.
        i.   A company's market offering often includes tangible goods and services.
        ii. At one extreme, the offer may consist of a pure tangible good. At the other extreme are pure services, for which the offer consists primarily of a service.
    e. To differentiate their offers, beyond simply making products and delivering services, companies are staging, marketing, and delivering memorable customer experiences.
    f. Companies that market experiences realize that customers are really buying much more than just products and services. They are buying what those offers will do for them.

    Levels of Products and Services
    g. Product planners need to think about products and services on three levels. See Figure 8.1. Each level adds more customer value.
        i.   The most basic level is the core benefit, which addressed the question: *What is the buyer really buying?*
        ii. At the second level, product planners must turn the core benefit into an actual product. They need to develop product and service features, design, a quality level, a brand name, and packaging.
        iii. Finally, product planners must build an augmented product around the core benefit and actual product by offering additional customer services and benefits.
    h. Consumers see products as complex bundles of benefits that satisfy their needs.

Product and Service Classifications

i. Products and services fall into two broad classes based on the types of consumers that use them.

    i. Consumer products are products and services bought by final consumers for personal consumption. Marketers usually classify these products and services further based on how consumers go about buying them. See Table 8.1.

        a. Convenience products are consumer products and services that the customer usually buys frequently, immediately, and with a minimum of comparison and buying effort.

        b. Shopping products are less frequently purchased consumer products and services that customers compare carefully on suitability, quality, price, and style. When buying shopping products and services, consumers spend much time and effort in gathering information and making comparisons.

        c. Specialty products are consumer products and services with unique characteristics or brand identification for which a significant group of buyers is willing to make a special purchase effort. Buyers do not normally compare specialty products. They invest only the time needed to reach dealers carrying the wanted products.

        d. Unsought products are consumer products that the consumer either does not know about or knows about but does not normally think of buying. Most major innovations are unsought until the consumer becomes aware of them through advertising. Unsought products require a lot of advertising, personal selling, and other marketing efforts.

    ii. Industrial products are those purchased for further processing or for use in conducting a business. The distinction between a consumer product and an industrial product is based on the purpose for which the product is bought.

        a. Materials and parts include raw materials and manufactured materials and parts.

        b. Capital items are industrial products that aid in the buyer's production or operations, including installations and accessory equipment. Installations consist of major purchases such as buildings and fixed equipment. Accessory equipment includes portable factory equipment and tools, and office equipment.

        c. Supplies and services include operating supplies, and repair and maintenance items, as well as maintenance and repair services and business advisory services.

    iii. Organizations often carry out activities to "sell" the organization itself. Corporate image advertising is a major tool companies use to market themselves to various publics.

    iv. Person marketing consists of activities undertaken to create, maintain, or change attitudes or behavior toward particular people.

    v. Place marketing involves activities undertaken to create, maintain, or change attitudes or behavior toward particular places.

    vi. Ideas can also be marketed. In one sense, all marketing is the marketing of an idea. Here, however, we narrow our focus to the marketing of social ideas.

        a. This area has been called social marketing, defined by the Social Marketing Institute as the use of commercial marketing concepts and tools in programs designed to influence individuals' behavior to improve their well-being and that of society.

3. **Product and Service Decisions**

    a. Marketers make product and service decisions at three levels.

Individual Product and Service Decisions

    b. Figure 8.2 shows the important decisions in the development and marketing of individual products and services.

        i. Developing a product or service involves defining the benefits it will offer.

            a. Product quality is one of the marketer's major positioning tools. Quality has a direct impact on product or service performance; thus, it is closely linked to customer value and satisfaction.

                1. In the narrowest sense, quality can be defined as "freedom from defects." Most customer-centered companies go beyond this narrow definition. Instead, they define quality in terms of creating customer value and satisfaction.

                2. Total quality management (TQM) is an approach in which all the company's people are involved in constantly improving the quality of products, services, and business processes.

                3. In developing a product, the marketer must first choose a quality level that will support the product's position in the target market. Here, product quality means performance quality—the ability of a product to perform its functions.

                4. High quality also can mean high levels of quality consistency. Here, product quality means conformance quality—freedom from defects and consistency in delivering a targeted level of performance.

            b. A product can be offered with varying features.

        1. A stripped-down model, one without any extras, is the starting point.

        2. The company can create higher-level models by adding more features. Features are a competitive tool for differentiating the company's product from competitors' products.

        3. The company can assess each feature's value to customers versus its cost to the company. Features that customers value little in relation to costs should be dropped; those that customers value highly in relation to costs should be added.

    c. Another way to add customer value is through distinctive product style and design.

        1. Style simply describes the appearance of a product.

        2. Design is more than skin deep—it goes to the very heart of a product.

        3. Good design begins with a deep understanding of customer needs. It involves shaping the customers' product or service experience.

    d. Product designers should think less about product attributes and technical specifications and more about how customers will use and benefit from the product.

  ii. A brand is a name, term, sign, symbol, or design, or a combination of these, that identifies the maker or seller of a product or service.

    a. Branding helps buyers in many ways. Brand names help consumers identify products that might benefit them. Brands also tell the buyer something about product quality.

    b. The seller's brand name and trademark provide legal protection for unique product features that otherwise might be copied by competitors.

    c. Building and managing brands is perhaps the marketer's most important task.

 iii. Packaging involves designing and producing the container or wrapper for the product.

    a. The package includes a product's primary container.

    b. It may also include a secondary package that is thrown away when the product is about to be used.

    c. It can include a shipping package necessary to store, identify, and ship the product.

    d. Increased competition and clutter on retail store shelves means that packages must now perform many sales tasks—from attracting attention, to describing the product, to making the sale.

    e. Innovative packaging can give a company an advantage over competitors.

      f. In recent years, product safety has also become a major packaging concern. In making packaging decisions, the company also must heed growing environmental concerns.

  iv. Labels may range from simple tags attached to products to complex graphics that are part of the package.

      a. The label identifies the product or brand.

      b. The label might also describe several things about the product.

      c. The label might promote the product through attractive graphics.

      d. Labeling has been affected in recent times by unit pricing (stating the price per unit of standard measure), open dating (stating the expected shelf life of the product), and nutritional labeling (stating the nutritional values in the product).

  v. Customer service is another element of product strategy.

      a. A company usually includes some support services that can be a minor or a major part of the total offering.

      b. The company should periodically survey customers to assess the value of current services and to obtain ideas for new ones.

      c. It should next assess the costs of providing these services.

      d. It can then develop a package of services that will both delight customers and yield profits to the company.

      e. Many companies are using a sophisticated mix of phone, e-mail, fax, Internet, and interactive voice and data technologies to provide support services that were not possible before.

Product Line Decisions

c. A product line is a group of products that are closely related because they function in a similar manner, are sold to the same customer groups, are marketed through the same types of outlets, or fall within given price ranges.

d. The major product line decision involves product line length—the number of items in the product line.

  i. The line is too short if the manager can increase profits by adding items.

  ii. The line is too long if the manager can increase profits by dropping items.

  iii. Product line length is influenced by company objectives and resources.

      a. One objective might be to allow for upselling.

      b. Another objective might be to allow for cross-selling.

      c. Still another objective might be to protect against economic swings.

    iv. A company can lengthen its product line in two ways.
        a. Product line stretching occurs when a company lengthens its product line beyond its current range. Companies located at the upper end of the market can stretch their lines downward. Companies at the lower end of a market can stretch their lines upward. Companies in the middle range of the market may decide to stretch their lines in both directions.
    v. Product line filling is adding more items within the present range of the line.
        a. There are several reasons for product line filling: reaching for extra profits, satisfying dealers, using excess capacity, being the leading full-line company, and plugging holes to keep out competitors.

Product Mix Decisions

e. A product mix (or product assortment) consists of all the product lines and items that a particular seller offers for sale.

f. A company's product mix has four important dimensions.
    i. Product mix width refers to the number of different product lines the company carries.
    ii. Product line depth refers to the number of versions offered of each product in the line.
    iii. The consistency of the product mix refers to how closely related the various product lines are in end use, production requirements, distribution channels, or some other way.
    iv. These product mix dimensions provide the handles for defining the company's product strategy. The company can increase its business in four ways.
        a. It can add new product lines, widening its product mix.
        b. The company can lengthen its existing product lines to become a more full-line company.
        c. It can add more versions of each product and thus deepen its product mix.
        d. It can pursue more product line consistency—or less—depending on whether it wants to have a strong reputation in a single field or in several fields.

4. **Branding Strategy: Building Strong Brands**
    a. Some analysts see brands as the major enduring asset of a company, outlasting the company's specific products and facilities.

Brand Equity

b. Brands are more than just names and symbols. Brands represent consumers' perceptions and feelings about a product and its performance—everything that the product or service means to consumers.

c. Brand equity is the positive differential effect that knowing the brand name has on customer response to the product or service. A measure of a brand's equity is the extent to which customers are willing to pay more for the brand.

d. A brand with strong brand equity is a very valuable asset. Brand valuation is the process of estimating the total financial value of a brand. Measuring such value is difficult.

e. High brand equity provides a company with many competitive advantages.

  i. A powerful brand enjoys a high level of consumer brand awareness and loyalty.

  ii. Because consumers expect stores to carry the brand, the company has more leverage in bargaining with resellers.

  iii. Because the brand name carries high credibility, the company can more easily launch line and brand extensions.

f. A powerful brand forms the basis for building strong and profitable customer relationships. Therefore, the fundamental asset underlying brand equity is customer equity—the value of the customer relationships that the brand creates.

Building Strong Brands

g. Figure 8.3 shows the major brand strategy decisions.

  i. Marketers need to position their brands clearly in target customers' minds. They can position brands at any of three levels.

    a. At the lowest level, they can position the brand on product attributes.

    b. A brand can be better positioned by associating its name with a desirable benefit.

    c. The strongest brands go beyond attribute or benefit position. They are positioned on strong beliefs and values.

    d. When positioning a brand, the marketer should establish a mission for the brand and a vision of what the brand must be and do. A brand is the company's promise to deliver a specific set of features, benefits, services, and experiences consistently to the buyers.

  ii. A good name can add greatly to a product's success. However, finding the best brand name is a difficult task.

    a. Desirable qualities for a brand name include the following:

      1. It should suggest something about the product's benefits and qualities.

      2. It should be easy to pronounce, recognize, and remember. Short names help.

      3. The brand name should be distinctive.

      4. It should be extendable.

      5. The name should translate easily into foreign languages.

103

        6. It should be capable of registration and legal protection.

    b. Once chosen, the brand name must be protected.

iii. A manufacturer has four brand sponsorship options.

    a. The product may be launched as a manufacturer's brand (or national brand).

    b. The manufacturer may sell to resellers who give it a private brand (also called a *store brand* or *distributor brand*).

    c. Other manufacturers market license brands.

    d. Two companies can join forces and co-brand a product.

iv. Manufacturers' brands have long dominated the retail scene. In recent times, however, an increasing number of retailers and wholesalers have created their own private brands (or store brands).

    a. In U.S. supermarkets, taken as a single brand, private-label products are the number one, two, or three brand in more than 40 percent of all grocery store product categories. In all, they capture more than a 20 percent share of sales in U.S. supermarkets, drug chains, and mass merchandise stores. Private-label apparel captures a 36 percent share of all U.S. apparel sales.

    b. In the so-called battle of the brands between manufacturers' and private brands, retailers have many advantages.

        1. They control what products they stock, where they go on the shelf, what prices they charge, and which ones they will feature in local circulars.

        2. Most retailers also charge manufacturers slotting fees—payments from the manufacturers before retailers will accept new products and find "slots" for them on their shelves.

    c. Private brands can be hard to establish and costly to stock and promote. However, they also yield higher profit margins for the reseller.

    d. To fend off private brands, leading brand marketers will have to invest in RandD to bring out new brands, new features, and continuous quality improvements.

v. Most manufacturers take years and spend millions to create their own brand names. However, some companies license names or symbols previously created by other manufacturers, names of well-known celebrities, or characters from popular movies and books.

    a. Name and character licensing has grown rapidly in recent years. Annual retail sales of licensed products in the United States and Canada have grown from only $4 billion in 1977 to $55 billion in 1987 and more than $105 billion today.

      b. The fastest-growing licensing category is corporate brand licensing, as more and more for-profit and not-for-profit organizations are licensing their names to generate additional revenues and brand recognition.

vi. Although companies have been co-branding products for many years, there has been a recent resurgence in co-branded products.

      a. Co-branding occurs when two established brand names of different companies are used on the same product.

      b. Co-branding offers many advantages. Because each brand dominates in a different category, the combined brands create broader consumer appeal and greater brand equity. Co-branding also allows a company to expand its existing brand into a category it might otherwise have difficulty entering alone.

      c. Co-branding also has limitations. Such relationships usually involve complex legal contracts and licenses. Co-branding partners must carefully coordinate their advertising, sales promotion, and other marketing efforts. When co-branding, each partner must trust the other will take good care of its brand.

vii. A company has four choices when it comes to developing brands. See Figure 8.4.

      a. Line extensions occur when a company introduces additional items in a given product category under the same brand name, such as new flavors, forms, colors, ingredients, or package sizes.

            1. A company might introduce line extensions as a low-cost, low-risk way to introduce new products.

            2. Or it might want to meet consumer desires for variety, to use excess capacity, or simply to command more shelf space from resellers.

            3. Line extensions involve some risks. An overextended brand name might lose its specific meaning, or heavily extended brands can cause consumer confusion or frustration. Another risk is that sales of an extension may come at the expense of other items in the line.

      b. A brand extension involves the use of a successful brand name to launch new or modified products in a new category.

            1. A brand extension gives a new product instant recognition and faster acceptance. It also saves the high advertising costs usually required to build a new brand name.

2. At the same time, a brand extension strategy involves some risk. The extension may confuse the image of the main brand. And if a brand extension fails, it may harm consumer attitudes toward the other products carrying the same brand name. Furthermore, a brand name may not be appropriate to a particular new product, even if it is well made and satisfying.

c. Multibranding offers a way to establish different features and appeal to different buying motives. It also allows a company to lock up more reseller shelf space.

1. A major drawback of multibranding is that each brand might obtain only a small market share, and none may be very profitable. The company may end up spreading its resources over many brands instead of building a few brands to a highly profitable level.

d. A company might believe that the power of its existing brand name is waning and a new brand name is needed. Or a company may create a new brand name when it enters a new product category for which none of the company's current brand names is appropriate.

1. As with multibranding, offering too many new brands can result in a company spreading its resources too thin. And in some industries, such as consumer-packaged goods, consumers and retailers have become concerned that there are already too many brands, with too few differences between them.

Managing Brands

h. Companies must manage their brands carefully. First, the brand's positioning must be continuously communicated to consumers.

i. Brands are not maintained by advertising but by the brand experience.

i. Today, customers come to know a brand through a wide range of contacts and touchpoints. These include advertising, but also personal experience with the brand, word-of-mouth, personal interactions with company people, telephone interactions, company Web pages, and many others.

j. The brand's positioning will not take hold fully unless everyone in the company lives the brand.

k. Some companies are now setting up brand asset management teams to manage their major brands.

l. Companies need to periodically audit their brands' strengths and weaknesses.

i. The brand audit may turn up brands that need to be repositioned because of changing customer preferences or new competitors.

      ii. Some cases call for completely rebranding a product, service, or company.

      iii. However, building a new image and reeducating customers can be a huge undertaking.

5.   **Services Marketing**

    a. Services now account for 74 percent of U.S. gross domestic product and nearly 60 percent of personal consumption expenditures. Whereas service jobs accounted for 55 percent of all U.S. jobs in 1970, today they account for 82 percent of total employment.

    b. Service industries vary greatly.

      i. Governments offer services through courts, employment services, hospitals, military services, police and fire departments, postal service, and schools.

      ii. Private not-for-profit organizations offer services through museums, charities, churches, colleges, foundations, and hospitals.

      iii. A large number of business organizations offer services.

<u>Nature and Characteristics of Services</u>

    c. A company must consider four special service characteristics when designing marketing programs. See Figure 8.5.

      i. Service intangibility means that services cannot be seen, tasted, felt, heard, or smelled before they are bought.

        a. To reduce uncertainty, buyers look for "signals" of service quality. They draw conclusions about quality from the place, people, price, equipment, and communications that they can see.

        b. The service provider's task is to make the service tangible in one or more ways and to send the right signals about quality. One analyst calls this evidence management, in which the service organization presents its customers with organized, honest evidence of its capabilities.

      ii. Service inseparability means that services cannot be separated from their providers, whether the providers are people or machines.

      iii. Service variability means that the quality of services depends on who provides them as well as when, where, and how they are provided.

      iv. Service perishability means that services cannot be stored for later sale or use. The perishability of services is not a problem when demand is steady. However, when demand fluctuates, service firms often have difficult problems.

Marketing Strategies for Service Firms

d. Because services differ from tangible products, they often require additional marketing approaches.

e. In a service business, the customer and front-line service employees interact to create the service. Thus, service providers must interact effectively with customers to create superior value during service encounters.

f. The service-profit chain links service firm profits with employee and customer satisfaction. This chain consists of five links.

    i. Internal service quality

    ii. Satisfied and productive service employees

    iii. Greater service value

    iv. Satisfied and loyal customers

    v. Healthy service profits and growth

g. Reaching service profits and growth goals begins with taking care of those who take care of customers. The idea is that happy employees will unleash their enthusiasm on customers, creating even greater customer satisfaction.

h. Figure 8.6 shows that service marketing also requires internal marketing and interactive marketing.

    i. Internal marketing means that the service firm must effectively train and motivate its customer-contact employees and supporting service people to work as a team to provide customer satisfaction. Internal marketing must precede external marketing.

    ii. Interactive marketing means that service quality depends heavily on the quality of the buyer-seller interaction during the service encounter. In services marketing, service quality depends on both the service deliverer and the quality of the delivery.

i. Service companies face three major marketing tasks.

    i. The solution to price competition is to develop a differentiated offer, delivery, and image.

        a. The offer can include innovative features that set one company's offer apart from competitors' offers.

        b. Service companies can differentiate their service delivery by having more able and reliable customer-contact people, by developing a superior physical environment in which the service product is delivered, or by designing a superior delivery process.

        c. Service companies also can work on differentiating their images through symbols and branding.

    ii. One of the major ways a service firm can differentiate itself is by delivering consistently higher quality than its competitors do.

        a. Service quality is harder to define and judge than is product quality.

       b. The first step is to empower front-line service employees—to give them the authority, responsibility, and incentives they need to recognize, care about, and tend to customer needs.

   iii. With their costs rising rapidly, service firms are under great pressure to increase service productivity. They can do so in several ways.

       a. They can train current employees better or hire new ones who will work harder or more skillfully.

       b. They can increase the quantity of their service by giving up some quality.

       c. The services provider can harness the power of technology.

       d. Companies must avoid pushing productivity so hard that doing so reduces quality. Attempts to industrialize a service or to cut costs can make a service company more efficient in the short run. But they can also reduce its longer-run ability to innovate, maintain service quality, or respond to consumer needs and desires.

Student Exercises

1.   Key Term: Product

What is a product? A product is defined as ANYTHING that can be offered to a market for attention, acquisition, use, or consumption that might satisfy a need or a want. So, as you can see, "product" has a very broad definition. Keep in mind that products are more than just tangible goods. Consider your college or university. What products does your school have?

2.   Key Term: Core Benefit

What is the buyer really buying? This is the most basic level of customer value a product provides. This is the core benefit. When product planners are thinking about products to offer in the marketplace, it is necessary to think of the product at this most basic of levels. Take a look at Canon digital cameras (www.canonusa.com). At its most basic level, what are the core benefits Canon is offering to consumers of its cameras?

3.   Key Term: Convenience Products

Consumer products are products and services bought by final consumers for their personal use. Marketers typically classify these products into three levels, based on how the consumer goes about buying them. Convenience goods are those products (and services) that consumers typically buy frequently, immediately, and without much product comparison or buying effort. Look at the homepage of Procter and Gamble (www.pg.com). Examine all of the different products and brands that they offer to consumers. Which of these product categories would you classify as convenience products?

4.   Key Term: Unsought Products

Unsought products present unique challenges to marketers. These are products that the consumer either does not know about or knows about but does not normally think of buying. The use of the modern windmill to generate electricity for the home is one such typically unsought product. Take a look at http://wind.dynalias.com and www.windmill.com for basic information on this technology and available products. How would you try to "get the word out" regarding this product?

5.   Key Term: Place Marketing

Place marketing involves activities undertaken to create, maintain, or change attitudes or behaviors toward particular places. Towns, cities, states, regions, or even entire countries compete to attract visitors, conventions, industries, and new residents. The New Orleans and Mississippi Gulf Coast areas are still reeling from the devastating effects of Hurricane Katrina. Take a look at the web marketing efforts of New Orleans (www.neworleansonline.com) and the Mississippi Gulf Coast region (www.gulfcoast.org). What are these regions doing to try and entice travelers back to visit?

6.   Key Term: Product Quality

One of the primary positioning tools available to the marketer is product quality. Product quality can be defined in many ways, but it really centers on creating customer satisfaction and customer value. The American Society for Quality defines quality as the characteristics of a product or service that bear on its ability to satisfy stated or implied customer needs. How would you rate the quality of your school's products?

7.   Key Term: Branding

The name, term, sign, symbol, or design that identifies the maker or the seller of a product of services is knows as its brand. Branding can definitely add value to a product. Brands help consumers identify products that might benefit them. Additionally, brands say something about product quality and consistency. Buyers who always buy the same brands always know what they are getting. What do the automotive brands Toyota (www.toyotausa.com), Kia (www.kia.com), and Volvo (www.volvocars.us) say to you about the products?

8.   Key Term: Packaging

Traditionally, the primary function of the package was to protect and hold the product. Companies are realizing the power of good packaging to create instant consumer recognition of the company and/or the brand. Not too long ago, the package was just considered something to hold the actual product; however, today, the package is an integral part of the product. Find a product for which you believe the packaging is a very meaningful and integral part of that product.

9.   Key Term: Product Line

A product line is a group of products that are closely related because they function in a similar manner, are sold to the same customer groups, are marketed through the same types of outlets, or fall within given price ranges. Look at the J. Peterman Company (www.jpeterman.com). What product lines does this merchant carry?

10.   Key Term: Brand Extension

A brand extension extends a current brand name to new or modified products in a new category. A brand extension gives a new product instant recognition and faster acceptance. However, if not carefully considered, a brand extension may confuse the image of the main brand, damaging its credibility. Read about Sea Ray boats (www.searay.com). If you were Sea Ray and considering a brand extension, what type of product might you consider?

Marketing ADventure Exercises

1.   Ad Interpretation Challenge: Product
      Ad: Services and B2B—Leo's

A product is defined as anything that can be offered to a market for attention, acquisition, use, or consumption that might satisfy a need or a want. Is Leo's Sports Club a product?

2.   Ad Interpretation Challenge: Core Benefit
       Ad: Electronics—Fujifilm

When product planners are thinking about products to offer in the marketplace, it is necessary to think of the product at this most basic of levels. A product's core benefit is the basic problem-solving benefits or services consumers seek in the purchase of a product. Think about this ad for Fujifilm. What would you say is the core benefit being offered by this product?

3.   Ad Interpretation Challenge: Convenience Products
       Ad: Student Choice

Convenience goods are those products that consumers typically buy frequently, immediately, and without much product comparison or buying effort. Convenience products are usually low priced and marketers place them in many locations to make them readily available where customers shop. Find an ad that is promoting a convenience product.

4.   Ad Interpretation Challenge: Organization Marketing
       Ad: Nonprofit Corporate Images—The Archdiocese

Many times, organizations carry out activities to sell the organization itself. Organization marketing consists of activities undertaken to create, maintain, or change the attitudes and behavior of target consumers toward an organization. Consider this ad for the Archdiocese. How does this type of marketing differ from traditional product marketing?

5.   Ad Interpretation Challenge: Social Marketing
       Ad: Student Choice

Social marketing is, in essence, the marketing of social ideas. The Social Marketing Institute defines social marketing as the use of commercial marketing concepts and tools in programs designed to influence individuals' behavior to improve their well-being and that of society. Find an ad that exemplifies social marketing. What are the ideals the ad is forwarding?

6.   Ad Interpretation Challenge: Product Features
       Ad: Food and Beverage—Tabasco

Features are a competitive tool for differentiating a company's product from those offered by the competition. One unique feature can effectively distance a company's product from its competition, giving it that competitive advantage. Look at the ad for Tabasco. What is the unique feature of this product that the company hopes sets it apart from all others?

7.   Ad Interpretation Challenge: Packaging
      Ad: Student Choice

At one time, the primary function of the package was to protect and hold the product. Companies are realizing the power of good packaging to create instant consumer recognition of the company and/or the brand. Today, the package is an integral part of the product. Find an ad for a product for which you believe the packaging is a very meaningful and integral part of that product.

8.   Ad Interpretation Challenge: Product Line
      Ad: Autos—Jaguar

A product line is a group of products that are closely related because they function in a similar manner, are sold to the same customer groups, are marketed through the same types of outlets, or fall within given price ranges. A company can lengthen its product line by stretching. Product line stretching occurs when a company lengthens its product line beyond what it is currently offering. A company can stretch its line upward, downward, or both directions. A company must me mindful not to stretch its line to the extent that its core customers rebel. Sometimes a company can go too far, by lengthening its product line to include versions of the product its consumers do not recognize as belonging. Consider Jaguar. What dangers, if any, do you believe Jaguar is facing by lengthening its product line?

9.   Ad Interpretation Challenge: Product Mix
      Ad: Apparel—Levi's

The product mix (or product portfolio) is the set of all product lines and items that a particular seller offers for sale. Take a look at the Levis' ads offered. Also, log on to their website (www.us.levi.com). Examine the consistency of their product mix.

10.   Ad Interpretation Challenge: Brand Extensions
      Ad: Autos—Honda

A brand extension extends a current brand name to new or modified products in a new category. A brand extension gives a new product instant recognition and faster acceptance. However, if not carefully considered, a brand extension may confuse the image of the main brand, damaging its credibility. Take a look at the ads for Honda (both car and motorcycle). How do you believe Honda was able to successfully extend their brand from one form of transportation to another form (or forms) of transportation, in the U.S. market?

Chapter 9
New-Product Development and Product Life-Cycle Strategies

Learning Objectives

1. Explain how companies find and develop new-product ideas.
2. List and define the steps in the new-product development process.
3. Describe the stages of the product life cycle.
4. Describe how marketing strategies change during the product's life cycle.
5. Discuss two additional product issues: socially responsible product decisions and international product and services marketing.

Chapter Overview

Organizations must develop new products and services. A company has to be good at developing new products. It also must manage them in the face of changing tastes, technologies, and competition. As a reason to change, the company must realize that products face limited life spans and must be replaced by newer products. In addition, new products can fail. The risks of innovation can be as great as the rewards.

The key to successful innovation is in a total company effort, strong planning, and a systematic new-product development process. The new-product development process consists of eight stages: idea generation, idea screening, concept development and testing, marketing strategy development, business analysis, product development, test marketing, and commercialization. At each stage, a decision must be made as to whether the idea should be further developed or dropped. The company wants to minimize the chances of poor ideas moving forward or good ideas being rejected.

Each product has a life cycle marked by a changing set of problems and opportunities. The sales of a typical product follow an S-shaped curve made up of five stages. These stages are the product-development stage, the introduction stage, the growth stage, the maturity stage, and the decline stage. As the product passes through these stages, the marketing planner must adjust the organization's strategies and be aware of changing problems, threats, and opportunities. The planner must adjust the firm's marketing mix to these changes and be able to predict when significant changes will occur. Managing change is a true marketing management art and one necessary for the organization to be successful in the long-term.

The chapter concludes with a discussion of the special challenges faced by marketers when they attempt to market products and services abroad. The international marketer faces the difficult decision of knowing when to standardize or differentiate products and services. This chapter gives useful guidelines to help make this difficult decision.

Chapter Outline

1. **Introduction**
   a. When it comes to innovation, Apple has its foot on the accelerator. Apple was an early leader in the personal computer market during the late 1970s and early 1980s.
   b. After losing founder Steve Jobs in 1985, Apple's creativity, market share, and profits plunged.
   c. In 1997, Jobs returned to mount one of the greatest turnarounds of all time. The success of Apple since then has been based on groundbreaking new products such as the Mac OS X operating system, the iTunes music player and store, and the iPod.
   d. A company has to be good at developing and managing new products. Every product seems to go through a life cycle—it is born, goes through several phases, and eventually dies as new products come along that better serve consumer needs.
   e. The product life cycle presents two major challenges.
      i. First, because all products eventually decline, a firm must be good at developing new products to replace aging ones (the challenge of new-product development).
      ii. Second, the firm must be good at adapting its marketing strategies in the face of changing tastes, technologies, and competition as products pass through life-cycle stages (the challenge of product life-cycle strategies).

2. **New-Product Development Strategy**
   a. A firm can obtain new products in two ways.
      i. One is through acquisition—by buying a whole company, a patent, or a license to produce someone else's product.
      ii. The other is through new-product development in the company's own research and development department. By new products we mean original products, product improvements, product modifications, and new brands that the firm develops through its own research and development efforts.
   b. One source estimates that of the staggering 30,000 new consumer food, beverage, and beauty products to hit the market each year, 70 to 90 percent fail within the first 12 months.
   c. Why do so many products fail? There are several reasons.
      i. Although an idea may be good, the market size may have been overestimated.
      ii. Perhaps the product was not designed as well as it should have been.
      iii. Or maybe it was incorrectly positioned in the market, priced too high, or advertised poorly.
      iv. A high-level executive might push a favorite idea despite poor marketing research findings.

115

    v. Sometimes the costs of product development are higher than expected, and sometimes competitors fight back harder than expected.

  d. In all, to create successful new products, a company must understand its consumers, markets, and competitors and develop products that deliver superior value to customers.

3. **The New-Product Development Process**

  a. It must carry out strong new-product planning and set up a systematic new-product development process for finding and growing new products. Figure 9.1 shows the eight major steps in this process.

Idea Generation

  b. New-product development starts with idea generation—the systematic search for new-product ideas. A company typically has to generate many ideas in order to find a few good ones.

    i. Using internal sources, the company can find new ideas through formal research and development. Companies sometimes look for creative innovation approaches that overcome barriers to the free flow of new-product ideas.

    ii. Good new-product ideas also come from watching and listening to customers.

      a. The company can analyze customer questions and complaints to find new products that better solve consumer problems.

      b. Company engineers or salespeople can meet with and work alongside customers to get suggestions and ideas.

      c. The company can conduct surveys or focus groups to learn about consumer needs and wants.

      d. Consumers often create new products and uses on their own, and companies can benefit by putting them on the market.

      e. Some companies even give customers the tools and resources to design their own products.

      f. Companies must be careful not to rely too heavily on customer input when developing new products. For some products, especially highly technical ones, customers may not know what they need.

    iii. Competitors are another good source of new-product ideas.

      a. Companies watch competitors' ads to get clues about their new products.

      b. They buy competing new products, take them apart to see how they work, analyze their sales, and decide whether they should bring out a new product of their own.

    iv. Distributors and suppliers can also contribute many good new-product ideas.

        a. Resellers are close to the market and can pass along information about consumer problems and new-product possibilities.

        b. Suppliers can tell the company about new concepts, techniques, and materials that can be used to develop new products.

    v. Other idea sources include trade magazines, shows, and seminars; government agencies; new-product consultants; advertising agencies; marketing research firms; university and commercial laboratories; and inventors.

c. The search for new-product ideas should be systematic rather than haphazard. Otherwise, few new ideas will surface and many good ideas will sputter and die.

d. Top management can avoid these problems by installing an idea management system that directs the flow of new ideas to a central point where they can be collected, reviewed, and evaluated.

Idea Screening

e. The purpose of idea generation is to create a large number of ideas. The first idea-reducing stage is idea screening that helps spot good ideas and drop poor ones as soon as possible.

    i. Product development costs rise greatly in later stages, so the company wants to go ahead only with the product ideas that will turn into profitable products.

f. Many companies require their executives to write up new-product ideas on a standard form that can be reviewed by a new-product committee.

    i. The write-up describes the product, the target market, and the competition.

    ii. It makes some rough estimates of market size, product price, development time and costs, manufacturing costs, and rate of return.

    iii. The committee then evaluates the idea against a set of general criteria.

Concept Development and Testing

g. An attractive idea must be developed into a product concept.

    i. A product idea is an idea for a possible product that the company can see itself offering to the market.

    ii. A product concept is a detailed version of the idea stated in meaningful consumer terms.

    iii. A product image is the way consumers perceive an actual or potential product.

h. The company's task is to develop a new product into alternative product concepts, find out how attractive each concept is to customers, and choose the best one.

i. Concept testing calls for testing new-product concepts with groups of target consumers. The concepts may be presented to consumers symbolically or physically.

    i. For some concept tests, a word or picture description might be sufficient. However, a more concrete and physical presentation of the concept will increase the reliability of the concept test.

    ii. After being exposed to the concept, consumers then may be asked to react to it by answering questions such as those in Table 9.1. The answers will help the company decide which concept has the strongest appeal.

    iii. Many firms routinely test new-product concepts with consumers before attempting to turn them into actual new products.

Marketing Strategy Development

j. The next step is marketing strategy development, designing an initial marketing strategy for introducing this product to the market.

    i. The marketing strategy statement consists of three parts.

        a. The first part describes the target market; the planning product positioning; and the sales, market share, and profit goals for the first few years.

        b. The second part of the marketing strategy statement outlines the product's planned price, distribution, and marketing budget for the first year.

        c. The third part of the marketing strategy statement describes the planning of long-run sales, profit goals, and marketing mix strategy.

Business Analysis

k. Business analysis involves a review of the sales, costs, and profit projections for a new product to find out whether they satisfy the company's objectives. If they do, the product can move to the product development stage.

Product Development

l. If the product concept passes the business test, it moves into product development. Here RandD or engineering develops the product concept into a physical product. The product development step now calls for a large jump in investment. It will show whether the product idea can be turned into a workable product.

    i. Developing a successful prototype can take days, weeks, months, or even years.

ii. Often products undergo rigorous tests to make sure that they perform safely and effectively, or that consumers will find value in them.

Test Marketing

m. If the product passes functional and consumer tests, the next step is test marketing, the stages at which the product and marketing program are introduced into more realistic market settings.
  i. Test marketing gives the marketer experience with marketing the product before going to the great expense of full introduction.
  ii. It lets the company test the product and its entire marketing program—positioning strategy, advertising, distribution, pricing, branding and packaging, and budget levels.
n. The amount of test marketing needed varies with each new product.
  i. When the costs of developing and introducing the product are low, or when management is already confident about the new product, the company may do little or no test marketing.
  ii. When introducing a new product requires a big investment, or when management is not sure of the product or marketing program, a company may do a lot of test marketing.
  iii. Although test marketing costs can be high, they are often small when compared with the costs of making a major mistake.
  iv. Still, test marketing does not guarantee success.
o. When using test marketing, consumer products companies usually choose one of three approaches.
  i. Using standard test markets, the company finds a small number of representative test cities, conducts a full marketing campaign in these cities, and uses store audits, consumer and distributor surveys, and other measures to gauge product performance.
      a. Standard test markets have some drawbacks. They can be very costly and they may take a long time—some last as long as three to five years. Competitors can monitor test market results or even interfere with them by cutting their prices in test cities, increasing their promotion, or even buying up the product being tested. Finally, test markets give competitors a look at the company's new product well before it is introduced nationally.
      b. Despite these disadvantages, standard test markets are still the most widely used approach for major in-market testing. However, many companies today are shifting toward quicker and cheaper controlled and simulated test marketing methods.

ii. Several research firms keep controlled panels of stores that have agreed to carry new products for a fee. Controlled test marketing systems like ACNielsen's Scantrack and Information Resources Inc.'s (IRI) BehaviorScan track individual consumer behavior for new products from the television set to the checkout counter.

    a. Controlled test markets usually cost less than standard test markets. Also, because retail distribution is "forced" in the first week of the test, controlled test markets can be completed much more quickly than standard test markets.

    b. As in standard test markets, controlled test markets allow competitors to get a look at the company's new product, and some companies are concerned that the limited number of controlled test markets used by the research services may not be representative of their products' markets or target consumers.

    c. However, the research firms are experienced in projecting test market results to broader markets and can usually account for biases in the test markets used.

iii. Companies can also test new products in a simulated shopping environment. The company or research firm shows ads and promotions for a variety of products, including the new product being tested, to a sample of consumers. It gives consumers a small amount of money and invites them to a real or laboratory store where they may keep the money or use it to buy items. The researchers note how many consumers buy the new product and competing brands.

    a. This simulation provides a measure of trial and the commercial's effectiveness against competing commercials. The researchers then ask consumers the reasons for their purchase or non-purchase. Some weeks later, they interview the consumers by phone to determine product attitudes, usage, satisfaction, and repurchase intentions. Using sophisticated computer models, the researchers then project national sales from results of the simulated test market.

    b. Simulated test markets overcome some of the disadvantages of standard and controlled test markets. They usually cost much less, can be run in eight weeks, and keep the new product out of competitors' view.

    c. Yet because of their small samples and simulated shopping environments, many marketers do not think that simulated test markets are as accurate or reliable as larger, real-world tests.

    d. Still, simulated test markets are used widely, often as pretest" markets. Because they are fast and inexpensive, they can be run to quickly assess a new product or its marketing program.

Commercialization

p. If the company goes ahead with commercialization—introducing the new product into the market—it will face high costs.
    i. The company may have to build or rent a manufacturing facility.
    ii. And it may have to spend, in the case of a new consumer packaged good, between \$10 million and \$200 million for advertising, sales promotion, and other marketing efforts in the first year.
q. The company launching a new product must first decide on introduction timing.
r. Next, the company must decide where to launch the new product—in a single location, a region, the national market, or the international market.

4.   **Managing New-Product Development**
    a. The new-product development process involves more than just going through a set of steps as per Figure 9-1. It requires that companies take a holistic approach to managing the process.

Customer-Centered New-Product Development

b. *Customer-centered new-product development* focuses on finding new ways to solve customer problems and create more customer-satisfying experiences.
c. The most successful new products are ones that are differentiated.

Team-Based New-Product Development

d. Many companies organize their new-product development process into the orderly sequence of steps shown in Figure 9.1, starting with idea generation and ending with commercialization.
e. Under this sequential product development approach, one company department works individually to complete its stage of the process before passing the new product along to the next department and stage.
f. In order to get their new products to market more quickly, many companies are adopting a faster, team-oriented approach called *team-based* product development.
    i. Under this approach, company departments work closely together through cross-functional teams, overlapping the steps in the product development process to save time and increase effectiveness.
    ii. Instead of passing the new product from department to department, the company assembles a team of people from various departments that stay with the new product from start to finish.
    iii. This approach does have some limitations.

> **a.** Superfast product development can be riskier and more costly than the slower, more orderly sequential approach.
>
> **b.** It often creates increased organizational tension and confusion.
>
> **c.** And the company must take care that rushing a product to market doesn't adversely affect its quality—the objective is not only to create products faster, but also to create them better.

iv. Despite the drawbacks, in rapidly changing industries facing increasingly shorter product life cycles, the rewards of fast and flexible product development far exceed the risks.

Systematic New-Product Development

g. To facilitate in minimizing the risk of new product failure, companies should install an innovation management system to collect, review, evaluate, and manage new-product ideas.

h. The innovation-management system yields two favorable outcomes.

> **i.** It helps to create an innovation-oriented company culture.
>
> **ii.** It will yield a larger number of new-product ideas.

5. Product Life-Cycle Strategies

a. After launching the new product, management wants the product to enjoy a long and happy life. Figure 9.2 shows a typical product life cycle (PLC), the course that a product's sales and profits take over its lifetime.

> **i.** Product development begins when the company finds and develops a new-product idea. During product development, sales are zero and the company's investment costs mount.
>
> **ii.** Introduction is a period of slow sales growth as the product is introduced in the market. Profits are nonexistent in this stage because of the heavy expenses of product introduction.
>
> **iii.** Growth is a period of rapid market acceptance and increasing profits.
>
> **iv.** Maturity is a period of slowdown in sales growth because the product has achieved acceptance by most potential buyers. Profits level off or decline because of increased marketing outlays to defend the product against competition.
>
> **v.** Decline is the period when sales fall off and profits drop.

b. Not all products follow this product life cycle. Some products are introduced and die quickly; others stay in the mature stage for a long, long time. Some enter the decline stage and are then cycled back into the growth stage through strong promotion or repositioning.

c. The PLC concept can describe a product class, a product form, or a brand. The PLC concept applies differently in each case.

> **i.** Product classes have the longest life cycles—the sales of many product classes stay in the maturity stage for a long time.
>
> **ii.** Product forms, in contrast, tend to have the standard PLC shape.

      iii. A specific brand's life cycle can change quickly because of changing competitive attacks and responses.

d. The PLC concept also can be applied to what are known as styles, fashions, and fads. Their special life cycles are shown in Figure 9.3.

      i. A style is a basic and distinctive mode of expression.

      ii. A fashion is a currently accepted or popular style in a given field.

      iii. Fads are temporary periods of unusually high sales driven by consumer enthusiasm and immediate product or brand popularity.

e. Marketers can apply the PLC concept as a useful framework for describing how products and markets work. But using the PLC concept for forecasting product performance or for developing marketing strategies presents some practical problems.

      i. Managers may have trouble identifying which stage of the PLC the product is in or pinpointing when the product moves into the next stage.

      ii. They may find it hard to determine the factors that affect the product's movement through the stages.

      iii. In practice, it is difficult to forecast the sales level at each PLC stage, the length of each stage, and the shape of the PLC curve.

f. Using the PLC concept to develop marketing strategy also can be difficult because strategy is both a cause and a result of the product's life cycle. The product's current PLC position suggests the best marketing strategies, and the resulting marketing strategies affect product performance in later life-cycle stages.

Introduction Stage

g. The introduction stage starts when the new product is first launched.

h. In this stage, as compared to other stages, profits are negative or low because of the low sales and high distribution and promotion stage.

i. A company, especially the market pioneer, must choose a launch strategy that is consistent with the intended product positioning. It should realize that the initial strategy is just the first step in a grander marketing plan for the product's entire life cycle.

Growth Stage

j. If the new product satisfies the market, it will enter a growth stage, in which sales start climbing quickly.

      i. The early adopters will continue to buy, and later buyers will start following their lead, especially if they hear favorable word of mouth.

      ii. Attracted by the opportunities for profit, new competitors will enter the market. They will introduce new product features, and the market will expand.

k. Profits increase during the growth stage, as promotion costs are spread over a large volume and as unit manufacturing costs fall.

l. The firm uses several strategies to sustain rapid market growth as long as possible.

    i. It improves product quality and adds new product features and models.

    ii. It enters new market segments and new distribution channels.

    iii. It shifts some advertising from building product awareness to building product conviction and purchase, and it lowers prices at the right time to attract more buyers.

m. In the growth stage, the firm faces a trade-off between high market share and high current profit.

<u>Maturity Stage</u>

n. At some point, a product's sales growth will slow down, and the product will enter a maturity stage.

    i. This maturity stage normally lasts longer than the previous stages, and it poses strong challenges to marketing management.

    ii. Most products are in the maturity stage of the life cycle, and therefore most of marketing management deals with the mature product.

o. Although many products in the mature stage appear to remain unchanged for long periods, most successful ones are actually evolving to meet changing consumer needs.

p. Product managers should do more than simply ride along with or defend their mature products. They should consider modifying the marketing, product, and marketing mix.

    i. In modifying the market, the company tries to increase the consumption of the current product. Or the company may reposition the brand to appeal to a larger or faster-growing market segment. The manager may also look for ways to increase usage among present customers.

    ii. The company might also try modifying the product—changing characteristics such as quality, features, or style to attract new users and to inspire more usage.

    iii. Finally, the company can try modifying the marketing mix—improving sales by changing one or more marketing mix elements.

        a. It can cut prices to attract new users and competitors' customers.

        b. It can launch a better advertising campaign or use aggressive sales promotions—trade deals, cents-off, premiums, and contests.

        c. In addition to pricing and promotion, the company can also move into large market channels, using mass merchandisers, if these channels are growing.

        d. The company can offer new or improved services to buyers.

Decline Stage

q. The sales of most product forms and brands eventually dip. The decline may be slow. Or sales may plunge to zero, or they may drop to a low level where they continue for many years. This is the decline stage.

r. Sales may decline for many reasons, including technological advances, shifts in consumer tastes, and increased competition.

s. Carrying a weak product can be very costly to a firm, and not just in profit terms.

    i. A weak product may take up too much of management's time.

    ii. It often requires frequent price and inventory adjustments.

    iii. It requires advertising and sales force attention that might be better used to make "healthy" products more profitable.

t. Companies need to pay more attention to their aging products.

    i. The firm's first task is to identify those products in the decline stage by regularly reviewing sales, market shares, costs, and profit trends.

    ii. Then, management must decide whether to maintain, harvest, or drop each of these declining products.

        a. Management may decide to maintain its brand without change in the hope that competitors leave the industry.

        b. Or management may decide to reposition or reformulate the brand in hopes of moving it back into the growth stage of the product life cycle.

        c. Management may decide to harvest the product that means reducing various costs and hoping that sales hold up. If successful, harvesting will increase the company's profits in the short run.

        d. Management may decide to drop the product from the line. It can sell it to another firm or simply liquidate it at salvage value.

u. Table 9.2 summarizes the key characteristics of each stage of the product life cycle. The table also lists the marketing objectives and strategies for each.

6. **Additional Product Considerations**

a. There are two additional product policy considerations to take note of.

Product Decisions and Social Responsibility

b. Marketers should consider carefully public policy issues and regulations involving acquiring or dropping products, patent protection, product quality and safety, and product warranties.

    i. Government may prevent companies from adding products through acquisitions if the effect threatens to lessen competition.

    ii. Companies dropping products must be aware that they have legal obligations, written or implied, to their suppliers, dealers, and customers who have a stake in the dropped product.

      iii. Companies must obey U.S. patent laws when developing new products.

  c. Manufacturers must comply with specific laws regarding product quality and safety.

      i. The Federal Food, Drug, and Cosmetic Act protects consumers from unsafe and adulterated food, drugs, and cosmetics.

      ii. Various acts provide for the inspection of sanitary conditions in the meat- and poultry-processing industries.

      iii. Safety legislation has been passed to regulate fabrics, chemical substances, automobiles, toys, drugs, and poisons.

      iv. The Consumer Product Safety Act of 1972 established a Consumer Product Safety Commission that has the authority to ban or seize potentially harmful products and set severe penalties for violation of the law.

  d. If consumers have been injured by a product that has been designed defectively, they can sue manufacturers or dealers.

  e. Many manufacturers offer written product warranties to convince customers of their products' quality.

      i. To protect consumers, Congress passed the Magnuson-Moss Warranty Act in 1975. The act requires that full warranties meet certain minimum standards, including repair "within a reasonable time and without charge" or a replacement or full refund if the product does not work "after a reasonable number of attempts" at repair.

International Product and Services Marketing

  f. International product and service marketers face special challenges.

      i. First, they must figure out what products and services to introduce and in which countries.

      ii. Then, they must decide how much to standardize or adapt their products and services for world markets.

         a. On the one hand, companies would like to standardize their offerings.

            1. Standardization helps a company to develop a consistent worldwide image. It also lowers manufacturing costs and eliminates duplication of research and development, advertising, and product design efforts.

            2. On the other hand, consumers around the world differ in their cultures, attitudes, and buying behaviors. And markets vary in their economic conditions, competition, legal requirements, and physical environments. Companies must usually respond to these differences by adapting their product offerings.

    iii. Packaging also presents new challenges for international marketers.
- **a.** Packaging issues can be subtle. For example, names, labels, and colors may not translate easily from one country to another.
- **b.** Packaging may also have to be tailored to meet the physical characteristics of consumers in various parts of the world.

    iv. Service marketers also face special challenges when going global.
- **a.** Some service industries have a long history of international operations.
- **b.** Professional and business service industries such as accounting, management consulting, and advertising have only recently globalized. The international growth of these firms followed the globalization of the client companies they serve. Retailers are among the latest service businesses to go global.
- **c.** Service companies wanting to operate in other countries are not always welcomed with open arms. Whereas manufacturers usually face straightforward tariff, quota, or currency restrictions when attempting to sell their products in another country, service providers are likely to face more subtle barriers. Despite such difficulties, the trend toward growth of global service companies will continue.

Student Exercises

1.   Key Term: New Product Development

New product development is the development of original products, product improvement, product innovations, and new brands through the firm's own R&D efforts. Innovation can be very risky and very expensive. About 90 percent of all new products fail. Review the information regarding Apple's new iPhone (www.apple.com/iphone). What do you think of this product? Do you believe it will "revolutionize" the cell phone market, as Apple states, or will it not live up to expectations?

2.   Key Term: Idea Generation

Companies must develop new products, but the odds are stacked against them. To have a chance at success, a company must carry out strong new-product planning and set up a systematic new-product development process for finding and growing new products. The first stage in this process is known as idea generation. Idea generation is the systematic search for new product ideas. Take a look at the work Frog Design has done for Victoria's Secret (www.frogdesign.com) in the revitalization of its retail design system for its new New York store. How do you believe the stage of idea generation played a part in this revitalization?

3.   Key Term: Concept Development

An attractive product idea must be developed into a product concept. A product concept is a detailed version of the new product idea stated in meaningful terms the consumer understands. Typically, a company will develop alternative product concepts and then find out how attractive each concept is to the customer, choosing the best one for further development. Look again at the Apple iPhone (www.apple.com/iphone). Develop three alternative product concepts for the iPhone Apple may have wanted to consider.

4.   Key Term: Test Marketing

Test marketing is the stage at which the product and marketing program are introduced into more realistic market settings. Test marketing gives the marketer experience with marketing the product before going to the great expense of full introduction. It allows the company to test the product and it entire marketing program. Imagine you were the marketer of a fashion-forward jean, different from anything currently on the market. You are preparing to test market your jeans before going nationwide. Where and how might you consider conducting your test market?

5.   Key Term: Product Life Cycle

The course of a product's sales and profits over its lifetime is known as the Product Life Cycle. It involves five distinct stages – product development, introduction, growth, maturity, and decline. Find a product that represents each of these stages.

6.   Key Term: Fashion

A fashion is a currently accepted or popular style in a given field. Fashions tend to grow slowly, remain popular for an extended period of time, and slowly decline to be replaced by the next fashion. Everyone knows of Morton Salt and the Morton Salt Girl. Go to www.mortonsalt.com. Take a look at how the dress of the little girl has changed through the years in response to changing American fashion.

7.   Key Term: Decline Stage

The last stage of the product life cycle is the decline stage. Products experiencing sales decline and profit decay occupy this unenviable stage. Take a look at the home audio component offering of Pioneer Electronics (www.pioneerelectronics.com). What product or products would you consider to occupy the decline stage?

8.   Key Term: Fads

Fads are temporary periods of unusually high sales driven by consumer enthusiasm and immediate product or brand popularity. Fads don't last long. Two recent fads of the fashion industry were the sailor look and the poncho. Both of these were introduced to great fanfare. Both experienced rapid run-ups in sales. Both saw their sales quickly come crashing down. What is a product do you consider to be a fad today?

9.   Key Term: Introduction Stage

The introduction stage begins when the product is first launched into the marketplace. Introducing a product takes time, and sales are likely to be slow. At this stage, profits are low (or negative) due to the low sales and the need to spend high sums of money to attract customers and build inventories. It takes time to develop adequate sales to lift a product to the next stage. Companies introducing the Blu-ray DVD disk and players are experiencing these uncomfortable growing pains. Take a look at www.blu-ray.com to learn more about this new technology. What is necessary for Blu-ray to move out of the introduction stage and on to the growth stage?

10.   Key Term: Social Responsibility

Marketers must carefully consider public policy issues and regulations involving introducing, acquiring, marketing, or dropping products or product quality and safety. Businesses are corporate citizens and, as such, must act with the well-being of the consumer in mind. How is Miller Brewing Company (www.millerbrewing.com) responding to the public policy issues surrounding underage drinking?

Marketing ADventure Exercises

1.   Ad Interpretation Challenge: Idea Generation
       Ad: Food & Beverage – Altoids

New-product development begins with idea generation – the systematic search for new-product ideas. Typically, companies have to generate many ideas in order to find a few good ones. Altoids, an unusual breath mint, is one of those "good" ideas. Your job is to take Altoids to the "next level." Using the currently available versions of Altoids, what new product ideas can you generate?

2.   Ad Interpretation Challenge: Idea Screening
        Ad: Food & Beverage – Heinz

The basic purpose of idea generation is to generate a large number of potential product ideas. The basic purpose of idea screening is to reduce that large number to a more manageable number. Idea screening helps spot potentially good products and drops the unworkable ones early on. Take a look at Heinz (www.heinz.com). Go to their new product introductions and take a look at the newest products in the Heinz line. Are there any products here that you would have had screened out during the idea screening stage?

3.   Ad Interpretation Challenge: Concept Testing
        Ad: Food & Beverage – Gatorade

Concept testing calls for testing new-product concepts with groups of target customers. The concepts can be presented to customers either physically or symbolically. Think about Gatorade. (You can go to www.gatorade.com to learn more about their products.) Imagine that Gatorade were considering introducing a version of their best-selling thirst quencher that was in capsule format. The product concept reads: "Gatorade in an easy to swallow capsule." Think about how you might present this concept symbolically (in words) to consumers for the purpose of conducting a concept test.

4.   Ad Interpretation Challenge: Test Marketing
        Ad: Electronics – Motorola

The stage of the new-product development process in which the product and marketing program are introduced into more realistic market settings is known as the test market. Test marketing gives the marketer a little experience with marketing the product before going to the great expense of full introduction. Consider this ad for Motorola V8088 cell phone. How might Motorola have test marketed this product prior to its national introduction?

5.   Ad Interpretation Challenge: Commercialization
        Ad: Student Choice

If the company chooses to go ahead after the test marketing stage and launch the new product into the market, they are entering the commercialization phase. Commercialization, a very expensive stage, is the final stage of the new-product development process. Commercialization is the introduction of a new product into the market. Find an ad that is designed to assist in this commercialization process. Find an ad that is "introducing" a new product to the marketplace.

6.   Ad Interpretation Challenge: Fashion
      Ad: Apparel - Student Choice

A fad is a currently accepted or popular style in a given field. Fashions tend to grow slowly, remain popular for a while, and then decline slowly. However, the underlying product remains. Look through the apparel ads offered. Find one that you believe is promoting a fashion.

7.   Ad Interpretation Challenge: Introduction Stage
      Ad: Student Choice

The introduction stage begins when the product is first launched and introduced to the market. No doubt, introduction takes time, and sales growth is bound to be slow initially. During this phase, competitors are few. The basic promotion strategy is to induce consumer trial of the product. Find an ad that is promoting consumer trial.

8.   Ad Interpretation Challenge: Growth Stage
      Ad: Electronics - LG

The growth stage of the product life cycle is characterized by products which are experiencing rapidly rising sales, an expanding distribution system, and an increasing number of competitors. Products in this stage typically appeal to the early adopter. Flat screen televisions (i.e., LCD or plasma) are a growth stage product. Take a look at this ad for flat FRONT televisions (they still have a picture tube, but the front of the screen is flat) manufactured by LG – a product in the mature stage. How would you alter this ad to indicate a product occupying the growth stage?

9.   Ad Interpretation Challenge: Decline Stage
      Ad: Electronics – Fuji Film

It is inevitable that, at some point, a product's sales will slow down and then begin to go down. At this point, the product enters into the decline phase of the product life cycle. Here, you find many producers with many products to sell; however, the numbers are less than when the product was in the mature stage. If you were the marketer of Fuji Film, a product one would consider definitely in the decline stage of the product life cycle, how would you attempt to make you product viable?

10.   Ad Interpretation Challenge: Social Responsibility
      Ad: Student Choice

Corporations are social institutions. As such, they must exhibit stewardship of our fragile planet and its limited resources. Marketers must be socially aware and socially responsible. Find an ad that is exhibiting the marketers believe in their social responsibility.

Chapter 10
Pricing Products: Understanding and Capturing Customer Value

Learning Objectives

1. Answer the question, "What is price?" and discuss the importance of pricing in today's fast-changing environment.
2. Discuss the importance of understanding customer value perceptions when setting prices.
3. Discuss the importance of company and product costs in setting prices.
4. Identify and define the other important internal and external factors affecting a firm's pricing.

Chapter Overview

Price goes by many names in our economy. In the narrowest sense, price is the amount of money charged for a product or service. This meaning, however, has been broadened. Today, despite the increased role of nonprice factors in the modern marketing process, price remains an important element in the marketing mix.

The most important aspect to consider when setting price is customer value. When customers buy something, they are exchanging something of value in order to get something of value. For this reason, various value-oriented pricing strategies can be employed, including value-based pricing, good-value pricing, and value-added pricing.

In addition to customer value, company costs are important in considering the setting of price. Both fixed costs and variables costs can affect the optimal price. Such costs are also important in calculating break-even points and target profit.

Additionally, other internal and external factors affect price. Internal factors include the firm's marketing objectives, marketing mix strategy, and organizational factors. External factors that influence pricing decisions include the nature of market and demand, competition, and other environmental factors like the economy, reseller needs, and government actions. In the end, the consumer decides whether the company has set the right price.

Chapter Outline

1. **Introduction**
   a. Toys "R" Us took the toy industry by storm by growing its market share to 25 percent in the 1980s and 1990s. It did this by offering variety, convenience, and everyday low prices year round.

b. Now, Toys "R" Us is getting a taste of its own medicine. Wal-Mart has been undercutting it on price for the better part of the last decade. Wal-Mart has surpassed Toys "R" Us in terms of market share.

c. Companies today face a fierce and fast-changing pricing environment. The challenge is to find the price that will let the company make a fair profit by harvesting the customer value it creates.

2. What Is Price?

a. In the narrowest sense, price is the amount of money charged for a product or service. More broadly, price is the sum of all the values that consumers exchange for the benefits of having or using the product or service.

b. Price is the only element in the marketing mix that produces revenue; all other elements represent costs. Price is also one of the most flexible elements of the marketing mix.

c. Pricing is the number one problem facing many marketing executives. Yet many companies do not handle pricing well.

　　i. One frequent problem is that companies are too quick to reduce prices in order to get a sale rather than convince buyers that their products are worth a higher price.

　　ii. Other common mistakes include pricing that is too cost oriented rather than customer-value oriented, and pricing that does not take the rest of the marketing mix into account.

3. Factors to Consider When Setting Prices

a. A company's pricing decisions are affected by both internal company factors and external environment factors. See Figure 10.1.

Value-Based Pricing

b. Pricing decisions must start with customer value because customers will ultimately decide whether the product's price is right.

c. Value-based pricing uses buyers' perceptions of value, not the seller's cost, as the key to pricing. Value-based pricing means that the marketer cannot design a product and marketing program and then set the price. Price is considered along with the other marketing mix variables before the marketing program is set.

d. Figure 10.2 compares cost-based pricing with value-based pricing.

　　i. Cost-based pricing is product driven.

　　ii. Value-based pricing reverses this process. The company sets its target price based on customer perceptions of the product value.

e. A company using value-based pricing must find out what value buyers assign to different competitive offers. Measuring perceived value can be difficult.

　　i. Sometimes, companies ask consumers how much they would pay for a basic product and for each benefit added to the offer.

　　ii. Or a company might conduct experiments to test the perceived value of different product offers.

f. There has been a fundamental shift in consumer attitudes toward price and quality. Good-value pricing is defined as offering just the right combination of quality and good service at a fair price.

g. In many cases, this has involved introducing less expensive versions of established, brand name products.

    i. An important type of value pricing at the retail level is everyday low pricing (EDLP). This involves charging a constant, everyday low price with few or no temporary price discounts.

    ii. In contrast, high-low pricing involves charging higher prices on an everyday basis but running frequent promotions to lower prices temporarily on selected items.

    iii. The king of EDLP is Wal-Mart, which practically defined the concept.

h. In many business-to-business marketing situations, the challenge is to build the company's pricing power—its power to escape price competition and to justify higher prices and margins without losing market share.

    i. To retain pricing power, a firm must retain or build the value of its marketing offer.

    ii. In such cases, many companies adopt value-added pricing strategies. Rather than cutting prices to match competitors, they attach value-added services to differentiate their offers and thus support higher margins.

Company and Product Costs

i. Costs set the floor for the price that the company can charge.

j. Cost-based pricing involves setting prices based on the costs for producing, distributing, and selling the product plus a fair rate of return for its effort and risk.

    i. A company's costs take two forms.

        a. Fixed costs (also known as *overhead*) are costs that do not vary with production or sales level.

        b. Variable costs vary directly with the level of production.

        c. Total costs are the sum of the fixed and variable costs for any given level of production.

    ii. Management wants to charge a price that will at least cover the total product costs at a given level of production.

    iii. If it costs the company more than competitors to produce and sell its product, the company will have to charge a higher price and make less profit, putting it at a competitive disadvantage.

    iv. To price wisely, management needs to know how its costs vary with different levels of production.

        a. Figure 10.3A shows the typical short-run average cost curve (SRAC).

        b. Figure 10.3B shows the long-run average cost curve (LRAC).

    v. Average cost tends to fall with accumulated production experience. This is shown in Figure 10.4. This drop in the average cost with accumulated production experience is called the experience curve (or the learning curve).

        a. A single-minded focus on reducing costs and exploiting the experience curve will not always work. The aggressive pricing might give the product a cheap image. The strategy also assumes that competitors are weak and not willing to fight it out by meeting the company's price cuts. Finally, while the company is building volume under one technology, a competitor may find a lower-cost technology that lets it start at prices lower than those of the market leader, who still operates on the old experience curve.

k. The simplest pricing method is cost-plus pricing—adding a standard markup to cost of the product.

    i. Unit cost is calculated as follows:

$$\text{Unit cost} = \text{Variable cost} + \frac{\text{Fixed costs}}{\text{Unit sales}}$$

    ii. Supposing a manufacturer wants to earn a certain percentage as a markup, the following would be applied:

$$\text{Markup price} = \frac{\text{Unit cost}}{(1 - \text{Desired return on sales})}$$

    iii. Does using standard markups to set prices make sense? Generally, not. Any pricing method that ignores demand and competitor prices is not likely to lead to the best price.

    iv. Markup pricing remains popular for many reasons.

        a. Sellers are more certain about costs than about demand. By tying the price to cost, sellers simplify pricing—they do not have to make frequent adjustments as demand changes.

        b. When all firms in the industry use this pricing method, prices tend to be similar and price competition is thus minimized.

        c. Many people feel that cost-plus pricing is fairer to both buyers and sellers. Sellers earn a fair return on their investment but do not take advantage of buyers when buyers' demand becomes great.

l. Another cost-oriented pricing approach is break-even pricing, or a variation called target profit pricing.

    i. The firm tries to determine the price at which it will break even or make the target profit it is seeking.

    ii. Target pricing uses the concept of a break-even chart that shows the total cost and total revenue expected at different sales volume levels. Figure 10.5 shows a break-even chart.

   iii. Break-even volume can be calculated using the following formula:

$$\text{Break-even volume} = \frac{\text{Fixed cost}}{\text{Price - Variable cost}}$$

    iv. The manufacturer should consider different prices and estimate break-even volumes, probable demand, and profits for each. This is done in Table 10.1.

Other Internal and External Factors Affecting Price Decisions

m. Whereas costs set the lower limit of prices, customer perceptions of value set the upper limit. However, the company must consider a number of other internal and external factors. These include the overall marketing strategy, objectives, and mix.

n. Before setting price, the company must decide on its strategy for the product. If the company has selected its target market and positioning carefully, then its marketing mix strategy, including price, will be fairly straightforward. Pricing strategy is largely determined by decisions on market positioning.

o. General pricing objectives include survival, current profit maximization, market share leadership, or customer retention and relationship building.

p. Price decisions must be coordinated with product design, distribution, and promotion decisions to form a consistent and effective marketing program. Decisions made of other marketing mix variables may affect pricing decisions. Companies often position their products on price and then tailor other marketing mix decisions to the prices they want to charge.

    i. Target costing reverses the usual process of first designing a new product, determining its cost, and then setting a price. It starts with an ideal selling price based on customer considerations, and then targets costs that will ensure that the price is met.

   ii. Other companies de-emphasize price and use other marketing mix tools to create nonprice positions. Often, the best strategy is not to charge the lowest price, but rather to differentiate the marketing offer to make it worth a higher price.

        a. If the product is positioned on nonprice factors, then decisions about quality, promotion, and distribution will strongly affect price.

        b. If price is a crucial positioning factor, then price will strongly affect decisions made about the other marketing mix elements.

q. Within the organization, management must decide who sets the price. In small companies, this may be set by top management. In industrial markets, salespeople may play a role. Still other industries utilize pricing departments.

r. The seller's pricing freedom also varies with different types of markets and the relationship between price and demand.

    i. Under pure competition, the market consists of many buyers and sellers trading in a uniform commodity. No single buyer or seller has much effect on the going market price.

    ii. Under monopolistic competition, the market consists of many buyers and sellers who trade over a range of prices rather than a single market price. A range of prices occurs because sellers can differentiate their offers to buyers.

    iii. Under oligopolistic competition, the market consists of a few sellers who are highly sensitive to each other's pricing and marketing strategies. There are few sellers because it is difficult for new sellers to enter the market.

    iv. In a pure monopoly, the market consists of one seller. In a regulated monopoly, the government permits the company to set rates that will yield a "fair return." Nonregulated monopolies are free to price at what the market will bear. However, they do not always charge the full price for a number of reasons: a desire not to attract competition, a desire to penetrate the market faster with a low price, or a fear of government regulation.

s. In the end, the consumer will decide whether a product's price is right. Pricing decisions, like other marketing mix decisions, must be buyer oriented.

    i. Each price the company might charge will lead to a different level of demand.

    ii. The relationship between the price charged and the resulting demand level is shown in the demand curve in Figure 10.6. The demand curve shows the number of units the market will buy in a given time period at different prices that might be charged.

    iii. In the normal case, demand and price are inversely related; that is, the higher the price, the lower the demand. In the case of prestige goods, the demand curve sometimes slopes upward. Still, if the company charges too high a price, the level of demand will be lower.

t. Marketers also need to know price elasticity—how responsive demand will be to a change in price.

    i. The price elasticity of demand is given by the following formula:

$$\text{Price elasticity of demand} = \frac{\% \text{ change in quantity demanded}}{\% \text{ change in price}}$$

        ii. What determines the price elasticity of demand? Buyers are less price sensitive when the product they are buying is unique or when it is high in quality, prestige, or exclusiveness. They are less price sensitive when substitute products are hard to find or when they cannot easily compare the quality of substitutes. Finally, buyers are less price sensitive when the total expenditure for a product is low relative to their income or when the cost is shared by another party.

        iii. If the demand is elastic rather than inelastic, sellers will consider lowering their prices.

    u. In setting its prices, the company must also consider competitors' costs and prices and possible competitor reactions to the company's own pricing moves.

    v. In assessing competitors' pricing strategies, the company should ask several questions:

        i. How does the company's market offering compare with competitors' offerings in terms of customer value?

        ii. How strong are current competitors and what are their current pricing strategies?

        iii. How does the competitive landscape influence customer price sensitivity?

    w. When setting prices, the company also must consider a number of other factors in its external environment.

        i. Economic conditions can have a strong impact on the firm's pricing strategies.

        ii. The company must also consider what impact its prices will have on other parties in its environment, such as resellers.

        iii. The government is an important external influence on pricing decisions.

        iv. Social concerns may have to be taken into account.

Student Exercises

1.   Key Term: Price

Price is defined as the amount of money charged for a product or service, or the sum of the values that consumer exchange for the benefits having or using the product or service. It is the only element of the marketing mix that produces revenue. Go to Hewlett-Packard home page (www.hp.com) and build for yourself the ultimate laptop computer. Determine the actual monetary price you would be charged, after all of the deals and discounts.

2.   Key Term: Price

Yes, it is the same term as given in Exercise 1; however, here it takes on a totally different dimension. Consider your decision to come to school. You paid (and are paying) a price (both tangible and intangible) for that decision. What price did you pay for this service (education) you are receiving?

3.   Key Term: Value-Based Pricing

Good pricing begins with a complete understanding of the value that a product or service creates for the customer. Value-based pricing uses the buyer's perception of value, not the seller's cost, as the key to pricing. Your text uses the example of the Bentley Continental automobile as an example of value-based pricing. Find another relatively expensive product that you believe is practicing value-based pricing.

4.   Key Term: Good-Value Pricing

More and more, marketers have been adopting good-value pricing strategies. In such a pricing strategy, marketers offer just the right combination of quality and good service at a lower, fair price. Go to a Wal-Mart store or look at Wal-Mart online (www.walmart.com). Find products that you believe the marketers have employed good-value pricing.

5.   Key Term: Value-Added Pricing

Value-added pricing is the practice of attaching value-added features and services to differentiate a company's offerings and to support charging higher prices. Lexus automobiles (www.lexus.com) (the luxury division of Toyota) utilize value-added pricing. The company charges premium prices for their cars. In addition to building and providing a high quality automobile, what value-added features and/or services do they provide to the customer?

6.   Key Term: Fixed Costs

Fixed costs are costs that do not vary with production or sales volume. Take a look at Tomasini Fine Linens (www.tomasini.cc), a high-end linen manufacturer based in Los Angeles. What are some of the fixed costs with which this company is faced?

7.   Key Term: Variable Costs

Variable costs vary directly with production volume. Typically, these are costs associated with the materials used in the manufacturer of the product. You only use the items if you make the product. Again, examine Tomasini Fine Linens (www.tomasini.cc) and the products they manufacture and market. What are some of the variable costs involved?

8.   Key Term: Cost-Based Pricing

Adding a standard markup to the cost of a product is known as cost-based pricing. It is the simplest form of pricing around. You just determine how much is costs you to produce the item and then you add a standard markup for profit. Consider Hot Springs Portable Spas (www.hotsprings.com). Would a company such as this utilize cost-based pricing?

9.   Key Term: Oligopolistic Competition

Under oligopolistic competition, the market consists of a few large sellers who are very aware of each other's pricing and marketing strategies. They are few sellers in the market because it is difficult for new sellers to successfully enter the market. Outside of cars and computers (examples used in your text), what is a market dominated by oligopolistic competition?

10.   Key Term: Pure Monopoly

In a pure monopoly, the market consists of just one seller. Nonregulated monopolies are free to price their products at what the market will bear. What is an example of a nonregulated monopoly today?

Marketing ADventure Exercises

1.   Ad Interpretation Challenge: Price
        Ad: Services and B2B—University of Toronto

Price is the amount of money charged for a product or service, or the sum of the values that consumers exchange for the benefits of having or using the product or service. Look at this ad for the University of Toronto. What is the "price" the student must pay to attend?

2.   Ad Interpretation Challenge: Value-based Pricing
        Ad: Autos—Jaguar

Remember, "good value" and "low cost" are not necessarily the same thing. Value-based pricing is setting prices based on the buyer's perception of value rather than on the seller's cost. Consider the ad for Jaguar. How could a consumer consider this product a good value?

3.   Ad Interpretation Challenge: Good-Value Pricing
        Ad: General Retail—Target

More and more, marketers have adopted a policy of good-value pricing. Good-value pricing is offering to the consumer just the right combination of quality and good service at a reasonable price. Wal-Mart is the king of good-value pricing with its use of EDLP (everyday low pricing). How is Target able to compete in the battle of good-value pricing?

4.   Ad Interpretation Challenge: Cost-based Pricing
        Ad: Autos—Mercedes

Adding a standard markup to the cost of a product is known as cost-based pricing. It is the simplest form of pricing around. You just determine how much it costs you to produce the item and then you add a standard markup for profit. Consider Mercedes. Would a company such as this utilize cost-based pricing?

5.   Ad Interpretation Challenge: Fixed Costs
        Ad: Travel and Tourism—American Airlines

Fixed costs are costs that do not vary much with production or sales volume. These are costs the manufacturer must pay regardless of these factors. Think about American Airlines. What are some of the fixed costs with which this company is faced?

6.   Ad Interpretation Challenge: Variable Costs
        Ad: Travel and Tourism—American Airlines

Variable costs vary directly with production volume. Typically, these are costs associated with the materials used in the manufacturer of the product or service. Again, think about American Airlines. What are some of the variable costs with which this company is faced?

7.   Ad Interpretation Challenge: Cost-Plus Pricing
        Ad: Student Choice

Adding a standard markup to the cost of a product or service is known as cost-plus pricing. It is the simplest form of pricing around. You just determine how much is costs you to produce the item and then you add a standard markup for profit. Find an ad for a product or company that would use cost-plus pricing.

8.   Ad Interpretation Challenge: Monopolistic Competition
        Ad: Food and Beverage—Heinz

When a market consists of many buyers and sellers who trade over a range of prices rather than a single market price, monopolistic competition exists. Buyers see differences in sellers' products and make purchase decisions accordingly. How does Heinz ketchup compete in this monopolistic competitive environment?

9.   Ad Interpretation Challenge: Inelastic Demand
        Ad: Student Choice

The less elastic the demand for a product, the more it makes sense for the seller to raise the price of the product. Buyers are less price sensitive when the product they are buying is unique or when it is high in quality. Find an ad for a product which would most likely have an inelastic demand.

10.   Ad Interpretation Challenge: Elastic Demand
        Ad: Student Choice

The more elastic the demand for a product or service, the more it makes sense to possibly lower the price of your product. Because of elastic demand, the lower the price, the greater the demand created for the product or service. Find an ad for a product or service which you believe experiences elastic demand.

Chapter 11
Pricing Products: Pricing Strategies

Learning Objectives

1. Describe the major strategies for pricing imitative and new products.
2. Explain how companies find a set of prices that maximize the profits from the total product mix.
3. Discuss how companies adjust their prices to take into account different types of customers and situations.
4. Discuss the key issues related to initiating and responding to price changes.

Chapter Overview

Because pricing is a dynamic process, companies must design a pricing structure that covers all their products and a variety of constantly changing conditions (such as changes that occur as the product progresses through the stages of the product life cycle). Two primary strategies (market-skimming and market-penetration pricing) are thoroughly discussed in this chapter.

The marketer wishing to explore pricing strategy options will find a wealth of alternatives from which to choose. The first major option will be pricing with respect to the product mix. Numerous forms of product-mix pricing strategies are examined within the context of the competitive environment. Examples include product-line pricing, optional-product pricing, captive-product pricing, by-product pricing, and product-bundle pricing. The average marketer does not use all of these methods; however, by studying the options available, the marketer enhances his or her ability to be creative with respect to pricing within the context of the product mix.

Sometimes, however, the firm must make adjustments in their pricing process and strategy. These adjustments are made to account for differences in consumer segments and changing situations. Adjustments can occur through discounts and allowances or by the desire to segment markets by price. Additionally, price has a psychological aspect that allows for adjustments just as geographical, promotional, and international relationships can alter pricing methods and strategies. The chapter explores each of these areas in some detail.

Reactions to price changes must be carefully studied. The reactions come from the firm, the consumer, the distribution channel, and the competition. Response must be carefully measured and be appropriate if marketing success is to be achieved. In conclusion, the chapter also touches on public policy with respect to pricing. Pricing does not occur within a vacuum. Once a price has been made (or adjusted), other components of the environment are affected. The reader will find that this chapter provides an excellent reference base from which to develop sound pricing strategy and policy.

143

Chapter Outline

1. **Introduction**
   a. Ryanair of Ireland has figured out a way to one-up the low fare airlines: offer air flights for free. Yes, zero cost. It is already flying one-quarter of its customers for free and is shooting for more than half by the end of the decade.
   b. Ryanair accomplishes this by charging for everything but air flight service. Beverages, magazines, and bag check are all revenue producing extras. But Ryanair is also selling ad space on the backs of seats.
   c. Pricing decisions are subject to an incredibly complex array of environmental and competitive forces. A company sets not a single price, but rather a pricing structure that covers different items in its line. This pricing structure changes over time as products move through their life cycles.

2. **New-Product Pricing Strategies**
   a. Companies bringing out a new product face the challenge of setting prices for the first time. They can choose between two broad strategies.

   Market-Skimming Pricing
   b. Many companies that invent new products set high initial prices to "skim" revenues layer-by-layer from the market. This is called market-skimming pricing.
   c. Market skimming makes sense only under certain conditions.
      i. First, the product's quality and image must support its higher price, and enough buyers must want the product at that price.
      ii. Second, the costs of producing a smaller volume cannot be so high that they cancel the advantage of charging more.
      iii. Finally, competitors should not be able to enter the market easily and undercut the high price.

   Market-Penetration Pricing
   d. Rather than setting a high price to skim off small but profitable market segments, some companies use market-penetration pricing. They set a low initial price in order to penetrate the market quickly and deeply—to attract a large number of buyers quickly and win a large market share.
   e. Several conditions must be met for this low-price strategy to work.
      i. The market must be highly price sensitive so that a low price produces more market growth.
      ii. Production and distribution costs must fall as sales volume increases.
      iii. The low price must help keep out the competition, and the penetration pricer must maintain its low-price position—otherwise, the price advantage may be only temporary.

3. **Product Mix Pricing Strategies**
   a. The strategy for setting a product's price often has to be changed when the product is part of a product mix. In this case, the firm looks for a set of prices that maximizes the profits on the total product mix.
   b. The five product mix pricing situations are summarized in Table 11.1.

Product Line Pricing

   c. Companies usually develop product lines rather than single products.
   d. In product line pricing, management must decide on the price steps to set between the various products in a line.
      i. The price steps should take into account cost differences between the products in the line, customer evaluations of their different features, and competitors' prices. In many industries, sellers use well-established price points for the products in their line.
      ii. The seller's task is to establish perceived quality differences that support the price differences.

Optional-Product Pricing

   e. Many companies use optional-product pricing—offering to sell optional or accessory products along with their main product.
   f. Pricing these options is a sticky problem. The company has to decide which items to include in the base price and which to offer as options.

Captive-Product Pricing

   g. Companies that make products that must be used along with a main product are using captive-product pricing. Producers of the main products often price them low and set high markups on the supplies.
   h. In the case of services, this strategy is called two-part pricing. The price of the service is broken into a fixed fee plus a variable usage rate.
      i. The service firm must decide how much to charge for the basic service and how much for the variable usage.
      ii. The fixed amount should be low enough to induce usage of the service; profit can be made on the variable fees.

By-Product Pricing

   i. Using by-product pricing, a manufacturer will seek a market for by-products and should accept any price that covers more than the cost of storing and delivering them.
   j. By-products can even turn out to be profitable.

Product Bundle Pricing

   k. Using product bundle pricing, sellers often combine several of their products and offer the bundle at a reduced price.
   l. Price bundling can promote the sales of products consumers might not otherwise buy, but the combined price must be low enough to get them to buy the bundle.

4. Price-Adjustment Strategies

a. Companies usually adjust their basic prices to account for various customer differences and changing situations.

b. The six price adjustment strategies are summarized in Table 11.2.

Discount and Allowance Pricing

c. Most companies adjust their basic price to reward customers for certain responses, such as early payment of bills, volume purchases, and off-season buying.

d. The many forms of discounts include a cash discount—a price reduction to buyers who pay their bills promptly.

    i. A typical example is "2/10, net 30," which means that although payment is due within 30 days, the buyer can deduct 2 percent if the bill is paid within 10 days.

    ii. A quantity discount is a price reduction to buyers who buy large volumes. Such discounts provide an incentive to the customer to buy more from one given seller, rather than from many different sources.

    iii. A functional discount (also called a *trade discount*) is offered by the seller to trade-channel members who perform certain functions, such as selling, storing, and record keeping.

    iv. A seasonal discount is a price reduction to buyers who buy merchandise or services out of season.

    v. Allowances are another type of reduction from list price.

        a. Trade-in allowances are price reductions given for turning in an old item when buying a new one.

        b. Promotional allowances are payments or price reductions to reward dealers for participating in advertising and sales support programs.

Segmented Pricing

e. Companies will often adjust their basic prices to allow for differences in customers, products, and locations.

f. In segmented pricing, the company sells a product or service at two or more prices, even though the difference in prices is not based on differences in costs.

    i. Under customer-segment pricing, different customers pay different prices for the same product or service.

    ii. Under product form pricing, different versions of the product are priced differently but not according to differences in their costs.

    iii. Under location pricing, a company charges different prices for different locations, even though the cost of offering each location is the same.

    iv. Using time pricing, a firm varies its prices by the season, the month, the day, and even the hour.

g. Segmented pricing goes by many names.

> **i.** Some in the airline industry call it revenue management.
> **ii.** Airlines, hotels, and restaurants call it yield management.

h. For segmented pricing to be an effective strategy, certain conditions must exist.

> **i.** The market must be segmentable, and the segments must show different degrees of demand.
> **ii.** The costs of segmenting and watching the market cannot exceed the extra revenue obtained from the price difference.
> **iii.** The segmented pricing must also be legal.

Psychological Pricing

i. Price says something about the product. For example, many consumers use price to judge quality.

j. In using psychological pricing, sellers consider the psychology of prices and not simply the economics.

k. Another aspect of psychological pricing is reference prices—prices that buyers carry in their minds and refer to when looking at a given product.

> **i.** The reference price might be formed by noting current prices, remembering past prices, or assessing the buying situation.
> **ii.** Sellers can influence or use these consumers' reference prices when setting price.

l. For most purchases, consumers don't have all the skill or information they need to figure out whether they are paying a good price. They may rely on certain cues that signal whether a price is high or low.

m. Even small differences in price can signal product differences.

Promotional Pricing

n. With promotional pricing, companies will temporarily price their products below list price and sometimes even below cost to create buying excitement and urgency.

o. Promotional pricing takes several forms.

> **i.** Supermarkets and department stores will price a few products as loss leaders to attract customers to the store in the hope that they will buy other items at normal markups.
> **ii.** Sellers will also use special-event pricing in certain seasons to draw more customers.
> **iii.** Manufacturers sometimes offer cash rebates to consumers who buy the product from dealers within a specified time; the manufacturer sends the rebate directly to the customer.
> **iv.** Some manufacturers offer low-interest financing, longer warranties, or free maintenance to reduce the consumer's "price."
> **v.** The seller may simply offer discounts from normal prices to increase sales and reduce inventories.

p. Promotional pricing can have adverse effects.

      i. Used too frequently and copied by competitors, price promotions can create "deal-prone" customers who wait until brands go on sale before buying them.

      ii. Constantly reduced prices can erode a brand's value in the eyes of customers.

      iii. Marketers sometimes use price promotions as a quick fix instead of sweating through the difficult process of developing effective longer-term strategies for building their brands.

      iv. The frequent use of promotional pricing can also lead to industry price wars. Such price wars usually play into the hands of only one or a few competitors—those with the most efficient operations.

Geographical Pricing

q. A company also must decide how to price its products for customers located in different parts of the country or world.

      i. FOB-origin pricing is a practice that means the goods are placed free on board (hence, FOB) a carrier. At that point the title and responsibility pass to the customer, who pays the freight from the factory to the destination.

      ii. Uniform-delivered pricing is the opposite of FOB pricing. Here, the company charges the same price plus freight to all customers, regardless of their location. The freight charge is set at the average freight cost.

      iii. Zone pricing falls between FOB-origin pricing and uniform-delivered pricing. The company sets up two or more zones. All customers within a given zone pay a single total price; the more distance the zone, the higher the price.

      iv. Using basing-point pricing, the seller selects a given city as a "basing point" and charges all customers the freight cost from that city to the customer location, regardless of the city from which the goods are actually shipped. Some companies set up multiple basing points to create more flexibility: they quote freight charges from the basing-point city nearest to the customer.

      v. The seller who is anxious to do business with a certain customer or geographical area might use freight-absorption pricing. Using this strategy, the seller absorbs all or part of the actual freight charges in order to get the desired business.

      vi. Dynamic pricing offers many advantages for marketers. Internet sellers can mine their databases to gauge a specific shopper's desires, measure his or her means, instantaneously tailor products to fit that shopper's behavior, and price products accordingly. Many B2B marketers monitor inventories, costs, and demand at any given moment and adjust prices instantly. Buyers also benefit from the Web and dynamic pricing.

International Pricing

r. Companies that market their products internationally must decide what prices to charge in the different countries in which they operate.

    i. In some cases, a company can set a uniform worldwide price.

    ii. However, most companies adjust their prices to reflect local market conditions and cost considerations.

s. The price that a company should charge in a specific country depends on many factors, including economic conditions, competitive situations, laws and regulations, and development of the wholesaling and retailing system.

    i. Consumer perceptions and preferences also may vary from country to country, calling for different prices.

    ii. Or the company may have different marketing objectives in various world markets that require changes in pricing strategy.

t. Costs play an important role in setting international prices. Travelers abroad are often surprised to find that goods that are relatively inexpensive at home may carry outrageously higher price tags in other countries.

    i. In some cases, such price escalation may result from differences in selling strategies or market conditions.

    ii. In most instances, however, it is simply a result of the higher costs of selling in another country—the additional costs of product modifications, shipping and insurance, import tariffs and taxes, exchange rate fluctuations, and physical distribution.

5. **Price Changes**

    a. Companies often face situations in which they must initiate price changes or respond to price changes by competitors.

Initiating Price Changes

    b. Several situations may lead a firm to consider cutting its price.

        i. One such circumstance is excess capacity. In this case, the firm needs more business and cannot get it through increased sales effort, product improvement, or other measures.

        ii. Another situation leading to price changes is falling market share in the face of strong price competition.

        iii. A company may also cut prices in a drive to dominate the market through lower costs. Either the company starts with lower costs than its competitors, or it cuts prices in the hope of gaining market share that will further cut costs through larger volume.

    c. A successful price increase can greatly increase profits.

        i. A major factor in price increases is cost inflation. Rising costs squeeze profit margins and lead companies to pass cost increases along to customers.

        ii. Another factor leading to price increases is over demand. When a company cannot supply all that its customers need, it can raise prices, ration products to customers, or both.

d. Companies can increase their prices in a number of ways to keep up with rising costs.
  - **i.** Prices can be raised almost invisibly by dropping discounts and adding higher-priced units to the line.
  - **ii.** Or prices can be pushed up openly.
  - **iii.** In passing price increases on to customers, the company must avoid being perceived as a price gouger.
  - **iv.** Companies also need to think of who will bear the brunt of increased prices.
    - **a.** There are some techniques for avoiding this problem. One is to maintain a sense of fairness surrounding any price increase.
    - **b.** Price increases should be supported by company communications telling customers why prices are being increased.
    - **c.** Whenever possible, the company should consider ways to meet higher costs or demand without raising prices.

e. Customers do not always interpret prices in a straightforward way. They may view a price cut in several ways.
  - **i.** They might think the company is abandoning their market.
  - **ii.** They might believe the quality has been reduced.
  - **iii.** They might think the price will come down even further and that it will pay to wait and see.

f. A price increase, which would normally lower sales, may have some positive meanings for buyers.
  - **i.** They might think that the item is very "hot" and may be unobtainable unless they buy it soon.
  - **ii.** Or they might think that the item is an unusually good product.
  - **iii.** Or, they might think the company is being greedy and just charging what the market will bear.

g. A firm considering a price change has to worry about the reactions of its competitors as well as those of its customers. Competitors are most likely to react when the number of firms involved is small, when the product is uniform, and when the buyers are well informed.

h. The company must guess each competitor's likely reaction.
  - **i.** If all competitors behave alike, this amounts to analyzing only a typical competitor.
  - **ii.** In contrast, if the competitors do not behave alike, then separate analyses are necessary.

Responding to Price Changes

i. Figure 11.1 shows the ways a company might assess and respond to a competitor's price cut.

j. If a company decides that effective action can and should be taken, it might make any of four responses.

     i. It could reduce its price to match the competitor's price.

         a. It may decide that the market is price sensitive and that it would lose too much market share to the lower-priced competitor.

         b. It might worry that recapturing lost market share later would be too hard.

         c. Cutting the price will reduce the company's profits in the short run.

         d. Some companies might also reduce their product quality, services, and marketing communications to retain profit margins, but this will ultimately hurt long-run market share.

     ii. The company should try to maintain its quality as it cuts prices.

     iii. Alternatively, the company might maintain its price but raise the perceived value of its offer. It could improve its communications, stressing the relative quality of its product over that of the lower-price competitor.

     iv. Or the company might improve quality and increase price, moving its brand into a higher-price position. The higher quality justifies the higher price that in turn preserves the company's higher margins.

     v. Finally, the company might launch a low-price "fighting brand"—adding a lower-price item to the line or creating a separate lower-price brand. This is necessary if the particular market segment being lost is price sensitive and will not respond to arguments of higher quality.

6. **Public Policy and Pricing**

    a. Price competition is a core element of our free-market economy. In setting prices, companies are not usually free to charge whatever prices they wish.

       i. Many federal, state, and even local laws govern the rules of fair play in pricing.

       ii. The most important pieces of legislation affecting pricing are the Sherman, Clayton, and Robinson-Patman acts, initially adopted to curb the formation of monopolies and to regulate business practices that might unfairly restrain trade.

    b. Figure 11.2 shows the major public policy issues in pricing.

Pricing Within Channel Levels

    c. Federal legislation on price-fixing states that sellers must set prices without talking to competitors. Otherwise, price collusion is suspected.

    d. Sellers are also prohibited from using predatory pricing—selling below cost with the intention of punishing a competitor or gaining higher long-run profits by putting competitors out of business. This protects small sellers from larger ones who might sell items below cost temporarily or in a specific locale to drive them out of business.

Pricing Across Channel Levels

e. The Robinson-Patman Act seeks to prevent unfair price discrimination by ensuring that sellers offer the same price terms to customers at a given level of trade.

f. Price discrimination is allowed if the seller can prove that its costs are different when selling to different retailers. Or the seller can discriminate in its pricing if the seller manufactures different qualities of the same product for different retailers. The seller has to prove that these differences are proportional.

g. Retail price maintenance is also prohibited—a manufacturer cannot require dealers to charge a specified retail price for its product. Although the seller can propose a manufacturer's suggested retail price to dealers, it cannot refuse to sell to a dealer who takes independent pricing action, nor can it punish the dealer by shipping late or denying advertising allowances.

h. Deceptive pricing occurs when a seller states prices or price savings that mislead consumers or are not actually available to consumers. This might involve bogus reference or comparison prices, as when a retailer sets artificially high "regular" prices then announces "sale" prices close to its previous everyday prices.

    i. The FTC's *Guide Against Deceptive Pricing* warns sellers not to advertise a price reduction unless it is a savings from the usual retail price, not to advertise "factory" or "wholesale" prices unless such prices are what they are claimed to be, and not to advertise comparable value prices on imperfect goods.

    ii. Other deceptive pricing issues include scanner fraud and price confusion.

        a. The widespread use of scanner-based computer checkouts has led to increasing complaints of retailers overcharging their customers.

        b. Price confusion results when firms employ pricing methods that make it difficult for consumers to understand just what price they are really paying.

    iii. Many federal and state statutes regulate against deceptive pricing practices.

        a. Reputable sellers go beyond what is required by law.

        b. Treating customers fairly and making certain that they fully understand prices and pricing terms is an important part of building strong and lasting customer relationships.

Student Exercises

1.   Key Term: Market-Skimming Pricing

When you set a price high for a new product to skim maximum revenues layer by layer from the segments willing to pay the high price, you are employing a market-skimming pricing strategy. Your text provides a good example of market-skimming pricing in the discussion regarding HDTV. Find another such example of a new product.

2.   Key Term: Market-Penetration Pricing

Market-penetration pricing is when a marketer sets a low price for a new product in order to attract a large number of buyers and a large market share. They set a low initial price in order to penetrate the market quickly and deeply. Look at the website for JR Cigars (www.jrcigars.com). JR Cigars is the largest seller of high quality cigars in the United States. How would you say they have used market-penetration pricing to their advantage?

3.   Key Term: Product-Line Pricing

Companies typically develop product lines rather than just one single product. It makes sense for them to offer multiple versions of a product, each with its own combination of consumer benefits and features to match the varying needs of customers. In product-line pricing, management must decide on the price steps to set between the various versions of the product. Apple's iPod is a great example. Examine the various iPod offerings (www.apple.com) and specify the differences between products their pricing.

4.   Key Term: Optional-Product Pricing

Many companies use optional-product pricing—offering to sell optional or accessory products along with their main product. Cars are a great example of optional-product pricing. Typically, you begin with the base car and then add on all of the bell-and-whistles that make it uniquely yours. Build yourself a SAAB (www.saabusa.com) and see how much the price changes from the base, once you add on items you believe you can not live without.

5.   Key Term: Captive-Product Pricing

There exist some secondary products that are only used in conjunction with the main product. These are known as captive products and the pricing of them is known as captive-product pricing. If you own the main product you have to buy the secondary product. Your text gives the example of razor blade cartridges and ink cartridges. Find other products that are priced using this strategy.

6.   Key Term: By-Product Pricing

By-product pricing is setting a price for by-products in order to make the main product's price more attractive. In the production of many products, there are often by-products left over. If you can not get rid of these leftovers it will impact the price of the main product. In some instances, by-products have turned out to be profitable. Your text uses the example of MeadWestvaco. Find another example of a by-product that has become a profitable product in its own right.

7.   Key Term: Product Bundle Pricing

Using product bundle pricing, sellers often combine several of their products and offer the bundle at a reduced prices. Price bundling can promote the sales of products the consumer might not otherwise buy. Look at the website for Expedia, the online travel services company (www.expedia.com). Explore their site and examine the ways in which they use product bundle pricing to boost sales.

8.   Key Term: Psychological Pricing

Psychological pricing is a pricing approach that considers the psychology of prices and not simply the economics—the price is used to say something about the product. For example, consumers usually perceive higher-priced products as having higher quality. Even though the products may be virtually identical, in the absence of additional information, most consumers will choose the higher-priced version. Take a look at the web pages for Nordstrom's Department Stores (www.nordstroms.com). Go to men's dress shirts and look at the different versions of the classic white dress shirt. Which ones do you believe are of the highest quality?

9.   Key Term: Reference Price

Prices that the consumer may carry with them (either in their minds or written down) and refer to when looking at a given product are known as reference prices. Sellers have realized the importance of such prices and now will many times provide the customer with a reference price. Buyers should be careful about over-relying on such seller-provided references. Log on to Overstock (www.overstock.com) and spend some time reviewing their use of reference pricing. How effective do you believe its use to be?

10.   Key Term: Promotional Pricing

Promotional pricing is temporarily pricing products below the list price to increase short-term sales by creating a sense of excitement or urgency. Look around and find a retail merchant that makes good use of promotional pricing.

Marketing ADventure Exercises

1. Ad Interpretation Challenge: Market-Skimming Pricing
    Ad: Electronics—Sony HS Series

When you set a price high for a new product to skim maximum revenues layer-by-layer from the segments willing to pay the high price, you are employing a market-skimming pricing strategy. Take a look at this ad for the Sony HS Series projection television. Do you believe this product would employ market-skimming pricing?

2. Ad Interpretation Challenge: Market-Penetration Pricing
    Ad: Student Choice

Market-penetration pricing is when a marketer sets a low price for a new product in order to attract a large number of buyers and quickly capture a large market share. They set a low initial price in order to penetrate the market quickly and deeply. Find an ad for a product that you believe would do well with market-penetration pricing.

3. Ad Interpretation Challenge: Product Line Pricing
    Ad: Apparel—Levi's

Setting the price steps between various products in a product line based on cost differences between the products, customer evaluations of different features, and competitors' prices is known as product line pricing. How has Levi's employed product line pricing in jeans?

4. Ad Interpretation Challenge: Optional-Product Pricing
    Ad: Autos—Ford

Many companies use optional-product pricing—offering to sell optional or accessory products for use with and along with their main product. Cars are a great example of optional-product pricing. Typically, you begin with the base car and then add on all of the bell-and-whistles that make it uniquely yours. Consider the ads for Ford (or for any car). How do the ads typically inform you that the vehicle is priced utilizing the optional-product pricing strategy?

5. Ad Interpretation Challenge: Captive-Product Pricing
    Ad: Student Choice

Captive-product pricing is the pricing of optional or accessory products along with the main product. These are products that are made to be used along with the main product and cannot, in fact, be used independently. Find an ad for a product that would typically employ captive-product pricing.

6.   Ad Interpretation Challenge: Product Bundle Pricing
        Ad: Cosmetics and Pharmaceuticals—Edge

Using product bundle pricing, sellers will often combine several of their products and offer the bundle to the consumer at a reduced price. In this manner, sellers may be able to sell items to consumers they would normally purchase singularly. Think about the ad for Edge shaving gel. How might this product be bundled with other products to create an appealing package for the customer?

7.   Ad Interpretation Challenge: Psychological Pricing
        Ad: Cosmetics and Pharmaceuticals—Edge

Price says something about the product. In using psychological pricing, sellers consider the psychology of prices and not simply the economics. How might the marketers of Edge shaving gel use psychological pricing to convey a message of quality to consumers?

8.   Ad Interpretation Challenge: Reference Prices
        Ad: General Retail—World's Biggest

Reference prices are the prices that consumers carry with them in their minds and refer to when looking at a given product. Merchants can help the consumer in this by having reference prices readily available to shoppers for comparison purposes. Consider the ads for World's Biggest Bookstore. How are they using the concept of reference prices?

9.   Ad Interpretation Challenge: Promotional Pricing
        Ad: Student Choice

Promotional pricing is the temporary pricing of products below the list price for the purpose of creating a buying excitement and urgency. Such pricing serves to get customers into the store. Find an ad for a product that could make good use of promotional pricing.

10.   Ad Interpretation Challenge: Dynamic Pricing
        Ad: Travel and Tourism—AeroMexico

Dynamic pricing is adjusting prices continually to meet the characteristics and needs of individual customers and situations. How might AeroMexcio use dynamic pricing?

Chapter 12
Marketing Channels and Supply Chain Management

Learning Objectives

1. Explain why companies use marketing channels and discuss the functions these channels perform.
2. Discuss how channel members interact and how they organize to perform the work of the channel.
3. Identify the major channel alternatives open to a company.
4. Explain how companies select, motivate, and evaluate channel members.
5. Discuss the nature and importance of marketing logistics and integrated supply chain management.

Chapter Overview

Distribution channels have been identified as being a set of independent organizations involved in the process of making a product or service available for use or consumption by the consumer or business user. Making decisions involving distribution channels are among the most complex and challenging decisions facing the firm. Each channel system (and there can be several) creates a different level of sales and costs. Unlike flexible elements of the marketing mix (price decisions, for example), once a distribution channel has been chosen, the firm must usually stick with their choice for some time. In addition, the chosen channel strongly affects, and is affected by, the other elements in the marketing mix.

Strategic planners limit their options if they consider only one channel choice. Each firm needs to identify alternative ways to reach its market. There are many means available. Some of the choices include the range of direct selling to multiple intermediary levels (that may involve several distribution relationships). Each of these options has advantages and disadvantages associated with them. Vertical and horizontal systems are more sophisticated than the basic channel alternatives and each is explained in context with contemporary usage. E-commerce and the use of the Internet have also impacted channel choice and strategy in a profound way.

Channel design begins with assessing customer channel-service needs and company channel objectives and constraints. The company then identifies the major channel alternatives in terms of the types of intermediaries, the number of intermediaries, and the channel responsibilities of each. No system, no matter how well it has been planned, is without conflict. If quality service and low cost are to be delivered, management of distribution conflict is a necessity. Because distribution relationships tend to be long-term in nature, the choice of channel partners is very important and should be taken very seriously.

In today's global marketplace, selling a product is sometimes easier than getting it to customers. Therefore, marketing logistics and supply chain management is receiving increased attention from strategic planners. The task of marketing logistics systems is to minimize the total cost of providing a desired level of customer services while bringing those services to the customer with the maximum amount of speed. Major logistics functions of warehousing, inventory management, transportation, and logistics information management are discussed and explored. The chapter concludes by discussing integrated logistics management within the firm and the relationships of distribution partners that are necessary to make an effective and profitable distribution network.

Chapter Outline

1. **Introduction**
   a. Caterpillar sells more than 300 products in nearly 200 countries, generating sales of almost $23 billion annually. It captures 27 percent of the worldwide construction-equipment business, more than double that of number two Komatsu.
   b. Many factors contribute to Caterpillar's enduring success—high-quality products, flexible and efficient manufacturing, and a steady stream of innovative new products. Yet these are not the most important reasons for Caterpillar's dominance.
   c. Instead, Caterpillar credits its focus on customers and its corps of 200 outstanding independent dealers worldwide, who do a superb job of taking care of every customer need.
   d. In the heavy-equipment industry, in which equipment downtime can mean big losses, Caterpillar's exceptional service gives it a huge advantage in winning and keeping customers.
   e. The close working relationship between Caterpillar and its dealers comes down to more than just formal contracts and business agreements. The powerful partnership rests on a handful of basic principles and practices.
      i. Dealer profitability
      ii. Extraordinary dealer support
      iii. Communications
      iv. Dealer performance
      v. Personal relationships
   f. Caterpillar's superb distribution system serves as a major source of competitive advantage.
   g. Most firms cannot bring value to customers by themselves. Instead, they must work closely with other firms in a larger value delivery network.

2. **Supply Chains and the Value Delivery Network**
   a. Producing a product or service and making it available to buyers requires building relationships not just with customers, but also with key suppliers and resellers in the company's supply chain.

158

       i. This supply chain consists of "upstream" and "downstream" partners. Upstream from the company is the set of firms that supply the raw materials, components, parts, information, finances, and expertise needed to create a product or service.

       ii. Marketers, however, have traditionally focused on the "downstream" side of the supply chain—on the marketing channels or distribution channels that look forward toward the customer. Downstream marketing channel partners, such as wholesalers and retailers, form a vital connection between the firm and its customers.

      iii. Both upstream and downstream partners may also be part of other firms' supply chains. But it is the unique design of each company's supply chain that enables it to deliver superior value to customers.

  b. The term *supply chain* may be too limited—it takes a make-and-sell view of the business.

       i. A better term would be *demand chain* because it suggests a sense-and-respond view of the market. Under this view, planning starts with the needs of target customers, to which the company responds by organizing a chain of resources and activities with the goal of creating customer value.

       ii. Even a demand-chain view of a business may be too limited, because it takes a step-by-step, linear view of purchase-production-consumption activities.

      iii. Most large companies today are engaged in building and managing a continuously evolving value delivery network.

  c. A value delivery network is made up of the company, suppliers, distributors, and ultimately customers who "partner" with each other to improve the performance of the entire system.

  d. To bring value to customers, companies need upstream supplier partners just as they need downstream channel partners. Increasingly, marketers are participating in and influencing their company's upstream activities as well as their downstream activities. More than marketing channel managers, they are becoming full network managers.

3. **The Nature and Importance of Marketing Channels**

  a. Few producers sell their goods directly to the final users. Instead, most use intermediaries to bring their products to market. They try to forge a marketing channel (or distribution channel)—a set of interdependent organizations involved in the process of making a product or service available for use or consumption by the consumer or business user.

  b. A company's channel decisions directly affect every other marketing decision.

  c. Companies often pay too little attention to their distribution channels, sometimes with damaging results. In contrast, many companies have used imaginative distribution systems to gain a competitive advantage.

d. Distribution channel decisions often involve long-term commitments to other firms.

How Channel Members Add Value

e. Figure 12.1 shows how using intermediaries can provide economies.

    i. Figure 12.1A shows three manufacturers, each using direct marketing to reach three customers. This system requires nine different contacts.

    ii. Figure 12.1B shows the three manufacturers working through one distributor that contacts the three customers. This system requires only six contacts. In this way, intermediaries reduce the amount of work that must be done by both producers and consumers.

f. From the economic system's point of view, the role of marketing intermediaries is to transform the assortments of products made by producers into the assortments wanted by consumers.

    i. Producers make narrow assortments of products in large quantities, but consumers want broad assortments of products in small quantities.

    ii. In the marketing channels, intermediaries buy large quantities from many producers and break them down into the smaller quantities and broader assortments wanted by consumers.

    iii. Thus, intermediaries play an important role in matching supply and demand.

g. In making products and services available to consumers, channel members add value by bridging the major time, place, and possession gaps that separate goods and services from those who would use them. Members of the marketing channel perform many key functions.

    i. Information: Gathering and distributing marketing research and intelligence

    ii. Promotion: Developing and spreading persuasive communications about an offer

    iii. Contact: Finding and communicating with prospective buyers

    iv. Matching: Shaping and fitting the offer to the buyer's needs, including activities such as manufacturing, grading, assembling, and packaging

    v. Reaching an agreement on price and other terms of the offer so that ownership or possession can be transferred

    vi. Physical distribution: Transporting and storing goods

    vii. Financing: Acquiring and using funds to cover the costs of the channel work

    viii. Risk taking: Assuming the risks of carrying out the channel work

h. The question is not whether these functions need to be performed—they must be—but rather who will perform them.

Number of Channel Levels

i. Each layer of marketing intermediaries that performs some work in bringing the product and its ownership closer to the final buyer is a channel level. Because the producer and the final consumer both perform some work, they are part of every channel.

j. The number of intermediary levels indicates the length of a channel. Figure 12.2A shows several consumer distribution channels of different lengths.

    i. Channel 1, called a direct marketing channel, has no intermediary levels; the company sells directly to consumers.

    ii. The remaining channels in Figure 12.2A are indirect marketing channels, containing one or more intermediaries.

    iii. Figure 12.2B shows some common business distribution channels.

        a. The business marketer can use its own sales force to sell directly to business customers.

        b. Or it can sell to various types of intermediaries, who in turn sell to these customers.

    iv. From the producer's point of view, a greater number of levels means less control and greater channel complexity.

    v. Moreover, all of the institutions in the channel are connected by several types of flows. These include the physical flow of products, the flow of ownership, the payment flow, the information flow, and the promotion flow. These flows can make even channels with only one or a few levels very complex.

4. **Channel Behavior and Organization**

    a. Some channel systems consist only of information interactions among loosely organized firms. Others consist of formal interactions guided by strong organization structures. Moreover, channel systems do not stand still—new types of intermediaries emerge and whole new channel systems evolve.

Channel Behavior

b. A marketing channel consists of firms that have partnered for their common good. Each channel member depends on the others.

c. Each channel member plays a specialized role in the channel.

d. Ideally, because the success of individual channel members depends on overall channel success, all channel firms should work together smoothly.

    i. They should understand and accept their roles, coordinate their activities, and cooperate to attain overall channel goals.

    ii. However, individual channel members rarely take such a broad view. Cooperating to achieve overall channel goals sometimes means giving up individual company goals. They often disagree on who should do what and for what rewards. Such disagreements over goals, roles, and rewards generate channel conflict.

      a. Horizontal conflict occurs among firms at the same level of the chain.

      b. Vertical conflict, conflict between different levels of the same channel, is even more common.

  iii. Some conflict in the channel takes the form of healthy competition. Such competition can be good for the channel—without it, the channel could become passive and non-innovative. But severe or prolonged conflict can disrupt channel effectiveness and cause lasting harm to channel relationships.

Vertical Marketing Systems

e. For the channel as a whole to perform well, each channel member's role must be specified and channel conflict must be managed. The channel will perform better if it includes a firm, agency, or mechanism that provides leadership and has the power to assign roles and manage conflict.

f. Historically, conventional distribution channels have lacked such leadership and power, often resulting in damaging conflict and poor performance. Figure 12.3 contrasts two types of channel arrangements.

  i. A conventional distribution channel consists of one or more independent producers, wholesalers, and retailers. Each is a separate business seeking to maximize its own profits, even at the expense of the system as a whole. No channel member has much control over the other members, and no formal means exists for assigning roles and resolving channel conflict.

  ii. In contrast, a vertical marketing system (VMS) consists of producers, wholesalers, and retailers acting as a unified system. One channel member owns the others, has contracts with them, or wields so much power that they must all cooperate. The VMS can be dominated by the producer, the wholesaler, or the retailer.

g. There are three types of VMSs.

  i. A corporate VMS integrates successive stages of production and distribution under single ownership. Coordination and conflict management are attained through regular organizational channels.

  ii. A contractual VMS consists of independent firms at different levels of production and distribution who join together through contracts to obtain more economies or sales impact than each could achieve alone. Coordination and conflict management are attained through contractual agreements among channel members.

      a. The franchise organization is the most common type of contractual relationship—a channel member called a franchisor links several stages in the production-distribution process. There are three types of franchises.

          1. The first is the manufacturer-sponsored retailer franchise system—for example, Ford and its network of independent franchised dealers.

2. The second type is the manufacturer-sponsored wholesaler franchise system—Coca-Cola licenses bottlers (wholesalers) in various markets who buy Coca-Cola syrup concentrate and then bottle and sell the finished product to retailers in local markets.

3. The third type is the serve-firm-sponsored retailer franchise system—examples are found in the auto-rental business, the fast-food service business, and the motel business.

b. In an administered VMS, leadership is assumed not through common ownership or contractual ties, but through the size and power of one or a few dominant channel members. Manufacturers of a top brand can obtain strong trade cooperation and support from resellers.

Horizontal Marketing Systems

h. Another channel development is the horizontal marketing system, in which two or more companies at one level join together to follow a new marketing opportunity. By working together, companies can combine their financial production or marketing resources to accomplish more than any one company could alone.

i. Companies might join forces with competitors or noncompetitors. They might work with each other on a temporary or permanent basis, or they may create a separate company.

j. Such channel arrangements also work well globally.

Multichannel Distribution Systems

k. Today, with the proliferation of customer segments and channel possibilities, more and more companies have adopted multichannel distribution systems—often called hybrid marketing channels. Such multichannel marketing occurs when a single firm sets up two or more marketing channels to reach one or more customer segments. Figure 12.4 shows a hybrid channel.

l. These days, almost every large company and many small ones distribute through multiple channels.

m. Multichannel distribution systems offer many advantages to companies facing large and complex markets.

i. With each new channel, the company expands its sales and market coverage and gains opportunities to tailor its products and services to the specific needs of diverse customer segments.

ii. But such multichannel systems are harder to control, and they generate conflict as more channels compete for customers and sales.

Changing Channel Organization

n. Changes in technology and the explosive growth of direct and online marketing are having a profound impact on the nature and design of marketing channels.

o. One major trend is toward disintermediation—a big term with a clear message and important consequences. Disintermediation means that more and more, product and service producers are bypassing intermediaries and going directly to final buyers, or that radically new types of channel intermediaries are emerging to displace traditional ones.

p. Disintermediation presents problems and opportunities for both producers and intermediaries.

   i. To avoid being swept aside, traditional intermediaries must find new ways to add value in the supply chain.

   ii. To remain competitive, product and service producers must develop new channel opportunities, such as the Internet and other direct channels.

   iii. However, developing those channels often brings them into direct competition with their established channels, resulting in conflict.

   iv. To ease this problem, companies often look for ways to make going direct a plus for both the company and its channel partner.

5. **Channel Design Decisions**

   a. In designing marketing channels, manufacturers struggle between what is ideal and what is practical.

      i. A new firm with limited capital usually starts by selling to a limited market.

      ii. If successful, the new firm might branch out to new markets through the existing intermediaries. In smaller markets, the firm might sell directly to retailers; in larger markets, it might sell through distributors.

      iii. In this way, channel systems often evolve to meet market opportunities and conditions.

   b. For maximum effectiveness, channel analysis and decision making should be more purposeful.

Analyzing Consumer Needs

   c. Designing the marketing channel starts with finding out what target consumers want from the channel.

   d. Providing the fastest delivery, greatest assortment, and most services may not be possible or practical.

      i. The company and its channel members may not have the resources or skills needed to provide all the desired services.

      ii. Providing higher levels of service results in higher costs for the channel and higher prices for consumers.

iii. The company must balance consumer needs not only against the feasibility and costs of meeting these needs but also against customer price preferences.

Setting Channel Objectives

e. Companies should state their marketing channel objectives in terms of targeted levels of customer service.

    i. Usually, a company can identify several segments wanting different levels of service.

    ii. The company should decide which segments to serve and the best channels to use in each case.

    iii. In each segment, the company wants to minimize the total channel cost of meeting customer service requirements.

f. The company's channel objectives are also influenced by the nature of the company, its products, its marketing intermediaries, its competitors, and the environment.

g. Environmental factors such as economic conditions and legal constraints may affect channel objectives and designs.

Identifying Major Alternatives

h. When the company has defined its channel objectives, it should next identify its major channel alternatives in terms of types of intermediaries, the number of intermediaries, and the responsibilities of each channel member.

    i. A firm should identify the types of channel members available to carry out its channel work. The following channel alternatives might emerge:

        a. Company sales force: Expand the company's direct sales force.

        b. Manufacturer's agency: Hire manufacturer's agents—independent firms whose sales forces handle related products from many companies.

        c. Industrial distributors: Find distributors in the different regions or industries who will buy and carry the new line.

    ii. Companies must also determine the number of channel members to use at each level. Three strategies are available.

        a. Producers of convenience products and common raw materials typically seek intensive distribution—a strategy in which they stock their products in as many outlets as possible. These products must be available where and when consumers want them.

  b. By contrast, some producers purposely limit the number of intermediaries handling their products. The extreme form of this practice is exclusive distribution, in which the producer gives only a limited number of dealers the exclusive right to distribute its products in their territories. Exclusive distribution is often found in the distribution of luxury automobiles and prestigious women's clothing.

  c. Between intensive and exclusive distribution lies selective distribution—the use of more than one, but fewer than all, of the intermediaries who are willing to carry a company's products. By using selective distribution, producers can develop good working relationships with selected channel members and expect a better-than-average selling effort. Selective distribution gives producers good market coverage with more control and less cost than does intensive distribution.

iii. The producer and intermediaries need to agree on the terms and responsibilities of each channel member.

  a. They should agree on price policies, conditions of sale, territorial rights, and specific services to be performed by each party. The producer should establish a list price and a fair set of discounts for intermediaries.

  b. It must define each channel member's territory, and it should be careful about where it places new resellers.

  c. Mutual services and duties need to be spelled out carefully, especially in franchise and exclusive distribution channels.

Evaluating the Major Alternatives

i. Each alternative should be evaluated against economic, control, and adaptive criteria.

  i. Using economic criteria, a company compares the likely sales, costs, and profitability of different channel alternatives.

  ii. The company must also consider control issues. Using intermediaries usually means giving them some control over the marketing of the product, and some intermediaries take more control than others. Other things being equal, the company prefers to keep as much control as possible.

  iii. Finally, the company must apply adaptive criteria. Channels often involve long-term commitments, yet the company wants to keep the channel as flexible as it can so that it can adapt to environmental changes. Thus, to be considered, a channel involving long-term commitments should be greatly superior on economic and control grounds.

Designing International Distribution Channels

j. International marketers face many additional complexities in designing their channels. Each country has its own unique distribution system that has evolved over time and changes very slowly.

k. These channel systems scan vary widely from country to country. Thus, global marketers must usually adapt their channel strategies to the existing structures within each country.

    i. In some markets, the distribution system is complex and hard to penetrate, consisting of many layers and large numbers of intermediaries.

    ii. At the other extreme, distribution systems in developing countries may be scattered and inefficient, or altogether lacking.

l. Designing efficient and effective channel systems between and within various country markets poses a difficult challenge.

6. Channel Management Decisions

    a. Once the company has reviewed its channel alternatives and decided on the best channel design, it must implement and manage the chosen channel.

Selecting Channel Members

    b. Producers vary in their ability to attract qualified marketing intermediaries. Some producers have no trouble signing up channel members. At the other extreme are producers who have to work hard to line up enough qualified intermediaries.

    c. When selecting intermediaries, the company should determine what characteristics distinguish the better ones.

        i. It will want to evaluate each channel member's years in business, other lines carried, growth and profit records, cooperativeness, and reputation.

        ii. If the intermediaries are sales agents, the company will want to evaluate the number and character of other lines carried and the size and quality of the sales force.

        iii. If the intermediary is a retail store that wants exclusive or selective distribution, the company will want to evaluate the store's customers, location, and future growth potential.

Managing and Motivating Channel Members

    d. Once selected, channel members must be continuously managed and motivated to do their best. The company must sell not only through the intermediaries but also to and with them.

        i. Most companies see their intermediaries as first-line customers and partners.

        ii. They practice strong partner relationship management (PRM) to forge long-term partnerships with channel members.

e. In managing its channels, a company must convince distributors that they can succeed better by working together as a part of a cohesive value delivery system.

f. Many companies are now installing integrated high-tech PRM systems to coordinate their whole-channel marketing efforts. Just as they use customer relationship management (CRM) software systems to help manage relationships with important customers, companies can now use PRM software to help recruit, train, organize, manage, motivate, and evaluate relationships with channel partners.

Evaluating Channel Partners

g. The producer must regularly check channel member performance against standards such as sales quotas, average inventory levels, customer delivery time, treatment of damaged and lost goods, cooperation in company promotion and training programs, and services to the customer.

    i. The company should recognize and reward intermediaries who are performing well and adding good value for consumers.

    ii. Those who are performing poorly should be assisted or, as a last resort, replaced.

    iii. A company may periodically "requalify" its intermediaries and prune the weaker ones.

h. Manufacturers need to be sensitive to their dealers. Those who treat their dealers poorly risk not only losing dealer support but also cause some legal problems.

7. **Public Policy and Distribution Decisions**

a. For the most part, companies are legally free to develop whatever channel arrangements suit them. Most channel law deals with the mutual rights and duties of the channel members once they have formed a relationship.

b. When the seller allows only certain outlets to carry its products, this strategy is called exclusive distribution. When the seller requires that these dealers not handle competitors' products, its strategy is called exclusive dealing.

    i. Both parties can benefit from exclusive arrangements: The seller obtains more loyal and dependable outlets, and the dealers obtain a steady source of supply and stronger seller support.

    ii. But exclusive arrangements also exclude other producers from selling to these dealers.

        a. This situation brings exclusive dealing contracts under the scope of the Clayton Act of 1914.

        b. They are legal as long as they do not substantially lessen competition or tend to create a monopoly and as long as both parties enter into the agreement voluntarily.

    iii. Exclusive dealing often includes exclusive territorial agreements. The producer may agree not to sell to other dealers in a given area, or the buyer may agree to sell only in its own territory.

        a. The first practice is normal under franchise systems as a way to increase dealer enthusiasm and commitment.

        b. The second practice, whereby the producer tries to keep a dealer from selling outside its territory, has become a major legal issue.

    iv. Producers of a strong brand sometimes sell it to dealers only if the dealers will take some or all of the rest of the line.

        a. This is called full-line forcing.

        b. Such tying agreements are not necessarily illegal, but they do violate the Clayton Act if they tend to lessen competition substantially.

c. Producers are free to select their dealers, but their right to terminate dealers is somewhat restricted.

    i. In general, sellers can drop dealers "for cause."

    ii. They cannot drop dealers if, for example, the dealers refuse to cooperate in a doubtful legal arrangement, such as exclusive dealing or tying agreements.

8. Marketing Logistics and Supply Chain Management

a. In today's global marketplace, selling a product is sometimes easier than getting it to customers. Companies must decide on the best way to store, handle, and move their products and services so that they are available to customers in the right assortments, at the right time, and in the right place.

Nature and Importance of Marketing Logistics

b. Marketing logistics—also called *physical distribution*—involves planning, implementing, and controlling the physical flow of goods, services, and related information from points of origin to points of consumption to meet customer requirements at a profit.

c. Marketing logistics involves not only outbound distribution (moving products from the factory to resellers and ultimately to customers) but also inbound distribution (moving products and materials from suppliers to the factory) and reverse distribution (moving broken, unwanted, or excess products returned by consumers or resellers).

    i. That is, it involves entire supply chain management—managing upstream and downstream value-added flows of materials, final goods, and related information among suppliers, the company, resellers, and final consumers, as shown in Figure 12.5.

    ii. The logistics manager's task is to coordinate activities of suppliers, purchasing agents, marketers, channel members, and customers.

d. Companies today are placing greater emphasis on logistics for several reasons.

    i. Companies gain a powerful competitive advantage by using improved logistics to give customers better service or lower prices.

    ii. Improved logistics can yield tremendous cost savings to both the company and its customers.

    iii. The explosion in product variety has created a need for improved logistics management.

    iv. Improvements in information technology have created opportunities for major gains in distribution efficiency.

Goals of the Logistics System

e. Unfortunately, no logistics system can both maximize customer service and minimize distribution costs.

    i. Maximum customer service implies rapid delivery, large inventories, flexible assortments, liberal return policies, and other services—all of which raise distribution costs.

    ii. In contrast, minimum distribution costs imply slower delivery, smaller inventories, and larger shipping lots—which represent a lower level of overall customer service.

f. The goal of marketing logistics should be to provide a targeted level of customer service at the least cost.

    i. A company must first research the importance of various distribution services to customers and then set desired service levels for each segment.

    ii. The objective is to maximize profits, not sales.

Major Logistics Functions

g. Given a set of logistics objectives, the company is ready to design a logistics system that will minimize the cost of attaining these objectives.

h. Production and consumption cycles rarely match. So most companies must store their tangible goods while they wait to be sold.

    i. The storage function overcomes differences in needed quantities and timing, ensuring that products are available when customers are ready to buy them.

    ii. A company must decide on how many and what types of warehouses it needs and where they will be located.

        a. Storage warehouses store goods for moderate to long periods.

        b. Distribution centers are designed to move goods rather than just store them. They are large and highly automated warehouses designed to receive goods from various plants and suppliers, take orders, fill them efficiently, and deliver goods to customers as quickly as possible.

i. Inventory management also affects customer satisfaction. Here, managers must maintain the delicate balance between carrying too little inventory and carrying too much.

    i. With too little stock, the firm risks not having products when customers want to buy. To remedy this, the firm may need costly emergency shipments or production.

      ii. Carrying too much inventory results in higher-than-necessary inventory carrying costs and stock obsolescence. Thus, in managing inventory, firms must balance the costs of carrying larger inventories against resulting sales and profits.

      iii. Many companies have greatly reduced their inventories and related costs through just-in-time logistics systems. With such systems, producers and retailers carry only small inventories of parts or merchandise, often only enough for a few days of operations.

j. The choice of transportation carriers affects the pricing products, delivery performance, and condition of the goods when they arrive—all of which will affect customer satisfaction. In shipping goods to its warehouses, dealers, and customers, the company can choose among five main transportation modes.

      i. Trucks have increased their share of transportation steadily and now account for nearly 41 percent of total cargo ton-miles (more than 65 percent of actual tonnage). Trucks are highly flexible in their routing and time schedules, and they can usually offer faster service than railroads. They are efficient for short hauls of high-value merchandise.

      ii. Railroads account for 37 percent of total cargo ton-miles moved. They are one of the most cost-effective modes for shipping large amounts of bulk products over long distances.

      iii. Water carriers, which account for about 10 percent of cargo ton-miles, transport large amounts of goods by ships and barges on U.S. coastal and inland waterways. Although the cost of water transportation is very low for shipping bulky, low-value, nonperishable products, water transportation is the slowest mode and may be affected by the weather.

      iv. Pipelines are a specialized means of shipping petroleum, natural gas, and chemicals from sources to markets. Most pipelines are used by their owners to ship their own products.

      v. Although air carries transport less than 1 percent of the nation's goods, they are an important transportation mode. Airfreight rates are much higher than rail or truck rates, but airfreight is ideal when speed is needed or distant markets have to be reached.

      vi. The Internet carries digital products from producer to customer via satellite, cable modem, or telephone wire.

k. Shippers also use intermodal transportation—combining two or more modes of transportation.

      i. Piggyback describes the use of rail and trucks.

      ii. Fishyback describes water and trucks.

      iii. Trainship is water and rail.

      iv. Airtruck is air and trucks.

l. Companies manage their supply chains through information. Channel partners often link up to share information and to make better joint logistics decisions. From a logistics perspective, information flows such as customer orders, billing, inventory levels, and even customer data are closely linked to channel performance.

m. Information can be shared and managed in many ways.
  i. Through mail
  ii. Through telephone
  iii. Through salespeople
  iv. Through electronic data interchange (EDI), the computerized exchange of data between organizations

n. In some cases, suppliers might actually be asked to generate orders and arrange deliveries for their customers.
  i. Many large retailers set up vendor-managed inventory (VMI) systems or continuous inventory replenishment systems.

Integrated Logistics Management

o. Today, more and more companies are adopting the concept of integrated logistics management. This concept recognizes that providing better customer service and trimming distribution costs require teamwork, both inside the company and among all the marketing channel organizations.

p. In most companies, responsibility for various logistics activities is assigned to many different functional units. Too often, each function tries to optimize its own logistics performance without regard for the activities of other functions.
  i. The goal of integrated supply chain management is to harmonize all of the company's logistics decisions. Close working relationships among functions can be achieved in several ways.
    a. Some companies have created permanent logistics committees.
    b. Companies can also create management positions that link the logistics activities of functional areas.
    c. Many companies have a vice president of logistics with cross-functional authority.
    d. Companies can employ sophisticated, systemwide supply chain management software, now available from a wide range of suppliers.

q. Companies must do more than improve their own logistics. They must also work with other channel partners to improve whole-channel distribution. The members of a distribution channel are linked closely in creating customer value and building customer relationships.
  i. Smart companies coordinate their logistics strategies and forge strong partnerships with suppliers and customers to improve customer service and reduce channel costs.
  ii. Many companies have created cross-functional, cross-company teams.

      iii. Other companies partner through shared projects.

  r. A growing number of firms now outsource some or all of their logistics to third-party logistics (3PL) providers such as UPS Supply Chain Services, Ryder Systems, FedEx Logistics, Roadway Logistics Services, or Emroy Global Logistics.

      i. Such integrated logistics companies perform any or all of the functions required to get their clients' product to market.

      ii. Companies use third-party logistics providers for several reasons.

         a. Because getting the product to market is their main focus, these providers can often do it more efficiently and at lower cost.

         b. Outsourcing logistics frees a company to focus more intensely on its core business.

         c. Integrated logistics companies understand increasingly complex logistics environments.

Student Exercises

1.   Key Term: Value Delivery Network

A value delivery network is the network made up of the company, suppliers, distributors, and ultimately customers who partner with each other to improve the performance of the entire system. Take a look at Mountain Valley Spring Company (www.mountainvalleyspring.com). Mountain Valley Spring is a well-known producer of premium spring water. Review their site. Make a list of the members of their "partner community."

2.   Key Term: Marketing Channel

Very few producers really sell their goods directly to the final user. Most use some kind of intermediary to bring their products to market. The set of independent organizations that help make a product or service available for use or consumption by the consumer (or business user) is known as the marketing channel. What marketing channel does computer manufacturer Gateway (www.gateway.com) uses to get their product to the ultimate (final) consumer?

3.   Key Term: Direct Marketing Channel

A direct marketing channel is a marketing channel that has no intermediary levels. The company sells directly to the consumer. Your texts points out Mary Kay cosmetics and Amway as examples of the direct marketing channel. Find two more.

4.   Key Term: Indirect Marketing Channel

An indirect marketing channel is any form of marketing channel that is not direct from the company to the customer. Indirect marketing channels involve one or more layers of intermediaries. Go to Starbuck's homepage (www.starbucks.com). What are the different indirect marketing channels Starbucks uses to get its products to the coffee drinker?

5.   Key Term: Horizontal Channel Conflict

Channel conflict occurs when there is disagreement among marketing channel members on goals and roles. Horizontal channel conflict occurs between firms at the same level of the channel. Think about the gas station where you typically buy gas. How could they come in conflict with other local stations owned by the same company?

6.   Key Term: Vertical Channel Conflict

Vertical channel conflict occurs between different levels of the same channel. It occurs even more frequently than does horizontal channel conflict. Your text gives you the example Goodyear using different channels to sell its tires. Take a look at Subway (www.subway.com). Currently, you can find a Subway store almost anywhere, it seems. Think of another form of distribution that Subway might enter in to that would potentially create vertical channel conflict with its existing stores.

7.   Key Term: Conventional Distribution Channel

A conventional distribution channel is a channel consisting of one or more independent producers, wholesalers, and retailers, each a separate business seeking to maximize its own profits even at the expense of profits for the system as a whole. No one channel member has much control over any of the other channel members. Every member is out for what is good for them, without regard to other channel members. Consider Green Giant vegetables (www.greengiant.com). Describe the conventional distribution channel you believe this company would use to get their frozen and canned vegetables to you, the consumer.

8.   Key Term: Vertical Marketing System (VMS)

A vertical marketing system consists of producers, wholesalers, and retailers acting as a unified system—in contrast to the adversarial nature of a conventional distribution channel. The VMS may be dominated by the producer, the wholesaler, or the retailer. Take a look at Goodyear (www.goodyear.com). Your text talks a lot about the relationship of Goodyear and its dealers. Describe the VMS used by Goodyear.

9.   Key Term: Administered VMS

An administered VMS is a vertical marketing system that coordinates successive stages of production and distribution, not through common ownership or contractual ties, but through the size or power of one of the members. Other than the examples of administered VMS given in your text think of another.

10.   Key Term: Exclusive Distribution

When a manufacturer gives a limited number of dealers the exclusive right to distribute the company's products in their territories it is known as exclusive distribution. Exclusive distribution is often found in the distribution of luxury automobiles and prestige women's clothing. The dealers of these products are few and far between. Exclusive distribution aids in enhancing the product image and contributes to larger markups. Find another product that makes use of an exclusive distribution channel.

Marketing ADventure Exercises

1.   Ad Interpretation Challenge: Value Delivery Network
      Ad: Apparel—Puma

A value delivery network is the network made up of the company, suppliers, distributors, and ultimately customers who partner with each other to improve the performance of the entire system. The idea of such a network is to improve the performance of the network with the result being higher profits for the channel members and a fair price to the consumer. Think about this Puma ad. Make a list of all members of value delivery network that would have an impact on this product.

2.   Ad Interpretation Challenge: Direct Marketing Channel
      Ad: Student Choice

A direct marketing channel has no intermediaries. The product goes from the company to the final consumer. Find an ad for a product that is sold through the direct marketing channel.

3.   Ad Interpretation Challenge: Channel Conflict
      Ad: Food and Beverage—Cool Drinking Water

Disagreements often occur among channel members on goals and roles—who should do what and who should get what. Describe the possible channel conflicts that you believe could arise regarding the marketing of this product.

4.   Ad Interpretation Challenge: Vertical Channel Conflict
          Ad: Electronics—LG

Vertical conflict is conflict between two members at different levels in the channel. Vertical conflict is a very common occurrence. Companies must manage this conflict to keep it from getting out of hand. Think about LG Electronics. How might they unwittingly create vertical conflict?

5.   Ad Interpretation Challenge: Horizontal Channel Conflict
          Ad: Autos—Ford

Horizontal channel conflict occurs among firms at the same level of the channel. Give a situation in which a Ford dealer might express horizontal channel disagreement with Ford Inc.

6.   Ad Interpretation Challenge: Vertical Marketing System
          Ad: Student Choice

A vertical marketing system is a distribution channel structure in which all channel member's work as a unified system. One channel member owns the others, has contracts with them, or has so much power that they all cooperate. Find an example of an ad for a company that would likely utilize a VMS.

7.   Ad Interpretation Challenge: Vertical Marketing System—Student Decision
          Ad: General Retail—Hallmark

Review the information on vertical marketing systems (VMS). Remember, in a VMS, one channel member owns the others, has contracts with them, or has so much power that they all cooperate. Three basic types of VMS exist—corporate, franchise, or administered. Study Hallmark, Inc. (www.hallmark.com). Pay particular attention to the relationship between Hallmark (the company) and Hallmark stores. What type of VMS does Hallmark employ?

8.   Ad Interpretation Challenge: Administered VMS
          Ad: General Retail—Target

An administered VMS is a vertical marketing system that coordinates successive stages of production and distribution, not through common ownership or contractual ties, but through the size and power of one of the parties. Consider Target. Why would you say Target operates an administered VMS?

9.   Ad Interpretation Challenge: Multichannel Distribution Systems
       Ad: General Retail—Hallmark

A multichannel distribution system is a distribution system in which a single firm sets ups two or more marketing channels to reach one or more customer segments. More and more companies are turning to such distribution systems as customer segments and channel possibilities have proliferated. What multiple channels of distribution does Hallmark employ?

10.   Ad Interpretation Challenge: Intensive Distribution
       Ad: Student Choice

Intensive distribution occurs when the company stocks their product in as many outlets as possible. The goal is to have the product everywhere that consumers may be. You want the product to be readily available so the consumer does not have to search for it. Find an ad for a product that you would consider a candidate for intensive distribution.

Chapter 13
Retailing and Wholesaling

Learning Objectives

1. Explain the roles of retailers and wholesalers in the distribution channel.
2. Describe the major types of retailers and give examples of each.
3. Identify the major types of wholesalers and give examples of each.
4. Explain the marketing decisions facing retailers and wholesalers.

Chapter Overview

Retailing and wholesaling consist of many organizations bringing goods and services from the point of production to the point of use. Retailing by definition includes all the activities involved in selling goods and services directly to final consumers for their personal, non-business use. Retailers can be classified as store retailers and non-store retailers. Store retailers can be further classified by the amount of service they provide, the product line sold, relative prices charged, and retail organization format (control of outlets). Non-store retailers are described as being in direct marketing, catalogs, telephone, home TV shopping shows, home and office parties, door-to-door contact, automatic vending, online services and the Internet, and other direct retailing approaches.

Retailing decisions involve the constant search for new marketing strategies to attract and hold customers. Considerations are the target market and positioning decision, the product assortment and services decision, the price decision, the promotion decision, and the place decision. All of these decisions are examined closely in the chapter. Numerous examples provide explanations of several options that are available in all the afore-mentioned areas.

Retailers operate in a harsh and fast-changing environment that offers threats as well as opportunities. New retail forms continue to emerge to meet new situations and consumer needs, but the life cycle of new retail forms is getting shorter. In addition to the traditional forms of retailing, consumers now have an array of nontraditional alternatives to choose from, including mail order, television, phone, and online shopping. The last major trend that seems to be of interest to business strategists and marketers is the rise of huge mass merchandisers and specialty superstores. These forms will have a pronounced effect on the way retailing is conducted in the future.

Wholesaling, unlike retailing, deals with the sale of goods and services that will be resold by and/or used by the business customer itself. One way to study and understand wholesaling is to examine the functions that are performed by the wholesalers. These functions include selling and promoting, buying and assortment building, bulk-breaking, warehousing, transportation, financing, risk bearing, supplying market information, performing management services, and providing advice for customers.

Wholesalers can be divided into numerous groups. Three primary types of wholesalers are merchant wholesalers, agents and brokers, and manufacturer and retailer sales branches and offices. Each of these general types (and their numerous subdivisions) are explained and detailed. The chapter also explains how wholesalers use target market and positioning information and make marketing mix decisions in a rapidly changing domestic and global marketing environment.

Chapter Outline

1. **Introduction**
   a. Whole Foods is a small, but growing grocery chain that is succeeding in spite of grocery giants like Wal-Mart and Kroger.
   b. Whole Foods positions itself as a provider of organic, natural, and gourmet foods, with a dose of social responsibility.
   c. Whole Foods caters to upscale customers. By doing this, they can offer a premium product at premium prices and achieve higher margins than typical grocers.
   d. The Whole Foods story provides many insights into the workings of one of today's most successful new retailers. This chapter looks at retailing and wholesaling.

2. **Retailing**
   a. Retailing includes all the activities involved in selling products or services directly to final consumers for their personal, non-business use. Most retailing is done by retailers—businesses whose sales come primarily from retailing.
   b. Although most retailing is done in retail stores, in recent years non-store retailing has been growing much faster than has store retailing.

   Types of Retailers
   c. The most important types of retail stores are described in Table 13.1. They can be classified in terms of several characteristics.
      i. Differing products require different amounts of service, and customer service preferences vary. Retailers may offer one of three levels of service.
         a. Self-service retailers serve customers who are willing to perform their own "locate-compare-select" process to save money. Self-service is the basis of all discount operations and is typically used by sellers of convenience goods and nationally branded, fast-moving shopping goods.
         b. Limited-service retailers provide more sales assistance because they carry more shopping goods about which customers need information.

    c. In full-service retailers, such as specialty stores and first-class department stores, salespeople assist customers in every phase of the shopping process.

  ii. Retailers can be classified by the length and breadth of their product assortments.

    a. Specialty stores carry narrow product lines with deep assortments within those lines.

    b. Department stores carry a wide variety of product lines.

    c. Supermarkets are the most frequently shopped type of retail store.

    d. Convenience stores are small stores that carry a limited line of high-turnover convenience goods.

    e. Superstores are much larger than regular supermarkets and offer a large assortment of routinely purchased food products, nonfood items, and services.

      1. Supercenters are combination food and discount stores that emphasize cross merchandising.

      2. Category killers feature stores the size of airplane hangars that carry a very deep assortment of a particular line with a knowledgeable staff.

      3. Hypermarkets are huge superstores, perhaps as large as six football fields. They have been very successful in Europe and other world markets, but have met with little success in the United States.

    f. Service retailers include hotels and motels, banks, airlines, colleges, hospitals, movie theaters, tennis clubs, bowling alleys, restaurants, repair services, hair care shops, and dry cleaners.

  iii. Retailers can be classified according to the prices they charge (see Table 13.1).

    a. A discount store sells standard merchandise at lower prices by accepting lower margins and selling higher volume.

    b. When the major discount stores traded up, a new wave of off-price retailers moved in to fill the low-price, high-volume gap. Ordinary discounters buy at regular wholesale prices and accept lower margins to keep prices down. In contrast, off-price retailers buy at less-than-regular wholesale prices and charge consumers less than retail. There are three main types of off-price retailers.

      1. Independent off-price retailers either are owned and run by entrepreneurs or are divisions of larger retail corporations.

      2. Factory outlets sometimes group together in factory outlet malls and value-retail centers, where dozens of outlet stores offer prices as low as 50 percent below retail on a wide range of items.

iv. Warehouse clubs (or wholesale clubs or membership warehouses) operate in huge, drafty, warehouse-like facilities and offer few frills. Customers themselves must wrestle furniture, heavy appliances, and other large items to the checkout The major types of retail organizations are described in Table 13.2.

    a. Chain stores are two or more outlets that are commonly owned and controlled. Their size allows them to buy in large quantities at lower prices and gain promotional economies.

        1. A voluntary chain is a wholesaler-sponsored group of independent retailers that engages in group buying and common merchandising.

        2. A retailer cooperative is a group of independent retailers that bands together to set up a jointly owned, central wholesale operation and conducts joint merchandising and promotion efforts. These organizations give independents the buying and promotion economies they need to meet the prices of corporate chains.

        3. Another form of contractual retail organization is a franchise. The main difference between franchise organizations and other contractual systems is that franchise systems are normally based on some unique product or service; on a method of doing business; or on the trade name, goodwill, or patent that the franchiser has developed.

        4. Merchandising conglomerates are corporations that combine several different retailing forms under central ownership.

Retailer Marketing Decisions

d. Retailers are always searching for new marketing strategies to attract and hold customers.

e. As shown in Figure 13.1, retailers face major marketing decisions.

    i. Retailers must first define their target markets and then decide how they will position themselves in these markets. Until they define and profile their markets, retailers cannot make consistent decisions about product assortment, services, pricing, advertising, store décor, or any of the other decisions that must support their positions.

    ii. Retailers must decide on three major product variables.

        a. The retailer's product assortment should differentiate the retailer while matching target shoppers' expectations.

            1. One strategy is to offer merchandise that no other competitor carries.

> **2.** The retailer can feature blockbuster merchandising events.
>
> **3.** The retailer can offer surprise merchandise.
>
> **4.** The retailer can differentiate itself by offering a highly targeted product assortment.

> **b.** The services mix can also help set one retailer apart from another.
>
> **c.** The store's atmosphere is another element in the reseller's product arsenal.

iii. A retailer's price policy must fit its target market and positioning, product and service assortment, and competition. Most retailers seek either high markups on lower volume (most specialty stores) or low markups on higher volume (mass merchandisers and discount stores).

iv. Retailers use any or all of the promotion tools—advertising, personal selling, sales promotion, public relations, and direct marketing—to reach consumers.

v. Retailers often point to three critical factors in retailing success—location, location, and location. It's very important that retailers select locations that are accessible to the target market in areas that are consistent with the retailer's positioning.

> **a.** Central business districts were the main form of retail cluster until the 1950s.
>
> **b.** A shopping center is a group of retail businesses planned, developed, owned, and managed as a unit.
>
> > **1.** A regional shopping center, or regional shopping mall, contains from 40 to more than 200 stores.
> >
> > **2.** A community shopping center contains between 15 and 40 retail stores.
> >
> > **3.** Most shopping centers are neighborhood shopping centers or strip malls that generally contain between five and 15 stores.
> >
> > **4.** A recent addition to the shopping center scene is the so-called power center. These huge unenclosed shopping centers consist of a long strip of retail stores, including large, freestanding anchors.

The Future of Retailing

f. Retailers operate in a harsh and fast-changing environment that offers threats as well as opportunities. For example, the industry suffers from chronic overcapacity, resulting in fierce competition for customer dollars.

g. New retail forms continue to emerge to meet new situations and consumer needs, but the life cycle of new retail forms is getting shorter. Department stores took about 100 years to reach the mature stage of the life cycle; more recent forms, such as warehouse stores, reach maturity in about 10 years.

h. Many retailing innovations are partially explained by the Wheel of Retailing concept.

    i. According to this concept, many new types of retailing forms begin as low-margin, low-price, low-status operations. They challenge established retailers that have become "fat" by letting their costs and margins increase.

    ii. The new retailers' success leads them to upgrade their facilities and offer more services.

    iii. In turn, their costs increase, forcing them to increase their prices.

    iv. Eventually, the new retailers become like the conventional retailers they replaced.

    v. The cycle begins again when still newer types of retailers evolve with lower costs and prices.

i. Consumers now have an array of alternatives, including mail order, television, phone, and online shopping. Americans are increasingly avoiding the hassles and crowds at malls by doing more of their shopping by phone or computer.

    i. Most store retailers have no developed direct retailing channels.

    ii. Online retailing is the newest form of non-store retailing. Although the pace has slowed, today's online retailing is alive, well, and growing.

j. Today's retailers are increasingly selling the same products at the same prices to the same consumers in competition with a wider variety of other retailers.

    i. This merging of consumers, products, prices, and retailers is called retail convergence.

    ii. Such convergence means greater competition for retailers and greater difficulty in differentiating offerings.

    iii. Yet the news is not all bad. Many small, independent retailers are thriving. They are finding that sheer size and marketing muscle are often no match for the personal touch that small stores can provide or the specialty niches that small stores fill for a devoted customer base.

k. The rise of huge mass merchandisers and specialty superstores, the formation of vertical marketing systems, and a rash of retail mergers and acquisitions have created a core of superpower megaretailers.

    i. The megaretailers are shifting the balance of power between retailers and producers.

    ii. A relative handful of retailers now control access to enormous numbers of consumers, giving them the upper hand in their dealings with manufacturers.

l. Retail technologies are becoming critically important as competitive tools. Progressive retailers are using advanced information technology and software systems to produce better forecasts, control inventory costs, order electronically from suppliers, send e-mail between stores, and even sell to customers within stores.

       i. They are adopting checkout scanning systems, online transaction processing, electronic data interchange, in-store television, and improved merchandise handling systems.

       ii. Many retailers now routinely use technologies such as touch screen kiosks, electronic shelf labels and signs, handheld shopping assistants, smart cards, self-scanning systems, and virtual reality displays.

  m. Retailers with unique formats and strong brand positioning are increasingly moving into other countries. Many are expanding internationally to escape mature and saturated home markets.

       i. U.S. retailers are still significantly behind Europe and Asia when it comes to global expansion.

       ii. Only 18 percent of the top U.S. retailers operate globally, compared to 40 percent of European retailers and 31 percent of Asian retailers.

  n. With the rise in the number of people living alone, working at home, or living in isolated and sprawling suburbs, there has been a resurgence of establishments that, regardless of the product or service they offer, also provide a place for people to get together.

3. **Wholesaling**

  a. Wholesaling includes all activities involved in selling goods and services to those buying for resale or business use. We call wholesalers those firms engaged primarily in wholesaling activity.

  b. Wholesalers buy mostly from producers and sell mostly to retailers, industrial consumers, and other wholesalers. As a result, many of the nation's largest and most important wholesalers are largely unknown to final consumers.

  c. Wholesalers add value by performing one or more of the following channel functions.

       i. Selling and promoting: Wholesalers' sales forces help manufacturers reach many small customers at a low cost.

       ii. Buying and assortment building: Wholesalers can select items and build assortments needed by their customers.

      iii. Bulk-breaking: Wholesalers save their customers money by buying in carload lots and breaking bulk.

      iv. Warehousing: Wholesalers hold inventory, thereby reducing the inventory costs and risks of suppliers and customers.

      v. Transportation: Wholesalers can provide quicker delivery to buyers because they are closer than the producers.

      vi. Financing: Wholesalers finance their customers by giving credit, and they finance their suppliers by ordering early and paying bills on time.

     vii. Risk bearing: Wholesalers absorb risk by taking title and bearing the cost of theft, damage, spoilage, and obsolescence.

> **viii.** Market information: Wholesalers give information to suppliers and customers about competitors, new products, and price developments.
>
> **ix.** Management services and advice: Wholesalers often help retailers train their salesclerks, improve store layouts and displays, and set up accounting and inventory control systems.

Types of Wholesalers

d. Wholesalers fall into three major groups (see Table 13.3).

> **i.** Merchant wholesalers are the largest single group of wholesalers, accounting for roughly 50 percent of all wholesaling. They include two broad types.
>
>> **a.** Full-service wholesalers provide a full set of services.
>>
>> **b.** Limited-service wholesalers offer fewer services to their suppliers and customers. The several different types of limited-service wholesalers perform varied specialized functions in the distribution channel.
>>
>>> **1.** A broker brings buyers and sellers together and assists in negotiations.
>>>
>>> **2.** Agents represent buyers or sellers on a more permanent basis. Manufacturers' agents are the most common type of agent wholesaler.
>>>
>>> **3.** The third major type of wholesaling is that done in manufacturers' sales branches and offices by sellers or buyers themselves rather than through independent wholesalers.

Wholesaler Marketing Decisions

e. Wholesalers now face growing competitive pressures, more demanding customers, new technologies, and more direct-buying programs on the part of large industrial, institutional, and retail buyers.

> **i.** As a result, they have had to take a fresh look at the marketing strategies.
>
> **ii.** As with retailers, their marketing decisions include choices of target markets, positioning, and the market mix. See Figure 13.2.

f. Like retailers, wholesalers must define their target markets and position themselves effectively.

> **i.** They can choose a target group by size of customer (only large retailers), type of customer (convenience stores only), need for service (customers who need credit), or other factors.
>
> **ii.** Within the target group, they can identify the more profitable customers, design stronger offers, and build better relationships with them.

g. Wholesalers must decide on product assortment and services, prices, promotion, and place.

  i. The wholesaler's "product" is the assortment of products and services that it offers.

  ii. Wholesalers are under great pressure to carry a full line and to stock enough for immediate delivery. But this practice can damage profits.

  iii. Wholesalers today are cutting down on the number of lines they carry, choosing to carry only the more profitable ones.

  iv. Price is an important wholesaler decision. Wholesalers usually mark up the cost of goods by a standard percentage—say 20 percent. Expenses may run 17 percent of the gross margin, leaving a profit margin of 3 percent. In grocery wholesaling, the average profit margin is often less than 2 percent.

  v. Although promotion can be critical to wholesaler success, most wholesalers are not promotion minded. Their use of trade advertising, sales promotion, personal selling, and public relations is largely scattered and unplanned.

  vi. Place is important—wholesalers must choose their locations, facilities, and Web locations carefully. Wholesalers typically locate in low-rent, low-tax areas and tend to invest little money in their buildings, equipment, and systems.

Trends in Wholesaling

h. As the wholesaling industry moves into the twenty-first century, it faces considerable challenges. The industry remains vulnerable to one of the most enduring trends of the last decade—fierce resistance to price increases and the winnowing out of suppliers who are not adding value based on cost and quality.

i. The distinction between large retailers and large wholesalers continues to blur.

  i. Many retailers now operate formats such as wholesale clubs and hypermarkets that perform many wholesale functions.

  ii. In return, many large wholesalers are setting up their own retailing operations.

j. Wholesalers will continue to increase the services they provide to retailers—retail pricing, cooperative advertising, marketing and management information reports, accounting services, online transactions, and others.

k. Facing slow growth in their domestic markets and such developments as the North American Free Trade Agreement, many large wholesalers are now going global.

Student Exercises

1.   Key Term: Retailing

Retailing is defined as all activities involved in selling goods or services directly to the final consumer for their personal, nonbusiness use. Look at Amazon (www.amazon.com) and National Cap and Set Screw Company (www.natlcap.com). Do both of these companies engage in retailing?

2.   Key Term: Self-Service Retailers

Self-service retailers serve customers who are willing to perform their own "locate-compare-select" process to save money. Self-service is the basis of all discount operations and is typically used by sellers of convenience goods and nationally branded, fast-moving shopping goods. This chapter opens with a discussion of Whole Foods. Would you consider Whole Foods a self-service retailer?

3.   Key Term: Specialty Store

Specialty stores carry narrow product lines with deep assortments within those lines. What are two specialty store chains?

4.   Key Term: Category Killer

A category killer is a giant specialty store that carries a very deep assortment of a particular line and is staffed by knowledgeable employees. In recent years category killers have experienced explosive growth. Category killers have come to dominate the retail landscape in recent years. Take a look at some category killers. Do you see any vulnerability which could cause them concern?

5.   Key Term: Superstores

A store much larger than a regular supermarket that offers a large assortment of routinely purchased food products, nonfood items, and services is commonly known as a superstore. Wal-Mart, Target, and Meijer (among others) all offer this supersized combination discount and grocery store. They are growing at the rate of 25% annually. Where is their weakness?

6.   Key Term: Discount Store

A discount store sells standard merchandise at lower prices by accepting lower margins and selling higher volume. In recent years, discount stores have been moving gradually upscale, selling higher quality merchandise and charging slightly higher prices. Your text spotlights Wal-Mart Stores (www.walmart.com). Take a look at Wal-Mart and briefly review their history, How has the focus of their stores changed over the years?

7.   Key Term: Factory Outlet

An off-price retail operation that is owned and operated by a manufacturer and that normally carries the manufacturer's surplus, discontinued, or irregular goods is known as a factory outlet. Factory outlet stores (and malls) have become one of the hottest growth areas in retailing. Take a look at Prime Outlets (www.primeoutlets.com), one of the largest operators of outlet mall in the country. How does the factory outlet mall differ from a traditional mall?

8.   Key Term: Power Center

A shopping center is a group of retail businesses planned, developed, owned, and managed as a unit. A power center is a huge unenclosed shopping center consisting of a long strip of retail stores, including large free-standing anchor stores. Each store has its own outside entrance. Why do you believe such centers have become increasingly popular in recent years?

9.   Key Term: The Wheel-of-Retailing Concept

The wheel-of-retailing concept is a concept of retailing that states new types of retailers typically begin as low-margin, low-price, low-status operations but later evolve into higher-priced, higher-service operations, eventually becoming like the conventional retailers they replaced. Think of an example of a retail format that has progressed through at least a portion of the wheel-of-retailing.

10.   Key Term: International Retailing

Retailers with unique formats and strong brand positioning are increasingly moving into other countries. Many are expanding internationally to escape mature and saturated markets at home. They feel they must expand internationally to continue to grow. Think of some of the issues these retailers may face.

Marketing ADventure Exercises

1.   Ad Interpretation Challenge: Self-Service Retailer
        Ad: Cosmetics and Pharmaceuticals—Edge

Self-service retailers serve customers who are willing to perform their own "locate-compare-select" process to save money. Self-service is the basis of all discount operations and is typically used by sellers of convenience goods and nationally branded, fast-moving shopping goods. Edge shaving gel is a typical product found in a self-service retailer. What type of information should the packaging of this product provide to assist the consumer in the "locate-compare-select" process?

2.   Ad Interpretation Challenge: Specialty Store
      Ad: Student Choice

A specialty store is a retail store that carries a narrow product line with a deep assortment within that line. The increasing use of market segmentation, market targeting, and product specialization has resulted in a greater need for stores that focus on specific products and segments. Find an ad for a retailer that you would consider a specialty store.

3.   Ad Interpretation Challenge: Department Store
      Ad: Electronics—LG

A department store is a retail organization that carries a wide variety of product lines—each line is operated as a separate department managed by specialist buyers or merchandisers. In recent years, department stores have been squeezed by both the discounters and the specialty stores. Why might you find a product such as this LG television in a department store?

4.   Ad Interpretation Challenge: Supermarket
      Ad: Food and Beverage—Heinz

Large, low-cost, low-margin, high-volume, self-service stores that carry a wide variety of grocery and household products are known as supermarkets. Why is it necessary to sell products such as Heinz ketchup through such stores?

5.   Ad Interpretation Challenge: Category Killer
      Ad: General Retail –World's Biggest

The category killer is a relatively new type of retail format. Category killers are in essence giant specialty stores that carry a very deep assortment of a particular line of product and are staffed by knowledgeable employees. What advantages does the consumer gain from shopping a store such as World's Biggest Bookstore?

6.   Ad Interpretation Challenge: Discount Stores
      Ad: Student Choice

Discount stores are retailers that sell standard merchandise at lower prices by accepting lower margins and making up for it by higher volume. Of the offered ads, find one for a discount store.

7.   Ad Interpretation Challenge: Off-Price Retailers
      Ad: Apparel—Levis

Off-price retailers are a type of retailer that buys at less-than-regular wholesale prices and sell at less than retail. Off-price retailers are a relatively new retail format that has come into existence as the traditional discount store has traded up. Under what situation would a product such as Levi's New Collection Diamond Jeans wind up at an off-price retailer?

8.   Ad Interpretation Challenge: Franchise
        Ad: Student Choice

A franchise is a contractual association between a manufacturer, wholesaler, or service organization (a franchiser) and independent businesspeople (franchisees) who buy the right to own and operate one or more units in the franchise system. Franchises now control over 40 percent of all U.S. sales. Locate an ad for a U.S.–based franchise.

9.   Ad Interpretation Challenge: Retail Positioning
        Ad: General Retail—Target

Retailers must define their target markets and positioning clearly. Otherwise, they do not project a clear image to the consumer. Wal-Mart has successfully positioned itself as the low-cost provider. How can Target successfully compete?

10.   Ad Interpretation Challenge: The Wheel-of-Retailing Concept
        Ad: General Retail—Worlds Biggest

The wheel-of-retailing concept states that new types of retailers typically begin as low-margin, low-price, low-status operations but later evolve into higher-priced, higher-service operations, eventually becoming like the conventional retailers they replaced. World's Biggest Bookstore seems to be in the beginning stages of the wheel. If they are not careful, how might they evolve and eventually become obsolete?

Chapter 14
Communicating Customer Value:
Integrated Marketing Communications Strategy

Learning Objectives

1. Discuss the process and advantages of integrated marketing communications in communicating customer value.
2. Define the five promotional tools and discuss the factors that must be considered in shaping the overall promotion mix.
3. Outline the steps in developing effective marketing communications.
4. Explain the methods for setting the promotion budget and factors that affect the design of the promotion mix.

Chapter Overview

Modern marketing calls for more than just developing a good product, pricing it attractively, and making it available to target customers. Companies must also communicate with their customers and there should be controlled direction to those communications. Promotion provides the primary communication function. As one of the four major elements of the marketing mix, promotion uses advertising, sales promotion, public relations, personal selling, and direct marketing to achieve the company's communication objectives.

During the past several decades, companies around the world have perfected the art of mass marketing. The companies must recognize that the face of marketing communications is constantly changing and, to be effective in the future, the marketer must learn to utilize the new emerging communication techniques. The growth and challenges of the electronic promotional communication form are great. The use of computer technology, a desire to get close to the consumer, and an increased use of direct marketing databases has set the stage for increased integrated marketing communications. Under this concept, the company carefully integrates and coordinates its many communication channels—mass media advertising, personal selling, sales promotion, public relations, direct marketing, packaging, and others—to deliver a clear, consistent, and compelling message about the organization and its products. Integrated marketing communications produce better communications consistency and greater sales impact.

Integrated marketing communications involves identifying the target audience and shaping a well-coordinated promotional program to elicit the desired audience response. Too often, marketing communications focus on overcoming immediate awareness, image, or preference problems rather than managing the customer relationship over time. To aid in accomplishing this objective, the chapter presents a communication model that has been time-tested. Good communication will result if managers follow this model.

Building on the aforementioned communications model, the chapter describes the steps in developing effective communication. The steps outlined in this chapter are to identify the target audience (who does the marketer wish to communication with), determine the response sought (objectives of the communication), design a message, choose the media through which to send the message, and collect feedback. Once these steps have been put in place, a marketer can feel more comfortable with communication efforts and begin to concentrate on developing sound communications and promotion strategy.

One of the most important decisions to be made by the organization is how much to spend on promotion. The chapter discusses several approaches to the organization of a promotional budget and a mix of tools to accomplish the organization's promotional objectives. There are various strategies that can be considered by the promotional planner. The primary strategies of *push* and *pull* are described. In addition, the buyer-readiness stage and the product life-cycle stage are also considered.

The chapter concludes by examining the forces that are requiring the organization and its promotional element to be socially responsible in all marketing efforts. People at all levels of the organization must be aware of the growing body of legal and ethical issues surrounding marketing communications.

Chapter Outline

1. **Introduction**
   a. Crispin Porter + Bogusky (CPB) is an agency that takes a very unorthodox approach to creating promotional campaigns. This is apparent in the manner in which it pitched ideas to Virgin Atlantic Airways.
   b. A few years earlier, CPB took similar approaches with BMW. BMW had acquired the British-made MINI automobile brand. BMW assigned the MINI unit a paltry marketing budget and a staff just big enough to fill, well a MINI.
   c. At a time when big-budget SUVs and monster trucks ruled the road, how could the company get consumers interested in the quirky little MINI? The answer: a very creative integrated marketing and promotion campaign.
   d. MINI USA and CPB decided to position the diminutive MINI as an anything-but-ordinary kind of car. To develop this positioning, MINI USA and CPB needed an anything-but-ordinary communications campaign. They assembled a rich mix of unconventional media, carefully integrated to create personality for the car and a tremendous buzz of excitement among consumers.
   e. MINI sales are now running better than 80 percent above the company's original projections. And the inexpensive, offbeat communications campaign has become one of the most celebrated marketing efforts in recent years, scooping up numerous advertising industry awards.
   f. Modern marketing calls for more than just developing a good product, pricing it attractively, and making it available to target customers.

       i. Companies must also communicate with current and prospective customers, and what they communicate should not be left to chance.

       ii. All of their communications efforts must be blended into a consistent and coordinated communications program.

2. **The Promotional Mix**

   a. A company's total marketing communications mix—also called its *promotion mix*—consists of the specific blend of advertising, sales promotion, public relations, personal selling, and direct-marketing tools that the company uses to pursue its advertising and marketing objectives.

   b. Definitions of the five major promotion tools are:

       i. Advertising: Any paid form of nonpersonal presentation and promotion of ideas, goods, or services by an identified sponsor

       ii. Sales promotion: Short-term incentives to encourage the purchase or sale of a product or service

       iii. Public relations: Building good relations with the company's various publics by obtaining favorable publicity, building up a good corporate image, and handling or heading off unfavorable rumors, stories, and events

       iv. Personal selling: Personal presentation by the firm's sales force for the purpose of making sales and building customer relationships

       v. Direct marketing: Direct connections with carefully targeted individual consumers to both obtain an immediate response and cultivate lasting customer relationships—using telephone, mail, fax, e-mail, the Internet, and other tools to communicate directly with specific customers.

   c. At the same time, communication goes beyond these specific promotion tools.

       i. The product's design, its price, the shape and color of its package, and the stores that sell it—all communicate something to buyers.

       ii. Thus, although the promotion mix is the company's primary communication activity, the entire marketing mix—promotion and product, price, and place—must be coordinated for greatest communication impact.

3. **Integrated Marketing Communications**

   a. As we move into the twenty-first century, marketing managers face some new marketing communications realities.

The New Marketing Communications Landscape

   b. Two major factors are changing the face of today's marketing communications.

      i. First, as mass markets have fragmented, marketers are shifting away from mass marketing. More and more, they are developing focused marketing programs designed to build closer relationships with customers in more narrowly defined micromarkets.

      ii. Second, vast improvements in information technology are speeding the movement toward segmented marketing.

c. Given this new communications environment, marketers must rethink the roles of various media and promotion mix tools.

      i. Market fragmentation has resulted in media fragmentation—in an explosion of more focused media that better match today's targeting strategies.

      ii. In all, companies are doing less broadcasting and more narrowcasting.

      iii. Marketers are losing confidence in television advertising and focusing their efforts on more targeted, cost-effective, interactive, and engaging media.

<u>The Need for Integrated Marketing Communications</u>

d. Customers don't distinguish between message sources the way marketers do.

      i. In the consumer's mind, advertising messages from different media and different promotional approaches all become part of a single message about the company.

      ii. Conflicting messages from these different sources can result in confused company images and brand positions.

e. Companies fail to integrate their various communications channels. Mass-media advertisements say one thing, while a price promotion sends a different signal and a product label creates still another message. Company sales literature says something altogether different and the company's Web site seems out of sync with everything else.

f. The problem is that these communications often come from different company sources.

      i. Recently, such functional separation has been a problem for companies and their Internet communications.

g. All the communication tools must be carefully integrated into the broader marketing communications mix. Today, the best bet is to wed the emotional pitch and impact of traditional brand marketing with the interactivity and real service offered online.

h. Today, more companies are adopting the concept of integrated marketing communications (IMC).

      i. Under this concept, as illustrated in Figure 14.1, the company carefully integrates and coordinates its many communications channels to deliver a clear, consistent, and compelling message about the organization and its brands.

      ii. IMC builds brand identity and strong customer relationships by tying together all of the company's messages and images. Brand messages and positioning are coordinated across all communication activities and media.

      iii. IMC calls for recognizing all contact points where the customer may encounter the company, its products, and its brands. Each brand contact will deliver a message, whether good, bad, or indifferent. The company must strive to deliver a consistent and positive message with each contact.

4. **A View of the Communication Process**

    a. Integrated marketing communications involves identifying the target audience and shaping a well-coordinated promotional program to obtain the desired audience response.

    b. Today, marketers are moving toward viewing communications as managing the customer relationship over time.

    c. Because customers differ, communications programs need to be developed for specific segments, niches, and even individuals.

    d. The communications process should start with an audit of all the potential contacts target customers may have with the company and its brands.

    e. To communicate effectively, marketers need to understand how communication works. Communication involves the nine elements shown in Figure 14.2

      i. Sender: The party sending the message to another party

      ii. Encoding: The process of putting thought into symbolic form

      iii. Message: The set of symbols that the sender transmits

      iv. Media: The communication channels through which the message moves from sender to receiver

      v. Decoding: The process by which the receiver assigns meaning to the symbols encoded by the sender

      vi. Receiver: The party receiving the message sent by another party

      vii. Response: The reactions of the receiver after being exposed to the message

      viii. Feedback: The part of the receiver's response communicated back to the sender

      ix. Noise: The unplanned static or distortion during the communication process that results in the receiver's getting a different message than the one the sender sent

    f. For a message to be effective, the sender's encoding process must mesh with the receiver's decoding process. Thus, the best messages consist of words and other symbols that are familiar to the receiver.

    g. This model points out several key factors in good communication.

      i. Senders need to know what audiences they wish to reach and what responses they want.

      ii. They must be good at encoding messages that take into account how the target audience decodes them.

      iii. They must send messages through media that reach target audiences, and they must develop feedback channels so that they can assess the audience's response to the message.

5. **Steps in Developing Effective Communication**

    a. There are several steps in developing an effective integrated communications and promotion program.

Identifying the Target Audience

    b. A marketing communicator starts with a clear target audience in mind.

       i. The audience may be potential buyers or current users, those who make the buying decision or those who influence it. The audience may be individuals, groups, special publics, or the general public.

      ii. The target audience will heavily affect the communicator's decisions on what will be said, how it will be said, when it will be said, where it will be said, and who will say it.

Determining the Communication Objectives

    c. Once the target audience has been defined, the marketing communicator must decide what response is sought.

    d. The marketing communicator needs to know where the target audience now stands and to what stage it needs to be moved. The target audience may be in any of six buyer-readiness stages, the stages consumers normally pass through on their way to making a purchase. See Figure 14.3.

       i. The communicator must first build awareness and knowledge.

      ii. Assuming target consumers know about the product, how do they feel about it? These stages include liking (feeling favorable about the product), preference, (preferring it to other brands), and conviction (believing that the product is best for them).

     iii. Some members of the target market might be convinced about the product, but not quite get around to making the purchase. The communicator must lead these consumers to take the final step. Actions might include offering special promotional prices, rebates, or premiums.

Designing a Message

    e. Having defined the desired audience response, the communicator turns to developing an effective message.

    f. The message should get Attention, hold Interest, arouse Desire, and obtain Action (a framework known as the AIDA model).

    g. In putting the message together, the marketing communicator must decide what to say and how to say it.

       i. The communicator has to figure out an appeal or theme that will produce the desired response. There are three types of appeals.

      a. Rational appeals relate to the audience's self-interest. They show that the product will produce the desired benefits.

      b. Emotional appeals attempt to stir up either negative or positive emotions that can motivate purchase.

            1. Communicators may use positive emotional appeals such as love, pride, joy, and humor.

                  a. Properly used, humor can capture attention, make people feel good, and a give a brand personality.

                  b. However, advertisers must be careful when using humor. Used poorly, it can detract from comprehension, wear out its welcome fast, overshadow the product, or even irritate consumers.

            2. Communicators can also use negative emotional appeals, such as fear, guilt, and shame that get people to do things they should or to stop doing things they shouldn't.

      c. Moral appeals are directed to the audience's sense of what is "right" and "proper." They are often used to urge people to support social causes such as a cleaner environment, better race relations, equal rights for women, and aid to the disadvantaged.

  ii. The communicator must also decide how to handle three message structure issues.

      a. The first is whether to draw a conclusion or leave it to the audience. Recent research suggests that in many cases, rather than drawing a conclusion, the advertiser is better off asking questions and letting buyers come to their own conclusions.

      b. The second message structure issue is whether to present the strongest arguments first or last. Presenting them first gets strong attention but may lead to an anticlimactic ending.

      c. The third message structure issue is whether to present a one-sided argument (mentioning only the product's strengths) or a two-sided argument (touting the product's strengths while also admitting its shortcomings).

 iii. The marketing communicator also needs a strong format for the message.

      a. In a print ad, the communicator has to decide on the headline, copy, illustration, and color. To attract attention, advertisers use novelty and contrast; eye-catching pictures and headlines; distinctive formats; message size and position; and color, shape, and movement.

      b. If the message is to be carried on television or in person, then all these elements plus body language have to be planned. Presenters plan their facial expressions, gestures, dress, posture, and hairstyles.

      c. If the message is carried on the product or its package, the communicator has to watch texture, scent, color, size, and shape.

Choosing Media

h. The communicator now must select channels of communication.

    i. In personal communication channels, two or more people communicate directly with each other. They might communicate face to face, over the telephone, through the mail, or even through an Internet "chat." Personal communication channels are effective because they allow for personal addressing and feedback.

      a. Some personal communication channels are controlled directly by the company. For example, company salespeople contact buyers in the target market.

      b. But other personal communications about the product may reach buyers through channels not directly controlled by the company. Word-of-mouth influence has considerable effect in many areas.

      c. Companies can take steps to put personal communication channels to work for them.

        1. They can create marketing programs that will generate favorable word-of-mouth communications about their brands.

        2. Other companies create opinion leaders—people whose opinions are sought by others—by supplying influencers with the product on attractive terms or by educating them so that they can inform others. Buzz marketing involves cultivating opinion leaders and getting them to spread information about a product or service to others in their communities.

    ii. Nonpersonal communication channels are media that carry messages without personal contact or feedback.

      a. Major media include print media, broadcast media, display media, and online media.

      b. Atmospheres are designed environments that create or reinforce the buyer's leanings toward buying a product.

      c. Events are staged occurrences that communicate messages to target audiences.

      d. Nonpersonal communication affects buyers directly.

        1. Communications first flow from television, magazines, and other mass media to opinion leaders and then from these opinion leaders to others.

2. Thus, opinion leaders step between the mass media and their audiences and carry messages to people who are less exposed to media.

3. This suggests that mass communicators should aim their messages directly at opinion leaders, letting them carry the message to others.

Selecting the Message Source

i. The message's impact on the target audience is also affected by how the audience views the communicator. Messages delivered by highly credible sources are more persuasive.

   i. Marketers often hire celebrity endorsers to deliver their message. But companies must be careful when selecting celebrities to represent their brands.

   ii. Picking the wrong spokesperson can result in embarrassment and a tarnished image.

Collecting Feedback

j. After sending the message, the communicator must research its effect on the target audience. This involves asking the target audience members whether they remember the message, how many times they saw it, what points they recall, how they felt about the message, and their past and present attitudes toward the product and company.

k. The communicator would also like to measure behavior resulting from the message—how many people bought a product, talked to others about it, or visited the store.

l. Feedback on marketing communications may suggest changes in the promotion program or in the product offer itself.

6. **Setting the Total Promotion Budget and Mix**

   a. How does the company decide on the total promotion budget and its division among the major promotional tools to create the promotion mix?

Setting the Total Promotion Budget

b. One of the hardest marketing decisions facing a company is how much to spend on promotion. We look at four common methods used to set the total budget for advertising.

   i. Some companies use the affordable method.

      a. They set the promotion budget at the level they think the company can afford. Small businesses often use this method, reasoning that the company cannot spend more on advertising than it has. They start with total revenues, deduct operating expenses and capital outlays, and then devote some portion of the remaining funds to advertising.

      b. Unfortunately, this method of setting budgets completely ignores the effects of promotion on sales. It tends to place advertising last among spending priorities, even in situations in which advertising is critical to the firm's success.

      c. It leads to an uncertain annual promotion budget that makes long-range market planning difficult. Although the affordable method can result in overspending on advertising, it more often results in underspending.

ii. Other companies use the percentage-of-sales method, setting their promotion budget at a certain percentage of current or forecasted sales. Or they budget a percentage of the unit sales price.

      a. The percentage-of-sales method has advantages. It is simple to use and helps management think about the relationship between promotion spending, selling price, and profit per unit.

      b. However, the percentage-of-sales method has little to justify it. It wrongly views sales as the cause of promotion rather than as the result.

      c. The percentage-of-sales budget is based on availability of funds rather than on opportunities. It may prevent the increased spending sometimes needed to turn around falling sales. Because the budget varies with year-to-year sales, long-range planning is difficult.

      d. Finally, the method does not provide any basis for choosing a specific percentage, except what has been done in the past or what competitors are doing.

iii. Still other companies use the competitive-parity method, setting their promotion budgets to match competitors' outlays.

      a. They monitor competitors' advertising or get industry promotion spending estimates from publications or trade associations, and then set their budgets based on the industry average.

      b. Two arguments support this method.

            1. First, competitor's budgets represent the collective wisdom of the industry. Second, spending what competitors spend helps prevent promotion wars.

            2. Unfortunately, neither argument is valid. There are no grounds for believing that the competition has a better idea of what the company should be spending on promotion than does the company itself.

      c. Companies differ greatly, and each has its own special promotion needs. Finally, there is no evidence that budgets based on competitive parity prevent promotion wars.

      iv. The most logical budget-setting method is the objective-and-task method, whereby the company sets its promotion budget based on what it wants to accomplish with promotion.

           a. This budgeting method entails (1) defining specific promotion objectives, (2) determining the tasks needed to achieve these objectives, and (3) estimating the costs of performing these tasks. The sum of these costs is the proposed promotion budget.

           b. The advantage of the objective-and-task method is that it forces management to spell out its assumptions about the relationship between dollars spent and promotion results.

           c. But it also is the most difficult method to use. Often, it is hard to figure out which specific tasks will achieve stated objectives.

Shaping the Overall Communication Mix

c. The concept of integrated marketing communications suggests that the company must blend the promotion tools carefully into a coordinated promotion mix. Companies within the same industry differ greatly in the design of their promotion mixes.

d. Each promotion tool has unique characteristics and costs. Marketers must understand these characteristics in selecting their mix of tools.

      i. Advertising can reach masses of geographically dispersed buyers at a low cost per exposure, and it enables the seller to repeat the message many times.

           a. Beyond its reach, large-scale advertising says something positive about the seller's size, popularity, and success. Because of advertising's public nature, consumers tend to view advertised products as more legitimate. Advertising is very expressive—it allows the company to dramatize its products through the artful use of visuals, print, sound, and color.

           b. Advertising also has some shortcomings. Although it reaches many people quickly, advertising is impersonal and cannot be as directly persuasive as can company salespeople. For the most part, advertising can carry on only a one-way communication with the audience, and the audience does not feel that it has to pay attention or respond. In addition, advertising can be very costly.

      ii. Personal selling is the most effective tool at certain stages of the buying process, particularly in building up buyers' preferences, convictions, and actions. It involves personal interaction between two or more people, so each person can observe the other's needs and characteristics and make quick adjustments.

      a. Personal selling also allows all kinds of relationships to spring up, ranging from matter-of-fact selling relationships to personal friendships. The effective salesperson keeps the customer's interests at heart in order to build a long-term relationship. Finally, with personal selling, the buyer usually feels a greater need to listen and respond, even if the response is a polite "No thank you."

      b. These unique qualities come at a cost, however. A sales force requires a longer-term commitment than does advertising—advertising can be turned on and off, but sales force size is harder to change. Personal selling is also the company's most expensive promotion tool, costing companies $170 on average per sales call. U.S. firms spend up to three times as much on personal selling as they do on advertising.

iii. Sales promotion includes a wide assortment of tools—coupons, contests, cents-off deals, premiums, and others—all of which have many unique qualities.

      a. They attract consumer attention, offer strong incentives to purchase, and can be used to dramatize product offers and to boost sagging sales.

      b. Sales promotions invite and reward quick response.

      c. Sales promotion effects are often short-lived, however, and often are not as effective as advertising or personal selling in building long-run brand preference.

iv. Public relations is very believable—news stories, features, sponsorships, and events seem more real and believable to readers than ads do.

      a. Public relations can also reach many prospects who avoid salespeople and advertisements—the message gets to the buyers as "news" rather than as a sales-directed communication. And as with advertising, public relations can dramatize a company or product.

      b. Marketers tend to underuse public relations or to use it as an afterthought. Yet a well-thought-out public relations campaign used with other promotion mix elements can be very effective and economical.

v. Although there are many forms of direct marketing—telephone marketing, direct mail, online marketing, and others—they all share four distinctive characteristics.

      a. Direct marketing is nonpublic: The message is normally directed to a specific person.

      b. Direct marketing is immediate and customized: Messages can be prepared very quickly and can be tailored to appeal to specific consumers.

      c. Finally, direct marketing is interactive: It allows a dialogue between the marketing team and the consumer, and messages can be altered depending on the consumer's response. Thus, direct marketing is well suited to highly targeted marketing efforts and to building one-to-one customer relationships.

vi. Marketers can choose from two basic promotion mix strategies. Figure 14.4 contrasts the two strategies.

      a. A push strategy involves "pushing" the product through distribution channels to final consumers. The producer directs its marketing activities (primarily personal selling and trade promotions) toward channel members to induce them to carry the product and to promote it to final consumers.

      b. Using a pull strategy, the producer directs its marketing activities (primarily advertising and consumer promotion) toward final consumers to induce them to buy the product. If the pull strategy is effective, consumers will then demand the product from channel members, who will in turn demand it from producers. Thus, under a pull strategy, consumer demand "pulls" the product through the channels.

      c. Most large companies use some combination of both.

      d. Companies consider many factors when designing their promotion mix strategies, including type of product/market and the product life-cycle stage. For example, the importance of different promotion tools varies between consumer and business markets.

            1. Business-to-consumer (B2C) companies usually "pull" more, putting more of their funds into advertising, followed by sales promotion, personal selling, and then public relations. In contrast, business-to-business (B2B) marketers tend to "push" more, putting more of their funds into personal selling, followed by sales promotion, advertising, and public relations. In general, personal selling is used more heavily with expensive and risky goods and in markets with fewer and larger sellers.

            2. The effects of different promotion tools also vary with stages of the product life cycle.

               a. In the introduction stage, advertising and public relations are good for producing high awareness, and sales promotion is useful in promoting early trial. Personal selling must be used to get the trade to carry the product.

b. In the growth stage, advertising and public relations continue to be powerful influences, whereas sales promotion can be reduced because fewer incentives are needed.

c. In the mature stage, sales promotion again becomes important relative to advertising. Buyers know the brands, and advertising is needed only to remind them of the product.

d. In the decline stage, advertising is kept at a reminder level, public relations is dropped, and salespeople give the product only a little attention. Sales promotion, however, might continue strong.

Integrating the Promotion Mix

e. Having set the promotion budget and mix, the company must now take steps to see that all of the promotion mix elements are smoothly integrated. Here is a checklist for integrating the firm's marketing communications.

 i. Analyze trends—internal and external—that can affect the company's ability to do business.

 ii. Audit the pockets of communications spending throughout the organization.

 iii. Identify all contact points for the company and its brands.

 iv. Team up in communications planning.

 v. Create compatible themes, tones, and quality across all communications media.

 vi. Create performance measures that are shared by all communications elements.

 vii. Appoint a director responsible for the company's persuasive communications efforts.

7. **Socially Responsible Marketing Communication**

a. In shaping its promotion mix, a company must be aware of the large body of legal and ethical issues surrounding marketing communications.

 i. Most marketers work hard to communicate openly and honestly with consumers and resellers.

 ii. Still abuses may occur, and public policy makers have developed a substantial body of laws and regulations to govern advertising, sales promotion, personal selling, and direct-marketing activities.

b. By law, companies must avoid false or deceptive advertising. Advertisers must not make false claims, such as suggesting that a product cures something when it does not. They must avoid ads that have the capacity to deceive, even though no one actually may be deceived.

c. Sellers must avoid bait-and-switch advertising that attracts buyers under false pretenses.

d. A company's trade promotion activities are also closely regulated. For example, under the Robinson-Patman Act, sellers cannot favor certain customers through their use of trade promotions. They must make promotional allowances and services available to all resellers on proportionately equal terms.

e. Companies can use advertising and other forms of promotion to encourage and promote socially responsible programs and actions.

f. A company's salespeople must follow the rules of "fair competition." Most states have enacted deceptive sales acts that spell out what is not allowed.

    i. For example, salespeople may not lie to consumers or mislead them about the advantages of buying a product. To avoid bait-and-switch practices, salespeople's statements must match advertising claims.

    ii. Different rules apply to consumers who are called on at home versus those who go to a store in search of a product.

        a. Because people called on at home may be taken by surprise and may be especially vulnerable to high-pressure selling techniques, the Federal Trade Commission (FTC) has adopted a three-day, cooling-off rule to give special protection to customers who are not seeking products.

        b. Under this rule, customers who agree in their own homes to buy something costing more than $25 have 72 hours in which to cancel a contract or return merchandise and get their money back, no questions asked.

    iii. Much personal selling involves business-to-business trade. In selling to businesses, salespeople may not offer bribes to purchasing agents or to others who can influence a sale. They may not obtain or use technical or trade secrets of competitors through bribery or industrial espionage. Finally, salespeople must not disparage competitors or competing products by suggesting things that are not true.

Student Exercises

1.   Key Term: The Promotion Mix

The specific blend of advertising, sales promotion, public relations, personal selling, and direct-marketing tools that the company uses to persuasively communicate customer value and build customer relationships is known as the promotion mix. This blend is different for every company, with some companies heavily employing all facets of the mix, while other companies only make use of specific mix components. Take a look at your university. Describe the promotion mix it employees.

2.   Key Term: Integrated Marketing Communication

Under the concept of integrated marketing communication (IMC), the company carefully integrates its many communications channels to deliver a clear, consistent, and compelling message about the organization and its brands. IMC calls for recognizing all contact points where the customer may encounter the company and its brands. Take a look at the Apple iPhone (www.apple.com). How do you believe IMC can play a key role in the success of this new product?

3.   Key Term: Noise

Noise is defined as the unplanned static or distortion which occurs during the communication process. This static may result in the receiver's getting a different message than the one the sender sent or intended. Think about a local television commercial for your favorite Mexican restaurant. What noise might interfere with the viewer's reception of the ad??

4.   Key Term: Decoding

Decoding is the part of the communication process in which the receiver assigns meaning to the symbols encoded by the sender. For example, a reader views an ad and interprets the words and illustrations it contains. Sometimes this can go awry. Go to BCBG's website (www.bcbg.com). How might a viewer decode the message here in a manner contrary to that intended by BCBG?

5.   Key Term: Message Content—Rational Appeals

The marketer has to figure out an appeal or theme that will produce the desired response. The rational appeal is one possibility. In a rational appeal, the marketer tries to relate the audience's self-interest. They show that the product will produce the desired benefits. Take a look at Audi USA (www.audiusa.com). Think of a couple of rational appeals Audi might use to provide information to consumers.

6.   Key Term: Message Content—Emotional Appeals

The emotional appeal is another method a marketer may use to attempt to produce the desired response in the consumer. Emotional appeals attempt to stir up either positive or negative emotions that can motivate a consumer to action. Rogaine is a product designed to help rejuvenate hair growth. Log on to Rogaine's webpage (www.rogaine.com). How is the emotional appeal used by this company?

7.   Key Term: Personal Communication Channel

A personal communication channel is a channel through which two or more people communicate directly with each other—including face-to-face on the phone, through mail or email, or even through an internet "chat." Personal communication channels are effective because they allow for personal addressing and feedback. You walk into your local Best Buy store. What personal communication channels may come into play?

8.   Key Term: Word-of-Mouth Influence

Word-of-mouth influence is derived from personal communication about a product between target buyers and neighbors, friends, family members, and associates. Personal influence, such as word-of-mouth, carries great weight for products that are expensive, risky, or highly visible. Trip Advisor is an internet website devoted to providing customer reviews about destinations worldwide. This type of customer-driven site is of enormous value to many travelers considering a holiday at an unfamiliar site. Take a look at Trip Advisor (www.tripadvisor.com). Type in a search for a specific destination or hotel (such as the Sandals Resorts property in the Bahamas) and read some of the reviews. How might such information influence your travel decisions?

9.   Key Term: Buzz Marketing

Buzz marketing involves cultivating opinion leaders and getting them to spread information about a product or service to others in their communities. Consider the Palm Treo Smartphone (go to www.palm.com/us/ to learn about it). Why might buzz marketing be a viable method of supplying information to the market?

10.   Key Term: Nonpersonal Communication Channel

Nonpersonal communication channels are media that carry messages without personal contact or feedback. They include media, atmospheres, and events. Go back and look again at the Palm Treo Smartphone (www.palm.com/us/). What nonpersonal communication channels do you believe would be useful in getting information about this phone out?

Marketing ADventure Exercises

1.   Ad Interpretation Challenge: The Promotion Mix
       Ad: Advertising—Universal McCann

The promotion mix is the specific blend of advertising, sales promotion, public relations, personal selling, and direct marketing tools that the company uses to persuasively communicate customer value and build customer relationships. Look at this ad for Universal McCann. Are they limiting themselves?

2.   Ad Interpretation Challenge: Narrowcasting
        Ad: Auto—Audi

A proliferation of new media formats has generated a shift in the way many marketers are doing business. These new media include specialty magazines, cable television channels, video on demand, and product placement in television shows and movies. This allows marketers to more finely tune their promotional efforts to more carefully reach their target markets. All of this is contributing to companies doing less broadcasting and more narrowcasting. How might Audi utilize narrowcasting to more effectively get the word out regarding the new Audi A2?

3.   Ad Interpretation Challenge: Mass-Media Communication
        Ad: Student Choice

Mass-media communication allows marketers to reach large groups of people efficiently through the use of mass media, such as television or newspaper advertising. Find an ad for a product that could make good use of a mass-media communication strategy.

4.   Ad Interpretation Challenge: Integrated Marketing Communications (IMC)
        Ad: Auto—Chrysler

Under the concept of integrated marketing communication (IMC), the company carefully integrates its many communications channels to deliver a clear, consistent, and compelling message about the organization and its brands. IMC calls for recognizing all contact points where the customer may encounter the company and its brands. Each of these points of contact will deliver a message about the product. The goal of IMC is to have the same message delivered at each contact point. Consider this ad for Chrysler. How might IMC be utilized to standardize the message Chrysler is using?

5.   Ad Interpretation Challenge: Noise
        Ad: Newspaper and TV—Cartoon Network

Noise is unplanned static or distortion during the communication process, which results in the receiver getting a different message than the one the sender sent. Examine this magazine ad for the Cartoon Network. What possible noise could interfere with the proper interpretation of this ad?

6.   Ad Interpretation Challenge: Receiver
        Ad: Auto—Audi A2

The receiver is the party receiving the message sent by another party. The message creator must have in mind specifically who will be receiving the ad so that the most effective message can be created and the most useful delivery format utilized. Take a look at this ad for the Audi A2. Who is the intended receiver of this advertisement?

7.   Ad Interpretation Challenge: Buyer-Readiness Stages
        Ad: Auto—Mercedes C Class

Buyer-readiness stages are the stages that consumers normally pass through on their way to purchase, including awareness, knowledge, liking, preference, conviction, and purchase. Take a look at this ad for the new Mercedes C Class automobile. What buyer-readiness stage is this ad targeting?

8.   Ad Interpretation Challenge: Emotional Appeal
        Ad: Student Choice

Emotional appeals attempt to stir up either positive or negative emotions that can motivate purchase. Communicators may use positive emotional appeals such as love, pride, or joy. Find an ad for a product or service that is based on an emotional appeal.

9.   Ad Interpretation Challenge: Humorous Appeal
        Ad: Financial—Fame

Properly used, humor can capture attention, make people feel good, and give a brand personality. Take a look at this ad for F.A.M.E. How does it use humor to get its point across?

10.   Ad Interpretation Challenge: Word-of-Mouth Influence
        Ad: Auto—Ford

Word-of-mouth influence is derived from personal communication about a product between target buyers and neighbors, friends, family members, and associates. Personal influence, such as word-of-mouth, carries great weight for products that are expensive, risky, or highly visible. Consider Ford. If you were in the market for this product, how might word-of-mouth play a role in your decision?

Chapter 15
Advertising and Public Relations

Learning Objectives

1. Define the roles of advertising in the promotion mix.
2. Describe the major decisions involved in developing an advertising program.
3. Define the role of public relations in the promotion mix.
4. Explain how companies use public relations to communicate with their publics.

Chapter Overview

Three of the promotional mix elements (advertising, sales promotion, and public relations) are mass communication tools. Advertising is the first of these important elements to be discussed in the chapter. Advertising is described as being any paid form of nonpersonal presentation and promotion of ideas, goods, and services by an identified sponsor.

There are four important decisions to be accomplished as the marketer attempts to organize and direct the advertising function. Each of these decisions (setting objectives, budget decisions, advertising strategy [message decisions and media decisions], and evaluating advertising campaigns) is discussed in detail and explained within the context of building an advertising campaign. In addition, several forms of advertising, various advertising strategies, and descriptions of the mass media are presented to the reader. The marketing firm can undertake the advertising functions themselves or they can contract with an advertising agency to accomplish their advertising objective, planning, and implementation.

Public relations, the final mass communication tool described in this chapter, is an attempt to build good relations with the company's various publics by obtaining favorable publicity, building up a good "corporate image," and handling or heading off unfavorable rumors, stories, or events. The organization has a variety of tools at their disposal for accomplishing this feat. One of the overriding tasks of public relations is to control the exposure and relationship with the mass media. By focusing on consumer attitudes, awareness, and knowledge of the organization, the company is better prepared to succeed. Public relations has even been extended to the Internet and companies are beginning to explore ways to increase its effect in the newly emerging world of e-commerce.

Chapter Outline

1. **Introduction**
   a. GEICO was once a little known insurance company that served a select group of government employees and non-commissioned military officers.
   b. After Warren Buffet bought the company in 1996 and told the marketing group to "speed things up," things started to change. Promotional spending increased 30-fold, focusing on the now-familiar humor-appeal campaign featuring the lovable Gecko.
   c. In each of the last five years, GEICO has experienced double-digit market share gains. The company now serves more than seven million customers and is the fourth largest insurance company.
   d. To do this, they must skillfully use the mass-promotion tools of advertising, sales promotion, and public relations.

2. **Advertising**
   a. Advertising can be traced back to the very beginnings of recorded history. Archaeologists working in the countries around the Mediterranean Sea have dug up signs announcing various events and offers. The Romans painted walls to announce gladiator fights, and the Phoenicians painted pictures promoting their wares on large rocks along parade routes.
   b. Although advertising is used mostly by business firms, it also is used by a wide range of not-for-profit organizations, professionals, and social agencies that advertise their causes to various target publics.
   c. Advertising is a good way to inform and persuade.
   d. Marketing management must make four important decisions when developing an advertising program. See Figure 15.1.

   Setting Advertising Objectives
   e. The first step is to set advertising objectives. An advertising objective is a specific task to be accomplished with a specific target audience during a specific period of time.
   f. Advertising objectives can be classified by primary purpose—whether the aim is to inform, persuade, or remind. Table 15.1 lists examples of each of these objectives.
      i. Informative advertising is used heavily when introducing a new product category. In this case, the objective is to build primary demand.
      ii. Some persuasive advertising has become comparative advertising, in which a company directly or indirectly compares its brand with one or more other brands.
      iii. Reminder advertising is important for mature products—it keeps consumers thinking about the product.

<u>Setting the Advertising Budget</u>

g. After determining its advertising objectives, the company next sets its advertising budget for each product.

h. A brand's advertising budget often depends on its stage in the product life cycle.

    i. New products typically need large advertising budgets to build awareness and to gain consumer trial.

    ii. Mature brands usually require lower budgets as a ratio to sales.

    iii. Market share also impacts the amount of advertising needed: Because building the market or taking share from competitors requires larger advertising spending than does simply maintaining current share, low-share brands usually need more advertising spending as a percentage of sales.

i. Because so many factors affect advertising effectiveness, some controllable and others not, measuring the results of advertising spending remains an inexact science. In most cases, managers must rely on large doses of judgment along with more quantitative analysis when setting advertising budgets.

<u>Developing Advertising Strategy</u>

j. Advertising strategy consists of two major elements: creating advertising messages and selecting advertising media. In the past, companies often viewed media planning as secondary to the message-creation process.

k. Today, however, media fragmentation, soaring media costs, and more focused target marketing strategies have promoted the importance of the media-planning function. More and more, advertisers are orchestrating a closer harmony between their messages and the media that deliver them.

l. No matter how big the budget, advertising can succeed only if advertisements gain attention and communicate well. Good advertising messages are especially important in today's costly and cluttered advertising environment.

    i. If all this advertising clutter bothers some consumers, it also causes big problems for advertisers.

        a. Their ads are sandwiched in with a clutter of other commercials, announcements, and network promotions, totaling more than 15 minutes of non-program material per prime-time hour, more than 21 minutes per daytime hour.

        b. Until recently, television viewers were pretty much a captive audience of advertisers. With the growth in cable and satellite TV, VCRs, and remote-controls, today's viewers have many more options. Adding to the problem is the new wave of personal video recorders (PVRs) and personal television services—such as TiVo and ReplayTV—that have armed viewers with an arsenal of new-age zipping and zapping weapons.

    ii. Just to gain and hold attention, today's advertising messages must be better planned, more imaginative, more entertaining, and more rewarding to consumers.

        a. Many advertisers now see themselves as creating "advertainment"—ads that are both persuasive and entertaining.

        b. Some advertisers even create intentionally controversial ads to break through the clutter and gain attention for their products.

m. The first step in creating effective advertising messages is to plan a message strategy—to decide what general message will be communicated to consumers. The purpose of advertising is to get consumers to think about or react to the product or company in a certain way. People will react only if they believe that they will benefit from doing so. Thus, developing an effective message strategy begins with identifying customer benefits that can be used as advertising appeals.

n. Message strategy statements tend to be plain, straightforward outlines of benefits and positioning points that the advertiser wants to stress. The advertiser must next develop a compelling creative concept—or "big idea"—that will bring the message strategy to life in a distinctive and memorable way.

    i. The creative concept will guide the choice of specific appeals to be used in an advertising campaign. Advertising appeals should have three characteristics.

        a. First, they should be meaningful, pointing out benefits that make the product more desirable or interesting to consumers.

        b. Second, appeals must be believable—consumers must believe that the product or service will deliver the promised benefits.

        c. Appeals should also be distinctive—they should tell how the product is better than the competing brands.

o. The advertiser now has to turn the big idea into an actual ad execution that will capture the target market's attention and interest.

    i. Any message can be presented in different execution styles, such as the following:

        a. Slice of life: This style shows one or more "typical" people using the product in a normal setting.

        b. Lifestyle: This style shows how a product fits in with a particular lifestyle.

        c. Fantasy: This style creates a fantasy around the product or its use.

        d. Mood or image: This style builds a mood or image around the product, such as beauty, love, or serenity.

        e. Musical: This style shows one or more people or cartoon characters singing about the product.

      f. Personality symbol: This style creates a character that represents the product. The character might be animated or real.

      g. Technical expertise: This style shows the company's expertise in making the product.

      h. Scientific evidence: This style presents survey or scientific evidence that the brand is better or better liked than one or more other brands.

      i. Testimonial evidence or endorsement: This style features a highly believable or likable source endorsing the product.

    ii. The advertiser also must choose a tone for the ad.

   iii. The advertiser must use memorable and attention-getting words in the ad.

    iv. Finally, format elements make a difference in an ad's impact as well as in its cost. A small change in ad design can make a big difference in its effect.

      a. The illustration is the first thing the reader notices—it must be strong enough to draw attention.

      b. Next, the headline must effectively entice the right people to read the copy.

      c. Finally, the copy—the main block of text in the ad—must be simple but strong and convincing.

      d. These three elements must effectively work together.

p. To select media, the advertiser must decide on the reach and frequency needed to achieve advertising objectives.

    i. Reach is a measure of the percentage of people in the target market who are exposed to the ad campaign during a given period of time.

    ii. Frequency is a measure of how many times the average person in the target market is exposed to the message.

   iii. The advertiser also must decide on the desired media impact—the qualitative value of a message exposure through a given medium.

    iv. In general, the more reach, frequency, and impact the advertiser seeks, the higher the advertising budget will have to be.

q. The media planner has to know the reach, frequency, and impact of each of the major media types. As summarized in Table 15.2, the major media types are newspapers, television, direct mail, radio, magazines, outdoor, and the Internet. Each medium has advantages and limitations.

    i. Media planners consider many factors when making their media choices.

      a. The media habits of target consumers will affect media choice—advertisers look for media that reach target consumers effectively.

      b. So will the nature of the product.

      c. Different types of messages may require different media.

        d. Cost is another major factor in media choice. The media planner looks both at the total cost of using a medium and at the cost per exposure of reaching specific target customers.

    ii. Media impact and cost must be re-examined regularly.

    iii. An important trend affecting media selection is the rapid growth in the number of "media multi-taskers," people who absorb more than one medium at a time.

r. The media planner now must chose the best media vehicles—specific media within each general media type.

    i. Media planners must compute the cost per thousand persons reached by a vehicle.

    ii. The media planner must also consider the costs of producing ads for different media. Whereas newspaper ads may cost very little to produce, flashy television ads may cost millions.

    iii. In selecting media vehicles, the media planner must balance media cost measures against several media impact factors.

        a. First, the planner should balance costs against the media vehicle's audience quality.

        b. Second, the media planner should consider audience attention.

        c. Third, the planner should assess the vehicle's editorial quality.

s. The advertisers must also decide how to schedule the advertising over the course of a year.

    i. The firm can vary its advertising to follow a seasonal pattern, to oppose a seasonal pattern, or to be the same all year. Most firms do some seasonal advertising. Some do only seasonal advertising.

    ii. The advertiser has to choose the pattern of the ads.

        a. Continuity means scheduling ads evenly within a given period. Pulsing means scheduling ads unevenly over a given time period.

            1. The idea behind pulsing is to advertise heavily for a short period to build awareness that carries over to the next advertising period. Those who favor pulsing feel that it can be used to achieve the same impact as a steady schedule but at a much lower cost. However, some media planners believe that although pulsing achieves minimal awareness, it sacrifices depth of advertising communications.

    iii. Recent advances in technology have had a substantial impact on the media planning and buying functions.

a. Today, computer software applications called media optimizers allow media planners to evaluate vast combinations of television programs and prices. Such programs help advertisers to make better decisions about which mix of networks, programs, and day parts will yield the highest reach per ad dollar.

Evaluating Advertising

t. Advertising accountability and *return on advertising investment* have become increasingly important concepts for companies.

u. The advertising program should evaluate both the communication effects and the sales effects of advertising regularly. Measuring the communication effects of an ad—copy testing—tells whether the ad is communicating well.

    i. Copy testing can be done before or after an ad is printed or broadcast.

    ii. Before the ad is placed, the advertiser can show it to consumers, ask how they like it, and measure message recall or attitude changes resulting from it.

    iii. After the ad is run, the advertiser can measure how the ad affected consumer recall or product awareness.

v. The sales effects of advertising are often harder to measure than the communication effects. Sales are affected by many factors besides advertising—such as product features, price, and availability.

    i. One way to measure the sales effect of advertising is to compare past sales with past advertising expenditures.

    ii. Another way is through experiments.

Other Advertising Considerations

w. In developing advertising strategies and programs, the company must address two additional questions. First, how will the company organize its advertising function—who will perform which advertising tasks? Second, how will the company adapt its advertising strategies and programs to the complexities of international markets?

    i. Different companies organize in different ways to handle advertising.

        a. In small companies, advertising might be handled by someone in the sales department.

        b. Large companies set up advertising departments whose job it is to set the advertising budget, work with the ad agency, and handle other advertising not done by the agency.

            1. Advertising agencies were started in the mid- to late 1800s by salespeople and brokers who worked for the media and received a commission for selling advertising space to companies.

2. Today's agencies employ specialists who can often perform advertising tasks better than can the company's own staff. Agencies also bring an outside point of view to solving the company's problems, along with lots of experience from working with different clients and situations.

3. Many agencies have sought growth by diversifying into related marketing services. These new diversified agencies offer a complete list of integrated marketing and promotion services under one roof.

ii. International advertisers face many complexities not encountered by domestic advertisers.

    a. The most basic issue concerns the degree to which global advertising should be adapted to the unique characteristics of various country markets.

        1. Standardization produces many benefits—lower advertising costs, greater global advertising coordination, and a more consistent worldwide image.

        2. But it also has drawbacks. Most important, it ignores the fact that country markets differ greatly in their cultures, demographics, and economic conditions. Thus, most international advertisers "think globally but act locally." They develop global advertising strategies that make their worldwide advertising efforts more efficient and consistent. Then they adapt their advertising programs to make them more efficient and consistent.

    b. Global advertisers face several special problems.

        1. For instance, advertising media costs and availability differ vastly from country to country.

        2. Countries also differ in the extent to which they regulate advertising practices. Many countries have extensive systems of laws restricting how much a company can spend on advertising, the media used, the nature of advertising claims, and other aspects of the advertising program. Such restrictions often require advertisers to adapt their campaigns from country to country.

3. **Public Relations**
  a. Another major mass-promotion tool is public relations—building good relations with the company's various publics by obtaining favorable publicity, building up a good corporate image, and handling or heading off unfavorable rumors, stories, and events. Public relations departments may perform any or all of the following functions.
    i. Press relations or press agency: Creating and placing newsworthy information in the news media to attract attention to a person, product, or service
    ii. Product publicity: Publicizing specific products
    iii. Public affairs: Building and maintaining national or local community relations
    iv. Lobbying: Building and maintaining relations with legislators and government officials to influence legislation and regulation
    v. Investor relations: Maintaining relationships with shareholders and others in the financial community
    vi. Development: Public relations with donors or members of non-profit organizations to gain financial or volunteer support
  b. Public relations is used to promote products, people, places, ideas, activities, organizations, and even nations. Companies use public relations to build good relations with consumers, investors, the media, and their communities.

The Role and Impact of Public Relations
  c. Public relations can have a strong impact on public awareness at a much lower cost than advertising can. The company does not pay for space or time in the media. Rather, it pays for a staff to develop and circulate information and to manage events.
  d. Despite its potential strengths, public relations is sometimes described as a marketing stepchild because of its often limited and scattered use.
  e. Although public relations still captures only a small portion of the overall marketing budgets of most firms, PR is playing an increasingly important brand-building role.

Major Public Relations Tools
  f. Public relations professionals use several tools.
    i. PR professionals find or create favorable news about the company and its products or people.
    ii. Speeches can also create product and company publicity.
    iii. Another common PR tool is special events, ranging from news conferences, press tours, grand openings, and fireworks displays to laser shows, hot air balloon releases, multimedia presentations, start-studded spectaculars, or educational programs designed to reach and interest target publics.

iv. Many marketers are now designing buzz marketing campaigns that create excitement and generate favorable word-of-mouth communication for their brands.

v. Recently, mobile marketing—traveling promotional tours that bring the brand to consumers—has emerged as an effective way to build one-to-one relationships with targeted consumers.

vi. Public relations people also prepare written materials to reach and influence their target markets. These materials include annual reports, brochures, articles, and company newsletters and magazines.

vii. Audiovisual materials, such as films, slide-and-sound programs, and video and audio CDs, are being used increasingly as communication tools.

viii. Corporate identity materials can also help create a corporate identity that the public immediately recognizes.

ix. Companies can improve public goodwill by contributing money and time to public service activities.

x. A company's Web site can be a good public relations vehicle. Web sites can also be ideal for handling crisis situations.

Student Exercises

1.   Key Term: Advertising

Advertising is defined as any form of paid nonpersonal presentation and promotion of ideas, goods, or services by an identified sponsor. Advertising's goal is to move consumers through the buyer-readiness stages previously discussed. Advertising is a good way to inform and persuade. Take a look at Bucuti Beach Resort's website (www.bucuti.com/en/). The site is providing the viewer with information about the resort and about Aruba in general. Is this advertising?

2.   Key Term: Advertising Objectives

An advertising objective is a specific communication task to be accomplished with a specific target audience during a specific period of time. Advertising objectives are classified by their primary purpose—whether the aim is to inform, persuade, or remind. Go to SuperClubs website (www.superclubs.com). What is the primary advertising objective of their site?

3.   Key Term: Reminder Advertising

One of the three basic advertising objectives is to remind. Reminder advertising is particularly important for mature products—it helps to maintain customer relationships and keep customers thinking about the product. What is a product that benefits from the use of reminder advertising?

4.	Key Term: Breaking Through the Clutter

There is so much advertising in the marketplace today that it can become little more than noise to the eyes and ears of the consumer. It becomes bothersome to the consumer. Likewise, it becomes an issue for the advertisers. The proliferation of ads means that marketers must work extra hard to make sure their ads break through the clutter of the market and stand out from the pack. If you were the marketing executive in charge of advertising Jamaica, what would you do to break through the clutter so that consumers would notice and pay attention to your product (Jamaica)?

5.	Key Term: Creative Concept

The creative concept is the compelling "big idea" that will bring the advertising message strategy to life in a distinctive and memorable manner. At this stage, simple message ideas become great ad campaigns. The newest advertising campaign designed to bring visitors to Australia is an example of one of these "big ideas." Go to www.australia.com. Discuss what you consider to be this "big idea."

6.	Key Term: Execution Style

Advertisers must turn the big idea into an actual ad execution that will capture the target market's attention and interest. Execution style is the approach, style, tone, works, and format used for executing an advertising message. Take a look at Couples Resorts in Jamaica (www.couples.com). What execution style is being employed here?

7.	Key Term: Advertising Media

Advertising media is the vehicle through which the advertising messages are delivered to their intended audiences. The major advertising media types are television, newspapers, direct mail, magazines, radio, outdoor, and the internet. Each medium has advantages and limitations. Read a little bit about Scion (www.scion.com). What forms of media do you believe would be most effective in reaching the intended Scion audience?

8.	Key Term: Alternative Media

Alternative media are those forms of media outside of the traditionally accepted formats. For example, Real Marketing 15.2, from your text discusses various forms of these alternative media—everything from miniature billboards on shopping cards to painted cows. Think again about Scion (www.scion.com). What are some alternative media formats you can think of that might be useful in getting the Scion name out to potential consumers?

9.   Key Term: Public Relations

Public relations is the building of good relationships with the company's various publics by obtaining favorable publicity, building a good corporate image, and handling or heading off unfavorable rumors, stories, and events. Britney Spears is an entertainer who seems to spend quite a bit of time in the news. Take a look at her website (www.britneyspears.com). How does the pop princess use public relations to try and enhance her public image?

10.   Key Term: Lobbying

One of the functions of public relations may be lobbying—the building and maintaining of relations with legislators and government officials to influence legislation and regulation. Consider the National Rifle Association (NRA) (www.nra.org). What role does lobbying play in the overall public relations campaign of the NRA?

Marketing ADventure Exercises

1.   Ad Interpretation Challenge: Advertising
        Ad: Apparel—Levi's New Collection Diamond Jean

Advertising is defined as any form of paid nonpersonal presentation and promotion of ideas, goods, or services by an identified sponsor. Advertising's goal is to move consumers through the buyer-readiness stages previously discussed. Advertising is a good way to inform and persuade. Take a look at this ad for Levi's. Do you view this ad as a good way to inform and persuade the consumer?

2.   Ad Interpretation Challenge: Reminder Advertising
        Ad: Student Choice

One of the three basic advertising objectives is to remind. Reminder advertising is particularly important for mature products—it helps to maintain customer relationships and keep customers thinking about the product. Take a look at the offered ads. Find one for a mature product that you believe is using reminder advertising.

3.   Ad Interpretation Challenge: Informative Advertising
        Ad: Auto—Hyundai Lean Burn

Another of the basic advertising objectives is to inform. Informative advertising is used heavily when introducing a new product category. In this case, the objective is to build primary demand. Consider this ad for Hyundai's lean burn engine (a high-efficiency engine). Why would this ad be considered an informative ad?

4.   Ad Interpretation Challenge: Persuasive Advertising
        Ad: Electronics—LG

Still another of the basic advertising objectives is to persuade. Persuasive advertising takes on greater importance as competition increases. Here, the company's objective is to build selective demand. Look at the ad for LG. Is this ad based on the objective of persuasion?

5.   Ad Interpretation Challenge: Advertising Budget
        Ad: Apparel—Levi's New Collection Diamond Jean

The advertising budget is the dollars and other resources allocated to a product or company advertising program. A brand's advertising budget is often related to its stage in the product life cycle. Take a look at this ad for Levi's New Collection Diamond Jean. Where would you place this product in the product life cycle and, as a result, how much of an advertising budget is required?

6.   Ad Interpretation Challenge: Breaking Through the Clutter
        Ad: Student Choice

There is so much advertising in the marketplace today that it can become little more than noise to the eyes and ears of the consumer. It becomes bothersome to the consumer. Likewise, it becomes an issue for the advertisers. The proliferation of ads means that marketers must work extra hard to make sure their ads break through the clutter of the market and stand out from the pack. Look at the offered ads. Locate one that seems to do a good job of breaking through the clutter.

7.   Ad Interpretation Challenge: Madison & Vine
        Ad: General Retail—Hallmark

"Madison & Vine' is a term that has come to represent the merging of advertising and entertainment in an effort to break through the clutter and create new avenues for reaching consumers with more engaging messages. It is becoming ever more important to entertain consumers. Go to Hallmark's home page (www.hallmark.com). Click on the link that takes you to hoops&yoyo—one of their newer collections of characters. Peruse the site. You will see that hoops&yoyo has been used in advertising and now has a line of products you can purchase. How are hoops&yoyo a meeting of Madison & Vine?

8.   Ad Interpretation Challenge: Execution Style
        Ad: Auto—Honda Motorcycles

Advertisers must turn the big idea into an actual ad execution that will capture the target market's attention and interest. Execution style is the approach, style, tone, works, and format used for executing an advertising message. Look at the ads for Honda motorcycles. What execution style would you say is being used in all of these ads?

9.   Ad Interpretation Challenge: Advertising Media
       Ad: Autos—Audi

Advertising media is the vehicle through which advertising messages are delivered to their intended audiences. The major advertising media types are television, newspapers, direct mail, magazines, radio, outdoor, and the Internet. Each medium has advantages and limitations. Take a look at this ad. What medium would you suggest carry this ad?

10.   Ad Interpretation Challenge: Advertising Media
       Ad: Newspapers and TV—MTV Masters

Yes, it is the same topical area as covered in the previous exercise, but here we are considering a different advertisement with different consequences. Take a look at this ad for MTV Masters. If you could rework and reformat this ad, what possible media do you believe would be useful in disseminating this information?

Chapter 16
Personal Selling and Sales Promotion

Learning Objectives

1. Discuss the role of a company's salespeople in creating value for customers and building customer relationships.
2. Identify and explain the six major sales force management steps.
3. Discuss the personal selling process, distinguishing between transaction-oriented marketing and relationship marketing.
4. Explain how sales promotion campaigns are developed and implemented.

Chapter Overview

Robert Louis Stevenson once noted, "Everyone lives by selling something." Today, most companies use salespeople to bring their company's offering to the consuming or business publics. The salesperson's role is a key one in the organization. The high cost of maintaining a sales force means that management is especially interested in how to efficiently organize this vital element. Six basic steps or decisions are important to the sales management process. They are *designing sales force strategy and structure, recruiting and selecting salespeople, training salespeople, compensating salespeople, supervising salespeople,* and *evaluating salespeople.* The chapter thoroughly explains each of these critical steps in enriched detail.

As an element of the marketing mix (the promotional component), the sales force is very effective in achieving certain marketing, communication, and promotion objectives. The formal steps in the selling process that aid the accomplishment of these objectives are *prospecting and qualifying, the preapproach, the approach, presentation and demonstration, handling objections, the closing,* and *a follow-up.* If the salesperson follows these steps, he or she is more likely to be viewed as a problem solver rather than a hard-sell salesperson by the consumer.

Great salespeople have drive, discipline, and relationship-building skills. A relationship (rather than a transaction-oriented) approach in selling is a process of creating, maintaining, and enhancing strong, value-laden relationships with customers and other stakeholders. Relationships are more important than mere transactions. Transactions can be completed quickly (and sometimes only once), whereas relationships can last a lifetime (such as the relationship between the customer and his or her doctor or life insurance salesperson).

Sales promotion, as the second of the mass communication tools described in this chapter, is a process of providing short-term incentives to encourage purchase or sales of a product or service. Sales promotion offers the buyer reasons to buy now. In addition, sales promotion is also intended to stimulate reseller effectiveness. Sales promotion has grown rapidly in the recent past because of pressure to increase sales, increased competition, and the declining efficiency of the other mass communication methods. The chapter discusses the objectives of a sound sales promotion campaign and offers examples of the major tools for accomplishing those objectives.

Chapter Outline

1. **Introduction**
   a. Perhaps no industry felt the recent economic slowdown more than the technology sector—total information technology spending has been flat for several years. But despite the slump, CDW Corporation, the nation's largest reseller of technology products and services, is thriving.
   b. The company owes its success to its highly effective "clicks and people" direct marketing strategy. CDW's direct model combines good old-fashioned high-touch personal selling with a modern high-tech Web presence to build lasting one-to-one customer relationships.
   c. Whereas many of CDW's competitors chase after a relative handful of very large customers, CDW has traditionally targeted small and midsize businesses (SMBs). These smaller customers often need lots of advice and support.
   d. The major responsibility for building and managing customer relationships falls to CDW's sales force of nearly 2,000 account managers. Each customer is assigned an account manager, who helps the customer select the right products and technologies and keep them running smoothly.
   e. Account managers do more than just sell technology products and services. They work closely with customers to find solutions to their technology problems.
   f. Customers who want to access CDW's products and expertise without going through their account manager can do so easily at any of several CDW Web sites.
   g. When someone says "salesperson," you may still think of the stereotypical "traveling salesman"—the fast-talking, ever-smiling peddler who travels his territory foisting his wares on reluctant customers. Such stereotypes, however, are sadly out of date. Today, like CDW's account managers, most professional salespeople are well-educated, well-trained men and women who work to build valued customer relationships.
   h. In this chapter, we examine two more marketing communication and promotion tools—personal selling and direct marketing.

2. **Personal Selling**
   a. We will examine the role of personal selling in the organization, sales force management decisions, and the personal selling process.

   The Nature of Personal Selling
   b. Selling is one of the oldest professions in the world. The people who do the selling go by many names: salespeople, sales representatives, account executives, sales consultants, sales engineers, agents, district managers, and account development reps, to name just a few.
   c. People hold many stereotypes of salespeople—including some unfavorable ones. However, modern salespeople are a far cry from the unfortunate stereotypes. They listen to their customers, assess customer needs, and organize the company's efforts to solve customer problems.
   d. The term *salesperson* covers a wide range of positions.
       i. At one extreme, a salesperson might be largely an order taker, such as the department store salesperson standing behind the counter.
       ii. At the other extreme are order getters, whose positions demand creative selling and relationship building for products and services.

   The Role of the Sales Force
   e. Personal selling is the interpersonal arm of the promotion mix.
       i. It involves two-way, personal communication between salespeople and individual customers—whether face-to-face, by telephone, through video or Web conferences, or by other means.
       ii. Personal selling can be more effective than advertising in more complex selling situations.
       iii. The role of personal selling varies from company to company.
   f. The sales force serves as a critical link between a company and its customers.
       i. First, they represent the company to customers. They find and develop new customers and communicate information about the company's products and services.
       ii. At the same time, salespeople represent customers to the company, acting inside the firm as "champions" of customers' interests and managing the buyer-seller relationship.

3. **Managing the Sales Force**
   a. We define *sales force management* as the analysis, planning, implementation, and control of sales force activities.
   b. It includes designing sales force strategy and structure and recruiting, selecting, training, compensating, supervising, and evaluating the firm's salespeople. These major sales force management decisions are shown in Figure 16.1.

<u>Designing Sales Force Strategy and Structure</u>

c. Marketing managers face several sales force strategy and design questions.

    i. A company can divide up sales responsibilities along any of several lines.

        a. In the territorial sales force structure, each salesperson is assigned to an exclusive geographic area and sells the company's full line of products or services to all customers in that territory. A territorial sales organization is often supported by many levels of sales management positions.

        b. Salespeople must know their products—especially when the products are numerous and complex. This need, together with the growth of product management, has led many companies to adopt a product sales force structure, in which the sales force sells along product lines. The product structure can lead to problems, however, if a single large customer buys many different company products.

        c. More and more companies are now using a customer sales force structure, in which they organize the sales force along customer or industry lines. Separate sales forces may be set up for different industries, for serving current customers versus finding new ones, and for major accounts versus regular accounts. Organizing the sales force around customers can help a company build closer relationships with important customers.

        d. When a company sells a wide variety of products to many types of customers over a broad geographic area, it often combines several types of sales force structures. Salespeople can be specialized by customer and territory; by product and territory; by product and customer; or by territory, product, and customer. No single structure is best for all companies and situations.

    ii. Once the company has set its structure, it is ready to consider sales force size.

        a. Many companies use some form of workload approach to set sales force size.

            1. Using this approach, a company first groups accounts into different classes according to size, account status, or other factors related to the amount of effort required to maintain them.

            2. It then determines the number of salespeople needed to call on each class of accounts the desired number of times.

    iii. Sales management must also decide who will be involved in the selling effort and how various sales and sales support people will work together.

a. The company may have an outside sales force (or field sales force), an inside sales force, or both.

   1. Outside salespeople travel to call on customers. Inside salespeople conduct business from their offices via telephone or visits from prospective buyers.

   2. Inside salespeople include technical support people, sales, assistants, and telemarketers. The inside sales force frees outside salespeople to spend more time selling to major accounts and finding major new prospects.

   3. Inside salespeople may perform a wide range of functions, from direct selling and account service to customer analysis and acting as liaisons between outside salespeople and customers.

   4. Just as telemarketing is changing the way that many companies go to market, the Internet offers explosive potential for restructuring sales forces and conducting sales operations.

b. As products become more complex, and as customers grow larger and more demanding, a single salesperson simply can't handle all of a large customer's needs. Instead, most companies now are using team selling to service large, complex accounts.

   1. Companies are finding that sales teams can unearth problems, solutions, and sales opportunities that no individual salesperson could.

   2. Such teams might include experts from any area or level of the selling firm—sales, marketing, technical support services, RandD, engineering, operations, finance, and others. In many cases, the move to team selling mirrors similar changes in customers' buying organizations.

   3. Team selling does have some pitfalls. For example, selling teams can confuse or overwhelm customers who are used to working with only one salesperson. Salespeople who are used to having customers all to themselves may have trouble learning to work with and trust others on a team. Finally, difficulties in evaluating individual contributions to the team selling effort can create some sticky compensation issues.

Recruiting and Selecting Salespeople

d. At the heart of any successful sales force operation is the recruitment and selection of good salespeople.

e. The research of Gallup Management Consulting Group, a division of the well-known Gallup polling organization, suggests that the best salespeople possess four key talents: intrinsic motivation, disciplined work style, the ability to close a sale, and perhaps most important, the ability to build relationships with customers.

  i. Other skills mean little if a salesperson can't close the sale. It takes unyielding persistence.

  ii. Perhaps the most important in today's relationship-marketing environment, top salespeople are customer problem solvers and relationship builders. They have an instinctive understanding of their customers' needs.

f. When recruiting, companies should analyze the sales job itself and the characteristics of its most successful salespeople to identify the traits needed by a successful salesperson in their industry. Then, it must recruit the right salespeople.

g. The selection procedure can vary from a single informal interview to lengthy testing and interviewing.

  i. Many companies give formal tests to sales applicants.

  ii. Tests typically measure sales aptitude, analytical and organizational skills, personality traits, and other characteristics.

Training Salespeople

h. New salespeople may spend anywhere from a few weeks or months to a year or more in training. Then, most companies provide continuing sales training via seminars, sales meetings, and the Web throughout the salesperson's career.

i. Training programs have several goals.

  i. Salespeople need to know and identify with the company and its products, so most training programs begin by describing the company's objectives, organization, financial structure, facilities, and chief products and markets.

  ii. They also need to know about customers and competitors. So the training program teaches them about competitors' strategies and about different types of customers and their needs, buying motives, and buying habits.

  iii. Finally, because salespeople must know how to sell effectively, they are also trained in the basics of the selling process.

j. Today, most companies are adding Web-based training to their sales training programs. Such training may range from simple text-based product information, to Internet-based sales exercises that build sales skills, to sophisticated simulations that recreate the dynamics of real-life sales calls.

229

Compensating Salespeople

    k. Compensation is made up of several elements—a fixed amount, a variable amount, expenses, and fringe benefits.

        i. The fixed amount, usually a salary, gives the salesperson some stable income.

        ii. The variable amount, which might be commissions or bonuses based on sales performance, rewards the salesperson for greater effort and success.

        iii. Expense allowances, which repay salespeople for job-related expenses, let salespeople undertake needed and desirable selling efforts.

        iv. Fringe benefits—such as paid vacations, sickness or accident benefits, pensions, and life insurance—provide job security and satisfaction.

    l. Management must decide what mix of these compensation elements makes the most sense for each sales job.

        i. Different combinations of fixed and variable compensation give rise to four basic types of compensation plans—straight salary, straight commission, salary plus bonus, and salary plus commission.

        ii. The average plan consists of about 60 percent salary and 40 percent incentive pay.

    m. Compensation should direct the sales force toward activities that are consistent with overall marketing objectives. Table 16.1 illustrates how a company's compensation plan should reflect its overall marketing strategy.

Supervising and Motivating Salespeople

    n. Through supervision, the company directs and motivates the sales force to do a better job.

    o. Companies vary in how closely they supervise their salespeople.

        i. Many help their salespeople in identifying customer targets and setting call norms.

        ii. Some may also specify how much time the sales force should spend prospecting for new accounts and set other time management priorities.

        iii. One tool is the annual call plan that shows which customers and prospects to call on in which months and which activities to carry out.

        iv. Another tool is time-and-duty analysis. In addition to time spent selling, the salesperson spends time traveling, waiting, eating, taking breaks, and doing administrative chores.

            a. Figure 16.2 shows how salespeople spend their time. On average, actual face-to-face selling time accounts for less than 30 percent of total working time!

p. Many firms have adopted sales force automation systems, computerized sales force operations for more efficient order-entry transactions, improved customer service, and better salesperson decision-making support.

    i. Salespeople use laptops, handheld computing devices, and Web technologies, coupled with customer-contact software and customer relationship management (CRM) software, to profile customers and prospects, analyze and forecast sales, manage account relationships, schedule sales calls, make presentations, enter orders, check inventories and order status, prepare sales and expense reports, process correspondence, and carry out many other activities.

    ii. Sales force automation not only lowers sales force costs and improves productivity, but also improves the quality of sales management decisions.

    iii. Perhaps the fastest-growing sales force technology tool is the Internet. The most common uses include gathering competitive information, monitoring customer Web sites, and researching industries and specific customers.

q. Beyond directing salespeople, sales managers must also motivate them.

    i. Management can boost sales force morale and performance through its organizational climate, sales quotas, and positive incentives.

        a. Organizational climate describes the feeling that salespeople have about their opportunities, value, and rewards for a good performance.

        b. Many companies motivate their salespeople by setting quotas—standards stating the amount they should sell and how sales should be divided among the company's products. Compensation is often related to how well salespeople meet their quotas.

        c. Companies also use various positive incentives to increase sales force effort.

            1. Sales meetings provide social occasions, breaks from routine, chances to meet and talk with "company brass," and opportunities to air feelings and to identify with a larger group.

            2. Companies also sponsor sales contests to spur the sales force to make a selling effort above what would normally be expected.

Evaluating Salespeople

r. Good feedback means getting regular information about salespeople to evaluate their performance.

s. Management gets information about its salespeople in several ways.

    i. The most important source is sales reports, including weekly or monthly work plans and longer-term territory marketing plans.

    ii. Salespeople also write up their completed activities on call reports and turn in expense reports for which they are partly or wholly repaid.

    iii. Additional information comes from personal observation, customer surveys, and talks with other salespeople.

t. Using various sales force reports and other information, sales management evaluates members of the sales force.

    i. It evaluates salespeople on their ability to "plan their work and work their plan."

    ii. Formal evaluation forces management to develop and communicate clear standards for judging performance. It also provides salespeople with constructive feedback and motives them to perform well.

4. The Personal Selling Process

    a. The selling process consists of several steps that the salesperson must master. These steps focus on the goal of getting new customers and obtaining orders from them.

Steps in the Selling Process

    b. As shown in Figure 16.3, the selling process consists of seven steps.

        i. The first step in the selling process is prospecting—identifying qualified potential customers.

            a. Approaching the right potential customers is crucial to selling success.

            b. The salesperson must often approach many prospects to get just a few sales. Although the company supplies some leads, salespeople need skill in finding their own.

            c. Salespeople also need to know how to qualify leads—that is, how to identify the good ones and screen out the poor ones. Prospects can be qualified by looking at their financial ability, volume of business, special needs, location, and possibilities for growth.

        ii. Before calling on a prospect, the salesperson should learn as much as possible about the organization and its buyers. This step is known as the preapproach.

            a. The salesperson can consult standard industry and online sources, acquaintances, and others to learn about the company.

     b. The salesperson should set call objectives, which may be to qualify the prospect, to gather information, or to make an immediate sale.

     c. Another task is to decide on the best approach, which might be a personal visit, a phone call, or a letter.

     d. The best timing should be considered carefully because many prospects are busiest at certain times.

     e. Finally, the salesperson should give thought to an overall sales strategy for the account.

iii. During the approach step, the salesperson should know how to meet and greet the buyer and get the relationship off to a good start. This step involves the salesperson's appearance, opening lines, and the follow-up remarks.

iv. During the presentation step of the selling process, the salesperson tells the product "story" to the buyer, presenting customer benefits and showing how the product solves the customer's problems.

     a. The problem-solver salesperson fits better with today's marketing concept than does a hard-sell salesperson or the glad-handing extrovert.

     b. This need-satisfaction approach calls for good listening and problem-solving skills.

     c. The qualities that buyers dislike most in salespeople include being pushy, late, deceitful, and unprepared or disorganized.

     d. The qualities they value most include empathy, good listening, honesty, dependability, thoroughness, and follow-through.

     e. Today, advanced presentation technologies allow for full multimedia presentations to only one or a few people.

v. Customers almost always have objections during the presentation or when asked to place an order.

     a. The problem can be either logical or psychological, and objections are often unspoken.

     b. In handling objections, the salesperson should use a positive approach, seek out hidden objections, ask the buyer to clarify any objections, take objections as opportunities to provide more information, and turn the objections into reasons for buying.

vi. After handling the prospect's objections, the salesperson now tries to close the sale. Some salespeople do not get around to closing or do not handle it well.

     a. They may lack confidence, feel guilty about asking for the order, or fail to recognize the right moment to close the sale.

     b. Salespeople should know how to recognize closing signals from the buyer, including physical actions, comments, and questions.

      c. Salespeople can use one of several closing techniques. They can ask for the order, review points of agreement, offer to help write up the order, ask whether the buyer wants this model or that one, or note that the buyer will lose out if the order is not placed now.

   vii. The last step in the selling process—follow-up—is necessary if the salesperson wants to ensure customer satisfaction and repeat business.

      a. Right after closing, the salesperson should complete any details on delivery time, purchase terms, and other matters.

      b. The salesperson should schedule a follow-up call when the initial order is received, to make sure that there is proper installation, instruction, and servicing.

Personal Selling and Customer Relationship Management

c. The principles of personal selling as just described are transaction-oriented—their aim is to help salespeople close a specific sale with a customer. But in many cases, the company is not seeking simply a sale: It has targeted a major customer that it would like to win and keep.

d. The sales force usually plays an important role in building and managing profitable customer relationships.

e. Today's large customers favor suppliers who can sell and deliver a coordinated set of products and services to many locations, and who can work closely with customer teams to improve products and services.

5. **Sales Promotion**

   a. Sales promotion consists of short-term incentives to encourage purchase or sales of a product or service. Whereas advertising offers reasons to buy a product or service, sale promotion offers reasons to buy now.

Rapid Growth of Sales Promotion

b. Sales promotion tools are used by most organizations, including manufacturers, distributors, retailers, and not-for-profit institutions.

    i. They are targeted toward final buyers (consumer promotions), retailers and wholesalers (trade promotions), business customers (business promotions), and members of the sales force (sales for promotions).

c. Several factors have contributed to the rapid growth of sales promotion, particularly in consumer markets.

    i. First, inside the company, product managers face greater pressures to increase their current sales, and promotion is viewed as an effective short-run sales tool.

   ii. Second, externally, the company faces more competition and competing brands are less differentiated. Increasingly, competitors are using sales promotion to help differentiate their offers.

      iii. Third, advertising efficiency has declined because of rising costs, media clutter, and legal restraints.

      iv. Finally, consumers have become more deal oriented, and ever-larger retailers are demanding more deals from manufacturers.

d. The growing use of sales promotion has resulted in promotion clutter, similar to advertising clutter. Consumers are increasingly tuning out promotions, weakening their ability to trigger immediate purchase.

<u>Sales Promotion Objectives</u>

e. Sales promotion objectives vary widely.

      i. Sellers may use consumer promotions to increase short-term sales or to help build long-term market share.

      ii. Objectives for trade promotions include getting retailers to carry new items and more inventory, getting them to advertise the product and give it more shelf space, and getting them to buy ahead.

      iii. For the sales force, objectives include getting more sales force support for current or new products or getting salespeople to sign up new accounts.

      iv. Sales promotions are usually used together with advertising, personal selling, or other promotion mix tools.

f. In general, rather than creating only short-term sales or temporary brand switching, sales promotions should help to reinforce the product's position and build long-term customer relationships. Increasingly, marketers are avoiding "quick fix," price-only promotions in favor of promotions designed to build brand equity.

      i. Even price promotions can be designed to help build customer relationships. Examples include all of the "frequency marketing programs" and loyalty clubs that have mushroomed in recent years.

<u>Major Sales Promotion Tools</u>

g. Many tools can be used to accomplish sales promotion objectives.

      i. The main consumer promotion tools include the following:

         a. Samples are offers of a trial amount of a product. Sampling is the most effective—but most expensive—way to introduce a new product.

            1. Some samples are free; for others, the company charges a small amount to offset its cost.

            2. The sample might be delivered door-to-door, sent by mail, handed out in a store, attached to another product, or featured in an ad.

            3. Sometimes, samples are combined into sample packs that can then be used to promote other products and services.

         b. Coupons are certificates that give buyers a savings when they purchase specified products.

1. Coupons can promote early trial of a new brand or stimulate sales of a mature brand.

2. As a result of coupon clutter, redemption rates have been declining in recent years. Thus, most major consumer goods companies are issuing fewer coupons and targeting them more carefully.

3. Marketers are also cultivating new outlets for distributing coupons, such as supermarket shelf dispensers, electronic point-of-sale coupon printers, or "paperless coupon systems."

c. Cash refund offers (or rebates) are like coupons except that the price reduction occurs after the purchase rather than at the retail outlet. The consumer sends a "proof of purchase" to the manufacturer, who then refunds part of the purchase price by mail.

d. Price packs (also called *cents-off deals*) offer consumers savings off the regular price of a product.

1. The reduced prices are marked by the producer directly on the label or package.

2. Price packs can be single packages sold at a reduced price, or two related products banded together.

3. Price packs are very effective—even more so than coupons—in stimulating short-term sales.

e. Premiums are goods offered either free or at a low cost as an incentive to buy a product. A premium may come inside the package (in-pack), outside the package (on-pack), or through the mail.

f. Advertising specialties, also called *promotional products,* are useful articles imprinted with an advertiser's name, logo, or message that are given as gifts to consumers.

g. Patronage rewards are cash or other awards offered for the regular use of a certain company's products or services.

h. Point-of-purchase (POP) promotions include displays and demonstrations that take place at the point of purchase or sale.

i. Contests, sweepstakes, and games give consumers the chance to win something, such as cash, trips, or goods, by luck or through extra effort.

1. A contest calls for consumers to submit an entry to be judged by a panel that will select the best entries.

2. A sweepstakes calls for consumers to submit their names for a drawing.

3. A game presents consumers with something every time they buy that may or may not help them win a prize.

    ii. Manufacturers direct more sales promotion dollars toward retailers and wholesalers (78 percent) than to consumers (22 percent). Trade promotion tools can persuade resellers to carry a brand, give it shelf space, promote it in advertising, and push it to consumers.

    iii. Many of the tools used for consumer promotions can also be used as trade promotions.

        a. Or the manufacturer may offer a straight discount off the list price on each case purchased during a stated period of time (also called a *price-off, off-invoice,* or *off-list*).

        b. Manufacturers also may offer an allowance (usually so much off per case) in return for the retailer's agreement to feature the manufacturer's products in some way.

            1. An advertising allowance compensates retailers for advertising the product.

            2. A display allowance compensates them for using special displays.

        c. Manufacturers may offer free goods, which are extra cases of merchandise, to resellers who buy a certain quantity or who feature a certain flavor or size.

        d. They may offer push money—cash or gifts to dealers or their sales forces to "push" the manufacturer's goods.

        e. Manufacturers may give retailers free specialty advertising items that carry the company's name.

    iv. Companies spend billions of dollars each year on promotion to industrial customers. These business promotion tools are used to generate business leads, stimulate purchases, reward customers, and motivate salespeople. Business promotion includes many of the same tools used for consumer or trade promotions.

        a. Many companies and trade associates organize conventions and trade shows to promote their products. Firms selling to the industry show their products at the trade show.

            1. Vendors receive many benefits, such as opportunities to find new sales leads, contact customers, introduce new products, meet new customers, sell more to present customers, and educate customers with publications and audiovisual materials.

            2. Trade shows also help companies reach many prospects not reached through their sales forces.

        b. A sales contest is a contest for salespeople or dealers to motivate them to increase their sales performance over a given period.

            1. Sales contests motivate and recognize good company performers, who may receive trips, cash prizes, or other gifts.

2. Some companies award points for performance that the receiver can turn in for any of a variety of prizes.

Developing the Sales Promotion Program

h. The marketer must make several other decisions in order to define the full sales promotion program.

   i. First, the marketer must decide on the size of the incentive. A certain minimum incentive is necessary if the promotion is to succeed; a larger incentive will produce more sales response.

   ii. The marketer must also set conditions for participation. Incentives might be offered to everyone or only to select groups.

   iii. The marketer must then decide how to promote and distribute the promotion program itself.

   iv. The length of the promotion is also important. If the sales promotion period is too short, many prospects (who may not be buying during that time) will miss it. If the promotion is too long, the deal will lose some of its "act now" force.

   v. Evaluation is also very important.

      a. The most common evaluation method is to compare sales before, during, and after a promotion.

      b. Consumer research would also show the kinds of people who responded to the promotion and what they did after it ended.

         1. Surveys can provide information on how many consumers recall the promotion, what they thought of it, how many took advantage of it, and how it affected their buying.

         2. Sales promotions also can be evaluated through experiments that vary factors such as incentive value, length, and distribution method.

Student Exercises

1.   Key Term: Personal Selling

Personal selling is the personal presentation by the firm's sales force for the purpose of making sales and building customer relationships. Today, most salespeople are well-educated, well-trained professionals who work to build and maintain long-term customer relationships. To get an idea of the current state of professionalism in personal selling take a look at the Journal of Personal Selling and Sales Management. Specifically, clink on the link that gives a description of the journal. (http://jpssm.org/general/jrnldesc.htm)

2.   Key Term: Salesperson

A salesperson is an individual representing a company to customers by performing one or more of the following activities: prospecting, communicating, selling, servicing, information gathering, and relationship building. The term "salesperson" covers a wide range of positions. Think about the salespeople at your favorite department store in the local mall. What functions to they really fulfill?

3.   Key Term: Sales Force Management

Sales force management is the analysis, planning, implementation, and control of sales force activities. It includes designing sales force strategy and structure and recruiting, selecting, training, supervising, compensating, and evaluating the firm's salespeople. Look at Limited Brands (www.limited.com), parent company to seven retail brands including Limited Stores and Victoria's Secret. How does Limited Brands use their website to assist in sales force management?

4.   Key Term: Territorial Sales Force Structure

A sales force organization that assigns each salesperson to an exclusive geographic territory in which that salesperson sells the company's full line is known as a territorial sales force structure. Take a look at IMS Health (www.imshealth.com), a health care consulting service. Look closely at the information they provide for the use of a territorial sales force.

5.   Key Term: Product Sales Force Structure

Product sales force structure is a sales force organization under which salespeople specialize in selling only a portion of the company's products or lines. Under such a structure, salespeople become specialists in only a portion of the company's products; however, the depth of knowledge they have is great. Find a company you believe would be well suited for use of a product sales force structure.

6.   Key Term: Customer Sales Force Structure

Customer sales force structure is a sales force organization under which salespeople specialize in selling only to certain customers or industries. Separate sales forces may be set up for different industries. Organizing the sales force around customers can help a company build closer relationships with important customers. Take a look at Wal-Mart Stores (www.walmart.com). How have companies used customer sales force structure to build closer relations with the retailing giant?

7.   Key Term: Outside Sales Force

Outside sales people who travel to call on customers in the field are known as an outside sales force (or field sales force). Compared to a sales call from an inside sales person, outside sales calls are very expensive and time consuming, but sometimes necessary to deliver adequate customer contact. Find a company that you believe would employ and outside sales force.

8.   Key Term: Inside Sales Force

An inside sales force is comprised of inside salespeople who conduct business from their offices via telephone, the internet, or visits from prospective buyers. Some inside salespeople provide support services for the outside sales forces. Other inside salespeople do much more than just provide support. Look at Office Depot's educational institution's webpage (www.officedepot.com). Examine how they make good use of an inside sales force to service the educational market.

9.   Key Term: Prospecting

Prospecting is the first step in the personal selling process. This is the stage of the process in which the salesperson identifies qualified potential customers. If you were a company salesperson for Montecristo cigars (www.montecristo.com), looking for a new outlet, what all would go into your prospecting?

10.   Key Term: Sales Promotion

A sales promotion is a short-term incentive to encourage the purchase or sale of a product or service. Whereas advertising offers reasons to buy a product or service, sales promotion offers reason to buy NOW. Find an example of a sales promotion.

Marketing ADventure Exercises

1.   Ad Interpretation Challenge: Personal Selling
        Ad: Student Choice

Personal selling is the personal presentation by the firm's sales force for the purpose of making sales and building customer relationships. Today, most salespeople are well-educated, well-trained professionals who work to build and maintain long-term customer relationships. Choose an ad for a product or service that you believe would be best served through personal selling.

2.   Ad Interpretation Challenge: Salesperson
       Ad: General Retail – Target

A salesperson is an individual representing a company to customers by performing one of more of the following activities: prospecting, communicating, selling, servicing, information gathering, and relationship building. The term 'salesperson' covers a wide range of positions. At one extreme, a salesperson might be largely an order taker. At the other extreme are order getters. What type of salesperson do you believe Target Stores would typically employ?

3.   Ad Interpretation Challenge: Territorial Sales Force Structure
       Ad: Food & Beverage – Heinz

A sales force organization that assigns each salesperson to an exclusive geographic territory in which that salesperson sells the company's full line is known as a territorial sales force structure. Why would H.J. Heinz Company choose to use a territorial sales force structure?

4.   Ad Interpretation Challenge: Product Sales Force Structure
       Ad: Electronics - Sony

Product sales force structure is a sales force organization under which salespeople specialize in selling only a portion of the company's products or lines. Under such a structure, salespeople become specialists in only a portion of the company's products; however, the depth of knowledge they have is great. Consider Sony. Why would Sony choose to use a product sales force structure?

5.   Ad Interpretation Challenge: Customer Sales Force Structure
       Ad: Apparel – Levi's

A sales force organization under which salespeople specialize in selling only to certain customers or industries is known as a customer sales force structure. Separate sales forces may be set up for different industries or for servicing major accounts versus regular accounts. Think about Levi Strauss & Company. Under what conditions can you see this company using a customer sales force structure?

6.   Ad Interpretation Challenge: Inside Sales Force
       Ad: Financial – H&R Block

Inside salespeople who conduct business from their offices via telephone, the internet, or visits from prospective buyers are known as the inside sales force. Why would the sales force of H&R Block be characterized as an inside sales force?

7.   Ad Interpretation Challenge: Team Selling
        Ad: Student Choice

Team selling occurs when a company uses teams of people from sales, marketing, engineering, finance, technical support, and possibly even upper management to service large, complex accounts. Find an ad for a product (or company) that you believe could make good use of the team selling concept.

8.   Ad Interpretation Challenge: Prospecting
        Ad: Services & B2B - EMS

Prospecting is the first step in the personal selling process. This is the stage of the process in which the salesperson identifies qualified potential customers. Prospects can be qualified by looking at their financial ability, special needs, location, and possibilities for growth. Look at the EMS Urgent Mail ad. If you were EMS, what features would you be looking for in your prospects?

9.   Ad Interpretation Challenge: Presentation
        Ad: Autos – Mercedes Keys

The presentation is the step in the selling process in which the salesperson tells the "product story" to the buyer, highlighting customer benefits. Look at this ad for Mercedes. If you were using this ad to take the place of the salesperson presentation, what "product story" would this ad tell?

10.   Ad Interpretation Challenge: Sales Promotion
        Ad: Food & Beverage - Snickers

A sales promotion is a short-tem incentive to encourage the purchase or sale of a product or service. What type of sales promotion could Snickers use to encourage the purchase of their product?

Chapter 17
Direct and Online Marketing: Building Direct Customer Relationships

Learning Objectives

1. Define direct marketing and discuss its benefits to customers and companies.
2. Identify and discuss the major forms of direct marketing.
3. Explain how companies have responded to the Internet and other powerful new technologies with online marketing strategies.
4. Discuss how companies go about conducting online marketing to profitably deliver more value to customers.
5. Overview the public policy and ethical issues presented by direct marketing.

Chapter Overview

Today, there is a trend of moving away from targeting broadly with standardized messages and marketing efforts. More and more companies are adopting direct marketing as a primary approach. The desire to build one-to-one relationships is very strong. The second part of this chapter examines the nature, role, and growing applications of direct marketing.

Direct marketing consists of direct communications with carefully targeted individual consumers to obtain an immediate response. Interactivity is essential to this process. The marketing manager must remember that direct marketing is not new. Catalog companies, direct mailers, and telemarketers have been using the approach for years. However, improved database technologies and new media (computers, modems, fax machines, e-mail, the Internet, and online services) have changed the direction and nature of direct marketing. Most direct marketers see direct marketing as playing an even broader role than simply selling products and services.

Database marketing is most frequently used by business-to-business marketers and service retailers (hotels, banks, and airlines). Companies use their databases to identify prospects, to make decisions on which consumers will receive a particular offer, to deepen customer loyalty, and to reactivate customer purchases.

The chapter discusses the major forms of direct marketing communication—direct-mail marketing, catalog marketing, telephone marketing, direct-response television marketing, kiosk marketing, and various forms of direct marketing taking advantage of new technologies. Each method is explored in detail.

Another form of direct marketing, online marketing, is treated in great depth in the latter half of this chapter. To illustrate how the new digital age has developed, the chapter focuses on four major Internet domains—B2C (business to consumer), B2B (business to business), C2C (consumers to consumers), and C2B (consumers to businesses).

The reader will notice that companies of all types are now engaged in online marketing. Brick-and-mortar (brick-only), click-only, and click-and-mortar marketers are illustrated so various strategies and successes can be identified. Few companies today have not considered moving to the Net to conduct business. The methods selected to do this simply did not exist only a few years ago. The chapter demonstrates that by creating a Web site, placing ads online, setting up or participating in Web communities, or using online e-mail, a firm cannot only expand business but also reach out to the global marketplace.

Online marketing continues to offer great promise for the future. Its most ardent apostles still envision a time when the Internet and online marketing will replace magazines, newspapers, and even stores as sources for information and buying. To get to this place, however, certain challenges must be met. Limited consumer exposure and buying, skewed user demographics and psychographics, chaos and clutter, security, and ethical concerns are chief among the challenges. Despite these challenges, companies large and small are quickly integrating online marketing into their marketing strategies and mixes.

The chapter concludes with a discussion of how integrated direct marketing, public policy, and ethical issues will shape the advancement of direct marketing. The industry must not only establish standards but must learn to police itself (or government will do it for them).

Chapter Outline

1. **Introduction**
   a. Michael Dell took his 1984 computer business from college dorm room to "world's largest computer maker" in just two decades. The company dominates the PC industry.
   b. Despite expert skepticism, Dell has succeeded by selling PCs and accessories directly to customers.
   c. The direct model allows the following customer value benefits: product customization, low prices, fast delivery, and award-winning customer service.
   d. The same direct model that has contributed to Dell's success is now presenting barriers to progress.
   e. With the trend toward more narrowly targeted or one-to-one marketing, many companies are adopting direct marketing, either as a primary marketing approach or as a supplement to other approaches.
   f. Direct marketing consists of direct connections with carefully targeted individual consumers to both obtain an immediate response and cultivate lasting customer relationships.

2.   **The New Direct marketing Model**
   a.   Today, fired by rapid advances in database technologies and new marketing media—especially the Internet—direct marketing has undergone a dramatic transformation.
   b.   Most companies still use direct marketing as a supplementary channel or medium for marketing their goods. However, for many companies today, direct marketing is more than just a supplementary channel or medium.
      i.   For these companies, direct marketing—especially in its newest transformation, Internet marketing and online marketing—constitutes a new and complete model for doing business.
      ii. More than just another marketing channel or advertising medium, this new direct model is rapidly changing the way companies think about building relationships with customers.
      iii. Whereas most companies use direct marketing and the Internet as supplemental approaches, firms employing the direct model use it as the only approach.

3.   **Growth and Benefits of Direct Marketing**
   a.   Whether employed as a complete business model or as a supplement to a broader integrated marketing mix, direct marketing brings many benefits to both buyers and sellers.

Benefits to Buyers
   b.   For buyers, direct marketing is convenient, easy to use, and private.
      i.   From the comfort of their homes or offices, they can browse mail catalogs or company Web sites at any time of the day or night.
      ii. Direct marketing gives buyers ready access to a wealth of products and information, at home and around the globe.
      iii. Direct marketing channels give buyers access to a wealth of comparative information about companies, products, and competitors.
      iv. Finally, direct marketing is immediate and interactive—buyers can interact with sellers by phone or on the seller's Web site to create exactly the configuration of information, products, or services they desire, then order them on the spot.

Benefits to Sellers
   c.   For sellers, direct marketing is a powerful tool for building customer relationships.
      i.   Using database marketing, today's marketers can target small groups or individual consumers, tailor offers to individual needs, and promote these offers through personalized communications.
      ii. Direct marketing can also be timed to reach prospects at just the right moment. Because of its one-to-one, interactive nature, the Internet is an especially potent direct marketing tool.

iii. Direct marketing can offer sellers a low-cost, efficient alternative for reaching their markets.

iv. Direct marketing can also offer greater flexibility by allowing marketers to make ongoing adjustments to their prices, programs, and promotions.

d. As a result of these advantages to both buyers and sellers, direct marketing has become the fastest-growing form of marketing. Sales through traditional direct marketing channels (telephone marketing, direct mail, catalogs, direct-response television, and others) have been growing rapidly.

4. **Customer Databases and Direct Marketing**

a. Effective direct marketing begins with a good customer database. A customer database is an organized collection of comprehensive data about individual customers or prospects, including geographic, demographic, psychographic, and behavioral data. The database can be used to locate good potential customers, tailor products and services to the special needs of targeted consumers, and maintain long-term customer relationships.

i. A customer mailing list is simply a set of names, addresses, and telephone numbers.

ii. A customer database contains much more information.

iii. In business-to-business marketing, the salesperson's customer profile might contain the products and services the customer has bought, past volumes and prices, key contacts, competitive suppliers, status of current contracts, estimated customer spending for the next few years, and assessments of competitive strengths and weaknesses in selling and servicing the account.

iv. In consumer marketing, the customer database might contain a customer's demographics, psychographics, buying behavior, and other relevant information.

b. Armed with the information in their databases, companies can identify small groups of customers to receive fine-tuned marketing offers and communications.

c. Companies use their databases in many ways.

i. They can use a database to identify prospects and generate sales leads by advertising products or offers.

ii. Companies can use a database to deepen customer loyalty—they can build customers' interest and enthusiasm by remembering buyer preferences and sending appropriate information, gifts, or other materials.

iii. Or they can use the database to profile customers based on previous purchasing and to decide which customers should receive particular offers.

d. Like many other marketing tools, database marketing requires a special investment.

       i. Companies must invest in computer hardware, database software, analytical programs, communication links, and skilled personnel.

      ii. The database system must be user-friendly and available to various marketing groups, including those in product and brand management, new-product development, advertising and promotion, direct mail, telemarketing, Web marketing, field sales, order fulfillment, and customer service.

     iii. A well-managed database should lead to sales gains that will more than cover its costs.

5.   **Forms of Direct Marketing**

    a. The major forms of direct marketing are shown in Figure 17.1.

Direct-Mail Marketing

    b. Direct-mail marketing involves sending an offer, announcement, reminder, or other item to a person at a particular address.

       i. Using highly selective mailing lists, direct marketers send out millions of mail pieces each year.

      ii. Direct mail accounts for nearly 24 percent of all direct marketing media expenditures and more than 32 percent of direct marketing sales.

     iii. Direct mail is well suited to direct, one-to-one communication. It permits high target-market selectivity, can be personalized, is flexible, and allows easy measurement of results. Although the cost per thousand people reached is higher than with mass media such as television or magazines, the people who are reached are much better prospects.

     iv. The direct-mail industry constantly seeks new methods and approaches. For example, CDs are now among the fastest-growing direct-mail media.

      v. Until recently, all mail was paper based and handled by the U.S. Post Office or delivery services. Recently, however, three new forms of mail delivery have become popular: fax mail, e-mail, and voice mail.

     vi. These new forms deliver direct mail at incredible speed compared to the post office's "snail mail" pace. Yet, much like mail delivered through traditional channels, they may be resented as "junk mail" if sent to people who have no interest in them.

Catalog Marketing

    c. Advances in technology, along with the move toward personalized, one-to-one marketing, have resulted in exciting changes in catalog marketing.

       i. With the stampede to the Internet, more and more catalogs are going electronic. Most print catalogers have added Web-based catalogs to their marketing mixes, and a variety of new Web-only catalogers have emerged.

    ii. Ninety-seven percent of all catalog companies now present merchandise and take orders over the Internet. Web-based catalogs present a number of benefits over printed catalogs.

    iii. Web-based catalogs also present various challenges.

<u>Telephone Marketing</u>

d. Telephone marketing—using the telephone to sell directly to consumers and business customers—has become the major direct marketing communication tool.

    i. Telephone marketing now accounts for more than 39 percent of all direct marketing media expenditures and 35 percent of direct marketing sales.

    ii. Marketers use outbound telephone marketing to sell directly to consumers and businesses.

    iii. Inbound toll-free 800 numbers are used to receive orders from television and print ads, direct mail, or catalogs.

    iv. Properly designed and targeted telemarketing provides many benefits, including purchasing convenience and increased product and service information.

    v. However, the explosion in unsolicited telephone marketing has annoyed many consumers. Lawmakers around the country have responded with legislation ranging from banning unsolicited telemarketing calls during certain hours to letting households sign up for "Do Not Call" lists. Most telemarketers are recognizing such negative reactions and support some action against random and poorly targeted telemarketing.

<u>Direct-Response Television Marketing</u>

e. Direct-response television marketing takes one of two major forms.

    i. The first is direct-response advertising. Direct marketers air television spots, often 60 or 120 seconds long, that persuasively describe a product and give customers a toll-free number for ordering.

    ii. Television viewers often encounter 30-minute advertising programs, or infomercials, for a single product.

    iii. Some successful direct-response ads run for years and become classics.

    iv. Many companies have begun using infomercials to sell their wares over the phone, refer customers to retailers, send out coupons and product information, or attract buyers to their Web sites.

    v. Direct response TV commercials are usually cheaper to make and the media purchase is less costly. Moreover, results are easily measured. Unlike most media campaigns, direct-response ads always include a 1-800 number or Web address, making it easier for marketers to measure the impact of their pitches.

    vi. Home shopping channels, another form of direct-response television marketing, are television programs or entire channels dedicated to selling goods and services. With widespread distribution on cable and satellite television, the top three shopping networks combined now reach 248 million homes worldwide, selling more than $4 billion of goods each year.

Kiosk Marketing

f. Some companies place information and ordering machines—called kiosks (in contrast to vending machines that dispense actual products)—in stores, airports, and other locations.

    i. Business marketers also use kiosks.

    ii. As with about everything else these days, kiosks are also going online, as many companies merge the powers of the real and virtual worlds.

New Digital Direct Marketing Technologies

g. Because of various new technologies, direct marketers can reach and interact with consumers in a number of new ways.

    i. Mobile phone marketing has emerged as almost 200 million Americans now subscribe to a wireless service.

    ii. By 2010, U.S. podcasts will reach 50 million people. Podcast listeners and vodcast viewers tend to be higher income individuals.

    iii. Interactive TV is poised to grow as a direct marketing medium.

6. Online Marketing

Marketing and the Internet

a. Online marketing is the fastest-growing form of direct marketing. The digital age has opened the door for this form of direct marketing.

b. The Internet, a vast public Web of computer networks, connects users of all types all around the world to each other and to an amazingly large "information repository."

c. With the creation of the World Wide Web and Web browsers in the 1990s, the Internet was transformed from a mere communication tool into a certifiably revolutionary technology. Last year, Internet penetration in the United States reached 64 percent, with more than 205 million people now using the Internet.

Online Marketing Domains

d. The four major online marketing domains are shown in Figure 17.2.

e. The popular press has paid the most attention to B2C (business-to-consumer) online marketing—the online selling of goods and services to final consumers. Despite some gloomy predictions, online consumer buying continues to grow at a healthy rate.

      i. Today, almost two-thirds of U.S. households surf the Internet. And each year, more than 13 million Americans access the Internet for the first time.

     ii. Thus, increasingly, the Internet provides e-marketers with access to a broad range of demographic segments.

   iii. Growing Internet diversity continues to open new online marketing targeting opportunities for marketers. For example, the Web now reaches consumers in all age groups.

    iv. Internet consumers differ from traditional offline consumers in their approaches to buying and in their responses to marketing.

       a. The exchange process via the Internet has become more customer initiated and customer controlled.

       b. People who use the Internet place greater value on information and tend to respond negatively to messages aimed only at selling.

       c. Traditional marketing targets a somewhat passive audience. In contrast, e-marketing targets people who actively select which Web sites they will visit and what marketing information they will receive about which products and under what conditions.

     v. Consumers can find a Web site for buying almost anything. The Internet is most useful for products and services when the shopper seeks greater ordering convenience or lower costs. The Internet also provides great value to buyers looking for information about differences in product features and value.

f. Consumer goods sales via the Web are dwarfed by B2B (business-to-business) online marketing.

      i. In 2003, worldwide B2B online marketing reached almost $4 trillion, compared with just $282 billion in 2000.

     ii. One study estimates that as much as one-third of all U.S. B2B spending will occur online by 2006.

   iii. Most major business-to-business marketers now offer product information, customer purchasing, and customer support services online.

    iv. Some B2B online marketing takes place in open trading exchanges—huge e-marketspaces in which buyers and sellers find each other online, share information, and complete transactions efficiently.

     v. Increasingly, online sellers are setting up their own private trading exchanges. Open trading exchanges facilitate transactions between a wide range of online buyers and sellers. In contrast, a private trading exchange links a particular seller with its own trading partners.

g. Much C2C (consumer-to-consumer) online marketing and communication occurs on the Web between interested parties over a wide range of products and subjects. In some cases, the Internet provides an excellent means by which consumers can buy or exchange goods or information directly with one another.

h. Such C2C sites give people access to much larger audiences than the local flea market or newspaper classifieds (which, by the way, are now also going online).

i. In other cases, C2C involves interchanges of information through Internet forums that appeal to specific special-interest groups.

    i. Such activities may be organized for commercial or noncommercial purposes.

    ii. An example is Web logs, or *blogs*, which are growing in popularity and offer opportunities for individuals to exchange information on almost any topic.

    iii. Many marketers are now tapping into blogs as a medium for reaching carefully targeted consumers.

j. C2C means that online visitors don't just consume product information—increasingly, they create it. They join Internet interest groups to share information, with the result that "word of Web" is joining "word of mouth" as an important buying influence.

k. The final online marketing domain is C2B (consumer-to-business) online marketing. Thanks to the Internet, today's consumers are finding it easier to communicate with companies. Most companies now invite prospects and customers to send in suggestions and questions via company Web sites.

Types of Online Marketers

l. Companies of all types are now engaged in online marketing. The different types of online marketers are shown in Figure 17.3.

m. The Internet gave birth to a new species of online marketers—the click-only dot-coms—that operate only online without any brick-and-mortar presence. In addition, most traditional brick-and-mortar companies have now added online marketing operations, transforming themselves into click-and-mortar companies.

n. Click-only companies come in many shapes and sizes.

    i. They include e-tailers, dot-coms that sell products and services directly to final buyers via the Internet. This group also includes search engines and portals such as Yahoo!, Google, and Excite that began as search engines and later added services such as news, weather, stock reports, entertainment, and storefronts, hoping to become the first port of entry to the Internet.

    ii. Internet service providers (ISPs) such as AOL and Earthlink are click-only companies that provide Internet and e-mail connections for a fee.

   iii. Transaction sites, such as the auction site eBay, take commissions for transactions conducted on their sites.

   iv. Various content sites provide financial, research, and other information.

   v. Finally, enabler sites provide the hardware and software that enable Internet communication and commerce.

o. The hype surrounding such click-only Web businesses reached astronomical levels during the "dot-com gold rush" of the late 1990s, when avid investors drove dot-com stock prices to dizzying heights.

   i. Dot-coms failed for many reasons. Some rushed into the market without proper research or planning.

   ii. Many relied too heavily on spin and hype instead of developing sound marketing strategies.

   iii. The dot-coms tended to devote too much effort to acquiring new customers instead of building loyalty and purchase frequency among current customers.

   iv. At the same time, many click-only dot-coms are surviving and even prospering in today's marketspace.

p. At first, many established companies moved quickly to open Web sites providing information about their companies and products.

   i. However, most resisted adding online marketing to their sites. They worried that this would produce channel conflict—that selling their products or services online would be competing with their offline retailers and agents.

   ii. These companies struggled with the question of how to conduct online sales without cannibalizing the sales of their own stores, resellers, or agents.

   iii. However, they soon realized that the risks of losing business to online competitors were even greater than the risks of angering channel partners. If they didn't cannibalize these sales, online competitors soon would.

   iv. Thus, most established brick-and-mortar companies are now prospering as click-and-mortar companies.

     a. Most click-and-mortar marketers have found ways to resolve channel conflicts.

     b. Despite potential channel conflict issues, many click-and-mortar companies are now having more online success than their click-only competitors.

   v. What gives the click-and-mortar companies an advantage? They have large customer bases, deeper industry knowledge and experience, and good relationships with key suppliers. By combining online marketing and established brick-and-mortar operations, they can offer customers more options.

Setting Up an Online Marketing Presence

q. Companies can conduct online marketing in any of the four ways shown in Figure 17.4.

r. For most companies, the first step in conducting online marketing is to create a Web site.

    i. Web sites vary greatly in purpose and content. The most basic type is a corporate Web site.

        a. These sites are designed to build customer goodwill and to supplement other sales channels, rather than to sell the company's products directly.

        b. Corporate Web sites typically offer a rich variety of information and other features in an effort to answer customer questions, build closer customer relationships, and generate excitement about the company.

    ii. Other companies create a marketing Web site.

        a. These sites engage consumers in an interaction that will move them closer to a direct purchase or other marketing outcome.

        b. Such sites might include a catalog, shopping tips, and promotional features such as coupons, sales events, or contests.

        c. B2B marketers also make good use of marketing Web sites.

    iii. Creating a Web site is one thing; getting people to visit the site is another. The key is to create enough value and excitement to get consumers to come to the site, stick around, and come back again.

        a. Many online marketers spend heavily on good old-fashioned advertising and other offline marketing avenues to attract visitors to their sites.

        b. For low-interest products, the company can create a corporate Web site to answer customer questions, build goodwill and excitement, supplement selling efforts through other channels, and collect customer feedback.

        c. A key challenge is designing a Web site that is attractive on first view and interesting enough to encourage repeat visits. To attract new visitors and to encourage revisits, suggests one expert, online marketers should pay close attention to the seven Cs of effective Web site design.

    iv. At the very least, a Web site should be easy to use and physically attractive. Ultimately, however, Web sites must also be useful.

    v. From time to time, a company needs to reassess its Web site's attractiveness and usefulness. One way is to invite the opinion of site-design experts. But a better way is to have users themselves evaluate what they like and dislike about the site.

s. Online marketers can use online advertising to build their Internet brands or to attract visitors to their Web sites.

    i. Online ads pop up while Internet users are surfing online.

     a. Such ads include banner ads and tickers (banners that move across the screen).

     b. Other online ad formats include skyscrapers (tall, skinny ads at the side of a Web page) and rectangles (boxes that are much larger than a banner). Interstitials are online ads that pop up between changes on a Web site.

     c. Content sponsorships are another form of Internet promotion. Many companies gain name exposure on the Internet by sponsoring special content on various Web sites, such as news or financial information.

     d. Online marketers can also go online with microsites, limited areas on the Web managed and paid for by an external company.

     e. Finally, online marketers use viral marketing, the Internet version of word-of-mouth marketing. Viral marketing involves creating an e-mail message or other marketing event that is so infectious that customers will want to pass it along to their friends.

t. The popularity of forums and newsgroups has resulted in a rash of commercially sponsored Web sites called Web communities, which take advantage of the C2C properties of the Internet. Such sites allow members to congregate online and exchange views on issues of common interest.

     i. Visitors to these Internet neighborhoods develop a strong sense of community. Such communities are attractive to advertisers because they draw frequent, lengthy visits from consumers with common interests and well-defined demographics.

     ii. Web communities can be either social or work related.

u. E-mail has exploded onto the scene as an important e-marketing tool. A recent study of ad, brand, and marketing managers found that nearly half of all the B2B and B2C companies surveyed use e-mail marketing to reach customers.

     i. To compete effectively in this ever-more-cluttered e-mail environment, marketers are designing "enriched" e-mail messages—animated, interactive, and personalized messages full of streaming audio and video.

     ii. Then, they are targeting these attention-grabbers more carefully to those who want them and will act upon them.

     iii. As with other types of online marketing, companies must be careful that they don't cause resentment among Internet users who are already overloaded with "junk e-mail." The recent explosion of spam—unsolicited, unwanted commercial e-mail messages that clog up our e-mail boxes—has produced consumer frustration and anger.

The Promise and Challenge of Online Marketing

v. Online marketing continues to offer both great promise and many challenges for the future.

w. To be sure, online marketing will become a successful business model for some companies. However, for most companies, online marketing will remain just one important approach to the marketplace that works alongside other approaches in a fully integrated marketing mix.

7. **Integrated Direct Marketing**

a. Too often, a company's individual direct marketing efforts are not well integrated with one another or with other elements of its marketing and promotion mixes.

b. A more powerful approach is integrated direct marketing, which involves using carefully coordinated multiple-media, multiple-stage campaigns.

i. Such campaigns can greatly improve response. Whereas a direct-mail piece alone might generate a 2 percent response, adding a Web site and toll-free phone number might raise the response rate by 50 percent.

ii. Then, a well-designed outbound telemarketing effort might lift response by an additional 500 percent.

iii. Suddenly, a 2 percent response has grown to 15 percent or more by adding interactive marketing channels to a regular mailing.

8. **Public Policy and Ethical Issues in Direct Marketing**

a. Direct marketers and their customers usually enjoy mutually rewarding relationships. Occasionally, however, a darker side emerges.

Irritation, Unfairness, Deception, and Fraud

b. Direct marketing excesses sometimes annoy or offend consumers.

i. Most of us dislike direct-response TV commercials that are too loud, too long, and too insistent.

ii. Beyond irritating consumers, some direct marketers have been accused of taking unfair advantage of impulsive or less sophisticated buyers.

iii. Other direct marketers pretend to be conducting research surveys when they are actually asking leading questions to screen or persuade consumers.

Invasion of Privacy

c. Invasion of privacy is perhaps the toughest public policy issue now confronting the direct marketing industry.

    i.   These days, it seems that almost every time consumers enter a sweepstakes, apply for a credit card, take out a magazine subscription, or order products by mail, telephone, or the Internet, their names are entered into some company's already bulging database. Using sophisticated computer technologies, direct marketers can use these databases to "microtarget" their selling efforts.

    ii.   Consumers often benefit from such database marketing—they receive more offers that are closely matched to their interests. However, many critics worry that marketers may know too much about consumers' lives and that they may use this knowledge to take unfair advantage of consumers. At some point, they claim, the extensive use of databases intrudes on consumer privacy.

<u>A Need for Action</u>

d. Many organizations are taking action on issues of ethics and public policy.

    i.   For example, the federal and state governments are taking legislative action to regulate how Web operators obtain and use consumer information.

    ii.   In an effort to build consumer confidence in shopping direct, the Direct Marketing Association (DMA)—the largest association for businesses practicing direct, database, and interactive marketing, with more than 4,700 member companies—launched a "Privacy Promise to American Consumers."

        a. The Privacy Promise requires that all DMA members adhere to a carefully developed set of consumer privacy rules.

        b. Members must agree to notify customers when any personal information is rented, sold, or exchanged with others.

        c. They must also honor consumer requests to "opt out" of receiving further solicitations or having their contact information transferred to other marketers.

        d. Finally, they must abide by the DMA's Preference Service by removing the names of consumers who wish not to receive mail, telephone or e-mail offers.

Student Exercises

1.   Key Term: Direct Marketing

Direct marketing is a direct connection with carefully targeted individual consumers to both obtain an immediate response and cultivate lasting customer relationships. Direct marketing communicates directly with customers, often on a one-to-one interactive basis. Take a look at Gateway's website (www.gateway.com). How do they differentiate between direct marketing and more traditional in-store marketing?

2.   Key Term: Customer Database

An organized collection of comprehensive data about individual customers or prospects, including geographic, demographic, psychographic, and behavioral data is known as a customer database. Think about your school. What type of database do you think they have created regarding their students?

3.   Key Term: Direct-Mail Marketing

Direct-mail marketing is direct marketing by sending an offer, announcement, reminder, or other item to a person at a particular address through the mail. Direct mail is by far the largest direct marketing medium. Much direct mail is considered junk mail or spam by recipients. Take a look at a direct-mail marketer such as Columbia House (www.columbiahouse.com). What can they do to keep the recipients of their direct mail offers from viewing the direct-mail piece as junk mail?

4.   Key Term: Catalog Marketing

Direct marketing through print, video, or electronic catalogs that are mailed to select customers, made available in stores or presented online is known as catalog marketing. Advances in technology, along with the move toward more personalized marketing, has resulted in dynamic changes in catalog marketing. Take a look at a catalog from Victoria's Secret (either online at www.victoriassecret.com or a hard copy). Compare the product offering in the catalogs with what is offered in their stores.

5.   Key Term: Telephone Marketing

Telephone marketing is using the telephone to sell directly to customers. Telephone marketing accounts for approximately 22 percent of all direct marketing-driven business. Telephone marketing is not just outbound marketing. Much of the growth in telephone marketing has come from inbound marketing – the 800 numbers consumers can call in on to reach a company. Take a look at Butterball Turkey (www.butterball.com). They offer consumers an 800 number (1-800-BUTTERBALL). What is the purpose of this number and what types of information can you receive?

6.   Key Term: Direct-Response Television Marketing

Direct-response television marketing is direct marketing via television, including direct-response television advertising (or infomercials) and home shopping channels. It is a huge growth business. Go to the Home Shopping Network's homepage (www.hsn.com) and log on to "Watch HSNtv Live." Explain how HSN (and other similar marketers) generate product excitement and sales.

7.   Key Term: Kiosk Marketing

As consumers become more and more comfortable with computer and digital technologies, many companies are placing information and ordering machines (kiosks) in stores, airports, and other locations. These are not the same as vending machines, which dispense actual products. Airlines are increasingly turning to kiosk marketing in an effort to more efficiently service customers and decrease overall costs. Take a look at how Delta Airlines is using kiosk marketing. Go to the following link to learn about Delta's use of kiosks. www.delta.com/traveling_checkin/itineraries_checkin/options/index.jsp

8.   Key Term: Mobile Phone Marketing

Mobile phone marketing is viewed by many marketers as the next big thing. It is believed that, in the near future, almost 90 percent of major brands will be marketed via mobile phones. Take a look at the T-Mobile website (www.t-mobile.com). How T-Mobile using mobile phone marketing?

9.   Key Term: Internet

The internet is a vast public web of computer networks that connects users of all types all around the world to each other and to an amazingly large information repository. Internet usage continues to grow at a steady rate. One of the largest "virtual" stores is Amazon. Go to Amazon (www.amazon.com) and take a tour of all the product categories from which a customer can select products and services. How does this compare to traditional "brick and mortar" retailers?

10.   Key Term: Click-and-Mortar Companies

Click-and-mortar companies are traditional brick-and-mortar companies that have added online marketing to their operations. As the internet grew, established brick-and-mortar companies realized that to compete effectively with online competitors they had to go online themselves. Sears is one such company (www.sears.com). How does Sears use its online presence to compete with the online-only companies, such as Amazon?

Marketing ADventure Exercises

1.   Ad Interpretation Challenge: Direct Marketing
      Ad: Advertising – Studio Funk

Direct marketing is a direct connection with carefully targeted individual consumers to both obtain an immediate response and cultivate lasting customer relationships. Direct marketing communicates directly with customers, often on a one-to-one interactive basis. Consider Studio Funk. How could their "attention grabbing" radio commercials incorporate direct marketing

2.   Ad Interpretation Challenge: Customer Database
        Ad: Internet – El Sitio

A customer database is an organized collection of comprehensive data about individual customers or prospects, including geographic, demographic, psychographic, and behavioral data. How would El Sitio make use of a customer database in its business?

3.   Ad Interpretation Challenge: Direct-Mail Marketing
        Ad: Auto – Audi A3

Direct-mail marketing is direct marketing by sending an offer, announcement, reminder, or other item to a person at a particular address. What would Audi have to do with this magazine ad to make it acceptable as a direct-mail piece?

4.   Ad Interpretation Challenge: Catalog Marketing
        Ad: Travel & Tourism – Travel Price

Catalog marketing is direct marketing through print, video, or electronic catalogs that are mailed to select customers, made available in stores, or presented online. Why could Travel Price be said to use catalog marketing?

5.   Ad Interpretation Challenge: Telephone Marketing
        Ad: Travel & Tourism – Imperial Hotel

Telephone marketing accounts for approximately 22 percent of all direct marketing-driven business. It is using the telephone to market directly to consumers. Telephone marketing is not just outbound marketing. Much of the growth in telephone marketing has come from inbound marketing – the 800 numbers consumers can call in on to reach a company. Look at the ads for the Imperial Hotel. Is this a form of telephone marketing?

6.   Ad Interpretation Challenge: Direct-Response Television Marketing
        Ad: Newspaper & TV – MTV

Direct-response television marketing is direct marketing via television, including direct-response television advertising (or infomercials) and home shopping channels. It is definitely a growth business. How does MTV use direct-response television marketing?

7.   Ad Interpretation Challenge: Kiosk Marketing
        Ad: Travel & Tourism – American Airlines

Information and ordering machines (kiosks) are popping up everywhere, as consumers become more comfortable with computers and new technologies. Kiosks do not dispense actual products, as do vending machines. How does American Airlines currently make use of kiosks? (For more information, you can go to www.aa.com)

8.   Ad Interpretation Challenge: Mobile Phone Marketing
        Ad: Electronics – Axiom

With almost 200 million Americans new subscribing to wireless services, many marketers view mobile phones as the next big direct marketing medium. How could Axiom make use of mobile phone marketing?

9.   Ad Interpretation Challenge: Marketing Web Site
        Ad: Electronics – Polaroid

A marketing website is a website that engages consumers in interactions that will move them closer to a direct purchase or other marketing outcome. Consider Polaroid. Go to the Polaroid web site (www.polaroid.com). Is this a marketing website?

10.   Ad Interpretation Challenge: Spam
        Ad: Travel & Transportation – Aeromexico

Spam is unsolicited and unwanted commercial e-mail messages that clog up your e-mailboxes. It is a big problem and becoming bigger. Aeromexico wants to be able to communicate with its customers via e-mail, but it does not want to be viewed as spam. How would you suggest they overcome this hurtle?

Chapter 18
Creating Competitive Advantage

Learning Objectives

1. Discuss the need to understand competitors as well as customers through competitor analysis.
2. Explain the fundamentals of competitive marketing strategies based on creating value for customers.
3. Illustrate the need for balancing customer and competitor orientations in becoming a truly market-centered organization.

Chapter Overview

Two key trends in marketing for the twenty-first century are (a) the trend toward the use of relationship marketing to improve customer satisfaction and (b) the trend toward in-depth competitor analysis as a means of identifying the company's major competitors (using both an industry and market-based analysis) and closely examining and formulating strategies to deal with competitors' objectives, strategies, strengths and weaknesses, and reaction patterns.

To be successful, a company must consider its competitors as well as its actual and potential customers. In the process of performing a competitor analysis, the company carefully analyzes and gathers information on competitors' strategies and programs. A competitive intelligence system helps the company acquire and manage competitive information. The company must then choose a competitive marketing strategy of its own. The strategy chosen depends on the company's industry position and its objectives, opportunities, and resources. Several basic competitive strategies are outlined in the chapter. Some of these are time-tested and some are relatively new.

Four primary competitive positions are reviewed in the chapter. The first is that of the *market leader* that faces three challenges: expanding the total market, protecting market share, and expanding market share. The market leader is interested in finding ways to expand the total market because it will benefit most from any increased sales. The leader must also have an eye toward protecting its share. Several strategies for accomplishing this protection task are presented. Aggressive leaders also try to expand their own market share. The second position is that of the *market challenger*. This is a firm that aggressively tries to expand its market share by attacking the leader, other runner-up firms, or smaller firms in the industry. The third position is that of the *market follower,* which is designated as a runner-up firm that chooses not to rock the boat (usually out of fear that it stands to lose more than it might gain). Lastly, the *market nicher* is a position option open to smaller firms that serve some part of the market that is not likely to attract the attention of the larger firms. These firms often survive by being specialists in some function that is attractive to the marketplace.

The analysis of the four competitive position options presented in this chapter is a truly unique presentation and offers insight for every potential manager. This information can be used by every mid-level strategic planner who seeks insight into competitive strategy dynamics.

The chapter closes with a brief but insightful glance into how to balance customer and competitor orientations to achieve a dominant strategy position in the marketplace.

Chapter Outline

1. **Introduction**
   a. A Washington Mutual branch is more like a retail store than a bank. This format might seem unusual for a bank, but it's working for Washington Mutual.
   b. Washington Mutual's stunning success has resulted from its relentless dedication to a simple competitive marketing strategy: operational excellence. Washington Mutual creates value through a Wal-Mart-like strategy of offering convenience and low prices.
   c. WaMu's strategy focuses on building full customer relationships.
   d. To win in today's marketplace, companies must become adept not just in managing products, but in managing customer relationships in the face of determined competition. Building profitable customer relationships and gaining competitive advantage requires delivering more value and satisfaction to target consumers than competitors do.
   e. The first step is competitor analysis—the process of identifying, assessing, and selecting key competitors.
   f. The second step is developing competitive marketing strategies that strongly position the company against competitors and give it the greatest possible competitive advantage.

2. **Competitor Analysis**
   a. As shown in Figure 18.1, competitor analysis involves first identifying and assessing competitors and then selecting which competitors to attack or avoid.

   Identifying Competitors
   b. At the narrowest level, a company can define its competitors as other companies offering similar products and services to the same customers at similar prices.
      i. But companies actually face a much wider range of competitors. The company might define competitors as all firms making the same product or class of products.
      ii. Even more broadly, competitors might include all companies making products that supply the same service.

    iii. Finally, and still more broadly, competitors might include all companies that compete for the same consumer dollars.

c. Companies must avoid "competitor myopia." A company is more likely to be "buried" by its latent competitors than its current ones.

d. Companies can identify their competitors from the industry point of view. A company must understand the competitive patterns in its industry if it hopes to be an effective "player" in that industry.

e. Companies can also identify competitors from a market point of view. Here they define competitors as companies that are trying to satisfy the same customer need or build relationships with the same customer group.

f. In general, the market concept of competition opens the company's eyes to a broader set of actual and potential competitors.

    i. One approach is to profile the company's direct and indirect competitors by mapping the steps buyers take in obtaining and using the product.

    ii. Figure 18.2 illustrates one competitor map.

<u>Assessing Competitors</u>

g. Each competitor has a mix of objectives.

    i. The company wants to know the relative importance that a competitor places on current profitability, market share growth, cash flow, technological leadership, service leadership, and other goals.

    ii. Knowing a competitor's mix of objectives reveals whether the competitor is satisfied with its current situation and how it might react to different competitive actions.

h. A company must also monitor its competitors' objectives for various segments.

    i. If the company finds that a competitor has discovered a new segment, this might be an opportunity.

    ii. If it finds that competitors plan new moves into segments now served by the company, it will be forewarned and, hopefully, forearmed.

i. The more that one firm's strategy resembles another firm's strategy, the more the two firms compete. A strategic group is a group of firms in an industry following the same or a similar strategy in a given target market.

    i. Some important insights emerge from identifying strategic groups. For example, if a company enters one of the groups, the members of that group become its key competitors.

    ii. Although competition is intense within a strategic group, there is also rivalry among groups.

        a. First, some of the strategic groups may appeal to overlapping customer segments.

        b. Second, the customers may not see much difference in the offers of different groups.

    c. Finally, members of one strategic group might expand into new strategy segments.

iii. The company needs to look at all of the dimensions that identify strategic groups within the industry.

    a. It needs to know each competitor's product quality, features, and mix; customer services; pricing policy; distribution coverage; sales force strategy; and advertising and sales promotion programs.

    b. And it must study the details of each competitor's R&D, manufacturing, purchasing, financial, and other strategies.

iv. Marketers need to assess each competitor's strengths and weaknesses carefully in order to answer the critical question: What can our competitors do?

    a. As a first step, companies can gather data on each competitor's goals, strategies, and performance over the last few years. Admittedly, some of this information will be hard to obtain.

    b. Companies normally learn about their competitors' strengths and weaknesses through secondary data, personal experience, and word of mouth.

    c. They can also conduct primary marketing research with customers, suppliers, and dealers.

    d. Or they can benchmark themselves against other firms, comparing the company's products and processes to those of competitors or leading firms in other industries to find ways to improve quality and performance.

v. Next, the company wants to know, What will our competitors do?

    a. A competitor's objectives, strategies, and strengths and weaknesses go a long way toward explaining its likely actions. They also suggest its likely reactions to company moves such as price cuts, promotion increases, or new-product introductions.

    b. In addition, each competitor has a certain philosophy of doing business, a certain internal culture and guiding beliefs.

    c. Each competitor reacts differently.

        1. Some do not react quickly or strongly to a competitor's move. They may feel their customers are loyal, they may be slow in noticing the move, or they may lack the funds to react.

        2. Some competitors react only to certain types of moves and not to others.

        3. Other competitors react swiftly and strongly to any action.

        4. Knowing how major competitors react gives the company clues on how best to attack competitors or how best to defend the company's current positions.

Selecting Competitors to Attack and Avoid

j. The company can focus on one of several classes of competitors.

    i. Most companies prefer to compete against weak competitors. This requires fewer resources and less time. But in the process, the firm may gain little.

    ii. You could argue that the firm also should compete with strong competitors in order to sharpen its abilities.

k. A useful tool for assessing competitor strengths and weaknesses is customer value analysis.

    i. The aim of customer value analysis is to determine the benefits that target customer value and how customers rate the relative value of various competitors' offers.

    ii. In conducting a customer value analysis, the company first identifies the major attributes that customers value and the importance customers place on these attributes.

    iii. Next, it assesses the company's and competitor's performance on the valued attributes.

l. The key to gaining competitive advantage is to take each customer segment and examine how the company's offer compares to that of its major competitor.

m. Most companies will compete with close competitors—those that resemble them the most—rather than distant competitors. At the same time, the company may want to avoid trying to "destroy" a close competitor.

n. The existence of competitors results in several strategic benefits.

    i. Competitors may help increase total demand.

    ii. They may share the costs of market and product development and help to legitimize new technologies.

    iii. They may serve less-attractive segments or lead to more product differentiation.

    iv. Finally, they lower the antitrust risk and improve bargaining power versus labor or regulators.

o. However, a company may not view all of its competitors as beneficial. An industry often contains "good" competitors and "bad" competitors.

    i. Good competitors play by the rules of the industry.

    ii. Bad competitors, in contrast, break the rules. They try to buy share rather than earn it, take large risks, and in general shake up the industry.

    iii. The implication is that "good" competitors would like to shape an industry that consists of only well-behaved competitors. A company might be smart to support good competitors, aiming its attacks at bad competitors.

Designing a Competitive Intelligence System

p. The competitive intelligence system first identifies the vital types of competitive information and the best sources of this information.

q. Then, the system continuously collects information from the field and from published data.

r. Next the system checks the information for validity and reliability, interprets it, and organizes it in an appropriate way.

s. Finally, it sends key information to relevant decision makers and responds to inquiries from managers about competitors.

t. Smaller companies that cannot afford to set up formal competitive intelligence offices can assign specific executives to watch specific competitors.

3. **Competitive Strategies**

a. Having identified and evaluated its major competitors, the company now must design broad competitive marketing strategies by which it can gain competitive advantage by offering superior customer value.

Approaches to Marketing Strategy

b. No one strategy is best for all companies. Each company must determine what makes the most sense given its position in the industry and its objectives, opportunities, and resources. Even within a company, different strategies may be required for different businesses or products.

c. Many large firms develop formal competitive marketing strategies and implement them religiously. However, other companies develop strategy in a less formal and orderly fashion.

d. Approaches to marketing strategy and practice often pass through three stages.

    i. Entrepreneurial marketing: Most companies are started by individuals who live by their wits. They visualize an opportunity, construct flexible strategies on the backs of envelopes, and knock on every door to gain attention.

    ii. Formulated marketing: As small companies achieve success, they inevitably move toward more-formulated marketing. They develop formal marketing strategies and adhere to them closely.

    iii. Intrepreneurial marketing: Many large and mature companies get stuck in formulated marketing. They pour over the latest Nielsen numbers, scan market research reports, and try to fine-tune their competitive strategies and programs. These companies sometimes lose the marketing creativity and passion that they had at the start. They now need to re-establish within their companies the entrepreneurial spirit and actions that made them successful in the first place.

    iv. There will be constant tension between the formulated side of marketing and the creative side.

<u>Basic Competitive Strategies</u>

e. More than two decades ago, Michael Porter suggested four basic competitive positioning strategies that companies can follow—three winning strategies and one losing one.

    i. Overall cost leadership: Here, the company works hard to achieve the lowest production and distribution costs.

    ii. Differentiation: Here, the company concentrates on creating a highly differentiated product line and marketing program so that it comes across as the class leader in the industry.

    iii. Focus: Here, the company focuses its effort on serving a few market segments well rather than going after the whole market.

    iv. Companies that pursue a clear strategy—one of the above—will likely perform well. But firms that do not pursue a clear strategy—middle-of-the-roaders—do the worst.

f. More recently, two marketing consultants, Michael Treacy and Fred Wiersema, offered a new classification of competitive marketing strategies. They suggest that companies gain leadership positions by delivering superior value to their customers. Companies can pursue any of three strategies—called value disciplines—for delivering superior customer value.

    i. Operational excellence: The company provides superior value by leading its industry in price and convenience.

    ii. Customer intimacy: The company provides superior value by precisely segmenting its markets and tailoring its products or services to match exactly the needs of targeted customers.

    iii. Product leadership: The company provides superior value by offering a continuous stream of leading-edge products or services.

    iv. Some companies successfully pursue more than one value discipline at the same time. However, such companies are rare—few firms can be the best at more than one of these disciplines.

g. Treacy and Wiersema have found that leading companies focus on and excel at a single value discipline, while meeting industry standards on the other two. Such companies design their entire value delivery network to single-mindedly support the chosen discipline.

<u>Competitive Positions</u>

h. Firms competing in a given target market, at any point in time, differ in their objectives and resources. Some firms are large, others small. Some have many resources, others are strapped for funds. Some are old and established, others new and fresh.

i. Firms can base their competitive strategies on the roles they play in the target market—leader, challenger, follower, or nicher.

i. Suppose that an industry contains the firms shown in Figure 18.3. Forty percent of the market is in the hands of the market leader, the firm with the largest market share. Another 30 percent is in the hands of market challengers, runner-up firms that are fighting hard to increase their market share. Another 20 percent is in the hands of market followers, other runner-up firms that want to hold their share without rocking the boat. The remaining 10 percent is in the hands of market nichers, firms that serve small segments not being pursued by other firms.

ii. Table 18.1 shows specific marketing strategies that are available to market leaders, challengers, followers, and nichers. Remember, however, that these classifications often do not apply to a whole company, but only to its position in a specific industry.

Market Leader Strategies

j. Most industries contain an acknowledged market leader. The leader has the largest market share and usually leads the other firms in price changes, new-product introductions, distribution coverage, and promotion spending. Competitors focus on the leader as a company to challenge, imitate, or avoid.

k. To remain number one, leading firms can take any of three actions. First, they can find ways to expand total demand. Second, they can protect their current market share through good defensive and offensive actions. Third, they can try to expand their market share further, even if market size remains constant.

i. The leading firm normally gains the most when the total market expands.

a. Market leaders can expand the market by developing new users, new uses, and more usage of its products.

b. While trying to expand total market size, the leading firm also must protect its current business against competitors' attacks.

1. First, it must prevent or fix weaknesses that provide opportunities for competitors. It must always fulfill its value promise. Its prices must remain consistent with the value that customers see in the brand. It must work tirelessly to keep strong relationships with valued customers. The leader should "plug holes" so that competitors do not jump in.

2. But the best defense is a good offense, and the best response is continuous innovation. The leader keeps increasing its competitive effectiveness and value to customers. And when attacked by challengers, the market leader reacts decisively.

   ii. Market leaders also can grow by increasing their market shares further. Studies have shown that, on average, profitability rises with increasing market share.

      a. Some studies have found that many industries contain one or a few highly profitable large firms, several profitable and more focused firms, and a large number of medium-sized firms with poorer profit performance.

      b. It appears that profitability increases as a business gains share relative to competitors in its served market.

      c. Companies must not think, however, that gaining increased market share will improve profitability automatically. Much depends on their strategy for gaining increased share. There are many high-share companies with low profitability and many low-share companies with high profitability.

Market Challenger Strategies

l. Firms that are second, third, or lower in an industry are sometimes quite large. These runner-up firms can adopt one of two competitive strategies: They can challenge the leader and other competitors in an aggressive bid for more market share (market challengers). Or they can play along with competitors and not rock the boat (market followers).

   i. A market challenger must first define which competitors to challenge and its strategic objective.

      a. The challenger can attack the market leader, a high-risk but potentially high-gain strategy. Its goal might be to take over market leadership.

      b. Or the challenger's objective may simply be to wrest more market share.

      c. Alternatively, the challenger can avoid the leader and instead challenge firms its own size, or smaller local and regional firms. These smaller firms may be underfinanced and not serving their customers well. The challenger must choose its opponents carefully and have a clearly defined and attainable objective.

   ii. How can the market challenger best attack the chosen competitor and achieve its strategic objectives?

      a. It may launch a full frontal attack, matching the competitor's product, advertising, price, and distribution efforts. It attacks the competitor's strengths rather than its weaknesses. The outcome depends on who has the greater strength and endurance.

      b. Rather than challenging head-on, the challenger can make an indirect attack on the competitor's weaknesses or on gaps in the competitor's market coverage.

Market Follower Strategies

m. Not all runner-up companies want to challenge the market leader. Challenges are never taken lightly by the leader.

n. A follower can gain many advantages.

    i. The market leader often bears the huge expenses of developing new products and markets, expanding distribution, and educating the market.

    ii. By contrast, the market follower can learn from the leader's experience. It can copy or improve on the leader's products and programs, usually with much less investment. Although the follower will probably not overtake the leader, it often can be as profitable.

o. A market follower must know how to hold current customers and win a fair share of new ones.

    i. It must find the right balance between following closely enough to win customers from the market leader but following at enough of a distance to avoid retaliation.

    ii. Each follower tries to bring distinctive advantages to its target market.

    iii. The follower is often a major target of attack by challengers. Therefore, the market follower must keep its manufacturing costs low and its product quality and services high. It must also enter new markets as they open up.

Market Nicher Strategies

p. Almost every industry includes firms that specialize in serving market niches. Instead of pursuing the whole market, or even large segments, these firms target subsegments.

q. Nichers are often smaller firms with limited resources. But smaller divisions of larger firms also may pursue niching strategies.

r. Why is niching profitable? The main reason is that the market nicher ends up knowing the target customer group so well that it meets their needs better than other firms that casually sell to this niche.

    i. As a result, the nicher can charge a substantial markup over costs because of the added value.

    ii. Whereas the mass marketer achieves high volume, the nicher achieves high margins.

s. Nichers try to find one or more market niches that are safe and profitable.

    i. An ideal market niche is big enough to be profitable and has growth potential.

    ii. It is one that the firm can serve effectively.

    iii. Perhaps most important, the niche is of little interest to major competitors.

t. The key idea in niching is specialization. A market nicher can specialize along any of several market, customer, product, or marketing mix lines.

    i. For example, it can specialize in serving one type of end user.

      ii. The nicher can specialize in serving a given customer-size group.

      iii. Some nichers focus on one or a few specific customers, selling their entire output to a single company.

      iv. Still other nichers specialize by geographic market, selling only in a certain locality, region, or area of the world.

      v. Quality-price nichers operate at the low or high end of the market.

      vi. Finally, service nichers offer services not available from other firms.

u. Niching carries some major risks.

      i. For example, the market niche may dry up, or it might grow to the point that it attracts larger competitors.

      ii. That is why many companies practice multiple niching. By developing two or more niches, a company increases its chances for survival.

4.   **Balancing Customer and Competitor Orientations**

a. Whether a company is a market leader, challenger, follower, or nicher, it must watch its competitors closely and find the competitive marketing strategy that positions it most effectively. And it must continually adapt its strategies to the fast-changing competitive environment.

b. A competitor-centered company is one that spends most of its time tracking competitors' moves and market shares and trying to find strategies to counter them. This approach has some pluses and minuses.

      i. On the positive side, the company develops a fighter orientation, watches for weaknesses in its own position, and searches out competitors' weaknesses.

      ii. On the negative side, the company becomes too reactive. Rather than carrying out its own customer relationship strategy, it bases its own moves on competitors' moves. As a result, it may end up simply matching or extending industry practices rather than seeking innovative new ways to create more value for customers.

c. A customer-centered company, by contrast, focuses more on customer developments in designing its strategies.

      i. Clearly, the customer-centered company is in a better position to identify new opportunities and set long-run strategies that make sense.

      ii. By watching customer needs evolve, it can decide what customer groups and what emerging needs are the most important to serve.

d. In practice, today's companies must be market-centered companies, watching both their customers and their competitors. But they must not let competitor watching blind them to customer focusing.

e. Figure 18.4 shows that companies have moved through four orientations over the years.

      i. In the first stage, they were product oriented, paying little attention to either customers or competitors.

    ii. In the second stage, they became customer oriented and started to pay attention to customers.

    iii. In the third stage, when they started to pay attention to competitors, they became competitor oriented.

    iv. Today, companies need to be market oriented, paying balanced attention to both customers and competitors. Rather than simply watching competitors and trying to beat them on current ways of doing business, they need to watch customers and find innovative ways to build profitable customer relationships by delivering more value than competitors do.

Student Exercises

1.   Key Term: Competitive Advantage

Competitive advantage is an advantage over competitors gained by offering consumers greater value than competitors offer. What is the competitive advantage enjoyed by AT&T? Go to their website (www.att.com) to learn more about the company.

2.   Key Term: Competitor Analysis

Competitor analysis is the process of identifying key competitors; assessing their objectives, strategies, strengths and weaknesses, and reaction patterns; and selecting which competitors to attack or avoid. Learn about Lenovo computers (www.lenovo.com/us/en/). Identify their key competitors.

3.   Key Term: Strategic Groups

In most industries, the competitors can be sorted into groups that pursue different strategies. A strategic group is a group of firms in an industry following the same or similar strategies. Look at Palm (www.palm.com). What is the strategic group to which they belong and who are the other members?

4.   Key Term: Benchmarking

Benchmarking is the process of comparing the company's products and processes to those of competitors or leading firms in other industries to find ways to improve quality and performance. If you were in charge of marketing Corel Paint Shop Pro photo editing software (www.corel.com), who would you benchmark?

5.   Key Term: "Bad" Competitors

There are two types of competitors that a company with which a company may have to deal—"good" competitors and "bad" competitors. "Good" competitors play by the rules of the industry. "Bad" competitors, on the other hand, break some of those rules. They try to buy share, rather than earn it, take large risks, and play by their own rules. Your text highlights iTunes as a competitor that is viewed as bad by other industry players. Find another example.

6.   Key Term: Differentiation

Differentiation is a competitive positioning strategy where the company concentrates on creating a highly differentiated product line and marketing program so that it comes across as the class leader in the industry. Consider Apple (www.apple.com). How does Apple differentiate itself from its competition?

7.   Key Term: Focus

Focus is a differentiation strategy where the company concentrates its efforts on serving only a few market segments well, rather than going after the entire market. Find a company in the transportation industry that uses a focus differentiation strategy.

8.   Key Term: Customer Intimacy

Customer-intimate companies serve customers who are willing to pay a premium to get precisely what they want. These companies will do almost anything to build long-term customer loyalty and to capture customer lifetime value. Look at how Wyndham work to develop customer intimacy (www.wyndham.com).

9.   Key Term: Market Follower

A market follower is a runner-up firm that wants to hold its share in an industry without rocking the boat or taking unnecessary risks. Market followers follow the market from a safe distance, only taking risks when the results seem clear. Research the U.S. breakfast cereal market. What is a company that you would consider a follower in this market?

10.   Key Term: Market Nicher

Almost every industry includes firms that specialize in serving small market niches. Instead of pursuing the whole market, or even large segments, these firms target subsegments. Nichers are often smaller firms with limited resources. Consider again, the U.S. breakfast cereal market. What is a company that you would consider a market nicher?

Marketing ADventure Exercises

1. Ad Interpretation Challenge: Competitive Advantage
    Ad: Financial—MBNA

An advantage over competitors gained by offering consumers greater value than the competitors offer is known as competitive advantage. Take a look at this ad for MBNA. What is the competitive advantage MBNA has over its competition?

2. Ad Interpretation Challenge: Identifying Competitors
    Ad: Electronics—LG

Normally, identifying competitors would seem a simple task. At the narrowest level, a company can define its competitors as other companies offering similar products and services to the same customers at similar prices. Look at this ad for LG televisions and then go to their website (http://us.lge.com) to learn more about their product offering in televisions. Who would you identify as their major competitors in television?

3. Ad Interpretation Challenge: Strategic Groups
    Ad: Auto—Porsche

A strategic group is a group of firms in an industry following the same or similar strategies. While you will have competitors outside of the strategic group, your primary competitors are other firms within the strategic group. Consider Porsche. How would you describe the strategic group of which it is a member? What are some of the other firms that would make up its strategic group?

4. Ad Interpretation Challenge: Benchmarking
    Ad: Cosmetics and Pharmaceuticals—Mentadent

Benchmarking is the process of comparing a company's products and processes to those of competitors or leading firms in other industries to find ways to improve quality and performance. If you were the marketing manager for Mentadent toothpaste, a toothpaste with a relatively small market share, what companies would look to benchmark?

5. Ad Interpretation Challenge: Close Competitors
    Ad: Financial—Ameritrade

Competitors come in all sizes and strengths. Most companies will choose to compete with close competitors. Close competitors are those that most resemble your company. Close competitors are the competitors that are most like your company. What type of companies would be close competitors to Ameritrade?

6.   Ad Interpretation Challenge: Entrepreneurial Marketing Strategy
      Ad: Student Choice

Entrepreneurial marketing strategies are typically those strategies employed by young companies (although not always that young) looking to stand out, be recognized, and make a name. These are strategies that may be somewhat unorthodox, but are designed to take a chance and (hopefully) make a splash. Find an ad for a product or company that you believe is employing an entrepreneurial marketing strategy.

7.   Ad Interpretation Challenge: Differentiation
      Ad: Services and B2B—24 Hour Fitness

Differentiation is a competitive positioning strategy where the company concentrates on creating a highly differentiated product line and marketing program so that it comes across as the class leader in the industry. How does 24 Hour Fitness differentiate itself from its competitors?

8.   Ad Interpretation Challenge: Focus
      Ad: Apparel—Polartec

Using a focus strategy, a company focuses its efforts on serving a few market segments well rather than going after the whole market. Look at this ad for Polartec. How is this company effectively using a focus strategy to compete?

9.   Ad Interpretation Challenge: Product Leadership
      Ad: Student Choice

A company which employees a product leadership strategy provides superior value in its own way. It provides value to its customers by offering a continuous stream of leading-edge products or services. It aims to make its own and competing products obsolete. These companies typically serve customers who want state-of-the-art products and services, regardless of the costs in terms of price or inconvenience. Find an ad for such a company.

10.   Ad Interpretation Challenge: Market Leader Strategies
      Ad: General Retail—Hallmark

Most industries contain an acknowledged market leader. The leader has the largest market share and usually leads the other firms in price changes, new-product introductions, distribution coverage, and promotion spending. Hallmark is the acknowledged market leader in the greeting card market. What must Hallmark do to stay on top?

Chapter 19
The Global Marketplace

Learning Objectives

1. Discuss how the international trade system and economic, political-legal, and cultural environments affect a company's international marketing decisions.
2. Describe three key approaches to entering international markets.
3. Explain how companies adapt their marketing mixes for international markets.
4. Identify the three major forms of international marketing organization.

Chapter Overview

The world is shrinking rapidly with the advent of faster communication, transportation, and financial flows. In the twenty-first century, firms can no longer afford to pay attention only to their domestic market, no matter how large it is. Many industries are global industries, and those firms that operate globally achieve lower costs and higher brand awareness. At the same time, global marketing is risky because of variable exchange rates, unstable governments, protectionist tariffs and trade barriers, and other prohibitive factors.

Given the potential gains and risks of global marketing, companies need a systematic way to make their international marketing decisions. Decision areas that must be addressed are (1) deciding how to look at the global market environment, (2) deciding whether to go international, (3) deciding which markets to enter, (4) deciding how to enter the market, (5) deciding on the global marketing program, and (6) deciding on the global marketing organization. Each of these decisions must be seriously considered and answered if success is to be achieved in the international competitive arena. This chapter addresses each of these issues in a complete and detailed fashion.

All markets and industrial bases around the world are not the same. There are varying degrees of economic sophistication. The marketer must make plans for operations in subsistence economies, raw material exporting economies, industrializing economies, and established industrial economies separately if true marketing success is to be achieved. It would be easier on the decision maker if all the economies were like the United States. They, however, are not. Global marketing requires an extensive amount of learning and, in some instances, adaptation of the marketing mix to fit the particular situation and economy.

In addition to global challenges with consideration of the marketing mix, the marketer that wishes to go global must also consider a variety of options on how to align the organization with international partners. A variety of formats exist and primary types are discussed in this chapter. These considerations are different than those that the marketer faces in its own domestic environment. The end result of making these new global decisions is not only improvement in marketing skills, but improvement toward attaining a truly global organization.

Chapter Outline

1. **Introduction**
   a. What could be more American than basketball, right? The sport was invented in the United States and each year, tens of millions of fans participate on local, high school, college, and professional levels.
   b. But the growth of the NBA has leveled off. Like any major company that experiences this, the NBA is expanding onto the global court in order to maintain an aggressive growth campaign.
   c. Various opportunities exist for the NBA. With many non-U.S. athletes (e.g., Yao Ming, Dirk Nowitzky, and Tony Kukoc) playing for NBA teams, there is a strong potential for broadcasting games and selling merchandise in the home countries of such players.
   d. The NBA is investing heavily abroad with international offices, marketing campaigns, and international events.
   e. The NBA Europe Live is one of the most aggressive programs to date. NBA teams compete in exhibition games against host teams from Euroleague Basketball.
   f. China and Latin America also represent huge growth opportunities.
   g. As a result of its international marketing prowess, the NBA may be the first U.S. major league to open a franchise team outside of North America.
   h. In the past, U.S. companies paid little attention to international trade. Today, however, the situation is much different.

2. **Global Marketing in the Twenty-First Century**
   a. International trade is booming. Since 1969, the number of multinational corporations in the world has grown from 7,000 to more than 70,000. Of the largest 100 "economies" in the world, only 53 are countries. The remaining 47 are multinational corporations.
   b. World trade is growing at a 6 percent to 10 percent annual rate, compared to 2.5 percent to 4 percent for global gross domestic product. Imports of goods and services now account for 28 percent of GDP worldwide.
   c. Global competition is intensifying. Foreign firms are expanding aggressively into new international markets, and home markets are no longer as rich in opportunity. Few industries are now safe from foreign competition.

    d. Firms that stay at home to play it safe not only might lose their chances to enter other markets but also risk losing their home markets.

    e. Ironically, although the need for companies to go abroad is greater today than in the past, so are the risks.

        i. Companies that go global may face highly unstable governments and currencies, restrictive government policies and regulations, and high trade barriers.

        ii. Corruption is also an increasing problem—officials in several countries often award business not to the best bidder but to the highest briber.

    f. A global firm is one that, by operating in more than one country, gains marketing, production, R&D, and financial advantages that are not available to purely domestic competitors. The global company sees the world as one market.

    g. This does not mean that small and medium-size firms must operate in a dozen countries to succeed. These firms can practice global niching.

    h. The rapid move toward globalization means that all companies will have to answer some basic questions.

        i. What market position should we try to establish in our country, in our economic region, and globally?

        ii. Who will our global competitors be, and what are their strategies and resources?

        iii. Where should we produce or source our product?

        iv. What strategic alliances should we form with other firms around the world?

    i. As shown in Figure 19.1, a company faces six major decisions in international marketing.

3. **Looking at the Global Marketing Environment**

    a. Before deciding whether to operate internationally, a company must understand the international marketing environment. That environment has changed a great deal in the last two decades, creating both new opportunities and new problems.

The International Trade System

    b. U.S. companies looking abroad must start by understanding the international trade system. When selling to another country, a U.S. firm faces various trade restrictions.

        i. The most common is the tariff, a tax levied by a foreign government against certain imported products. The tariff may be designed either to raise revenue or to protect domestic firms.

        ii. The exporter also may face a quota, which sets limits on the amount of goods the importing country will accept in certain product categories. The purpose of the quota is to conserve on foreign exchange and to protect local industry and employment.

      iii. An embargo, or boycott, which totally bans some kinds of imports, is the strongest form of quota.

      iv. American firms may face exchange controls that limit the amount of foreign exchange and the exchange rate against other currencies.

      v. The company also may face nontariff trade barriers, such as biases against U.S. company bids or restrictive product standards or other rules that go against American product features.

c. At the same time, certain forces help trade between nations. Examples include the General Agreement on Tariffs and Trade (GATT) and various regional free trade agreements.

d. The General Agreement on Tariffs and Trade (GATT) is a 56-year-old treaty designed to promote world trade by reducing tariffs and other international trade barriers.

      i. Since the treaty's inception in 1948, member nations (currently numbering 149) have met in eight rounds of GATT negotiations to reassess trade barriers and set new rules for international trade. The first seven rounds of negotiations reduced the average worldwide tariffs on manufactured goods from 45 percent to just 5 percent.

      ii. The most recently completed GATT negotiations, dubbed the Uruguay Round, dragged on for seven long years before concluding in 1993.

            a. The benefits of the Uruguay Round will be felt for many years as the accord promotes long-term global trade growth.

                1. It reduced the world's remaining merchandise tariffs by 30 percent, boosting global merchandise trade by as much as 10 percent, or $270 billion in current dollars, by 2002.

                2. The agreement also extended GATT to cover trade in agriculture and a wide range of services, and it toughened international protection of copyrights, patents, trademarks, and other intellectual property.

            b. Beyond reducing trade barriers and setting global standards for trade, the Uruguay Round set up the World Trade Organization (WTO) to enforce GATT rules. In general, the WTO acts as an umbrella organization, overseeing GATT, mediating global disputes, and imposing trade sanctions.

            c. A new round of GATT negotiations, the Doha round, began in Doha, Qatar, in late 2001 and was expected to conclude in January 2005.

e. Certain countries have formed free trade zones or economic communities. These are groups of nations organized to work toward common goals in the regulation of international trade.

      i. One such community is the European Union (EU).

     a. Formed in 1957, the EU set out to create a single European market by reducing barriers to the free flow of products, services, finances, and labor among member countries and developing policies on trade with nonmember nations.

     b. Today, the EU represents one of the world's largest markets.

     c. European unification offers tremendous trade opportunities for U.S. and other non-European firms. However, it also poses threats.

          1. As a result of increased unification, European companies will grow bigger and more competitive.

          2. Perhaps an even greater concern, however, is that lower barriers inside Europe will create only thicker outside walls.

     d. In recent years, 12 member nations have taken a significant step toward unification by adopting the euro as a common currency.

     e. Even with the adoption of the euro, it is unlikely that the EU will ever go against 2,000 years of tradition and become the "United States of Europe."

  ii. In North America, the United States and Canada phased out trade barriers in 1989. In January 1994, the North American Free Trade Agreement (NAFTA) established a free trade zone among the United States, Mexico, and Canada.

     a. The agreement created a single market of 360 million people who produce and consume $6.7 trillion worth of goods and services.

     b. As it is implemented over a 15-year period, NAFTA will eliminate all trade barriers and investment restrictions among the three countries.

  iii. Other free trade areas have formed in Latin America and South America. For example, MERCOSUR now links six members, including full members Argentina, Brazil, Paraguay, and Uruguay and associate members Bolivia and Chile.

f. Although the recent trend toward free trade zones has caused great excitement and new market opportunities, some see it as a mixed blessing.

  i. For example, in the United States, unions fear that NAFTA will lead to the further exodus of manufacturing jobs to Mexico, where wage rates are much lower.

  ii. Environmentalists worry that companies that are unwilling to play by the strict rules of the U.S. Environmental Protection Agency will relocate in Mexico, where pollution regulation has been lax.

Economic Environment

g. The international marketer must study each country's economy. Two economic factors reflect the country's attractiveness as a market: the country's industrial structure and its income distribution.

h. The country's industrial structure shapes its product and service needs, income levels, and employment levels. There are four types of industrial structures.

    i. Subsistence economies: In a subsistence economy, the vast majority of people engage in simple agriculture. They consume most of their output and barter the rest for simple goods and services. They offer few market opportunities.

    ii. Raw material exporting economies: These economies are rich in one or more natural resources but poor in other ways. Much of their revenue comes from exporting these resources.

    iii. Industrializing economies: In an industrializing economy, manufacturing accounts for 10 percent to 20 percent of the country's economy. Industrialization typically creates a new rich class and a small but growing middle class, both demanding new types of imported goods.

    iv. Industrial economies: Industrial economies are major exporters of manufactured goods, services, and investment funds. They trade goods among themselves and also export them to other types of economies for raw materials and semifinished goods.

i. The second economic factor is the country's income distribution.

    i. Countries with subsistence economies may consist mostly of households with very low family incomes.

    ii. In contrast, industrialized nations may have low-, medium-, and high-income households.

    iii. Still other countries may have households with only either very low or very high incomes.

    iv. In many cases, poorer countries may have small but wealthy segments of upper-income consumers.

    v. Also, even in low-income and developing economies, people may find ways to buy products that are important to them.

Political-Legal Environment

j. Nations differ greatly in their political-legal environments. At least four political-legal factors should be considered when deciding whether to do business in a given country.

    i. In their attitudes toward international buying, some nations are quite receptive to foreign firms and others are quite hostile.

    ii. A second factor is government bureaucracy—the extent to which the host government runs an efficient system for helping foreign companies: efficient customs handling, good market information, and other factors that aid in doing business.

    iii. Political stability is another issue.

        a. Governments change hands, sometimes violently. Even without a change, a government may decide to respond to new popular feelings.

      b. The foreign company's property may be taken, its currency holdings may be blocked, or import quotas or new duties may be set.

      c. International marketers may find it profitable to do business in an unstable country, but the unstable situation will affect how they handle business and financial matters.

    iv. Finally, companies must also consider a country's monetary regulations.

      a. Sellers want to take profits in a currency of value to them.

      b. Short of this, sellers might accept a blocked currency—one whose removal from the country is restricted by the buyer's government—if they can buy other goods in that country that they need themselves or can sell elsewhere for a needed currency.

      c. Besides currency limits, a changing exchange rate also creates high risks for the seller.

k. Most international trade involves cash transactions. Yet many nations have too little hard currency to pay for their purchases from other countries. They may want to pay with other items instead of cash, which has led to a growing practice called countertrade.

    i. Countertrade makes up an estimated 20 percent of all world trade. It takes several forms.

      a. Barter involves the direct exchange of goods or services.

      b. Another form is compensation (or *buyback*), whereby the seller sells a plant, equipment, or technology to another country and agrees to take payment in the resulting products.

      c. Another form is counterpurchase, in which the seller receives full payment in cash but agrees to spend some of the money in the other country.

Cultural Environment

l. Each country has its own folkways, norms, and taboos. When designing global marketing strategies, companies must understand how culture affects consumer reactions in each of its world markets. In turn, they must also understand how their strategies affect local cultures.

    i. The seller must examine the ways consumers in different countries think about and use certain products before planning a marketing program. There are often surprises.

      a. Business norms and behavior also vary from country to country. American business executives need to be briefed on these factors before conducting business in another country.

      b. By the same token, companies that understand cultural nuances can use them to their advantage when positioning products internationally.

     ii. Whereas marketers worry about the impact of culture on their global marketing strategies, others may worry about the impact of marketing strategies on global cultures.

          a. For example, some critics argue that "globalization" really means "Americanization."

          b. Critics worry that the more people around the world are exposed to American lifestyles in the food they eat, the stores they shop, and the television shows and movies they watch, the more they will lose their individual cultural identities. They contend that exposure to American values and products erodes other cultures and westernizes the world.

          c. As a result, there is some amount of backlash against American brands worldwide. Despite this, most U.S. brands are doing very well internationally.

4. **Deciding Whether to Go International**

    a. Not all companies need to venture into international markets to survive.

       i. Operating domestically is easier and safer.

      ii. Managers don't need to learn another country's language and laws.

     iii. They don't have to deal with unstable currencies, face political and legal uncertainties, or redesign their products to suit different customer expectations.

     iv. However, companies that operate in global industries, where their strategic positions in specific markets are affected strongly by their overall global positions, must compete on a worldwide basis to succeed.

    b. Any of several factors might draw a company into the international arena.

       i. Global competitors might attack the company's domestic market by offering better products or lower prices.

      ii. The company might want to counterattack these competitors in their home markets to tie up their resources.

     iii. The company's domestic market might be stagnant or shrinking, and foreign markets may present higher sales and profit opportunities.

     iv. Or the company's customers might be expanding abroad and require international servicing.

    c. Before going abroad, the company must weigh several risks and answer many questions about its ability to operate globally.

       i. Can the company learn to understand the preferences and buyer behavior of consumers in other countries?

      ii. Can it offer competitively attractive products?

     iii. Will it be able to adapt to other countries' business cultures and deal effectively with foreign nationals?

     iv. Do the company's managers have the necessary international experience?

v. Has management considered the impact of regulations and the political environments of other countries?

d. Because of the difficulties of entering international markets, most companies do not act until some situation or event thrusts them into the global arena.

    i. Someone—a domestic exporter, a foreign importer, or a foreign government—may ask the company to sell abroad.

    ii. Or the company may be saddled with overcapacity and need to find additional markets for its goods.

5.   **Deciding Which Markets to Enter**

a. Before going abroad, the company should try to define its international marketing objectives and policies. It should decide what volume of foreign sales it wants.

    i. Most companies start small when they go abroad.

    ii. Some plan to stay small, seeing international sales as a small part of their business.

    iii. Other companies have bigger plans, seeing international business as equal to or even more important than their domestic business.

b. The company also needs to choose how many countries it wants to market in. Companies must be careful not to spread themselves too thin or to expand beyond their capabilities by operating in too many countries too soon.

c. Next, the company needs to decide on the types of countries to enter.

    i. A country's attractiveness depends on the product, geographical factors, income and population, political climate, and other factors.

    ii. The seller may prefer certain country groups or parts of the world.

d. After listing possible international markets, the company must screen and rank each one.

    i. Possible global markets should be ranked on several factors, including market size, market growth, cost of doing business, competitive advantage, and risk level.

    ii. The goal is to determine the potential of each market, using indicators such as those shown in Table 19.1.

    iii. Then the marketer must decide which markets offer the greatest long-run return on investment.

6.   **Deciding How to Enter the Market**

a. Once a company has decided to sell in a foreign country, it must determine the best mode of entry.

b. Figure 19.2 shows three market entry strategies, along with the options each one offers.

c. As the figure shows, each succeeding strategy involves more commitment and risk, but also more control and potential profits.

Exporting

d. The simplest way to enter a foreign market is through exporting.

    i. The company may passively export its surpluses from time to time, or it may make an active commitment to expand exports to a particular market.

    ii. In either case, the company produces all its goods in its home country. It may or may not modify them for the export market.

    iii. Exporting involves the least change in the company's product liens, organization, investments, or mission.

e. Companies typically start with indirect exporting, working through independent international marketing intermediaries.

    i. Indirect exporting involves less investment because the firm does not require an overseas marketing organization or set of contacts.

    ii. It also involves less risk. International intermediaries bring know-how and services to the relationship, so the seller normally makes fewer mistakes.

f. Sellers may eventually move into direct exporting, whereby they handle their own exports.

    i. The investment and risk are somewhat greater in this strategy, but so is the potential return. A company can conduct direct exporting in several ways.

        a. It can set up a domestic export department that carries out export activities.

        b. It can set up an overseas sales branch that handles sales, distribution, and perhaps promotion. The sales branch gives the seller more presence and program control in the foreign market and often serves as a display center and customer service center.

        c. The company can also send home-based salespeople abroad at certain times in order to find business.

        d. Finally, the company can do its exporting either through foreign-based distributors who buy and own the goods or through foreign-based agents who sell the goods on behalf of the company.

Joint Venturing

g. A second method of entering a foreign market is joint venturing—joining with foreign companies to produce or market products or services.

    i. Joint venturing differs from exporting in that the company joins with a host country partner to sell or market abroad.

    ii. It differs from direct investment in that an association is formed with someone in the foreign country.

h. There are four types of joint ventures.

    i. Licensing is a simple way for a manufacturer to enter international marketing.

    a. The company enters into an agreement with a licensee in the foreign market.

    b. For a fee or royalty, the licensee buys the right to use the company's manufacturing process, trademark, patent, trade secret, or other item of value.

    c. The company thus gains entry into the market at little risk; the licensee gains production expertise or a well-known product or name without having to start from scratch.

    d. Licensing has potential disadvantages. The firm has less control over the licensee than it would over its own production facilities. Furthermore, if the licensee is very successful, the firm has given up these profits, and if and when the contract ends, it may find it has created a competitor.

ii. Another option is contract manufacturing—the company contracts with manufacturers in the foreign market to produce its product or provide its service.

    a. The drawbacks of contract manufacturing are decreased control over the manufacturing process and loss of potential profits.

    b. The benefits are the chance to start faster, with less risk, and the later opportunity either to form a partnership with or to buy out the local manufacturer.

iii. Under management contracting, the domestic firm supplies management know-how to a foreign company that supplies the capital. The domestic firm exports management services rather than products.

    a. Management contracting is a low-risk method of getting into a foreign market, and it yields income from the beginning.

    b. The arrangement is even more attractive if the contracting firm has an option to buy some share in the managed company later on.

    c. The arrangement is not sensible, however, if the company can put its scarce management talent to better uses or if it can make greater profits by undertaking the whole venture.

    d. Management contracting also prevents the company from setting up its own operations for a period of time.

iv. Joint ownership ventures consist of one company joining forces with foreign investors to create a local business in which they share joint ownership and control.

    a. A company may buy an interest in a local firm, or the two parties may form a new business venture.

    b. Joint ownership may be needed for economic or political reasons.

1. The firm may lack the financial, physical, or managerial resources to undertake the venture alone.
2. Or a foreign government may require joint ownership as a condition for entry.

    c. Joint ownership has certain drawbacks.

1. The partners may disagree over investment, marketing, or other policies.
2. Whereas many U.S. firms like to reinvest earnings for growth, local firms often prefer to take out these earnings; and whereas U.S. firms emphasize the role of marketing, local investors may rely on selling.

Direct Investment

i. The biggest involvement in a foreign market comes through direct investment—the development of foreign-based assembly or manufacturing facilities.

    i. If a company has gained experience in exporting and if the foreign market is large enough, foreign production facilities offer many advantages.

        a. The firm may have lower costs in the form of cheaper labor or raw materials, foreign government investment incentives, and freight savings.

        b. The firm may improve its image in the host country because it creates jobs.

        c. Generally, a firm develops a deeper relationship with government, customers, local suppliers, and distributors, allowing it to adapt its products to the local market better.

        d. Finally, the firm keeps full control over the investment and therefore can develop manufacturing and marketing policies that serve its long-term international objectives.

    ii. The main disadvantage of direct investment is that the firm faces many risks, such as restricted or devalued currencies, falling markets, or government changes. In some cases, a firm has no choice but to accept these risks if it wants to operate in the host country.

7. **Deciding on the Global Marketing Program**

    a. Companies that operate in one or more foreign markets must decide how much, if at all, to adapt their marketing mixes to local conditions.

        i. At one extreme are global companies that use a standardized marketing mix, selling largely the same products and using the same marketing approaches worldwide.

      ii. At the other extreme is an adapted marketing mix. In this case, the producer adjusts the marketing mix elements to each target market, bearing more costs but hoping for a larger market share and return.

b. The question of whether to adapt or standardize the marketing mix has been much debated in recent years.

      i. On the one hand, some global marketers believe that technology is making the world a smaller place, and that consumer needs around the world are becoming more similar.

            a. This pàves the way for "global brands" and standardized global marketing.

            b. Global branding and standardization, in turn, result in greater brand power and reduced costs from economies of scale.

      ii. On the other hand, the marketing concept holds that marketing programs will be more effective if tailored to the unique needs of each targeted customer group.

            a. If this concept applies within a country, it should apply even more in international markets.

            b. Despite global convergence, consumers in different countries still have widely varied cultural backgrounds. They still differ significantly in their needs and wants, spending power, product preferences, and shopping patterns.

c. Global standardization is not an all-or-nothing proposition but rather a matter of degree.

      i. Most international marketers suggest that companies should "think globally but act locally"—that they should seek a balance between standardization and adaptation.

      ii. These marketers advocate a "glocal" strategy in which the firm standardizes certain core marketing elements and localizes others. The corporate level gives global strategic direction; local units focus on the individual consumer differences across global markets.

Product

d. Five strategies allow for adapting product and promotion to a global market. See Figure 19.3.

      i. Straight product extension means marketing a product in a foreign market without any change. The first step, however, should be to find out whether foreign consumers use that product and what form they prefer.

            a. Straight extension has been successful in some cases and disastrous in others.

            b. Straight extension is tempting because it involves no additional product development costs, manufacturing changes, or new promotion. But it can be costly in the long run if products fail to satisfy foreign consumers.

      ii. Product adaptation involves changing the product to meet local conditions or wants.

      iii. Product invention consists of creating something new for a specific country market. This strategy can take two forms.

          a. It might mean maintaining or reintroducing earlier product forms that happen to be well adapted to the needs of a given country.

          b. Or a company might create a new product to meet a need in a given country.

Promotion

e. Companies can either adopt the same promotion strategy they used in the home market or change it for each local market.

      i. Consider advertising messages. Some global companies use a standardized advertising theme around the world. Of course, even in highly standardized promotion campaigns, some small changes might be required to adjust for language and minor cultural differences.

      ii. Colors also are changed sometimes to avoid taboos in other countries.

      iii. Even names must be changed.

f. Other companies follow a strategy of communication adaptation, fully adapting their advertising messages to local markets.

g. Media also needs to be adapted internationally because media availability varies from country to country.

      i. TV advertising time is very limited in Europe, for instance, ranging from four hours a day in France to none in Scandinavian countries. Advertisers must buy time months in advance, and they have little control over airtimes.

      ii. Magazines also vary in effectiveness. For example, magazines are a major medium in Italy and a minor one in Austria.

      iii. Newspapers are national in the United Kingdom but are only local in Spain.

Price

h. Companies also face many problems when setting their international prices.

i. Regardless of how companies go about pricing their products, their foreign prices probably will be higher than their domestic prices for comparable products.

      i. A company may face price escalation. It must add the cost of transportation, tariffs, importer margin, wholesaler margin, and retailer margin to its factory price.

      ii. Depending on these added costs, the product may have to sell for two to five times as much in another country to make the same profit.

    j. Another problem involves setting a price for goods that a company ships to its foreign subsidiaries.

        i. If the company charges a foreign subsidiary too much, it may end up paying higher tariff duties even while paying lower income taxes in that country.

        ii. If the company charges its subsidiary too little, it can be charged with dumping.

            a. Dumping occurs when a company either charges less than its costs or less than it charges in its home market.

            b. Various governments are always watching for dumping abuses, and they often force companies to set the price charged by other competitors for the same or similar products.

    k. Recent economic and technological forces have had an impact on global pricing.

        i. For example, in the European Union, the transition to the euro is reducing the amount of price differentiation.

            a. As consumers recognize price differentiation by country, companies are being forced to harmonize prices throughout the countries that have adopted the single currency.

            b. Companies and marketers that offer the most unique or necessary products or services will be least affected by such "price transparency."

        ii. The Internet will also make global price differences more obvious. When firms sell their wares over the Internet, customers can see how much products sell for in different countries.

Distribution Channels

l. The international company must take a whole-channel view of the problem of distributing products to final consumers.

m. Figure 19.4 shows the three major links between the seller and the final buyer.

        i. The first link, the seller's headquarters organization, supervises the channels and is part of the channel itself.

        ii. The second link, channels between nations, moves the products to the borders of the foreign nations.

        iii. The third link, channels within nations, moves the products from their foreign entry point to the final consumers.

n. Channels of distribution within countries vary greatly from nation to nation.

        i. First, there are the large differences in the numbers and types of intermediaries serving each foreign market.

        ii. Another difference lies in the size and character of retail units abroad. Whereas large-scale retail chains dominate the U.S. scene, much retailing in other countries is done by many small, independent retailers.

8. **Deciding on the Global Marketing Organization**
   a. Companies manage their international marketing activities in at least three different ways.
      i. A firm normally gets into international marketing by simply shipping out its goods. If its international sales expand, the company organizes an export department with a sales manager and a few assistants.
         a. As sales increase, the export department can expand to include various marketing services so that it can actively go after business.
         b. If the firm moves into joint ventures or direct investment, the export department will no longer be adequate.
      ii. Many companies get involved in several international markets and ventures. A company may export to one country, license to another, have a joint ownership venture in a third, and own a subsidiary in a fourth. Sooner or later, it will create international divisions or subsidiaries to handle all its international activity. International divisions are organized in a variety of ways.
         a. An international division's corporate staff consists of marketing, manufacturing, research, finance, planning, and personnel specialists. It plans for and provides services to various operating units, which can be organized in one of three ways.
            1. They can be geographical organizations, with country managers who are responsible for sales-people, sales branches, distributors, and licensees in their respective countries.
            2. Or the operating units can be world product groups, each responsible for worldwide sales of different product groups.
            3. Finally, operating units can be international subsidiaries, each responsible for its own sales and profits.
      iii. Many firms have passed beyond the international division stage and become truly global organizations.
         a. They stop thinking of themselves as national marketers who sell abroad and start thinking of themselves as global marketers. The top corporate management and staff plan worldwide manufacturing facilities, marketing policies, financial flows, and logistical systems.
         b. The global operating units report directly to the chief executive or executive committee of the organization, not to the head of an international division. Executives are trained in worldwide operations, not just domestic or international.

      c. The company recruits management from many countries, buys components and supplies where they cost the least, and invests where the expected returns are the greatest.

      b. Moving into the twenty-first century, major companies must become more global if they hope to compete.

Student Exercises

1.   Key Term: Global Firm

A global firm is a firm that, by operating in more than one country, gains R&D, production, marketing, and financial advantages in its costs and reputation that are not available to purely domestic competitors. The global company sees the world as one market. Research Saab automobile (www.saab.com). Would you consider Saab to be a global firm?

2.   Key Term: GATT

The General Agreement on Tariffs and Trade (GATT) is a 59-year-old treaty designed to promote world trade by reducing tariffs and other international grade barriers. The World Trade Organization (WTO) has the primary responsibility for overseeing GATT. The latest round of GATT negotiations, the Doha Round, began in Doha, Qatar, in late 2001. Read about the recent developments in this round of negotiations (www.gatt.org).

3.   Key Term: Economic Community

An economic community is a groups of nations organized to work toward common goals in the regulation of international trade. One such community is the European Union (EU). Today, the EU represents one of the world's single largest markets. Learn more about the European Union by going to http://europa.eu/index_en.htm. Pay particular attention to the opportunities that exist for college students to study in the European Union and learn about the Community first-hand (http://ec.europa.eu/ploteus/portal/home.jsp)

4.   Key Term: NAFTA

In 1994, the North American Free Trade Agreement (NAFTA) established a free trade zone among the United States, Mexico, and Canada. The agreement created a single market of 435 million people. (Go to http://www.mac.doc.gov/nafta/ for more information). Assume you are a farmer in the U.S. wishing to get into the international arena by exporting to Mexico. How should NAFTA be of benefit to you?

5.   Key Term: Subsistence Economies

In a subsistence economy, the vast majority of people engage in simple agriculture. They consume most of their output and barter the rest for simple goods and services. While these economies offer few market opportunities, they do offer some. What types of goods and services might find a market in such economies?

6.   Key Term: Income Distribution

Income distribution is the spread of low-, medium-, and high-income households throughout a society. Many industrialized nations have a wide spread of income. In contrast, countries with subsistence economies may consist mostly of household with very low family incomes. Still other countries may have income distribution at only the high and low ends of the scale. Take a look at the income distribution for Mexico (one source is: http://www.photius.com/countries/mexico/) and compare it to the United States (www.census.gov). What similarities and differences do you note?

7.   Key Term: Exporting

Exporting is entering a foreign market by selling goods produced in the company's home country, often with little modification. Exporting involves the least change in the company's product lines, organization, investments, or mission. If you were a relatively small company (such as MikWright (www.mikwright.com)) just getting into the export game, how would you most likely choose to begin?

8.   Key Term: Licensing

Licensing is a method of entering a foreign market in which the company enters into an agreement with a licensee in the foreign market. Licensing is a simple way for a manufacturer to enter international marketing. Consider a company like Nordstrom (www.nordstrom.com). If Nordstrom was considering entering into a foreign market through licensing, what would be the risk?

9.   Key Term: Standardized Marketing Mix

A standardized marketing mix is an international marketing strategy for using basically the same product, advertising, distribution channels, and other marketing mix elements in all the company's international markets. Find a company that you believe practices a standardized marketing mix.

10.   Key Term: Communication Adaptation

Communication adaptation is a global communication strategy of fully adapting advertising messages to local markets. The same advertising messages do not work equally as well globally. Adaptation is typically necessary. Take a look at the homepage of Vaseline in the United Kingdom (www.vaseline.co.uk). How might this site and its contents be adapted for the U.S. market?

Marketing ADventure Exercises

1.   Ad Interpretation Challenge: Global Firm
       Ad: Auto – Audi

A global firm is a firm that, by operating in more than one country, gains R&D, production, marketing, and financial advantages in its costs and reputation that are not available to purely domestic competitors. The global company sees the world as one market, making adaptation to the marketing mix as is necessary for each market. Is Audi a true global company?

2.   Ad Interpretation Challenge: Tariffs
       Ad: Auto – Audi

Tariffs are basically taxes a government places on imported goods to either raise revenue or protect domestic produces (or both). Consider Audi. If the United States were to place high tariffs on the importation of German automobiles (such as Audi and Mercedes) in the country, what would be the negative impact on consumers?

3.   Ad Interpretation Challenge: GATT
       Ad: Student Choice

The GATT (General Agreement on Tariffs and Trade) is a decades-old treaty designed to promote world trade by reducing and eliminating tariffs and other international trade barriers. After reviewing the information regarding GATT, find an ad for a product that may well have benefited by the GATT treaty.

4.   Ad Interpretation Challenge: European Union
       Ad: Auto – Fiat

From its beginning in 1957, the European Union (EU) set out to create a single European market by reducing barriers to the free flow of products, services, finances, and labor among member countries and to develop policies on trade with nonmember countries. Consider the Italian company Fiat. If Fiat were having difficulty filling factory positions in Italy, how might Italy being a member of the EU be of value to them?

5.   Ad Interpretation Challenge: FTAA
        Ad: Food & Beverage – Brazilian Fruit

The yet to be established Free Trade Area of the Americas (FTAA) would create a mammoth free trade zone encompassing the 34 countries of North, Central, and South America. How might this benefit Brazil and its efforts to export more fruit to the U.S.?

6.   Ad Interpretation Challenge: Raw Material Exporting Economies
        Ad: Auto – Jaguar

Raw material exporting economies are economies rich in one or more natural resources but poor in other ways. Much of their revenue comes from exporting these resources. Why might Jaguar have a market in such an economy?

7.   Ad Interpretation Challenge: Industrializing Economies
        Ad: Student Choice

In an industrializing economy, manufacturing accounts for between 10 and 20 percent of the country's economy. Industrialization typically creates a new rich class and a small buy growing middle class. Find an ad for a product or service that would likely appeal to these emerging classes.

8.   Ad Interpretation Challenge: Cultural Environment
        Ad: Apparel – Levi's New Collection Diamond Jeans

Every county has its own folkways, norms, and taboos. What is easily acceptable in one country may be completely taboo in another. When developing global marketing strategies, companies must understand these cultural differences. Think about this ad for Levi's. Why might this advertisement not be acceptable in many Muslim cultures?

9.   Ad Interpretation Challenge: "Americanizing" the World
        Ad: Student Choice

There is a growing concern that some of the global marketing strategies of the largest firms are altering individual country cultures. The iconic symbols of large American multinational companies are becoming common place objects in cultures around the world. Critics worry that countries around the globe are losing their individual country cultures. Find an ad for a product that you believe has the potential to become an iconic global symbol of American culture.

10.   Ad Interpretation Challenge: Adapted Marketing Mix
        Ad: Apparel – Levi's New Collection Diamond Jeans

An adapted marketing mix is an international marketing strategy for adjusting the marketing mix elements to each international target market, bearing more costs but hoping for a larger market share and return. Look again at this ad for Levi's Diamond Jeans. How could you vary the marketing mix to make this product more acceptable to the Muslim community?

Chapter 20
Marketing Ethics and Social Responsibility

Learning Objectives

1. Identify the major social criticisms of marketing.
2. Define *consumerism* and *environmentalism* and explain how they affect marketing strategies.
3. Describe the principles of socially responsible marketing.
4. Explain the role of ethics in marketing.

Chapter Overview

This chapter examines the social effects of private marketing practices. A marketing system should sense, serve, and satisfy consumer needs and improve the quality of consumers' lives. In working to meet consumer needs, marketers may take some actions that are not approved of by all the consumers or publics within the social sector. Marketing managers must understand the criticism that the marketing function may encounter. By understanding the criticism, the manager is better prepared to respond to it in a proactive manner. Some of the criticism is justified; some is not.

The primary criticisms of the marketing function with respect to the impact on individual consumers have been categorized as being (1) high prices, (2) deceptive practices, (3) high-pressure selling, (4) shoddy or unsafe products, (5) planned obsolescence, and (6) poor service to disadvantaged consumers. These criticisms have come from a failure to meet individual consumer welfare needs.

A separate set of criticisms is directed toward the marketing function by society in general. Criticism from this larger public body includes comments on creating (1) false wants and too much materialism, (2) too few social goods, (3) cultural pollution, and (4) too much political power. In addition, critics have also pointed out that marketing's impact on businesses may not be good either. Marketing is accused of harming competitors and reducing competition by acquiring competitors, creating barriers to entry, and using unfair marketing practices.

Concerns about the marketing function have led action groups to participate in consumer and environmental movements and to form protest organizations. Marketing's response to action groups and social criticism has largely been positive and proactive. Many companies that were originally opposed to social movements and legislation that was created to address consumer complaints have now recognized a need for positive consumer information, education, and protection. The most successful of these firms have reorganized their companies to follow *enlightened marketing*. This concept is based on the principles of consumer orientation, innovation, value creation, social mission, and social orientation. Also, companies are increasingly responding to the need to provide company policies and guidelines to help their managers deal with questions and issues in marketing ethics. These policies generally cover issues in distributor relations, advertising standards, customer service, pricing, product development, and general ethical standards. Companies that are able to harness social change, understand it, and develop meaningful policies that help create new values in a socially responsible way will have dynamic growth and receive the sales reward from the consumer in the future.

Chapter Outline

1. **Introduction**
   a. Timberland is a company that is defying convention for publicly traded companies.
   b. Jeffrey Swartz, third-generation CEO, exemplifies the values that the company stands for. Timberland places social responsibility at the forefront of all business activities.
   c. Swartz is trying to use the resources, energy, and profits of the company to combat the social ills, help the environment, and improve conditions for laborers around the globe.
   d. A strong value is placed on service. Timberland grants employees 40 hours of paid leave per year to engage in volunteer service projects.
   e. The company is showing strong signs that the strategy is working, not just from a social standpoint, but from a financial one. Revenues, profits, and stock performance are all strong.
   f. Responsible marketers discover what consumers want and respond with marketing offers that create value for buyers in order to capture value in return. The marketing concept is a philosophy of customer value and mutual gain. Its practice leads the economy by an invisible hand to satisfy the many and changing needs of millions of consumers.
   g. Not all marketers follow the marketing concept, however. In fact, some companies use questionable marketing practices, and some marketing actions that seem innocent in themselves strongly affect the larger society. Consider the sale of cigarettes.

2. **Social Criticisms of Marketing**
   a. Marketing receives much criticism. Some of this criticism is justified; much is not. Social critics claim that certain marketing practices hurt individual consumers, society as a whole, and other business firms.

   <u>Marketing's Impact on Individual Consumers</u>
   b. Consumers have many concerns about how well the American marketing system services their interests.
   c. Many critics charge that the American marketing system causes prices to be higher than they would be under more "sensible" systems. They point to three factors.
      i. A long-standing charge is that greedy intermediaries mark up prices beyond the value of their services.
         a. Critics charge that there are too many intermediaries, that intermediaries are inefficient, or that they provide unnecessary or duplicate services. As a result, distribution costs too much, and consumers pay for these excessive costs in the form of higher prices.
         b. How do resellers answer these charges? They argue that intermediaries do work that would otherwise have to be done by manufacturers or consumers. Markups reflect services that consumers themselves want—more convenience, larger stores and assortments, more service, longer store hours, return privileges, and others. In fact, they argue, retail competition is so intense that margins are actually quite low. If some resellers try to charge too much relative to the value they add, other resellers will step in with lower prices.
      ii. Modern marketing is also accused of pushing up prices to finance heavy advertising and sales promotion.
         a. Marketers respond that advertising does add to product costs. But it also adds value by informing potential buyers of the availability and merits of a brand. Brand name products may cost more, but branding gives buyers assurances of consistent quality.
         b. Moreover, consumers can usually buy functional versions of products at lower prices. However, they want and are willing to pay more for products that also provide psychological benefits. Also, heavy advertising and promotion may be necessary for a firm to match competitors' efforts—the business would lose "share of mind" if it did not match competitive spending. At the same time, companies are cost-conscious about promotion and try to spend their money wisely.
      iii. Critics also charge that some companies mark up goods excessively. They point to the drug industry, where a pill costing 5 cents to make may cost the consumer $2 to buy.

      a. Marketers respond that most businesses try to deal fairly with consumers because they want to build customer relationships and repeat business. Most consumer abuses are unintentional.

      b. Marketers also respond that consumers often don't understand the reasons for high markups.

d. Marketers are sometimes accused of deceptive practices that lead consumers to believe they will get more value than they actually do. Deceptive practices fall into three groups.

      i. Deceptive pricing includes practices such as falsely advertising "factory" or "wholesale" prices or a large price reduction from a phony high retail list price.

      ii. Deceptive promotion includes practices such as misrepresenting the product's features or performance or luring the customers to the store for a bargain that is out of stock.

      iii. Deceptive packaging includes exaggerating package contents through subtle design, using misleading labeling, or describing size in misleading terms.

e. Deceptive practices have led to legislation and other consumer protection actions.

      i. For example, in 1938 Congress reacted to such blatant deceptions as Fleischmann's Yeast's claim to straighten crooked teeth by enacting the Wheeler-Lea Act, giving the Federal Trade Commission (FTC) power to regulate "unfair or deceptive acts or practices." The FTC has published several guidelines listing deceptive practices.

      ii. The toughest problem is defining what is "deceptive." The advertiser might claim that it is just "puffery"—innocent exaggeration for effect.

      iii. However, others claim that puffery and alluring imagery can harm consumers in subtle ways, and that consumers must be protected through education.

f. Marketers argue that most companies avoid deceptive practices because such practices harm their business in the long run.

      i. Profitable customer relationships are built on a foundation of value and trust.

      ii. If consumers do not get what they expect, they will switch to more reliable products.

g. Salespeople are sometimes accused of high-pressure selling that persuades people to buy goods they had no thought of buying.

      i. Marketers know that buyers often can be talked into buying unwanted or unneeded things.

         a. Laws require door-to-door and telephone salespeople to announce that they are selling a product. Buyers also have a "three-day cooling-off period" in which they can cancel a contract after rethinking it.

      b. In addition, consumers can complain to Better Business Bureaus or to state consumer protection agencies when they feel that undue selling pressure has been applied.

    ii. But in most cases, marketers have little to gain from high-pressure selling.

        a. Such tactics may work in one-time selling situations for short-term gain.

        b. However, most selling involves building long-term relationships with valued customers. High-pressure or deceptive selling can do serious damage to such relationships.

h. Another criticism is that products lack the needed quality.

    i. One complaint is that many products are not made well and services not performed well.

    ii. A second complaint is that many products deliver little benefit, or that they might even be harmful.

    iii. A third complaint concerns product safety.

        a. Product safety has been a problem for several reasons, including company indifference, increased product complexity, and poor quality control.

        b. For years, Consumers Union—the nonprofit testing and information organization that publishes the *Consumer Reports* magazine and Web site—has reported various hazards in tested products.

        c. However, most manufacturers want to produce quality goods. The way a company deals with product quality and safety problems can damage or help its reputation. Companies selling poor-quality or unsafe products risk damaging conflicts with consumer groups and regulators. Moreover, unsafe products can result in product liability suits and large awards for damages.

i. Critics also have charged that some producers follow a program of planned obsolescence, causing their products to become obsolete before they actually should need replacement.

    i. Other producers are accused of holding back attractive functional features, then introducing them later to make older models obsolete.

    ii. Marketers respond that consumers like style changes; they get tired of the old goods and want a new look in fashion or a new design in cars.

        a. No one has to buy the new look, and if too few people like it, it will simply fail.

        b. For most technical products, customers want the latest innovations, even if older models still work.

        c. Companies that withhold new features run the risk that competitors will introduce the new feature first and steal the market.

       iii. Companies do not design their products to break down earlier, because they do not want to lose customers to other brands. Instead, they seek constant improvement to ensure that products will consistently meet or exceed customer expectations.

j. Finally, the American marketing system has been accused of serving disadvantaged consumers poorly.

       i. For example, critics claim that the urban poor often have to shop in smaller stores that carry inferior goods and charge higher prices.

       ii. Clearly, better marketing systems must be built to service disadvantaged consumers.

          a. Moreover, disadvantaged consumers clearly need consumer protection.

          b. The FTC has taken action against merchants who advertise false values, sell old merchandise as new, or charge too much for credit.

          c. The commission is also trying to make it harder for merchants to win court judgments against low-income people who were wheedled into buying something.

Marketing's Impact on Society as a Whole

k. The American marketing system has been accused of adding to several "evils" in American society at large. Advertising has been a special target—so much so that the American Association of Advertising Agencies launched a campaign to defend advertising against what it felt to be common but untrue criticisms.

l. Critics have charged that the marketing system advocates too much interest in material possessions. People are judged by what they own rather than by who they are.

       i. In the new millennium, many social scientists have noted a reaction against the opulence and waste of the previous decades and a return to more basic values and social commitment.

       ii. The critics do not view this interest in material things as a natural state of mind but rather as a matter of false wants created by marketing. Businesses hire Madison Avenue (where the head-quarters of many advertising agencies are located) to stimulate people's desires for goods, and Madison Avenue uses the mass media to create materialistic models of the good life. Thus, marketing is seen as creating false wants that benefit industry more than they benefit consumers.

       iii. These criticisms overstate the power of business to create needs, however.

          a. People have strong defenses against advertising and other marketing tools.

          b. Marketers are most effective when they appeal to existing wants rather than when they attempt to create new ones.

      c. Furthermore, people seek information when making important purchases and often do not rely on single sources. Even minor purchases that may be affected by advertising messages lead to repeat purchases only if the product performs as promised.

      d. Finally, the high failure rate of new products shows that companies are not able to control demand.

    iv. On a deeper level, our wants and values are influenced not only by marketers but also by family, peer groups, religion, ethnic background, and education.

m. Business has been accused of overselling private goods at the expense of public goods.

    i. As private goods increase, they require more public services that are usually not forthcoming. For example, an increase in automobile ownership (private good) requires more highways, traffic control, parking spaces, and police services (public goods). The overselling of private goods results in "social costs."

    ii. A way must be found to restore a balance between private and public goods.

      a. One option is to make producers bear the full social costs of their operations. The government could require automobile manufacturers to build cars with even more safety features, more efficient engines, and better pollution control systems.

      b. A second option is to make consumers pay the social costs. For example, many cities around the world are starting to charge "congestion tolls" in an effort to reduce traffic congestion.

n. Critics charge the marketing system with creating cultural pollution. Our senses are being constantly assaulted by advertising.

    i. These interruptions continually pollute people's minds with messages of materialism, sex, power, or status. Although most people do not find advertising overly annoying, some critics call for sweeping changes.

    ii. Marketers answer the charges of "commercial noise" with these arguments.

      a. First, they hope that their ads reach primarily the target audience. But because of mass-communication channels, some ads are bound to reach people who have no interest in the product and are therefore bored or annoyed. People who buy magazines addressed to their interests rarely complain about the ads because the magazines advertise products of interest.

      b. Second, ads make much of television and radio free to users and keep down the costs of magazines and newspapers. Many people think commercials are a small price to pay for these benefits.

      c. Finally, today's consumers have alternatives.

o. Another criticism is that business wields too much political power.

    i. Advertisers are accused of holding too much power over the mass media, limiting media freedom to report independently and objectively.

    ii. American industries do promote and protect their own interests. They have a right to representation in Congress and the mass media, although their influence can become too great. Fortunately, many powerful business interests once thought to be untouchable have been tamed in the public interest.

    iii. Too much business power tends to result in counterforces that check and offset these powerful interests.

<u>Marketing's Impact on Other Businesses</u>

p. Critics also charge that a company's marketing practices can harm other companies and reduce competition. Three problems are involved: acquisitions of competitors, marketing practices that create barriers to entry, and unfair competitive marketing practices.

    i. Critics claim that firms are harmed and competition reduced when companies expand by acquiring competitors rather than by developing their own new products.

        a. Acquisition is a complex subject. Acquisitions can sometimes be good for society. The acquiring company may gain economies of scale that lead to lower costs and lower prices.

        b. A well-managed company may take over a poorly managed company and improve its efficiency.

    ii. Critics have also charged that marketing practices bar new companies from entering an industry. Large marketing companies can use patents and heavy promotion spending, and can tie up suppliers or dealers to drive out competitors.

    iii. Finally, some firms have in fact used unfair competitive marketing practices with the intention of hurting or destroying other firms.

        a. They may set their prices below costs, threaten to cut off business with suppliers, or discourage the buying of a competitor's products.

        b. Various laws work to prevent such predatory competition. It is difficult, however, to prove that the intent or action was really predatory.

3. **Citizen and Public Actions to Regulate Marketing**

    a. Because some people view business as the cause of many economic and social ills, grassroots movements have arisen from time to time to keep business in line.

Consumerism

b. American business firms have been the target of organized consumer movements on three occasions.

    i. The first consumer movement took place in the early 1900s. It was fueled by rising prices, Upton Sinclair's writings on conditions in the meat industry, and scandals in the drug industry.

    ii. The second consumer movement, in the mid-1930s, was sparked by an upturn in consumer prices during the Great Depression and another drug scandal.

    iii. The third movement began in the 1960s. Consumers had become better educated, products had become more complex and potentially hazardous, and people were unhappy with American institutions. Ralph Nader appeared on the scene to force many issues, and other well-known writers accused big businesses of wasteful and unethical practices.

c. But what is the consumer movement? Consumerism is an organized movement of citizens and government agencies to improve the rights and power of buyers in relation to sellers.

d. Traditional seller's rights include:

    i. The right to introduce any product in any size and style, provided it is not hazardous to personal health or safety—or, if it is, to include proper warnings and controls

    ii. The right to charge any price for the product, provided no discrimination exists among similar kinds of buyers

    iii. The right to spend any amount to promote the product, provided it is not defined as unfair competition

    iv. The right to use any product message, provided it is not misleading or dishonest in content or execution

    v. The right to use any buying incentive programs, provided they are not unfair or misleading

e. Traditional buyers' rights include:

    i. The right not to buy a product that is offered for sale

    ii. The right to expect the product to be safe

    iii. The right to expect the product to perform as claimed

f. Comparing these rights, many believe that the balance of power lies on the seller's side. True, the buyer can refuse to buy. But critics feel that the buyer has too little information, education, and protection to make wise decisions when facing sophisticated sellers.

g. Consumer advocates call for the following additional consumer rights:

    i. The right to be well informed about important aspects of the product

    ii. The right to be protected against questionable products and marketing practices

    iii. The right to influence products and marketing practices in ways that will improve the "quality of life"

h. Each proposed right has led to more specific proposals by consumerists.

      i. The right to be informed includes the right to know the true interest on a loan (truth in lending), the true cost per unit of a brand (unit pricing), the ingredients in a product (ingredient labeling), the nutritional value of foods (nutritional labeling), product freshness (open dating), and the true benefits of a product (truth in advertising).

      ii. Proposals related to consumer protection include strengthening consumer rights in cases of business fraud, requiring greater product safety, and giving more power to government agencies.

      iii. Proposals relating to quality of life include controlling the ingredients that go into certain products and packaging, reducing the level of advertising "noise," and putting consumer representatives on company boards to protect consumer interests.

i. Consumers have not only the right but also the responsibility to protect themselves instead of leaving this function to someone else.

      i. Consumers who believe they got a bad deal have several remedies available, including contacting the company or the media; contacting federal, state, or local agencies; and going to small-claims court.

Environmentalism

j. Whereas consumerists consider whether the marketing system is efficiently serving consumer wants, environmentalists are concerned with marketing's effects on the environment and with the costs of serving consumer needs and wants.

k. Environmentalism is an organized movement of concerned citizens, businesses, and government agencies to protect and improve people's living environment.

l. Environmentalists are not against marketing and consumption; they simply want people and organizations to operate with more care for the environment.

      i. The marketing system's goal, they assert, should not be to maximize consumption, consumer choice, or consumer satisfaction, but rather to maximize life quality.

      ii. And "life quality" means not only the quantity and quality of consumer goods and services, but also the quality of the environment.

      iii. Environmentalists want environmental costs included in both producer and consumer decision making.

m. The first wave of modern environmentalism in the United States was driven by environmental groups and concerned consumers in the 1960s and 1970s.

      i. They were concerned with damage to the ecosystem caused by strip-mining, forest depletion, acid rain, loss of the atmosphere's ozone layer, toxic wastes, and litter.

    ii. They also were concerned with the loss of recreational areas and with the increase in health problems caused by bad air, polluted water, and chemically treated food.

n. The second environmentalism wave was driven by government, which passed laws and regulations during the 1970s and 1980s governing industrial practices impacting the environment. This wave hit some industries hard.

o. The first two environmentalism waves have now merged into a third and stronger wave in which companies are accepting responsibility for doing no harm to the environment.

    i. They are shifting from protest to prevention, and from regulation to responsibility.

    ii. More and more companies are adopting policies of environmental sustainability—developing strategies that both sustain the environment and produce profits for the company.

    iii. Figure 20.1 shows a grid that companies can use to gauge their progress toward environmental sustainability.

        a. At the most basic level, a company can practice pollution prevention. This involves more than pollution control—cleaning up waste after it has been created. Pollution prevention means eliminating or minimizing waste before it is created.

        b. At the next level, companies can practice product stewardship—minimizing not just pollution from production but all environmental impacts through the full product life cycle. Many companies are adopting design for environment (DFE) practices that involve thinking ahead to design products that are easier to recover, reuse, or recycle.

        c. At the third level, companies look to the future and plan for new environment technologies. Many organizations that have made good sustainability headway are still limited by existing technologies. To develop fully sustainable strategies, they will need to develop new technologies.

        d. Finally, companies can develop a sustainability vision that serves as a guide to the future. It shows how the company's products and services, processes, and policies must evolve and what new technologies must be developed to get there. This vision of sustainability provides a framework for pollution control, product stewardship, and environmental technology.

     iv. Most companies today focus on the lower-left quadrant of the grid in Figure 20.1, investing most heavily in pollution prevention. Some forward-looking companies practice well-defined sustainability visions. A heavy emphasis on the top half suggests that a company has good environmental vision but lacks the skills needed to implement it. Thus, companies should work at developing all four dimensions of environmental sustainability.

   p. Environmentalism creates some special challenges for global marketers.

     i. As international trade barriers come down and global markets expand, environmental issues are having an ever-greater impact on international trade.

     ii. However, environmental policies still vary widely from country to country.

Public Actions to Regulate Marketing

   q. Citizen concerns about marketing practices will usually lead to public attention and legislative proposals.

   r. Figure 20.2 illustrates the major legal issues facing marketing management.

4. **Business Actions Toward Socially Responsible Marketing**

   a. At first, many companies opposed consumerism and environmentalism. They thought the criticisms were either unfair or unimportant.

     i. But by now, most companies have grown to accept the new consumer rights, at least in principle.

     ii. Many of these companies have responded positively to consumerism and environmentalism as a way to create greater customer value and to strengthen customer relationships.

Enlightened Marketing

   b. The philosophy of enlightened marketing holds that a company's marketing should support the best long-run performance of the marketing system. Enlightened marketing consists of five principles.

     i. Consumer-oriented marketing means that the company should view and organize its marketing activities from the consumer's point of view. It should work to sense, serve, and satisfy the needs of a defined group of customers. Only by seeing the world through its customers' eyes can the company build lasting and profitable customer relationships.

  ii. According to the principle of customer-value marketing, the company should put most of its resources into customer value-building marketing investments. Many things marketers do may raise sales in the short run but add less value than would actual improvements in the product's quality, features, or convenience. Enlightened marketing calls for building long-run consumer loyalty and relationships by continually improving the value consumers receive from the firm's marketing offer.

  iii. The principle of innovative marketing requires that the company continuously seek real product and marketing improvements. The company that overlooks new and better ways to do things will eventually lose customers to another company that has found a better way.

  iv. Sense-of-mission marketing means that the company should define its mission in broad social terms rather than narrow product terms. When a company defines a social mission, employees feel better about their work and have a clearer sense of direction.

  v. Following the principle of societal marketing, an enlightened company makes marketing decisions by considering consumers' wants and interest, the company's requirements, and society's long-run interests. The company is aware that neglecting consumer and societal long-run interests is a disservice to consumers and society.

    a. A societally oriented marketer wants to design products that are not only pleasing but also beneficial. The difference is shown in Figure 20.3. Products can be classified according to their degree of immediate consumer satisfaction and long-run consumer benefit.

      1. Deficient products, such as bad-tasting and ineffective medicine, have neither immediate appeal nor long-run benefits.

      2. Pleasing products give high immediate satisfaction but may hurt consumers in the long run. An example is cigarettes.

      3. Salutary products have low appeal but may benefit consumers in the long run—for instance, seat belts and air bags.

      4. Desirable products give both high immediate satisfaction and high long-run benefits, such as a tasty and nutritious breakfast food.

    b. Companies should try to turn all of their products into desirable products.

Marketing Ethics

c. Conscientious marketers face many moral dilemmas. The best thing to do is often unclear. Because not all managers have fine moral sensitivity, companies need to develop corporate marketing ethics policies—broad guidelines that everyone in the organization must follow.

d. The finest guidelines cannot resolve all the difficult ethical situations the marketer faces. Table 20.1 lists some difficult ethical situations marketers could face during their careers.

e. But what principle should guide companies and marketing managers on issues of ethics and social responsibility?

    i. One philosophy is that such issues are decided by the free market and legal system. Under this principle, companies and their managers are not responsible for making moral judgments. Companies can in good conscience do whatever the system allows.

    ii. A second philosophy puts responsibility not on the system but in the hands of individual companies and managers. This more enlightened philosophy suggests that a company should have a "social conscience." Companies and managers should apply high standards of ethics and morality when making corporate decisions, regardless of "what the system allows."

f. Each company and marketing manager must work out a philosophy of socially responsible and ethical behavior. Under the societal marketing concept, each manager must look beyond what is legal and allowed and develop standards based on personal integrity, corporate conscience, and long-run consumer welfare.

g. As with environmentalism, the issue of ethics provides special challenges for international marketers.

    i. Business standards and practices vary a great deal from one country to the next. For example, whereas bribes and kickbacks are illegal for U.S. firms, they are standard business practice in many South American countries.

    ii. The question arises as to whether a company must lower its ethical standards to compete effectively in countries with lower standards. In one study, two researchers posed this question to chief executives of large international companies and got a unanimous response: No.

h. For the sake of all the company's stakeholders—customers, suppliers, employees, shareholders, and the public—it is important to make a commitment to a common set of shared standards worldwide.

i. Many industrial and professional associations have suggested codes of ethics, and many companies are now adopting their own codes.

    i. For example, the American Marketing Association, an international association of marketing managers and scholars, developed the code of ethics shown in Table 20.2.

    ii. Companies are also developing programs to teach managers about important ethics issues and help them find the proper responses.

       iii. Furthermore, most major U.S. companies have appointed high-level ethics officers to champion ethics issues and to help resolve ethics problems and concerns facing employees.

    j. Still, written codes and ethics programs do not ensure ethical behavior. Ethics and social responsibility require a total corporate commitment. They must be a component of the overall corporate culture.

Student Exercises

1.   Key Term: High Advertising Costs

Marketers are always being accused of pushing up the prices on products to finance heavy advertising. A company may spend millions of dollars to advertise a product. Why can't they just cut back on the advertising and drop the price to the consumer? If you were responsible for the marketing of Dole pineapple (www.dole.com), how would you respond to such a statement?

2.   Key Term: Planned Obsolescence

Planned obsolescence is the practice of making products obsolete before they actually should need to be replaced. Critics charge that some producers continually change consumer concepts of acceptable styles to encourage more and earlier buying. Take a few minutes look at the new season of ready-to-wear fashion from BCBG (www.bcbg.com). How is it different from what you currently see being worn by women? Is BCBG engaging in planned obsolescence? How would marketers respond to this charge?

3.   Key Term: Consumerism

Consumerism is an organized movement of citizens and government agencies to improve the rights and power of buyers in relation to sellers. Consumers have not only the right but the responsibility to protect themselves instead of leaving this function entirely to someone else. Knowledge is one of the most powerful ways that the consumer can protect themselves. Knowing from whom you are buying, their reputation and standing in the market, provides the buyer with tremendous power. Look at the website for the Better Business Bureau (www.bbb.org). The Better Business Bureau provides the consumer with a wealth of information regarding merchants all around the country and in your home town. Take some time to look up some of your favorite companies.

4.   Key Term: Environmentalism

Environmentalists are concerned with marketing's effects on the environment. Environmentalism is an organized movement of concerned citizens, businesses, and government agencies to protect and improve people's living environment. Environmentalists want people and organizations to operate with more care and concern for the environment. Take a look at Green Globe (www.greenglobe.org). Green Globe is global environmental certification organization specializing in the hospitality industry. How do hotels benefit from this certification?

5.   Key Term: Environmental Sustainability

Environmental sustainability is a management approach that involves developing strategies that both sustain the environment and produce benefits for the company. Environmental sustainability takes on many forms. Review the Environmental Sustainability Grid from this chapter. Now, think about Patagonia (www.patagonia.com). Where does Patagonia fit on this grid?

6.   Key Term: Innovative Marketing

Innovative marketing is a principle of enlightened marketing that requires a company seek real product and marketing improvements. The company that overlooks new and better ways to do things will eventually lose customers to another company that has found a better way. Find a company that you believe exemplifies innovative marketing.

7.   Key Term: Sense-of-Mission Marketing

Sense-of-mission marketing is a principle of enlightened marketing that holds a company should define its mission in broad social terms rather than narrow product terms. Brands linked with broad social missions can serve the best long-run interests of both the brand and the consumer. Take a look at Starbucks (www.starbucks.com). How is there sense-of-mission made evident to consumers?

8.   Key Term: Societal Marketing

Societal marketing is a principle of enlightened marketing that holds a company should make marketing decisions by considering consumers' wants, the company's requirement, consumers' long-run interests, and society's long-run interests. Alert companies view societal problems as opportunities. Locate a company that practices societal marketing.

9.   Key Term: Pleasing Products

Pleasing products are products that give high immediate satisfaction but may hurt consumers in the long run. From a societal marketing standpoint, companies should question their long-term commitment to such products. Your text cites cigarettes and junk food as examples. What about alcohol? Do you believe alcohol fits into this category? Take a look at some of producers' websites (www.stoli.com; www.barcardi.com; www.millerlite.com) for more information.

10.   Key Term: Desirable Products

Products (or services) that give both high immediate satisfaction and high long-run benefits to consumers are known as desirable products. Companies should try to turn all of their products into desirable products. Do you believe Hard Rock Casinos (www.hardrock.com/casinos) to be a desirable product?

Marketing ADventure Exercises

1.   Ad Interpretation Challenge: Planned Obsolescence
        Ad: Apparel – Levi's New Collection Diamond Jeans

Critics have charged that some producers follow a program of planned obsolescence, causing their products to become obsolete before they actually should need replacement. Consider this ad for Levi's. Why might some say this is an ad for a planned obsolescence product?

2.   Ad Interpretation Challenge: "Shop till You Drop"
        Ad: Apparel – Johnsons

The term "shop till you drop" seems to have characterized the go-go 1980s and 1990s, when the drive for wealth and possessions hit new highs. Critics have charged that the marketing system urges too much interest in material possessions. How might this ad for Johnsons encourage this "shop till you drop" mentality?

3.   Ad Interpretation Challenge: "Congestion Toll"
        Ad: Auto – Porsche

 Business has been accused of overselling private goods at the expense of public goods. As private goods increase, they typically require more public services that are usually not forthcoming. A way must be found to restore a balance between private and public goods. Why might Porsche be subjected to a congestion toll in some cities?

4.   Ad Interpretation Challenge: Consumerism
      Ad: Food & Beverage – McDonalds

Consumerism is an organized movement of citizens and government agencies to improve the rights and power of buyers in relation to sellers. Consumers have not only the right but the responsibility to protect themselves instead of leaving this function entirely to someone else. How might McDonalds possibly find themselves on the wrong end of the consumerism movement?

5.   Ad Interpretation Challenge: Environmental Sustainability
      Ad: Apparel – Timberland

Environmental sustainability is a management approach that involves developing strategies that both sustain the environment and produce benefits for the company. Simply stated, environmental sustainability is about generating profits while helping to save the planet. Environmental sustainability takes on many forms. Go to Timberland's website (http://www.timberland.com/timberlandserve/timberlandserve_index.jsp) and learn about their belief in environmental sustainability.

6.   Ad Interpretation Challenge: Consumer-Oriented Marketing
      Ad: Student Choice

Consumer-oriented marketing means that the company should view and organize its marketing activities from the consumer's point of view. It should work hard to sense, serve, and satisfy the needs of a defined group of customers. Find an ad for a company that you believe practices consumer-oriented marketing.

7.   Ad Interpretation Challenge: Innovative Marketing
      Ad: Apparel – Polartec

The principle of innovative marketing requires that the company continuously seek real product and marketing improvements. Why does Polartec (www.polartec.com) fit here? Or does it?

8.   Ad Interpretation Challenge: Sense-of-Mission Marketing
      Ad: Travel & Tourism – Wild Drift

Sense-of-mission marketing is a principle of enlightened marketing that holds a company should define its mission in broad social terms rather than narrow product terms. Take a look at these ads for Wild Drift Adventures. How do you believe sense-of-mission marketing fits in with this company?

9.   Ad Interpretation Challenge: Pleasing Products
        Ad: Student Choice

Pleasing products are products that give high immediate satisfaction but may hurt consumers in the long run. From a societal marketing standpoint, companies should question their long-term commitment to such products. Locate an ad that is promoting a product you could consider as fitting into this category.

10.   Ad Interpretation Challenge: Marketing Ethics
        Ad: Auto – Jeep

Because not all managers have finely-tuned moral sensitivity, companies need to develop corporate marketing ethics policies. These are broad guidelines that everyone in the organization must follow. Consider Jeep. If Jeep were attempting to initiate business in another country (Saudi Arabia, for example), should they be held accountable to marketing ethics as practiced in the United States or marketing ethics as practiced in the foreign country?

Suggested Answers

Chapter 1

Student Exercises

1.   Apple: Right up front, Apple highlights "news" concerning their products—from an iPod on the international space station to praise from recent product reviews. This format helps to pull in new customers by showing Apple products as advanced, user-friendly, and "cool." Cingular: Prominently displayed on the home page is a graphic which alternates between touting the Cingular network as having the fewest dropped calls and claiming to have the best phones AND the best plans. What a great way to pull in new customers while reinforcing your present customers. American Cancer Society: The "I need information for…" link dominate on the ACS home page makes it easy for new visitors to quickly find the information they are seeking. Likewise, return guests are presented with links to take them to their personalized page.

2.   In this case, LaSalle Bank is presenting a "market offering" designed to provide information on and possible solutions to the problems around residents' lack of grocery stores and nutritious food choices.

3.   The HD-DVD does a much better job of connecting with the customer and focusing on customer-related benefits. Blu-ray just doesn't seem to be focused on benefits to the consumer. Too much emphasis is given to the technology and how great it is, while overlooking the customer.

4.   A quick review of their websites leads you to believe that Starbucks is targeting a more "sophisticated" coffee drinker by placing emphasis on its music offerings and the lushness of its stores. Caribou, on the other hand, comes across as targeting a more "outdoorsy," fun crowd. Caribou retail locations also follow this theme by their rustic décor and furnishings.

5.   Tobacco manufacturers are in a difficult position. Their primary product is one that has been shown to be harmful to their customers, with long-term use. On the other hand, to just stop the manufacture and marketing of the product, not only divests the companies of their livelihood but also deprives their customers of a product they desire. All the companies mentioned here are trying to walk this tightrope by providing their customers with lots of easily accessible information about the dangers of smoking and where to turn to for help if they are trying to give it up.

6.   Many universities today are offering condensed classes during traditional break periods (like Christmas or Spring Break). Schools are also offering more weekend and on-line classes, in an effort to better serve their increasingly diverse population.

7.   Several examples may come readily to mind, including airline partner alliances, such as SkyTeam (www.skyteam.com), OneWorld (www.oneworld.com), and Star Alliance (www.staralliance.com). Another notable example is the Caribbean Tourism Organization (www.doitcaribbean.com).

8.   Here you are looking for local companies that you believe have done a good job of maintaining and growing customers. The most successful companies are those that are able to acquire a customer relatively early on and then "grow" that customer. "Growing" a customer refers to having that customer return for more and more additional (hopefully, higher margin) products and/or services.

9.   When looking at how globalization has impacted you directly, don't just think about whether you believe you may someday be working overseas. Look at the labels in the clothes you wear. Think about the car you drive and where either the car or its components were made. It's hard to escape the impact of globalization in our lives. It truly is everywhere.

10.   When considering companies you believe have a social responsibility mindset, you might want to think about those who place their responsibility to society right up front. For example, take a look at companies such as Newman's Own (www.newmansown.com), Starbucks coffee (www.starbucks.com), Chevron (www.chevron.com), and Syngenta (www.syngenta.com).

Marketing ADventure Exercises

1. Ad Interpretation Challenge: New Marketing Frontiers
    Ad: Apparel—Levi's New Collection

Levi's have been negatively impacted by the move to more "fashion"-oriented jeans (for example, Citizens of Humanity and 7 for All Mankind). Levi has been viewed as a rather traditional company offering traditional products. This ad shows that the company's market offering includes the non-traditional, fashion-forward products today's consumers crave.

2. Ad Interpretation Challenge: Insightful Segmentation
    Ad: Electronics—Compaq

Compaq is appealing to the socially conscious consumer with this ad. They are targeting the consumer who wants and expects more from the companies they do business with than just a quality product. In essence, they are saying "We know you have a choice of many computer companies with which to do business. However, we are more than just a computer company; we are also a socially conscious member of our community, working to make life better for those with need."

3. Ad Interpretation Challenge: The Production Concept
    Ad: Student Choice

You should be looking for an ad that highlights the principles of the production concept—for example, an ad that focuses on a product's wide availability and/or affordability. Ad examples may include Pepsi and/or IKEA.

4. Ad Interpretation Challenge: The Marketing Concept
    Ad: Travel and Tourism—Leisure Entertainment—Bali

This ad is appealing to the basic hedonistic need that people have to just unwind and relax. The ad is successful because it, first, recognizes the consumer need and then, second, provides the reader with an avenue of satisfying this need.

5. Ad Interpretation Challenge: The Marketing Concept
    Ad: Student Choice

Keeping in mind the marketing concept is a customer-driven concept, you may want to consider either the ad for Polartec (Apparel – Polartec) or the ad for Tabasco (Food & Beverage – Tobasco). Both of these ads highlight the benefits to consumers from the use and consumption of the products.

6.   Ad Interpretation Challenge: What's Good for Society
        Ad: Auto—Hyundai Avante

The company is fulfilling its societal interests by producing and marketing a vehicle with exceptionally high fuel economy. At the same time, they are providing a product with appeal to the marketplace, thus resulting (hopefully) in increased sales.

7.   Ad Interpretation Challenge: Value
        Ad: General Retail—World's Biggest Bookstore

This ad just screams "Value!" By claiming to have book prices so low that even those who do not typically read can afford them, World's Biggest Bookstore is showing how they provide the customer with exceptional value.

8.   Ad Interpretation Challenge: Making the Customer Happy
        Ad: Auto—Volvo S60

This ad highlighting the Volvo S60 wears its customer loyalty (hence customer satisfaction) on its arm, literally. This is one example of an ad prominently exhibiting the central component of the ad. Other examples you might select include: Food and Beverage—Winterfresh and Autos—Mercedes.

9.   Ad Interpretation Challenge: Club Marketing Program
        Ad: Student Choice

You may want to consider the ad for MBNA (Financial—MBNA). This ad highlights a product that seeks customers with a common interest and works to create a member community—those customers loyal to Clemson University.

10.   Ad Interpretation Challenge: Increasing Lifetime Value and Customer Equity
        Ad: Auto—Jaguar

These ads seek to distinguish Jaguar from other competitors in the luxury automobile category by portraying Jaguars as different from the "run-of-the-mill" luxury auto. At the same time, the ads are a departure from previous Jaguar advertising by emphasizing a more youthful, playful image and deemphasizing the stogy traditional image that has for so long dominated Jaguar ads. As a result, the ads should appeal to younger consumers. The resulting hope is that these consumers will make their initial Jaguar purchase and then stay with the brand as they grow and mature in their lives.

Chapter 2

Student Exercises

1.   Recognizing the increasingly competitive global automobile environment, Ford has announced a plan to direct additional attention to worldwide markets and customers. Additionally, acknowledging the squeeze on profits, Ford has undertaken efforts to improve leverage of global assets and capabilities.

2.   All three of these mission statements emphasize putting the customer first. Starbucks, however, goes much further with their mission statement by emphasizing the relationship between the company, the environment, the customer, the supplier, and the communities in which they operate.

3.   Ford Motor Company is made up of a number of different products and businesses including: Ford, Mercury, Jaguar, Land Rover, and Ford Credit.

4.   Numerous possibilities exist that would fulfill this requirement. You might want to consider taking a look at either Waffle House (www.wafflehouse.com), which has now started accepting credit cards, or Subway (www.subway.com), which continues to rapidly open more and more locations.

5.   This is a wide-open question with multiple possible solutions. Take a look at either Monarch Beverage Company (www.monarchbeverages.com) or Quinenco S.A. (www.quinenco.cl) for two good examples.

6.   You might want to consider IBM (www.ibm.com) who recently sold its personal computer business to Levono (www.levono.com), a Chinese company. You may also wish to take a look at Alcoa (www.alcoa.com), which recently completed the sale of its specialty chemicals division.

7.   Without a doubt, Rolls Royce is targeting to the ultra-luxury car customer. They are directing themselves toward that consumer who wants the best, has the means to purchase the best, and is willing to do so. On the other hand, Chery, who is seeking to begin selling cars in the United States, is targeting the most financially cautious customer—those consumers who have very limited funds to spend on an automobile.

8.   Local restaurants can choose to position themselves in many ways. They may decide they want to be known as "home grown" and local, catering to the community and being a part of that community. Or, they may want to be known as an upscale establishment, where only the most social elite are welcome. Many other possible positioning strategies exist from which your favorite restaurant may choose.

9.   The product being offered, in the case of Southwest Airlines, is transportation. Just because it is not a physical entity does not mean it is not a product. Price is the amount of money customers have to pay in order to receive the product. In the case of airlines, this price is very volatile and changes frequently based on availability, time from departure, and a myriad of other variables. Place involves everything that Southwest does to make its product available to the consumer. Not only the airports, but the ticket counters and self-service kiosks. Finally, promotion is everything involved in communicating Southwest to the customer. This includes traditional television and billboard advertising. This also includes their easy to navigate website and their enthusiastic employees.

10.   When considering the SWOT analysis for your school, keep in mind that you need to view your school from a dispassionate or neutral point of view. Only in this manner can you truly see what challenges and problems it may be facing.

Marketing ADventure Exercises

1.   Ad Interpretation Challenge: The Mission Statement
       Ad: Apparel—Polartec

Polartec's mission statement could read something like this: "We seek to be the premier provider of high performance cold weather clothing for the extreme outdoor enthusiast."

2.   Ad Interpretation Challenge: Distinctive Competencies
       Ad: Apparel—Umbro

Football. Umbro is making the statement that they are the authority and/or leader in providing football (soccer) footwear. Their ads make very clear to the viewer that this is their distinctive competency.

3.   Ad Interpretation Challenge: Business Portfolio
       Ad: Food and Beverage—Pizza World

The new product the ad is promoting is a seafood pizza—a product not typically found in the collection of products offered by most pizza restaurants.

4.   Ad Interpretation Challenge: Stars
       Ad: Student Choice

Several examples exist. You may want to examine the ad for Sony's PlayStation (Electronics—PlayStation). Certainly, PlayStation would be considered a star in the gaming market, with its high-market share in a high-growth market.

5.   Ad Interpretation Challenge: Market Penetration
       Ad: General Retail—Drugmart

Drugmart is reaching out to its current market segment by informing them of home delivery of their drug order. In this way, they are attempting to set themselves apart from the competition and entice more of their current market segment to increase frequency of use.

6.   Ad Interpretation Challenge: Market Development
       Ad: Travel and Tourism—Turkish Airlines

With this ad, Turkish Airlines is introducing new and expanded service. The company does not appear to be reaching out to new market segments; rather, they are providing new services to their existing customers.

7.   Ad Interpretation Challenge: Value Chain
        Ad: Exhibits and Entertainment—D-Day (Melting Pot)

This ad is a great example of how a value chain actually works. In a value chain, the sum of the individual members is greater (and, thus, provides greater value) than the individual members. Through coordinated work together, the members of the D-Day forces were able to overcome incredible odds and carry the day—something none of the solo players would have been able to accomplish individually.

8.   Ad Interpretation Challenge: The Value-Delivery Network
        Ad: Internet—Shopnow

This ad shows how Shopnow acts as a clearinghouse for over 50,000 stores. This relationship allows the consumer to compare stores, products, and prices in one place. The ultimate goal is providing the customer with superior value.

9.   Ad Interpretation Challenge: Product Positioning
        Ad: Auto—Lincoln

SUVs have gotten a lot of attention lately, in part due to the ever-increasing price of gasoline and their relatively poor mileage performance. Lincoln shifts the emphasis to safety. In this ad Lincoln is positioning the Navigator as "big." Along with this large size comes occupant safety.

10.   Ad Interpretation Challenge: The Product
        Ad: Student Choice

You may want to consider the ad for Rimmel (Cosmetics and Pharmaceuticals—Rimmel) or Scholl (Cosmetics and Pharmaceuticals—Scholl). Both of these ads downplay the actual product; however, they still make certain you realize its importance.
Marketing ADventure Exercises

Chapter 3

Student Exercises

1.   While the microenvironment is going to vary from school to school, all are faced with some of the same basic microenvironmental actors, such as availability of qualified teachers and support personnel, alumni, quantity and quality of students (both current and potential), and the physical plant.

2.   From a review of Amazon.com's website, you will find that they partner with both the USPS and UPS to efficiently deliver their merchandise. Also, Amazon has partnered with and makes heavy use of banner advertising on sites such as Google.com and CNN.com in an effort to draw more customers to the Amazon site. Bebe, a moderately-pricy and trendy women's clothing store, makes exclusive use of UPS to deliver their products. Additionally, Bebe is a featured store occasionally on the Style Channel's "The Look for Less," providing the store with increased exposure and promotional opportunities.

3.   Many publics have an interest in or impact on your school. Your administrators must consider, among others, you (students), parents, the community, funding sources (private and public), alumni, and employers. This is many different people to try and take into consideration when making organizational decisions.

4.   There are so many possible answers to this question. You may want to consider taking a look at Curves Fitness (www.curves.com), a fitness center that caters to older women, and SeaRay (www.searay.com), a yacht manufacturing company whose primary clientele are baby boomer males.

5.   Just a casual look at the Scion website will let you know that this is not your typical car website or your typical car. Everything about the site screams Generation Y, from the use of language to the music played. Take the time to "build" your favorite car. This process reveals much that is geared toward the sensibilities of Gen Y.

6.   This is becoming a bit harder to do, as more and more companies recognize the changes and shifts in the American household. However, consider these two examples: Beaches Family Resorts (www.beaches.com) and McDonald's (www.mcdonalds.com). Find others.

7.   Abercrombie takes great care in the selection of their spokespersons and models to ensure they project the image of the company. That is not to say the spokespersons and models actually mirror the typical Abercrombie customer.

8.   These decisions are not contradictory to Engel's Law. All Jaguar and BMW are doing is making less expensive products available that appeal to consumers in less affluent income brackets. These customers typically spend the same percentage of their income on transportation as do consumers in higher income categories. By offering lower priced products, these companies are making it possible for more consumers to experience their products, while still maintaining spending on transportation at the same constant rate.

9.   There are so many recent accomplishments that it is difficult to name just four. However, you might want to consider camera phones (www.nokia.com, www.samsung.com as two examples), nanites used for microsurgery (www.nanobites.com), LASIK eye surgery to correct vision (www.fda.gov/cdrh/lasik), and the cloning of animals (www.time.com/time/newsfiles/cloning). Many more recent examples exist.

10.   How do you feel about this? The products are legal, yet we are increasingly seeing it targeted for restrictive regulations. Just because we may not personally like the product, does that give us (or others) the right to "unfairly" restrict its use? It's a debate that will continue for the foreseeable future.

Marketing ADventure Exercises

1.   Ad Interpretation Challenge: The Macroenvironment
      Ad: Auto—Hyundai Avante

Hyundai is positioning the Avante as a very fuel-efficient vehicle. Fuel efficiency today is about more than just saving a few dollars at the gas station (although that is certainly of great importance!). Fuel efficiency today (and Hyundai's lean burn technology) is also about saving the environment from undue emissions and, at the same time, helping to conserve a dwindling natural resource (petroleum).

2.   Ad Interpretation Challenge: The Macroenvironment
      Ad: Food and Beverage—McDonald's

Healthy living and healthy eating are two current cultural trends that can cause some difficulties for fast food companies known for producing and marketing calorie- and fat-intensive products. McDonald's is addressing these cultural issues partially by affiliating themselves with the Olympic games of Sydney.

3.   Ad Interpretation Challenge: Marketing Intermediaries
      Ad: Student Choice

Although several examples exist, you may want to take a look at the ad for Sedex (Services and B2B—Sedex) or the ads for the Italian postal system (Services and B2B—Posta).

4.   Ad Interpretation Challenge: Competition
      Ad: Student Choice

Consider the following as possible solutions to this question: Fiat's air conditioning (Auto—Fiat); Honda's claim of having the sportiest sedan (Auto—Honda); or LG's ad for its televisions (Electronics—LG).

5.   Ad Interpretation Challenge: Publics
      Ad: Auto—Cadillac Escalade

Although this ad is obviously appealing to the SUV owner (or potential owner) looking for more power and performance, Cadillac might also pay attention to Media Publics (as more and more negativity is written about gas-guzzling SUVs) and General Publics (as the public, in general, reexamines its love affair with high-performance vehicles).

6.   Ad Interpretation Challenge: Demography
        Ad: Travel and Tourism—Leisure Entertainment

The general aging of the U.S. population is the basis of this ad—from a standpoint of demography. As the baby boom generation continues to gray and reach retirement age, we are witnessing a large increase in expenditures on leisure activities, with "exotic" travel at the front of the list.

7.   Ad Interpretation Challenge: Baby Boomers
        Ad: Student Choice

Take a look at either the ad for Schwab (Financial—Schwab) that is using Ringo Starr of the Beatles fame as spokesperson or one of the two Jaguar ads (Auto—Jaguar) that are touting the understated elegance of this brand.

8.   Ad Interpretation Challenge: Generation Y
        Ad: Apparel—Levis New Collection

Generation Y (a.k.a., echo boomers) are those 72 million people born between 1977 and 2000. After several years of decline, this generation has given a new boom to the market for fashion clothing. They also have the money to spend on such items. Levi's has tailored their product offering to reach this generation by designing or redesigning much of their clothing to reflect a more "modern" time.

9.   Ad Interpretation Challenge: The "Traditional Family"
        Ad: Auto—Toyota

This ad is for a Toyota minivan—a family icon. The ad is stressing safety, surely an important factor to consider in the purchase of a family vehicle in which to carry the children.

10.   Ad Interpretation Challenge: Diversity
        Ad: Nonprofit Corporate Images—Nike

These three ads for Nike are all dealing with people with disabilities. Nike is saying "Yes, these people are different. But why are they REALLY different? They are different because they are achievers."

Chapter 4

Student Exercises

1.   Today, colleges and universities are continually reviewing course offerings—taking a look at what classes they are offering, when they are offered, and who is enrolling in them. From this and other information they are able to change or modify what and when courses are offered in an effort to better meet the needs of today's busy students.

2.   You would want to have available to you both secondary information (information that already exists somewhere) and primary information (information that is collected for the specific purpose at hand).

3.   The magazine presents secondary statistics on page 11 of the media kit. Here you will find all kinds of results derived from secondary research, including retail sales figures and sales tax estimates.

4.   Wow. There is so much information available here that it would be easy to end up with a case of information overload. Here you can find information pertaining to household composition, size, income, and health insurance—among much more. The government makes readily available a wealth of information that may be of great importance and use to marketers. All we have to do is take the time to look.

5.   It is truly amazing the capabilities of Zoomerang – and there are several other online survey houses that operate in a similar manner. You will have noticed the ease with which you were able to create your own online survey. Think how easy it can be to now conduct online survey research

6.   There are many ways to answer this question. You could, for example, make use of a focus group of children to delve into what kids like and dislike about the pizza-eating experience—maybe the chairs are too big for them or maybe the pizza slices are too large for their smaller mouths. Alternatively, you might employ a focus group to find in-depth insight into how your current customers view CiCi's relative to your primary competition.

7.   Keep in mind that you can not survey everyone. In determining who to sample, you must think of who would be most impacted if your school moved totally online—current students, prospective students? When considering how many people to sample, remember that the more people you sample the more it costs. However, typically speaking, the more you sample the better the information. Sample selection comes down to either probability or nonprobability sampling. Be sure to look at the advantages and disadvantages of each.

8.   You can pretty much look anywhere to fulfill this question. For many websites, when you initially sign up or register, you are required to fill out a registration and/or personal interest form. These are examples of online questionnaires.

9.   Harrah's Entertainment (highlighted in your text) uses data mining to manage day-to-day relationships with important customers at its properties around the world (see Real Marketing 4.1).

10.   You can use many of the techniques of marketing research in a less formal manner and with little or no expense. Among the many possibilities for informal and inexpensive research are just driving around the area to see what other coffee shops are around. While you are doing this, you can also get a feel for how much business they have and the type of customers that frequent them. Additionally, through observing the shops over time, you can get a feel for both busy and slack times.

Marketing ADventure Exercises

1.   Ad Interpretation Challenge: Marketing Information System
          Ad: Services and B2B—24 Hour Fitness

This is a company that is catering to the need of its customers to have access to a health club at any time of the day or night. You might want to check out their website for more information about them—www.24hourfitness.com. Through the use of a marketing information system, this company may have been able to pinpoint a weakness in the existing market for fitness clubs. They filled that niche by providing a club to which members have 24 hour access.

2.   Ad Interpretation Challenge: Internal Data
          Ad: Apparel—Puma

Puma and its customers are widely believed to be fanatics of football (soccer). A review of Puma's internal database would likely confirm this belief. Based on this, ads could be created which serve to highlight this passion, thereby helping to reinforce the image and draw others with like beliefs to the brand.

3.   Ad Interpretation Challenge: Internal Data
          Ad: Services and B2B—University of Toronto

As a routine matter, colleges and universities gather information about their graduates, compiling information such as for whom they work, where they are located, and how much they make. This information is useful for all kinds of things, such as staying in touch with you after you graduate and encouraging you to be active in your university's alumni association. Also, if you happen to have some graduates who have gone on to truly distinguish themselves, it can serve as a good way to entice future students.

4.   Ad Interpretation Challenge: Causal Research
          Ad: Student Choice

You might want to consider the ad for Advil (Cosmetics and Pharmaceuticals—Advil), which suggests that by taking Advil your splitting headache will go away. Also, take a look at the ad for Virgin Atlantic (Travel and Tourism—Virgin Atlantic). This ad leaves you with the idea that travel on Virgin will result in pleasure (hence, the smile).

5.   Ad Interpretation Challenge: Secondary Data
          Ad: Auto—Cadillac Escalade

This ad for Cadillac is promoting the new Escalade as the most powerful SUV in the world. Cadillac did not go out and actually measure the horsepower of every other available SUV in the world. Cadillac relied on previously published information to arrive at their conclusion. This previously published information is secondary data.

6.   Ad Interpretation Challenge: Primary Data
       Ad: Autos—Dunlop

Dunlop is saying that this particular advertised tire is an extremely quite tire. This is an example of findings from the company's primary research. The results of the research pertain to only this product. They are not making comparisons to any other company and/or product, which would most likely require the use of secondary data sources.

7.   Ad Interpretation Challenge: Ethnographic Research
       Ad: Student Choice

Consider the advertisements for the Audi A2 (Auto—Audi). These ads highlight the way the younger target market lives and spends time—areas in which ethnographic research excels.

8.   Ad Interpretation Challenge: Contact Methods—Personal
       Ad: Financial—Alliance

In this ad Lucy is questioning Snoopy about his financial affairs. This is a great example of using the personal contact method to collect information.

9.   Ad Interpretation Challenge: Data Mining
       Ad: Internet—EPage

EPage, a marketing research company, uses data mining to put its clients on "the same page" as their customers. Data mining has the potential to uncover information about the wants, desires, and dislikes of your customers that you may have easily overlooked.

10.   Ad Interpretation Challenge: Public Policy
       Ad: Nonprofit Corporate Images—Labatt

Labatt is addressing the issue of alcohol overindulgence. Alcoholic beverages are enjoyed by millions every day; however, a significant percentage have a problem in knowing when to stop. Labatt, along with alcoholic beverage producers everywhere, are facing this issue head-on and attempting to help the problem drinker by encouraging them to consume in moderation.

Chapter 5

Student Exercises

1. RJR presents their products to adults only. They provide information about the disadvantages of consuming their product and they provide information for those who are currently smoking but wish to cease. In so doing, RJR is acting as a good corporate citizen by making their product available to those who desire it, while, at the same time, assisting those who wish to give it up.

2. All schools are scrambling to adequately serve a number of diverse markets. For example, the nontraditional student now makes up a sizable portion of most college enrollments. Just a few years ago this was not the case. As a result, colleges and universities are offering more night and weekend classes to reach this important subculture. Nights and weekends allow the members of this group to continue their full-time employment while attending classes.

3. A quick review of their website makes it apparent that Chevrolet takes the Hispanic market very seriously. Right up front on the site is an option to have the entire site presented in Spanish. This is one of the easiest, yet most effective, methods for appealing to this submarket.

4. The mature market can be a very lucrative market for companies to tap into. The U.S. population of mature consumers will more than double in the next 25 years, to over 130 million. Many companies have found it very profitable to cater exclusively to this group. Possibly the most prominent company devoted to this important subsegment is AARP (www.aarp.com).

5. Bentleys are exclusive, high-priced automobiles. They definitely appeal to the Upper Class. Within the Upper Class, there are two subdivisions, Upper Uppers and Lower Uppers. You could make the argument that Bentleys appeal equally well to either.

6. Early on, Scion made a name by positioning their vehicles as young, exciting, and energetic alternatives to traditional automotive alternatives. On their homepage you will find many references to and photos of attractive, trendy young people—just the type person that Scion used to get the word out about the brand.

7. More and more companies today are using children as a conduit to reach parents. Take a look at some children's magazines, such as Nickelodeon Magazine (www.nick.com) or National Geographic Kids (www.nationalgeographic.com). Consider how some of the ads in these kid's magazines are actually there to sell products to adults—through influencing their kids.

8. Whether your lifestyle is active, sedentary, flamboyant, or demure, the way you live and spend money helps define who you really are.

9.   Safety and security are big business today. Companies that specialize in this lower level need have seen their business increase over the past years. Log on the ADT (www.adt.com) or Brinks (www.brinkshomesecurity.com) and take a look at what these companies (and this is only two of many) have to offer in the way of home security.

10.   L.L. Bean makes a big deal out of their guarantee. They guarantee everything purchased from them will be 100% satisfactory or they will give you your money back. While many merchants make similar claims, L.L. Bean goes further than most. Their customers have the opportunity to return anything to them AT ANY TIME for a replacement or a refund.

Marketing ADventure Exercises

1.   Ad Interpretation Challenge: Cultural Shifts
       Ad: Apparel—Levi's New Collection

Many people believed that Levi's missed the boat in the current trend of fashion jeans. New competitors entered the marketplace and took away some of Levi's fashion-conscious customers. Now they are fighting back. Their new line of rhinestone-studded jeans raises the bar for fashion-conscious customers.

2.   Ad Interpretation Challenge: Subcultures
       Ad: Autos—Chevy S10 Truck

The easiest way to see that this ad is geared to the Hispanic submarket is through language. The ad is presented in Spanish. If a company is serious about servicing this group, this is a minimum requirement.

3.   Ad Interpretation Challenge: Mature Consumers
       Ad: Student Choice

You need to look for products that seem to "fit" with this submarket of the population. Remember, they have the money to spend and the time to enjoy spending it. You might want to take a look at the ads for either Cadillac (Autos—Cadillac) or Leisure Entertainment (Bali) (Travel and Tourism—Leisure Entertainment).

4.   Ad Interpretation Challenge: Social Class
       Ad: Autos—Jaguar

It seems as though Jaguar has always had a bit of mystique here in the United States. By looking at these ads and reading the copy, it appears Jaguar is reaching out to the Upper Class. Within that class, there are two subclasses—the Upper Uppers and the Lower Uppers. Through a review of the definitions for these two subclasses, one can conclude Jaguar is directing their advertising to the Lower Uppers.

5.   Ad Interpretation Challenge: Opinion Leader
       Ad: Internet—Leaping Salmon

By providing early adopters of its products with additional incentives (such as discounts, free products, or cash), Leaping Salmon is encouraging these individuals to get out and tell others about the product. Keep in mind that early adopters are the opinion leaders.

6.   Ad Interpretation Challenge: Family
       Ad: Food and Beverage—McDonald's Happy Meal

This ad targets at least two members of the family buying organization—the parent and the child.

7.   Ad Interpretation Challenge: Life-Cycle
        Ad: Financial—MasterCard Home Alone

This ad is targeted toward younger, singles still living at home. To target a different stage of the life-cycle it would only be necessary to change to prop contained in the ad and the associated wording.

8.   Ad Interpretation Challenge: Brand Personality
        Ad: Student Choice

The brand personality trait of "sophistication" is characterized as "upper class and charming." For examples, look at the ads for Jaguar and Imperial hotel. The ads for Jaguar (Autos—Jaguar) and Imperial Hotel (Travel and Leisure—Imperial Hotel) both display the characteristics of sophistication.

9.   Ad Interpretation Challenge: Selective Attention
        Ad: Cosmetics and Pharmaceuticals—Schick

When you initially look at this ad for Schick, you may notice the woman in the swimsuit. Only when you take a closer look at the ad are you likely to see the Schick razor placed in the lower left-hand corner. This is the problem. Many times when we first see an ad, we do not pick up all of the information the marketers wants (and needs) us to.

10.   Ad Interpretation Challenge: Information Search
        Ad: Student Choice

Many of the ads will easily satisfy the requirements of this question. Differences primarily lie in the amount of information provided to the reader. At the minimal information end of the spectrum is the ad for Buenos Aires traffic laws (Nonprofit Corporate Image—Buenos Aires). The ad is not designed to give the viewer information with which to compare products. This ad is designed to provide the viewer with minimal crucial information. On the other hand, consider the ad for Fiat's air-conditioning (Autos—Fiat). This ad provides the reader with a quantity of information with which to make a direct comparison to other brands.

Chapter 6

Student Exercises

1.   Keep in mind that B2B marketers sell to other organizations—not the final consumer. Folgers Coffee is available through retail stores (e.g., Albertson's, Kroger, and Wal-Mart). You can't buy it directly from the company.

2.   Almost everything about this company operates as a result of derived demand. All of their products are used as components in further manufacturing or production. As a result of this, their business is driven by derived demand.

3.   Multiple organizations exist that can be used here. You may want to consider taking a look at either Target Stores (www.target.com) or Ocean Yachts (www.oceanyachtsinc.com) for ideas. Ocean Yachts takes a unique approach to supplier-partner development by providing public information about many of its primary suppliers.

4.   Most of the items established restaurants reorder would probably be on a straight rebuy basis. So, almost any of the products they use could fall into this category.

5.   Systems selling is one of major methods companies employ to gain and keep accounts. Companies that effectively use this technique are much more successful in maintaining long-term profitable relationships with their clients. One good example of systems selling is IBM (www.ibm.com).

6.   The answer to this exercise is unique to each individual. Within your family, the member who carries the most influence at the various stages of the buying process may be totally different from how influence is distributed in your classmate's family.

7.   The continually evolving regulatory environment surrounding the sell and consumption of cigarettes is having a significant impact on RJR buyers. More restrictions are being placed on public smoking. A smaller percentage of American adults smoke cigarettes on a regular basis. The RJR buyers must watch these factors (among others), determine the impact on the company and its customers, and try to turn these challenges into opportunities.

8.   Locating a company that is currently seeking proposals from qualified suppliers may require some searching on your part. You can look for such companies either in your home community, state, university town, or on the internet.

9.   You do not need a login name and password to address this question. Just take a look along the right-hand side of the page. Here, Office Depot outlines online purchasing for many different types of organizations.

10.   School cafeterias are not necessarily looking to make a profit. Typically they may be happy to just not loose too much money! School cafeterias want to provide good quality food to a large number of students in a short period of time. As a result, they seek to purchase large quantities of quality product at the lowest reasonable price to process and pass on to their customers (you, the student). The selections may not always seem that exciting, but they are economical.

Marketing ADventure Exercises

1. Ad Interpretation Challenge: Business Markets
    Ad: Service and B2B—SpeedStart

The ad is letting the viewer know that SpeedStart can help you cut through your problems and get to profits quicker. Appealing to profits is one of the principal methods of communicating to business markets.

2. Ad Interpretation Challenge: Derived Demand
    Ad: Electronics—Axiom

The demand for Nokia cell phones is, in part, derived from the demand for Axiom services. Axiom, as a telecommunications company, uses Nokia as its cell phone provider. As demand for Axiom services increase, so does the demand for Nokia phones. If demand for Axiom services were to decrease, so to would demand for Nokia handsets.

3. Ad Interpretation Challenge: Inelastic Demand
    Ad: Autos—Dunlop

Probably the most important component which goes into the creation of their product is rubber. A change in the cost of rubber is not going to cause Dunlop to buy less rubber, at least not in the short run.

4. Ad Interpretation Challenge: Straight Rebuy
    Ad: Services and B2B—EMS

Keep in mind that a straight rebuy happens when a company reorders and uses the same product or service. If a company had experienced good results from the use of EMS, they may well turn to EMS in the future for the exact same services again. This would be a straight rebuy.

5. Ad Interpretation Challenge: Systems Selling
    Ad: Services and B2B—Springbow

Springbow is offering a "one stop" shopping experience for the corporate buyer who is faced with challenges in the new digital world. From this ad, you can see that Springbow is positioning their company as a solution to any problem or series of problems that a company may have operating in this digital world.

6.   Ad Interpretation Challenge: Environmental Factors
        Ad: Services and B2B—Posta

The ads for Posta Prioritaria are addressing two environmental factors—competition and economic. Through the use of priority mail, the ad is suggesting you will have your letter delivered faster than your competition that is not using the service. Associatively, you can have your letter delivered fast for a very reasonable cost.

7.   Ad Interpretation Challenge: Problem Recognition
        Ad: Services and B2B—Varig

At times, delays in cargo shipments may be inevitable. However, when these delays become frequent, then a company may be faced with a serious delivery problem. Through this ad, Varig is highlighting this issue.

8.   Ad Interpretation Challenge: E-Procurement
        Ad: Student Choice

There are many companies whose products or services would satisfy this exercise. For just two examples, take a look at Energizer batteries (Electronics—Energizer) and Heinz ketchup (Food and Beverage—Heinz). Both of these products could easily be purchased through an online procurement system.

9.   Ad Interpretation Challenge: Institutional Markets
        Ad: Student Choice

You may want to consider the advertisements for either Aeromexico (Travel and Tourism—Aeromexico) or Virgin Atlantic (Travel and Tourism—Virgin). Both of these companies may serve as institutional markets for some products, for example food services.

10.   Ad Interpretation Challenge: Government Markets
        Ad: Electronics—Energizer

Take a look at the Energizer ad. They are positioning themselves as longer lasting than any other battery. That is the key. Energizer may be able to persuade the government buyer to accept the higher bid because they are providing a superior, longer lasting product.

Chapter 7

Student Exercises

1.   Bebe has keyed in on a very specific of the women's clothing market. They are reaching out to trendy, fashion conscious, moderately upscale, younger women. Their clothing line is very specific and typically appeals only to this market segment. They have wisely chosen to not try and be all things to all people.

2.   While Polaris would be very happy to sell snowmobiles to consumers living in Mobile, Alabama, it probably is not going to happen. Likewise, customers from Flint, Michigan are not the best prospects to purchase ATVs. Polaris Industries has made the wise (and obvious) decision to concentrate marketing efforts for snowmobiles in northern states of the U.S. At the same time, you would find the primary market for ATVs among southern and southwestern states, where the warm weather persists until late in the year.

3.   Cosmetic companies have begun to realize that there are a growing number of men who desire skin care products. While desiring quality skincare products, this newly emerging segment are not willing to just pick up a "women's" product to use. They have demanded products targeted specifically to them. Clinique (and other traditional cosmetic companies) have responded by launching lines of skincare products with a decidedly "male" look.

4.   On their website, Pottery Barn makes heavy use of lifestyle segmentation. One of the primary competitive features of their site is the ability of a customer to select the "room lifestyle" which most closely matches their own. Pottery Barn allows you to shop completed rooms to match your own personal style.   In this manner, Pottery Barn is letting the consumer self-select their merchandise on the basis of their lifestyle.

5.   You can probably think of many products here. Two you might want to consider are pumpkins (you see a lot of usage around Thanksgiving and Halloween) and turkeys (again, for Thanksgiving). While not wanting to decrease demand during their traditional sales or consumption periods, marketers would like to increase consumption of their products during other, slack periods. That is why you now see ads promoting the consumption of orange juice at times other than breakfast and turkey for more than Thanksgiving. Take a look at the National Turkey Federation's website for an example of promoting consumption of your product at "non-peak" times (www.eatturkey.com).

6.   Wyndham offers their customers many benefits and perks in an effort to maintain their loyalty. Chief among these is their frequent guest's club, Wyndham by Request. Wyndham takes great pains to be certain that their loyal customer is shown appreciation for that loyalty. This is the type of service that keeps customers coming back—again and again.

7.   A review of some of EBay's international sites shows that they have been adapted to meet local market requirements in several ways. First, the default language has been changed to the local language. Even for those countries which speak English, you will notice that the language has been adjusted to meet local dialects, word usages, and spellings. Also, in keeping with local customs and regulations, some items you may find for sell on the U.S. site are not available on the foreign site.

8.   Nielsen Media Research has a multitude of research reports available to cover all facets of the media. The type, quality, and quantity of segmentation data available from just this one source are most impressive. Keep in mind, while Nielsen may be the best known in the business, several others competing companies exist offering similar information.

9.   You might begin your search by looking at Putumayo Music (www.putumayo.com). Putumayo is the leading producer of World Music in the U.S. World Music makes up a very small portion of the overall recorded music industry. Instead of trying to compete in that larger music world, Putumayo has chosen to become a leader in a very small niche.

10.   On the Audi website, you have the option to "Build Your Audi." This technology allows you to "design" your ultimate Audi experience and then order it. In essence, you are able to design an automobile just to your specifications.

Marketing ADventure Exercises

1.   Ad Interpretation Challenge: Market Segmentation
      Ad: Apparel—Levi's Diamond Jeans

Based on this ad, you would have to say that Levi's Diamond Jeans are targeting a market segmented on the basis of demographics and psychographics. Specific demographic variables that seem to come into play here would be age (young women) and income (significant discretionary income). Likewise, lifestyle and personality traits would anchor the psychographic variables.

2.   Ad Interpretation Challenge: Geographic Segmentation
      Ad: Student Choice

Keep in mind that many companies are localizing their products, advertising, and promotions to the needs of individual regions of the country. Based on this, the ad for Fiat (Autos—Fiat) would be a good example of regional segmentation. The ad is highlighting the strength of the Fiat's air-conditioning. This is a product attribute especially salient to those consumers living in warmer climate regions.

3.   Ad Interpretation Challenge: Demographic Segmentation
      Ad: Services and B2B—University of Toronto

Obviously, age is the demographic segmentation variable in use in these ads. However, as the student population of colleges and universities continues to age, consideration must be given to using segmentation variables besides strictly age to divide the market.

4.   Ad Interpretation Challenge: Gender Segmentation
      Ad: Student Choice

Think along the stereotypes of men and women. Men have traditionally been viewed as aggressive, seeking power and prestige. The traditional view of women has been one of nurturing, caring, and peace maker. Based on these views, you might want to consider the ad for Nissan's Altima (Autos—Nissan Altima). This ad highlights the power and acceleration features of the new Altima—both features geared to appeal to the male market. To make this ad possibly more appealing to women, we could highlight features of safety and security.

5.   Ad Interpretation Challenge: Income Segmentation
      Ad: Autos—Hyundai

What Hyundai might want to do would be to focus their promotions on price, durability, and dependability

6.   Ad Interpretation Challenge: Psychographic Segmentation
        Ad: Apparel—Umbro

Umbro is appealing to the sports-minded individual. In doing so, Umbro is using basic lifestyle segmentation. Remember that a consumer's lifestyle is comprised of their activities, interests, and opinions. For Umbro, the activities in which consumer's engage are of primary importance—specifically football.

7.   Ad Interpretation Challenge: Occasions Based Segmentation
        Ad: Services and B2B: 24 Hour Fitness

By its name, you would expect 24 Hour Fitness to be open 24 hours a day. Most gyms and health clubs operate on a more limited schedule. Most of us are comfortable with such schedules. However, by offering a facility which operates 24 hours a day, 24 Hour Fitness is promoting the use of its facilities at times other than the traditionally accepted times. The hope would be greater enrollment and facility usage.

8.   Ad Interpretation Challenge: Undifferentiated Marketing
        Ad: Student Choice

You can't do it. None of ads here use this approach. Most modern marketers have strong reservations about this strategy. Mass marketers have a tough time competing with more focused firms that do a better job of satisfying the needs of specific market segments.

9.   Ad Interpretation Challenge: Niche Marketing
        Ad: Newspapers and TV—Football Channel

To be a player in the mainstream television market today would be a very difficult and expensive proposition. The number of competitors all offering basically the same programming is immense. It would be tough to find a way to stand out, be recognized, and make even a small profit. On the other hand, by concentrating all of your efforts in one category—in this case football—you have the unique opportunity to become the dominant competitor in a small field of competitors.

10.   Ad Interpretation Challenge: Individual Marketing
        Ad: Student Choice

One possible example you may look at is DBS (Financial—DBS). DBS, an early marketer of the debit card, is positioning the card as fulfilling the needs of each individual, regardless of what those needs may be or how they may differ from your neighbor's. Keep in mind that one of the characteristics of individual marketing is the tailoring of the product to the needs of the individual customer.

Chapter 8

Student Exercises

1.	How you answer this question depends on how you define your school's market. If the market your school is appealing to be the student, then the product is education. This educational product is manifested in the course offerings, times, and faculty. On the other hand, if you consider the market to be the organizations that hire the students upon graduation, then the product becomes the student themselves.

2.	Digital photography has become increasingly popular for many reasons. One reason is that it allows the photographer to experience something much closer to instant gratification, when compared to conventional film photography. With digital photography, you have the ability to take a photograph and almost instantly see the results of your creative work and to share this work with others.

3.	By clicking on the Products tab, you are shown all products and brands the company offers for general consumption. Keep in mind that convenience products are typically low in price, have widespread distribution, and benefit from mass promotion by the producer. Based on this, you might conclude that the vast majority of PandG products fall into this category—particularly products such as laundry, dish care, paper products, and oral care.

4.	Windmill power has been around for centuries, but has had only limited application in the modern world. The availability of units appropriate for single family homes represents a step forward in technology. The challenge facing manufacturers is letting people know of the viability of the product and technology and its appropriateness for home use. This will require a substantial commitment in advertising and personal selling to potential home owners and home builders. It's not an easy sell.

5.	Both are "Open for business!" That is the key message. New Orleans and the gulf coast region are encouraging visitors to come back and enjoy the many pleasures that made the regions so popular before. Neither is saying that everything is back to normal. However, they are saying that, as they continue the rebuilding process, now is the perfect time for the visitor to come see the progress and enjoy the area.

6.	To effectively rate the quality of your school's "products," you need to keep an open and unbiased mind. How well do you really believe your school is doing in creating good, qualified, competent graduates ready to enter the work force?

7.	How brands "speak" to you is a personal and individual experience. Marketers hope that their brands speak to you in the manner they intend! For example, Toyota – reliability, Kia – economy, Volvo – safety.

8.   While this is a completely individual decision, you will want to focus on products for which the packaging says something significant about its contents or the delivery of those contents. For example, Mentadent toothpaste (www.youareteethpeople.com) uses its packaging as a primary product attribute. For most consumers, one of the main motivations behind the purchase of this product is its unique form of product delivery.

9.   At a minimum, you can say that J. Peterman offers product lines comprised of men's clothing (shirts, pants, hats, etc.), women's clothing (dresses, skirts, shirts, pants), and items for the home (furniture, bar signs).

10.   In a brand extension it is important to always keep your primary brand and product in mind. Any extension you enter into to must maintain the credibility of that main brand. In Sea Ray's instance, they would probably want to remain with products connected in some manner to the marine industry, as that is where their strengths lie. Possibilities could include a line of Sea Ray branded marine instruments or Sea Ray branded dishes for use in your boat.

Marketing ADventure Exercises

1. Ad Interpretation Challenge: Product
   Ad: Services and B2B—Leo's

The answer to the question is "yes." Leo's Sports Club is a product. Products include more than just tangible goods. Broadly defined, products include physical objects, services, events, people, places, organizations, ideas, or a mix of these entities. Thus, although Leo's is certainly providing a service, it is a product.

2. Ad Interpretation Challenge: Core Benefit
   Ad: Electronics—Fujifilm

Fuji is offering the consumer a product with which to capture images. However, this is not the base, or core benefit. People buying Fuji film are buying memories. They are buying a product that will allow them to faithfully preserve their memories for a lifetime.

3. Ad Interpretation Challenge: Convenience Products
   Ad: Student Choice

There are many ads which fulfill the requirements of this question. Take a look at Kit Kat (Food and Beverage—Kit Kat) and Pepsi (Food and Beverage—Pepsi) for two examples. Marketers of convenience goods work to keep the image of the product fresh in the consumer's mind. As such, many of the advertisements for products of this type are heavy with imagery without delving too deeply into the specifics of the product.

4. Ad Interpretation Challenge: Organization Marketing
   Ad: Nonprofit Corporate Images—The Archdiocese

In essence, the marketing of the Archdiocese (an organization) and the marketing of a Nissan (a product) are exactly the same. The organization is interested in attracting new members. Nissan, on the other hand, is interested in selling more cars. The basic similarities in accomplishing these tasks are many.

5. Ad Interpretation Challenge: Social Marketing
   Ad: Student Choice

Promoting products and services that are good for the person and good for society is social marketing. There are numerous ads which are promoting such social concepts. Take a look at, for example, the ad for ABC Canada (Nonprofit Corporate Images—ABC Canada). ABC Canada is a nonprofit organization whose primary goal is to teach adults how to read and write. This is certainly an example of an organization whose goal is both to improve the well-being of the individual and of society.

6.   Ad Interpretation Challenge: Product Features
        Ad: Food and Beverage—Tabasco

Look at the Tabasco ad. That is a burned toothpick in the upper portion of the ad. Tabasco is using this to symbolize the heat strength of its product. One of the most desirable features of a hot sauce is the intensity of its heat. Tabasco is telling consumers it has that feature covered.

7.   Ad Interpretation Challenge: Packaging
        Ad: Student Choice

For this exercise, you will want to focus on ads for which the packaging says something significant about its contents or the delivery of those contents. In today's highly competitive marketplace, packaging can be just as important as the product it holds. As an example, take a look at the ad for Altoids (Food and Beverage—Altoids). The metal container used to hold the mint is as much an integral part of this product as is the mint itself.

8.   Ad Interpretation Challenge: Product Line
        Ad: Autos—Jaguar

Jaguar faces the most danger in moving its product line downward through the introduction of less expensive models. Prestige products are always at risk when a less-expensive version of the item is introduced.

9.   Ad Interpretation Challenge: Product Mix
        Ad: Apparel—Levi's

If you look at all the different product lines and items within those lines, you begin to understand the complexity of projecting a consistent corporate image. Ideally, a company desires for all of its products and product variations to act in concert in the projection of a single image. Levi's does a nice job of this.

10.   Ad Interpretation Challenge: Brand Extensions
        Ad: Autos—Honda

Honda has been very careful when considering brand extensions. Before moving to additional transportation forms, they made certain they were strong and well regarded by consumers in the current market. Only at that time, did they extend their brand to other forms of transportation. Also, Honda has been careful to remain primarily within the transportation category with its brand extensions, therefore, keeping brand dilution to a minimum.

Chapter 9

Student Exercises

1.   It is hard to say whether the iPhone will "revolutionize" the use of cell phones. While it certainly provides the consumer with several new and somewhat novel features – such as the ability to see album covers – one can question whether these features are "revolutionary" or "evolutionary."

2.   Frog Design would have used both internal and external idea sources in the course of this project. Internally, Frog would likely have turned to company executives and on-the-floor salespeople for insights into the mind of the Victoria's Secret customer. Good new product ideas also come from customers. So it would be safe to assume Frog turned to these customers for additional suggestions and ideas.

3.   There is no truly correct answer to this exercise. Just use your imagine to come up with other uses and/or features for the iPhone. For example,

Concept 1: A low-priced phone, offered in only one version, available through all service providers, that combines standard cell phone features (such as a camera, texting, and music capabilities), but using Apple technology.

Concept 2: A moderately-priced phone, offered with limited variations, available through only one or two service providers, which offers (in addition to the features of Concept 1) the ability to perform limited word processing and spreadsheet functions and interface with your home computer.

Concept 3: A high-end device that is infinitely customizable and is "built-to-order." This device would include everything from Concept 2, with the additions of GPS, directions on demand, locator beacon, and automatic phone book updates.

4.   Given the nature of the product, you would want to concentrate your test marketing to regions or cities known for their "fashion-forward" style. Markets such as Los Angeles, Miami, and New York come readily to mind. Having settled on your test market cities, you would turn your attention to retail outlets within those markets most frequented by your potential clientele. These areas then become the focus of your test market.

5.   Finding a product for the first stage – product development – may be the most challenging. Here you are dealing with a product that is not yet released to the market. For an example of a product in this stage, consider the Chevrolet Camaro – a car not yet introduced (www.chevrolet.com/performance).

6.   The Morton salt girl's dress has followed the trend of American women's fashion clothing. When dresses where longer, the Morton girl's dress was longer. When the fashion of dresses was shorter, the Morton girl's dress was shorter. The fashion forecast for women's dresses for the next couple of years is shorter, so we may see the dress on the Morton salt girl inch up.

7.   A review of their product offering draws your attention to the cassette players. Pioneer currently offers a couple of cassette players for the audio buff that still maintains a large collection of cassette tapes.

8.   Fads may be kind of hard to spot, because so many times they simply do not remain around that long. However, today, one may consider the military-inspired (camouflage) look so evident in women's clothing.

9.   Blu-ray technology is going to have to be adopted by more electronics manufacturing companies so that more players will be available in the marketplace to consumers – at lower prices. Also, consumers – the ultimate deciders of new product fate – must be convinced of the clear superiority of this product over existing DVDs and the new competing HD-DVD format.

10.   Miller produces a number of information packages designed to assist in helping parents to continue the dialogue with their teens about making responsible and healthy decisions about illegal underage drinking. Also, Miller Brewing provides signage to all merchants alerting patrons that proper I.D. will be required of them to purchase alcoholic beverages.

Marketing ADventure Exercises

1.   Ad Interpretation Challenge: Idea Generation
         Ad: Food and Beverage—Altoids

This becomes an imagination game. Through the use of brainstorming, you may come up with any number of potential product ideas. Some of your ideas may be as far fetched as a breath mint that lasts for 24 hours. On the other hand, you may generate relatively minor extensions of the current product mix. Maybe, a mint that immediately dissolves in your mouth, but is effective for a couple of hours.

2.   Ad Interpretation Challenge: Idea Screening
         Ad: Food and Beverage—Heinz

When looking at all of the products Heinz offers, it is probably easy to see some that you believe should never have made it into production. Keep in mind, though, that you need to look at these items on a larger scale, considering their potential regardless of your own personal likes and dislikes.

3.   Ad Interpretation Challenge: Concept Testing
         Ad: Food and Beverage—Gatorade

You might want to say something along the lines of: "An easy to swallow capsule, designed to be swallowed without water. When ingested, the capsule immediately disintegrates, releasing thirst-quenching nourishment throughout the body."

4.   Ad Interpretation Challenge: Test Marketing
         Ad: Electronics—Motorola

Motorola may have considered introducing this product through only one cell service provider. This would have allowed them the opportunity to experiment with pricing and promotion strategies before making the (expensive) decision to provide the phone to all service providers nationwide.

5.   Ad Interpretation Challenge: Commercialization
         Ad: Student Choice

If you are having trouble coming up with any ads for this exercise, you may want to take a look at the ad for Sony's projection television (Electronics—Sony) or the ad for Advantage card (Financial—Advantage Card). Read the copy on both of these ads. Both of these ads serve the purpose of introducing a new product to the market.

6.   Ad Interpretation Challenge: Fashion
          Ad: Apparel—Student Choice

Of the available ads, you would most likely settle on the ad for Levi's New Collection jeans. Here, Levi's has introduced a new variation on the traditional jean; they have added the currently fashionable rhinestone.

7.   Ad Interpretation Challenge: Introduction Stage
          Ad: Student Choice

There are several ads that you might select to fulfill the requirements of this question. Remember, you are looking for an ad that is designed to introduce the product to the market and to entice consumers to give it a try. For an example, take a look at Freedomland (Newspaper and TV—Freedomland).

8.   Ad Interpretation Challenge: Growth Stage
          Ad: Electronics—LG

If this were an ad for a LCD or plasma TV, the ad would be directed more toward the early adopter and not the middle majority. The ad would be designed to help build demand in the mass market, while still emphasizing the LG brand.

9.   Ad Interpretation Challenge: Decline Stage
          Ad: Electronics—Fujifilm

Products in the decline stage of the product life cycle are characterized by declining sales and as appealing to laggards. In this phase, you want to phase out weak versions of the product and only concentrate on the core product. Additionally, you may consider a price cut in an effort to keep sales high. Also, typically, advertising and sales promotions are reduced to minimal levels.

10.   Ad Interpretation Challenge: Social Responsibility
          Ad: Student Choice

As a possible example, look at Autos—Nissan. Specifically, take a look at the ad dealing highlighting the Nissan Primira—recognized as the most ecological vehicle on the market.

Chapter 10

Student Exercises

1.   After spending some time on the Hewlett-Packard home page (www.hp.com) and building the ultimate laptop computer, you have probably realized that the opinions are staggering. Build-to-order companies, such as HP, offer the demanding consumer a multitude of options and configurations to meet any need. In this way, HP (and others) is building greater customer loyalty and satisfaction.

2.   When making the decision to come to school, you paid a monetary price—and you continue to pay that every term. But, you have also paid a price in regards to income lost or deferred. You could have gone to work and earned an income straight out of high school, but you chose to not do that (in essence, paying a price) to continue your education.

3.   You need to be looking for products whose price may seem a bit out-of-line with the actual product. In such an instance, there must be more at work to add to the image of the product. Possible examples you may consider are Rolex watches (www.rolex.com) and Monolo Blahnik shoes (www.manoloblahnik.com).

4.   You should be able to find a multitude of products to fulfill the requirement of this exercise. Two examples you might consider are Levi Strauss Signature jeans (a less expensive version of the traditional Levi's jean) and eMachines computers (a less expensive brand of Gateway).

5.   By reviewing the website for Lexus, you will notice several value-added services for customers. For example, they have established a partnership with a collection of luxury hotels. These hotels offer special services or amenities exclusively to Lexus owners.

6.   Fixed costs (also known as overhead) do not vary with production or sales level. Examples with which Tomasini are faced include rent on the manufacturing facilities and offices, payments on equipment, utilities, insurance, and salaries. They have to pay these items no matter how much they sell.

7.   Remember, variable costs fluctuate with the quantity produced. Costs associated with materials used in production would be the primary variable costs for Tomasini. These materials would include the fabrics used to make to bedding and the pillow forms from which the final pillows are produced.

8.   No. Hot Springs Portable Spas would be wiser to use an alternative form of pricing their spas. Hot Springs spas are the number one selling brand of portable spas and hot tubs. From a review of their website, you will see they have a long history, loyal clients, and have consistently received good press. These factors push for a form of pricing other than cost-based.

9.   One good example you might consider is the oil industry. There are only a few major manufacturers and sellers in this industry. Their pricing always seems to be pretty consistent. It would be prohibitively expensive for new competitors to enter the marketplace.

10.   You will not find many large nonregulated monopolies around today. There is too much concern over consumer welfare to allow most truly monopolistic situations to continue for long periods of time. Given that they manufacture the vast majority of computer operating systems, many people consider Microsoft (www.microsoft.com) to be a nonregulated monopoly. However, others (including Microsoft) would argue they are not a monopoly. While they still sell the vast majority of PC operating systems, other competitors such as Linux (www.linux.com) and Apple (www.apple.com) are slowing making inroads.

Marketing ADventure Exercises

1. Ad Interpretation Challenge: Price
    Ad: Services and B2B—University of Toronto

Remember, price includes more than just a monetary exchange. In this case, price encompasses loss of time to attend classes and potential loss of income, if you were working. Price is everything you give up in exchange for the product or service.

2. Ad Interpretation Challenge: Value-based Pricing
    Ad: Autos—Jaguar

By reviewing the ad, you see that Jaguar is positioning itself as a sophisticated product, unlike the competing BMW (which would be considered simply a "grown up" product). Along with this level of sophistication comes a certain respect. Jaguar knows that this perceived respect is worth money, in the eyes of its customers. Based on this, Jaguar customers are willing to pay a premium for their cars while still maintaining they are receiving value.

3. Ad Interpretation Challenge: Good-Value Pricing
    Ad: General Retail—Target

Target has been able to effectively compete with Wal-Mart in the battle of good-value pricing by offering its customers a different mix from Wal-Mart of quality, service, and fair prices. Knowing that they cannot compete solely on the basis of price, Target has made the decision to offer customers good-value pricing by having quality products, with enhanced levels of customer service, at prices that are close to those offered by Wal-Mart.

4. Ad Interpretation Challenge: Cost-based Pricing
    Ad: Autos—Mercedes

The answer is probably not. Although Mercedes operates in the highly competitive luxury automobile market, they have established a long-standing reputation for quality, dependability, and engineering excellence. These are all product attributes for which the customer is willing to pay a premium.

5. Ad Interpretation Challenge: Fixed Costs
    Ad: Travel and Tourism—American Airlines

American Airlines, like all airlines in the United States, is faced with severe fixed costs. Some of the fixed costs confronting AA are payments for airplanes, wages and salaries of pilots, flight attendants, and ground personnel, fuel, and landing fees to airports. These costs remain relatively set regardless of how full their planes fly.

6.   Ad Interpretation Challenge: Variable Costs
        Ad: Travel and Tourism—American Airlines

Here we are looking for costs that change, or vary with how full they fly their planes. They do not have a tremendous number of variable costs. Some of the variable costs they do incur include food and drinks. Only if the volume of passengers increases dramatically would you see an increase in expenses for items such as fuel or personnel.

7.   Ad Interpretation Challenge: Cost-Plus Pricing
        Ad: Student Choice

Some of the best examples can be found in the section for financial services. You might want to look at RKMC or Bank of Montreal for examples.

8.   Ad Interpretation Challenge: Monopolistic Competition
        Ad: Food and Beverage—Heinz

Heinz is producing a basic commodity: ketchup. However, they have worked tirelessly to differentiate their version of ketchup from all other competitors. As a result, they have established a unique brand in the crowded ketchup market and can command higher prices from consumers.

9.   Ad Interpretation Challenge: Inelastic Demand
        Ad: Student Choice

You are looking for products that are unique or perceived as being high in quality. For one example, take a look at Altoids (Food and Beverage—Altoids). Altoids has long held a unique position in the breath mint market. Its "Curiously Strong Mints" stand out in a crowded breath mint market, as does its unique use of packaging.

10.   Ad Interpretation Challenge: Elastic Demand
        Ad: Student Choice

One that jumps out is for World's Biggest Bookstore (General Retail—World's Biggest Bookstore). The ad states that its prices are so low even people who do not read overly well buy from them. This store has based its existence on elastic demand.

Chapter 11

Student Exercises

1.   A lot of new technology-driven products employ a market-skimming pricing strategy. For example, take a look at the newest professionally-oriented EOS digital cameras from Canon (www.usa.canon.com) or look at the newest version of Apple's iPod (www.apple.com).

2.   Keep in mind that several conditions have to be met for market-penetration pricing to really work. The market must be highly price sensitive so that a low price produces more sales. Also, the low cost must help to keep out the competition. By pricing their products so low, JR Cigar has been able to greatly increase the volume of their business, resulting in greater overall sales and increased profits. Additionally, it has been difficult for competitors to effectively work against them due, in part, to the great volumes necessary to push the low prices.

3.   Currently, Apple is offering three different versions of its widely successful iPod. Within each category, they typically offer at least two varying units. Look at their website and you will see their prices are well defined and range from around $80 to over $350.

4.   Cars are a great example of optional-product pricing. You start off with the base car and then add on everything you want to make it uniquely yours. After adding on everything you want to your unique SAAB, you will most probably see the price rise dramatically. Does this make the car less attractive to you?

5.   One item that seems to always crop up in the purchase of a new computer and monitor is the cable to hook the monitor to the computer. It's the kind of necessary accessory item you would expect to be included as standard equipment, but it's not. It always cost you around $35.

6.   One example of a successful by-product is chicken wings. For years chicken wings were all but an unwanted by-product of production. Everyone was interested in breasts and legs. Chicken wings were viewed as a food of the lower classes. Today, "buffalo wings" of all kinds are extremely popular and profitable. Think about how much you paid for your last serving.

7.   Expedia offers the traveler the option of booking just a flight, a hotel, rental car, or any and all combinations of these services. Typically, the more services you allow them to handle for you, the greater your savings. Additionally, once you select a location, they will offer you a multitude of area attraction for which you can prepay your entrance fees and save. In these ways, Expedia is practicing product bundle pricing.

8.   By looking at the multitude of products offered, it is easy to become overwhelmed by the choices for a simple white dress shirt. Most of us, barring other knowledge, would select one of the shirts in the $85-$110 range as the highest quality. In reality, many of the less expensive shirts may be of close, if not equal quality.

9.   Overstock makes great use of "list prices." On every item for sell, they prominently provide the consumer with a reference price. This information is of great value to the shopper who may not be totally familiar with some of the brands offered.

10.   Many possibilities exist here. One of the best merchants at using promotional pricing is Best Buy (www.bestbuy.com). They do a great job of placing just enough items at a temporarily reduced price to keep the same customers coming back time after time.

Marketing ADventure Exercises

1.   Ad Interpretation Challenge: Market-Skimming Pricing
           Ad: Electronics—Sony HS Series

Yes. This product, when introduced, was one of the most technically advanced televisions on the market. Technology products will many times employ market-skimming pricing in an effort to recoup some of their massive financial outlays for research and development.

2.   Ad Interpretation Challenge: Market-Penetration Pricing
           Ad: Student Choice

One of the first responses that may come to mind is for Hyundai automobiles (Autos—Hyundai). Hyundai, a new automobile into the marketplace, is looking to become established rapidly and gain as much name recognition and market share as possible. Market-penetration pricing is the perfect avenue for them to pursue.

3.   Ad Interpretation Challenge: Product Line Pricing
           Ad: Apparel—Levi's

One of the first responses that may come to mind is for Hyundai automobiles (Autos—Hyundai). Hyundai, a new automobile into the marketplace, is looking to become established rapidly and gain as much name recognition and market share as possible. Market-penetration pricing is the perfect avenue for them to pursue.

4.   Ad Interpretation Challenge: Optional-Product Pricing
           Ad: Autos—Ford

Take a look at just about any car ad. When you read the fine print, you will notice something along the line of "possibly shown with optional equipment." This is the carmakers way of letting the consumer know that the auto they see may not be the base model. It may, in fact, be a vehicle with optional equipment and is priced accordingly.

5.   Ad Interpretation Challenge: Captive-Product Pricing
           Ad: Student Choice

One of the most obvious solutions to the exercise would be the ad for Schick razors (Cosmetics and Pharmaceuticals—Schick). Razors are typically sold independently, but are useless without the accessory blade cartridges, which are sold separately.

6.   Ad Interpretation Challenge: Product Bundle Pricing
      Ad: Cosmetics and Pharmaceuticals—Edge

One possibility would be to combine the Edge shaving gel with a razor and razor blade cartridges. This bundle would present to the consumer all that was needed for a clean, close shave in one convenient to purchase bundle.

7.   Ad Interpretation Challenge: Psychological Pricing
      Ad: Cosmetics and Pharmaceuticals—Edge

Edge shaving gel is typically priced at a premium to most other shaving creams and gels. For many consumers, there is a strong relationship between the price of a product and the perceived quality of that product. All other factors being equal, the consumer will typically consider the higher priced product to be of superior quality to the lower priced product.

8.   Ad Interpretation Challenge: Reference Prices
      Ad: General Retail—World's Biggest Bookstore

Their ads state that they have "Great books. Fantastic prices." This is giving the consumer a reference price cue. World's Biggest Bookstore is telling the consumer that their prices are great—much better than the typical retail price of a book.

9.   Ad Interpretation Challenge: Promotional Pricing
      Ad: Student Choice

Many of the products or businesses featured could be used to fulfill the requirement of this question. One example would be Pizza World (Food and Beverage—Pizza World). Pizza World could simply run their pizzas at a discount (for example, 20 percent off!) for the purpose of creating excitement, getting more customers into their store, and selling more pizzas.

10.   Ad Interpretation Challenge: Dynamic Pricing
      Ad: Travel and Tourism—Aeromexico

Airlines are heavy users of dynamic pricing strategies. Through a sophisticated system, they constantly monitor the sells activity for any given flight. If the flight is not filling up fast enough, the airline may temporarily reduce the price of tickets to stimulate traffic. If ticket sales are brisk, the airline may decide to raise prices in an effort to gain more revenue from each ticket sold.

Chapter 12

Student Exercises

1.   Members of the partner community must work effectively together to bring superior value to Mountain Valley's customers. These members include manufacturers and suppliers of the components used in production of their water and accessory products—bottle producers (plastic and glass), clothing suppliers, distributors nationwide, and (of course) their customers.

2.   Gateway gets their computers to the consumer through a variety of marketing channels. They sell directly through their website or through their retail stores. They sell through third party intermediaries—other retail establishments (such as Best Buy), and they sell through other online merchants such as Amazon.

3.   Two examples you might consider are Dell computers (www.dell.com) and Canon cameras and printers (www.canonusa.com). Both of these companies produce their products and then sell them directly to the final consumers.

4.   While the majority of Starbucks coffee is sold through its company owned stores, other indirect methods are in use. Starbucks sells much of its product through the indirect channel of supermarkets. Now, you can find many of your favorite Starbucks flavors at your local market.

5.   The easiest way for conflict to occur would be for one of the stations to lower the price of its gas. Drives do not seem to be overly loyal to particular gas stations. If one were to lower their price significantly, chances are you may migrate to them, leaving your "standard" station for the better price. In such a situation, horizontal channel conflict could occur.

6.   One thing that Subway might consider doing is to offer its products as additions to the delis of local supermarkets. Subway might also consider overnight delivery of their sandwiches from national corporate-owned stores directly to consumers nationwide. Both of these would likely generate vertical channel conflict.

7.   Green Giant does not use a conventional distribution channel. However, if Green Giant were to use a conventional distribution channel, they would sell their products to an independent wholesaler for the highest price they could get. This wholesaler would have only its own best interests in mind as it sought out the best deal it could make with a retail merchant to buy the product. This retailer (grocery store) would, in turn, price the product as high as possible in an effort to maximize their profit, with little regard for the consumer. The independent layers of the channel do not work together. In fact, many times they work at odds with one another in an effort to maximize their individual profits.

8.   Goodyear has two primary outlets for its tires: its own franchised outlets and mass-merchandisers (such as Wal-Mart). In both instances, the VMS is composed of only Goodyear and the retail merchant. In both instances, the level of communication and corporation between Goodyear and the retailer is very good, with the result being smooth product delivery and fair prices to channel members and consumers.

9.   You can think of almost any major manufacturer or retailer to answer this exercise. Examples may include Gibson Guitars (www.gibson.com), PetSmart (www.petsmart.com), and Lowes (www.lowes.com).

10.   The easiest thing to do is to think of products that are expensive. One that comes readily to mind is the Rolex watch (www.rolex.com). Rolex is very selective when it comes to awarding dealership rights. Part of the allure of the product is that it can not be found in too many places. If you are in the market for a Rolex watch, you are forced to seek out one of the limited number of retailers licensed to carry the product. Such limited distribution contributes to the feeling of exclusivity of owning a Rolex.

Marketing ADventure Exercises

1.   Ad Interpretation Challenge: Value Delivery Network
     Ad: Apparel—Puma

In order to cover everyone, there are a lot of companies that you can add to this list. The value delivery network is composed of Puma, its suppliers of footwear, possibly wholesalers, retailers of its products, and finally the customer.

2.   Ad Interpretation Challenge: Direct Marketing Channel
     Ad: Student Choice

You are looking for a product that would be sold by the company directly to the consumer. Possible answers are American Airlines (Travel and Tourism—American Airlines) and Samsung (Electronics—Samsung). Many travelers buy their airline tickets directly from the airline, cutting out or bypassing the traditional intermediary of the travel agent. Likewise, a popular trend is to purchase your electronic equipment, particularly computers and accessories directly from the company.

3.   Ad Interpretation Challenge: Channel Conflict
     Ad: Food and Beverage—Cool Drinking Water

There are all kinds of potential conflicts with this product, as there are with most. For example, this product is likely shipped from the producer to a wholesaler. This wholesaler then, in turn, ships cases of the water to the retailer. At this point, the retailer, will uncase the water and make individual units available to the consumer. At any stage of this process, disagreements are likely to emerge between different levels of the channel over timing, costs, rewards, or other issues.

4.   Ad Interpretation Challenge: Vertical Channel Conflict
     Ad: Electronics—LG

LG sells through retailers. Thus, the channel goes from LG to the retailer and then on to the final consumer. If LG were to make the decision to sell directly to the consumer, the potential for conflict would occur. Now, no longer would customers have to deal with a retailer (and pay the retailer's profit), they could go directly to the source and buy.

5.   Ad Interpretation Challenge: Horizontal Channel Conflict
     Ad: Autos—Ford

The most likely scenario in which this would occur would be if Ford were to allow another dealership to open close by the original dealer. In such a situation, you would have two dealers going (potentially) after the same clients.

6.   Ad Interpretation Challenge: Vertical Marketing System
          Ad: Student Choice

One good example of a company that would use a VMS is S. C. Johnson and Son, the makers of Edge shave gel (Cosmetics and Pharmaceuticals—Edge). S. C. Johnson and Son (www.edgeadvanced.com) is so large and has so much power they would have great influence over the downstream channel members.

7.   Ad Interpretation Challenge: Vertical Marketing System—Student Decision
          Ad: General Retail—Hallmark

Hallmark is using a variation of the contractual VMS known as the franchise organization. Specifically, Hallmark is engaging in a manufacturer-sponsored retailer franchise system.

8.   Ad Interpretation Challenge: Administered VMS
          Ad: General Retail—Target

Target, the second largest discount chain, has tremendous power in a VMS. Target purchases vast quantities of merchandise for sale in its stores. The company is so large that it is able to dictate channel terms to members further up the channel, many times back to the company, which manufactures the products.

9.   Ad Interpretation Challenge: Multichannel Distribution Systems
          Ad: General Retail—Hallmark

Hallmark utilizes three marketing channels to make up its multichannel distribution system. First, Hallmark products may be found in independent Hallmark stores. These are independent merchants partnering with Hallmark through a manufacturer-sponsored retail franchise system. Second, Hallmark products may be found in other retail locations (discount stores, grocery stores, etc.). Finally, the consumer may purchase Hallmark products directly from Hallmark, via the Web. This would be a direct marketing channel.

10.   Ad Interpretation Challenge: Intensive Distribution
          Ad: Student Choice

Intensive distribution is ideally suited for products of low value, which the consumer may purchase on a relatively frequent basis. Examples include Heinz ketchup (Food and Beverage—Heinz) and Listerine (Cosmetics and Pharmaceuticals—Listerine).

Chapter 13

Student Exercises

1.   No. Certainly, Amazon fulfills the requirements of engaging in retailing. However, National Cap and Set Screw Company does not engage in retailing. Remember, retailing is involved with getting the products or services to the final consumer for their personal, nonbusiness use. National Cap and Set Screw Company sell primarily to other manufacturers or organizations that use the products in creation of their own products.

2.   Yes. Even though the typical Whole Foods store has a greater level of customer service than the traditional grocery store, it is still primarily up to the customer to "locate-compare-select" the products they purchase.

3.   There are many chains you can select from to successfully complete this exercise. For examples, consider Victoria's Secret (www.victoriassecret.com) and Aloha Shirt Shop (www.alohashirtshop.com). Both of these companies carry only a very narrow product line. But, their assortment within that line is extensive.

4.   Category killers have really done great in recent years and there seems to be no stopping them. However, they are not invincible. One example is Toys R Us (www.toysrus.com). This category killer once dominated the toy market and was the largest seller of toys and games. Poor strategy execution left them vulnerable to the major superstores (e.g., Wal-Mart) which now control the majority of the toy market.

5.   Many people would say they have no weaknesses. But, for some, the sheer size of these stores is a turn off. Wal-Mart has recognized this issue and has attempted to counter it with the opening of the Wal-Mart Neighborhood Markets, miniature versions of Wal-Mart Supercenters appropriately sized for small neighborhoods.

6.   A brief review of Wal-Mart history will show that they began as a discount merchant in smaller towns, offering quality merchandise at significantly lower prices than the competition. Over the years, we have seen their stores locate in ever higher rent areas. Their merchandise mix has shifted to offer more higher-priced, designer-like products. This has been a conscious move to try and capture a somewhat higher level clientele.

7.   A review of Prime Outlets website will show you that the typical factory outlet mall is populated with company-owned stores selling merchandise at a substantial discount off the "regular" retail price. Physically, factory outlets are generally starker in appearance and offer the shopper fewer ancillary amenities—for example, smaller food courts.

8.   Power centers have grown in popularity as an alternative to the traditional enclosed shopping mall. Shoppers have become bored and are seeking variation and excitement in the shopping experience. Power centers have appeared to fill this void.

9.   The discount store is one example you might consider. Initially, discount stores entered the market as low-price, low-status, low-margin retailers. They were located in less than desirable locations and offered lower-quality merchandise. As time has progressed, they have moved into better locations (and are paying much higher rents). Now, they are operating as somewhat higher-status merchants, faced with higher costs, and, as a result, higher prices.

10.   Retailers moving into the international arena may be faced with a multitude of challenges, including language barriers and unknown cultures. Just these two issues may prove to be daunting challenges for the unprepared retailer.

Marketing ADventure Exercises

1.   Ad Interpretation Challenge: Self-Service Retailer
      Ad: Cosmetics and Pharmaceuticals—Edge

Consumers need information with which to make decisions. To be helpful, the Edge packaging should include very visible information about the product and its positive features.

2.   Ad Interpretation Challenge: Specialty Store
      Ad: Student Choice

The most obvious choice here would probably be Hallmark (General Retail—Hallmark). This is a retailer that specializes in greeting cards. Hallmark carries primarily greeting cards (with a few ancillary and related items) and has very deep assortment of cards from which the consumer may choose.

3.   Ad Interpretation Challenge: Department Store
      Ad: Electronics—LG

Department stores carry a wide range of merchandise. However, one of the differentiating factors of department stores is service. Department stores have long used service to customers to set themselves apart from other forms of retailing. For many consumers, customer information and help in making the best selection is a vital part of the shopping experience, particularly for big-ticket items such as televisions.

4.   Ad Interpretation Challenge: Supermarket
      Ad: Food and Beverage—Heinz

Heinz (and other convenience goods manufacturers) relies almost exclusively on supermarkets to make their products available to consumers. Heinz ketchup is a low-cost item, which provides only a low-margin to the merchant. This is a classic example of the type of products that need supermarkets to survive.

5.   Ad Interpretation Challenge: Category Killer
      Ad: General Retail—World's Biggest Bookstore

Category killers, such as World's Biggest Bookstore, offer the customer much greater selection within a particular product line—in this case books. Along with the deeper product line, comes knowledgeable employees who are there to answer the customer's detailed questions and to offer advice on products.

6.   Ad Interpretation Challenge: Discount Stores
        Ad: Student Choice

There is only one possibility here. Target (General Retail—Target) is a typical discount chain, albeit an upscale one.

7.   Ad Interpretation Challenge: Off-Price Retailers
        Ad: Apparel—Levi's

Off-price retailers typically stock last season's styles or factory overruns. Therefore, if Levi's New Collection Diamond Jeans did not sell during the season, they may very well find themselves at an off-price retailer come the beginning of the next fashion season.

8.   Ad Interpretation Challenge: Franchise
        Ad: Student Choice

There are several ads you can select to fulfill the requirements of this exercise. Two you might consider are McDonald's (Food and Beverage—McDonald's) and 24 Hour Fitness (Services and B2B—24 Hour Fitness).

9.   Ad Interpretation Challenge: Retail Positioning
        Ad: General Retail—Target

Target has done a very good job of competing with Wal-Mart, not by going head-to-head, but by positioning itself as an upscale alternative to the mass merchandiser of Wal-Mart. Now, the two discount behemoths are targeting very different markets and have distinctly different positions in the marketplace.

10.   Ad Interpretation Challenge: The Wheel-of-Retailing Concept
        Ad: General Retail—Worlds Biggest Bookstore

In the introductory stage of the wheel-of-retailing the merchant is a low-price, low-status operator. As time goes by and they become successful, there is a tendency for them to move into higher-priced goods, with higher-priced operations, losing some of the competitive tenacity that made them so successful early on.

Chapter 14

Student Exercises

1.   The promotion mix for your university is most likely a mix of several promotional tools. You may see that your school uses traditional advertising (such as billboards or newspaper ads). Along with this, they will likely have a "salesforce" (although they would never call them that). This salesforce are the recruiters for your school that go out to the high schools and community colleges to provide information about your school's course offerings.

2.   IMC ties together all of the company's messages and images. Apple could use IMC to help get the message out regarding the iPhone. Under IMC, they need to be certain that their television and print ads communicate the same basic message and that they do so with the same look and feel as other components of the program. Likewise, they would want their public relations materials to project the same image as their website.

3.   Noise is anything that interferes with the correct reception of the sender's message. In this example, the noise could come from many places. For example, local television ads are notorious for poor production quality. If there were the case for our favorite local Mexican restaurant, this poor production could overwhelm the intended message.

4.   BCBG is a marketer of high fashion women's clothing. They have products that cover the price scale from moderately priced to expensive. A quick review of their website might lead the viewer to believe that they only market to consumers at the upper ends of the socioeconomic scale and that they have nothing for the average or slightly-above average consumer. This would not be their intention and would not be the message they were intending to transmit.

5.   Remember, in a rational appeal, the messages typically show a product's quality, economy, value, or performance. Audi could key in on any of these attributes with their message.

6.   Rogaine appeals directly to consumer emotions by showing the happiness of a couple when the man has a full head of hair. Much of the content of this site is geared toward showing the reader how much better than can feel about themselves and how much happier they can be in relationships with a full head of newly grown hair.

7.   Keep in mind that a personal communication channel may be company controlled. With this in mind, the most common personal communication channel that would likely be employed is face-to-face. Best Buy is widely regarded as offering the consumer good in-store service. They make an effort to have highly trained salespeople and to make those salespeople easily accessible to the customer.

8.   Sites such as Trip Advisor provide the consumer with independent customer information, not controlled by the company. After reading a few of their customer reviews, you may realize that fabulous vacation destination you had always wanted to visit really may not be that grand.

9.   This product, one of a growing number of smartphone products, could do well through buzz marketing. To utilize buzz marketing, Palm would want to get a number of the units into the hands of influential members of its target market. These individuals would then serve as a primary information source for others of their cohort—providing them with seemingly unbiased word-of-mouth information.

10.   There are many possible nonpersonal communication channels Palm could consider. Primary in their consideration should be the use of media (magazines, e-mail, and websites). Also, possibly Palm may want to consider sponsoring events as another method of introducing Treo to the marketplace.

Marketing ADventure Exercises

1.   Ad Interpretation Challenge: The Promotion Mix
      Ad: Advertising—Universal McCann

From a review of this particular ad, Universal McCann appears to be concentrating solely on paid media forms of advertising. If this is in fact the case, then Universal McCann may be omitting many other portions of the promotion mix from their repertoire.

2.   Ad Interpretation Challenge: Narrowcasting
      Ad: Auto—Audi

The new A2 is targeted to a younger profile than the typical Audi automobile. Because of this, Audi might consider moving away from traditional television advertising and instead use product placements in television shows, movies, or video games.

3.   Ad Interpretation Challenge: Mass-Media Communication
      Ad: Student Choice

Many products, particularly convenience goods products, make good use of a mass-media communication strategy. You may want to take a look at Snickers (Food and Beverage—Snickers) and Energizer (Electronics—Energizer) for two examples. Both of these examples are for convenience goods products that appeal to a wide range of consumers across socioeconomic categories.

4.   Ad Interpretation Challenge: Integrated Marketing Communications (IMC)
      Ad: Auto—Chrysler

This ad is promoting the idea of Chrysler as a "bright idea." Utilizing IMC, company marketers would make certain that every communication channel used would convey the exact same idea in much the same manner. Consistency of image and consistency of delivery are important concepts of IMC.

5.   Ad Interpretation Challenge: Noise
      Ad: Newspaper and TV—Cartoon Network

Ad placement could be an issue here. One of the possible causes of noise in magazine advertising is the content surrounding the advertisement. If the content is unusually appealing or interesting, there may be a tendency for the reader to overlook the ad in an effort to continue the reading of the primary article.

6.   Ad Interpretation Challenge: Receiver
            Ad: Auto—Audi A2

Cearly, Audi is targeting younger consumers with this series of A2 ads. The style of the ads, from the models used to the wording used, indicates the intended receiver to be an early-20s individual.

7.   Ad Interpretation Challenge: Buyer-Readiness Stages
            Ad: Auto—Mercedes C Class

This is an ad for a new product—the C Class Mercedes. Based on this, and on the fact that the ad is not providing the consumer with much solid information, you would have to say the ad is targeting consumers in the awareness stage of the buyer-readiness continuum.

8.   Ad Interpretation Challenge: Emotional Appeal
            Ad: Student Choice

One good choice here is the ad for Hallmark cards (General Retail—Hallmark). This is an ad that uses the emotional appeal of love and belongingness to get its point across.

9.   Ad Interpretation Challenge: Humorous Appeal
            Ad: Financial—Fame

This ad relies on humor to make its point. Although everyone would like to be in show business, it is not a realistic goal for most of us. F.A.M.E. allows us to still feel like a part of the biz through investing in entertainment-oriented stocks. This ad makes light of this unrealistic goal many of us have.

10.   Ad Interpretation Challenge: Word-of-Mouth Influence
            Ad: Auto—Ford

If you were considering the purchase of a new Ford vehicle, word-of-mouth would likely play a large role in your search for information. You might turn to friends, colleagues, and family for their opinions regarding this brand.

Chapter 15

Student Exercises

1.   Yes. The purpose of their website is to present information and promote their property. These are the basic tenants of advertising.

2.   If you take the time to thoroughly review the information contained on the SuperClubs website, you will realize that the principle objective of the site is to inform, with a secondary objective being to persuade. The website takes great pains to explain the concept of "all-inclusive" and how SuperClubs competes in that arena.

3.   Just think of any mature product—a product whose growth rate has slowed substantially and is competing in a market that is experiencing low (in any) growth. Examples may include shaving creams (such as Edge shaving gel [www.edgeadvanced.com]) and breakfast cereals (such as Kellogg's Frosted Flakes [www.frostedflakes.com]).

4.   To many vacationers, a Caribbean island is a Caribbean island. They are all pretty much alike. As the marketing executive in charge of advertising Jamaica, you must make your product stand out from the pack. (Take a look at www.visitjamaica.com for some background and ideas.) You must make Jamaica seem different and unique from other sun and sand Caribbean destinations. Maybe you do this through concentrating on potential interactions between the visiting tourists and locals. Maybe you do this by concentrating on the cultural aspects of what Jamaica has to offer the visitor—such as reggae.

5.   The creative concept ("big idea") of the new Australia tourism campaign is "So where the bloody hell are you?" With this one sentence, Australia tourism has put forth an advertising message that, not only cuts through the advertising clutter, but is also memorable.

6.   Couples Resorts is selling romance. This is an island resort that is devoted to couples-only holidays. Knowing this and by reviewing their website, it is easy to see that Couples Resorts is using Mood or Image as the execution style of choice. This style builds a mood or image around the product or service. Few claims are made about the product, except through suggestion.

7.   Scion (a brand of Toyota Motors) is geared toward a younger car buying market. A review of the advantages and disadvantages of various media types will lead you to decide that to reach the Scion market, you would most likely rely on targeted magazine advertising and internet. Magazine advertising boasts high geographic and demographic selectivity, along with high credibility and prestige. Likewise, the internet delivers a demographically skewed audience—skewed towards younger clientele, just the type interested in products such as Scion.

8.   Alternative media formats have grown rapidly in recent years, as advertising clutter continues to rise. Marketers are looking for any way to allow information about their product to "pop" through the advertising clutter. Here, you are looking for alternative media formats that fit with the intended target market. It may be something as wild as placing the Scion name and logo on streets in the SoHo district of New York or as unusual as skydivers at a sporting event with parachutes embellished with the Scion logo.

9.   Through press releases and press relations, the singer provides her audience with positive information regarding her actions and activities. Further, through public affairs, attention is given to her efforts to give back to communities.

10.   A quick review of the NRA website will let you know that lobbying of government officials is a central component of their overall public relations campaign.

Marketing ADventure Exercises

1.   Ad Interpretation Challenge: Advertising
       Ad: Apparel—Levi's New Collection Diamond Jean

This ad is designed to show a side of Levi's that many consumers had not seen and were not aware of—Levi's as a fashion-forward apparel company. As such, this ad does a good job of capturing the viewer's attention and informing them of the "new" Levi's.

2.   Ad Interpretation Challenge: Reminder Advertising
       Ad: Student Choice

There are several ads here that will fulfill the requirements of this exercise. Remember, you are looking for an ad for a product in the mature stage of the product life cycle. That narrows the list down somewhat. You might consider either the ad for Snickers candy bars (Food and Beverage—Snickers) or the ad for Aim toothpaste (Cosmetics and Pharmaceuticals—Aim). Both of these ads are for products in the mature phase of the product life cycle. Also, the main purpose of these two ads is simply to keep the name of the product in the mind of the consumer.

3.   Ad Interpretation Challenge: Informative Advertising
       Ad: Auto—Hyundai Lean Burn

Informative advertising is used to tell the market about a new product or to communicate customer value. Informative advertising may also be used to assist in building a brand or company image. This ad for Hyundai does all of these things.

4.   Ad Interpretation Challenge: Persuasive Advertising
       Ad: Electronics—LG

Yes. This ad has at its heart persuasion. The ad is designed to encourage brand switching.

5.   Ad Interpretation Challenge: Advertising Budget
       Ad: Apparel—Levi's New Collection Diamond Jean

This product would be in the early stages of the product life cycle. As a result of this, it would be wise to provide a relatively large advertising budget. New products typically need large advertising budgets to build awareness and to gain consumer trial.

6.   Ad Interpretation Challenge: Breaking Through the Clutter
        Ad: Student Choice

What you are looking for is an ad that just simply stands out far and above its competition. This is certainly not an easy feat to accomplish. One example you may consider is the advertisement for Leisure Entertainment (Travel & Tourism—Leisure Entertainment). This ad does a good job of being unique. The use of a scantily clad dancer helps draw attention to an ad that otherwise may have gone unnoticed.

7.   Ad Interpretation Challenge: Madison & Vine
        Ad: General Retail—Hallmark

Hoops&yoyo were created as just another card character. However, their growing popularity caused the characters to be used as a method of communicating with the consumer. Their ads are so lively and unique they easily cut through the clutter and are noticeable. They entertain as they inform.

8.   Ad Interpretation Challenge: Execution Style
        Ad: Auto—Honda Motorcycles

Honda is making use of the lifestyle execution style in all of these motorcycle ads. The ads indicate that users of these products typically have a certain lifestyle and that lifestyle is depicted in the ads.

9.   Ad Interpretation Challenge: Advertising Media
        Ad: Autos—Audi

This ad for the Audi A2 would work best in a magazine. Magazine advertising has high geographic and demographic selectively. It has high credibility and prestige and high-quality reproduction (important for the detail in the pictures).

10.   Ad Interpretation Challenge: Advertising Media
        Ad: Newspapers and TV—MTV Masters

Look at the target market for this product. MTV appeals most heavily to younger adults and teens. By reviewing the advantages and limitations of the various forms of media, you can see that magazines, radio, and the Internet do the best jobs of segmenting the market on demographic factors.

Chapter 16

Student Exercises

1.   By spending just a minimal amount of time on the website for the Journal of Personal Selling and Sales Management you may well be surprised at the level of professionalism displayed. No longer are salespeople just someone you pull off the street to hawk items to unsuspecting consumers. Today's salesforce is highly trained and professional.

2.   Many times, salespeople in department stores are little more than "order takers." You will find them often standing behind a cash terminal waiting for you to approach them with your merchandise ready to check out. This function of a salesperson is pretty much at the lower end of the spectrum.

3.   When you go to Limited Brands website, click on Career Opportunities. Here, you will find various links directing you to Campus and Career Coaching. Both of these areas provide the reader with valuable information useful in considering a career with Limited Brands. In this way, Limited Brands is working to recruit talented individuals to its company. Recruitment is one of the early stages of sales force management.

4.   IMS provides services to clients to assist them is properly setting up and controlling a territorial sales force. Their website provides the reader with basic information on when it is appropriate to utilize a territorial sales force structure and a basic understanding of sales force deployment.

5.   You will want to look for a company with a wide product line composed of technically sophisticated or complex products. Pharmaceutical companies are one possibility, particularly if you divide their products into those taken by mouth (pills) and those injected (shots). These are two very different product lines which may require different types of expertise on the part of the sales force. For an example, take a look at the products offered by Merck Pharmaceuticals (www.merck.com).

6.   Many vendors have devoted special sales teams to interact solely with Wal-Mart. Some have gone so far as to locate offices close by the Bentonville, Arkansas home of the company in an effort to build and maintain the closest of relationships.

7.   Outside sales forces are particularly important for companies that market highly complex products. The face-to-face interaction allows for potentially greater understanding between the parties. Additionally, face-to-face interaction many times better facilitates the transfer of knowledge and understanding – important factors to consider when marketing technical and complex products. Companies such as Boeing (www.boeing.com) and AstraZeneca (www.astrazeneca.com) come readily to mind.

8.   Office Depot has sales specialists on call to answer and assist educational customers in fulfilling the needs of their organizations. A review of the Office Depot website reveals contact information for specialists dealing with different parts of the educational system so that, as a customer, you may be connected with the appropriate salesperson for your needs. In this manner, Office Depot does away with the necessity of an outside sales force.

9.   You are looking to add new retailers to your list. The first step of this process is prospecting. You would probably want to consider the merchants financial ability, volume of business, any special needs they may have, their location, and possibilities for growth.

10.   Sales promotions are everywhere. Pick up a local Sunday newspaper and take a look at the freestanding insert for Best Buy. (You can also see the local insert at www.bestbuy.com) No doubt, this advertising insert will be filled with offers on products that are only valid during the current week. This is a great example of sales promotion.

Marketing ADventure Exercises

1. Ad Interpretation Challenge: Personal Selling
    Ad: Student Choice

There are many possibilities you can select to fulfill the requirements of this question. Two that come to mind are Mercedes (Auto—Mercedes) and Royal Bank (Financial—Royal Bank). Automobiles need personal selling due to the complex nature of the product. Similarly, Royal Bank is promoting financing for businesses. Financial services have typically needed personal selling to explain the intricacies of the product.

2. Ad Interpretation Challenge: Salesperson
    Ad: General Retail—Target

Target stores would employ salespeople for the general purpose of order taking. Target, like most discount stores and many department stores, is primarily a self-service establishment. The role of the salesperson is reduced to nothing more than acting as a checkout person.

3. Ad Interpretation Challenge: Territorial Sales Force Structure
    Ad: Food and Beverage—Heinz

Heinz products are typically low-cost, high-volume products. With a territorial sales force structure, each salesperson is responsible for a geographic region and sells the entire line of company products. Such a structure is best suited to low cost, convenience goods products.

4. Ad Interpretation Challenge: Product Sales Force Structure
    Ad: Electronics—Sony

Sony offers a very wide range of products and product lines, some with seemingly little connection to others. Some of the lines Sony offers are highly specialized, technical, and diverse. With such a wide range of highly complex and diverse product lines, Sony would be wise to use a product sales force structure.

5. Ad Interpretation Challenge: Customer Sales Force Structure
    Ad: Apparel—Levi's

Levi Strauss would likely use a customer sales force structure to differentiate between major clients (such as Sears) and typical small merchants. By structuring their sales force in such a manner, Levi Strauss is better able to provide its primary clients with the level of service necessary.

6.　　Ad Interpretation Challenge: Inside Sales Force
　　　Ad: Financial—H&R Block

Typically, H&R Block does not go out actively soliciting business (using an outside sales force). Rather, they wait for potential business to seek them out. When prospective buyers enter and H&R Block establishment, it becomes the responsibility of the inside sales force to provide them with the information they need and (hopefully) sell them the products and services that are correct for their needs.

7.　　Ad Interpretation Challenge: Team Selling
　　　Ad: Student Choice

You need to be looking for companies that represent potentially large and complicated accounts. These are the type of accounts that would typically need more servicing than the traditional salesperson could provide. One possible example is Chevrolet (Autos— Chevy). For example, if you were a company responsible for providing Chevrolet with computers, you would likely choose to use a team selling approach. The size and complexity of the account would be daunting for one salesperson to have total responsibility for; multiple areas of expertise would be needed.

8.　　Ad Interpretation Challenge: Prospecting
　　　Ad: Services and B2B—EMS

In addition to all of the qualities already mentioned in the question, you would be very interested to determine the potential volume of business you could derive from EMS. This would be of vital importance later in the selling process as you were preparing to negotiate prices.

9.　　Ad Interpretation Challenge: Presentation
　　　Ad: Autos—Mercedes Keys

This ad is presenting the product to the consumer. The ad is highlighting the long history of Mercedes. The ad is saying, in essence, this is a car company that has been around for a long time and has a long proud history.

10.　　Ad Interpretation Challenge: Sales Promotion
　　　 Ad: Food and Beverage—Snickers

Remember, a sales promotion is a short-term incentive. There are many possibilities that Snickers could employ to boost sales of their candy bar. For example, they could run an ad with a coupon for "Buy 1, Get 1." Or, they might consider a special display in the candy aisle at your local grocery store. These are only two of a multitude of possible sales promotion ideas that could be employed.

Chapter 17

Student Exercises

1.   On the Gateway site you have the option of designing and purchasing a computer system but together just for you (direct marketing) or of being directed to a merchant where you can find a pre-packaged system (traditional in-store marketing). Gateway is one of a growing number of companies that are reaching out to consumers through multiple marketing avenues.

2.   Schools collect a wealth of data about their students, all of which may be "mined" for use later on. Some of the typical types of information collected include basic demographics (age, gender, ethnicity, home town, etc.), majors and specific classes taken.

3.   Columbia House sends out thousands of pieces of direct-mail yearly. While some of these mailing are targeted to past customers of the mail-order music and DVD site, many of the mailing are "cold calls" – mailing to consumers who have shown no prior interest in the company. By targeting their mailings only to those individuals who have shown interest in the products and services they offer, Columbia House could reduce their junk mail image somewhat.

4.   After visiting a Victoria's Secret store and perusing one of their catalogs, you will notice a dramatic difference in merchandise offered. While the stores have concentrated primarily on undergarments and lingerie, the catalog offering is a more varied. In the catalog, you will see, along with those items, a comprehensive line of clothing, shoes, and accessories. It is not possible for the retail stores to carry the wide array of merchandise available in the catalogs.

5.   A review of their website gives you some details on their customer help line. This line is available to consumers who have questions about turkey preparation and storage. You call the number and can be connected to an individual with specialized knowledge on turkeys. This is a form of telephone marketing. By providing the customer with needed information through an easy to use format, you increase the likelihood of repeat purchase.

6.   After watch HSNtv live on your PC for a few minutes, you can begin to understand just how they build product excitement. Every product is individually showcased and shown in its best possible form. Knowledgeable "hosts" provide on-air excitement and details about the product. Also, all products are marked down from their "list prices," further generating buyer excitement.

7.   Delta's online kiosks allow customers to perform many of the tasks themselves that were previously assigned to airline employees. Through a kiosk, customers can now check themselves in for a flight, change seats, make new reservations, even check in luggage.

8.   T-Mobile is currently making numerous services available to their customers. A quick tour of their website shows that you can purchase (from your cell phone handset) services such as ring-tones and wallpapers or access to the internet. All of this and more is available for purchase from your cell phone handset.

9.   Amazon offers a seemingly endless variety of product categories from which to choose. One of the best comparisons of Amazon's selection is to compare it to a very large mall. However, even that form of comparison is inadequate as the product selection available through Amazon is so much vaster.

10.   Sears uses its online presence in two ways to effectively compete with the click-only companies. First, the online version of Sears allows the customer to shop at anytime of the day or night. Therefore, they are not bounded by the traditional store operating hours. Second, by allowing its customers to shop from the convenience of their home (or office or school), Sears is providing a level of customer convenience they can not match with their stores. No longer does the typical Sears customer have to travel to visit a Sears store.

Marketing ADventure Exercises

1.   Ad Interpretation Challenge: Direct Marketing
        Ad: Advertising—Studio Funk

One thing that Studio Funk could do with their radio ads is to provide the listener with a Web address or toll-free number that could be used to directly communicate with the ad sponsor. In this way, the advertiser would be directly linked to the individual consumer.

2.   Ad Interpretation Challenge: Customer Database
        Ad: Internet—El Sitio

El Sitio boasts an online dating service (among other things). Knowledge of your customer is paramount to the success of any online dating venture. As a result, El Sitio would need a comprehensive database of member information from which to draw matches.

3.   Ad Interpretation Challenge: Direct-Mail Marketing
        Ad: Auto—Audi A3

Audi would not have to do much to make this a good direct-mail piece. However, to be effective as a direct-mail piece, this ad would have to be directed to someone in particular. It is important with direct-mail marketing that the effort be directed to a particular person at a particular address to assist in overcoming the "junk mail" image of so much direct-mail marketing.

4.   Ad Interpretation Challenge: Catalog Marketing
        Ad: Travel and Tourism—Travel Price

Go to their website (www.travelprice.es) and take a look around. You will see that they offer a multitude of travel and tourism options. The potential traveler only has to enter basic information, such as destination, to be presented with a wide range of options from their virtual catalog.

5.   Ad Interpretation Challenge: Telephone Marketing
        Ad: Travel and Tourism—Imperial Hotel

Yes. If you will look at the ads, you will realize the basic purpose of them is to generate telephone calls, which can then be turned into reservations. This is a great example of using a print advertisement to generate business through the telephone.

6.   Ad Interpretation Challenge: Direct-Response Television Marketing
          Ad: Newspaper and TV—MTV

Anytime that MTV asks viewers to text or call in to the network they are practicing direct-response television marketing.

7.   Ad Interpretation Challenge: Kiosk Marketing
          Ad: Travel and Tourism—American Airlines

The primary manner in which American Airlines is currently using kiosks is in allowing customers to check in for flights and check baggage. American also uses kiosks to allow customers to purchase tickets for future flights and change seating assignments.

8.   Ad Interpretation Challenge: Mobile Phone Marketing
          Ad: Electronics—Axiom

There are several services Axiom could make available to its customers by way of mobile phone marketing. Axiom could use mobile phone marketing to make available ring tones to its customers. Also, Axiom could sell wallpapers and Internet services.

9.   Ad Interpretation Challenge: Marketing Website
          Ad: Electronics—Polaroid

Yes this is a marketing website. The Polaroid site provides detailed information about Polaroid products. However, the site does more than just provide the consumer with information. Interested consumers have the opportunity to buy directly from the company, via their website, making this a marketing website.

10.   Ad Interpretation Challenge: Spam
          Ad: Travel and Transportation—Aeromexico

The easiest thing Aeromexico can do so as to not be viewed as "spamming" the consumer is simply to ask for permission to e-mail marketing information. By doing this, Aeromexico will have alerted its customers to its intention and will have received their permission to deliver marketing information to their e-mailbox.

Chapter 18

Student Exercises

1. The "new" AT&T, formed by a merging of Cingular and BellSouth, enjoy advantages its competitors currently do not have. Name recognition is the biggest competitive advantage AT&T holds over its competition. The AT&T name has been an American icon for about a century. It boasts name recognition among the highest of any brand name in the country.

2. Lenovo is a manufacturer of desktop and laptop computers geared primarily for business and industry. Their primary competitors are Dell (www.dell.com), Hewlett-Packard (www.hp.com), and Gateway (www.gateway.com).

3. Palm belongs to a strategic group that produces handheld organizers and communications devices. Other members of the group include Blackberry (www.blackberry.com) and Nokia (www.nokia.com), and Dell (www.dell.com).

4. You always want to look to the industry leader to benchmark. In this industry, Adobe Systems is the market leader for photo editing software. Other industry competitors include Apple (www.apple.com) and Microsoft (www.microsoft.com).

5. One example that may come to mind is Southwest Airlines. Long an industry outsider, Southwest refuses to play by some of the basic industry rules, such as allowing its flights to be listed on the reservation systems of other airlines or third-party sellers such as Expedia (www.expedia.com).

6. Apple has always been viewed as somewhat of a quirky company, different and unique from its competition. Apple perpetuates this image and earned a cult-like following among technophiles. Additionally, Apple has made a name by introducing products that are incredibly stylish as well as functional.

7. Cathay Pacific Airways is one such company. You can view their website at www.cathaypacific.com. Cathay Pacific has chosen a focus strategy and concentrates their efforts on the top tier of business travelers. This segment of the market values comfort and convenience over cost.

8. Wyndham Hotels and Resorts has created a program known as Wyndham ByRequest. Members of this program provide the company with some basic customer information. The company is then in a position to provide to that customer a level of service significantly above the average in the industry. Such high-level service keeps the well-paying customer coming back again and again.

9. The market leaders in this industry are Kellogg's and Post. Quaker Oats Company, while no doubt a powerful competitor, is seldom seen to rock the boat in this slow growing industry. Quaker Oats Company would be considered a market follower.

10.   A market nicher only goes after a small subset of the overall market. When you examine the companies that are competing in the breakfast cereal market, Healthy Choice (makers of Healthy Choice Apple & Almond Crunch Mueslix) stands out. This is a company that is only competing for breakfast customers who are health-conscious and willing to pay a premium for a healthy alternative breakfast cereal.

Marketing ADventure Exercises

1.   Ad Interpretation Challenge: Competitive Advantage
             Ad: Financial—MBNA

MBNA has an affinity card deal with Clemson University. Alumni and diehard fans of Clemson may be drawn to this credit card. The card allows them to show school spirit, while at the same time actually benefiting the school. For every purchase made on the card, a percentage of the purchase is rebated to the university.

2.   Ad Interpretation Challenge: Identifying Competitors
             Ad: Electronics—LG

LG (the world's largest manufacturer of flat panel televisions) does not operate without some major strong competitors. Principal among those competitors is Sony (www.sony.com) and Sharp (www.sharpusa.com), two of the largest marketers of flat panel televisions.

3.   Ad Interpretation Challenge: Strategic Groups
             Ad: Auto—Porsche

Porsche is an automobile manufacturer. However, more specifically, Porsche is the manufacturer of high-performance, high-price luxury automobiles. This strategic group is made up of similar manufacturers. This could possibly include BMW (www.bmwusa.com) and Mercedes (www.mbusa.com).

4.   Ad Interpretation Challenge: Benchmarking
             Ad: Cosmetics and Pharmaceuticals—Mentadent

You would want to benchmark against the largest players in the field, namely Crest (http://crest.com) and Colgate (www.colgate.com). You would want to closely examine their products and marketing strategies to see what they do best and how you might more effectively compete.

5.   Ad Interpretation Challenge: Close Competitors
             Ad: Financial—Ameritrade

Ameritrade (www.tdameritrade.com) is an online stock trading company. Close competitors would be other online trading companies, such as ETrade Financial (https://us.etrade.com). Companies such as this are most similar to Ameritrade. Traditional trading companies, such as Merrill Lynch (Financial—Merrill Lynch), while certainly competitors, are not as close.

6.   Ad Interpretation Challenge: Entrepreneurial Marketing Strategy
      Ad: Student Choice

One example that may stand out is for the University of Toronto (Services and B2B—University of Toronto). These ads are unique. They stand out in a crowded competitive landscape. They are edgy and risk takers.

7.   Ad Interpretation Challenge: Differentiation
      Ad: Services and B2B—24 Hour Fitness

The simplest answer to this question is that 24 Hour Fitness differentiates itself through it hours of operation. The company is open 24 hours a day, making itself very convenient to its customers.

8.   Ad Interpretation Challenge: Focus
      Ad: Apparel—Polartec

Polartec (http://polartec.com) has made the conscious decision to concentrate their efforts on a small segment of the overall clothing market. Polartec focuses on what they term "performance fabrics."

9.   Ad Interpretation Challenge: Product Leadership
      Ad: Student Choice

One possible answer to this exercise is Motorola (Electronics—Motorola). Motorola is a leader in cell phone production. Motorola is constantly innovating, changing the form, functions, and features of its cell phones. Its goal is to stay ahead of the competition and render its current phones obsolete.

10.   Ad Interpretation Challenge: Market Leader Strategies
      Ad: General Retail—Hallmark

Hallmark must maintain a constant watch on its competitors. Additionally, they must also watch for subtle changes or trends in the marketplace. Small trends, if not realized and capitalized on quickly, can become big trends that a competitor controls. Finally, Hallmark must work constantly to remain relevant in today's market. They cannot afford to be viewed as old fashioned or out of touch.

Chapter 19

Student Exercises

1.   Yes. Saab is a global company. The company (a wholly owned unit of General Motors) manufactures automobiles for the global community. By examining their global home page, you can see that they have a presence in many countries. They offer the same product in every country in which they operate, with only minimal variation to meet local requirement.

2.   By reading of the most recent developments in the latest round of GATT negotiations, the one thing that should stand out most vividly to you is the difficulty and complexity of these negotiations. All members have their own special interests to think about; yet, there does seem to be an overall desire to accomplish something worthwhile. Only time will tell.

3.   The European Union has achieved more in a shorter period of time than most outsiders thought to be possible. The elimination of tariffs and other barriers to trade has opened their markets, not only to each other, but to those outside of the Union to a degree previously unobtainable. By reviewing the information on foreign students studying in the EU, you will see that a multitude of study options exist. You should consider spending a semester abroad!

4.   Under the NAFTA treaty, all non-tariff barriers to agricultural trade between the United States and Mexico were eliminated. Because of this, it should be much more economical for you to export to Mexico.

5.   Even the poorest of countries need basic goods and services. Economies such as these may offer limited markets for clean drinking water and basic agricultural assistance.

6.   In Mexico, the top 10 percent of the population is responsible for about 33 percent of the income. Also, about 60 percent of the population can be classified as belonging to the lowest socioeconomic groups. When looking at the U.S., you will notice that the income is more evenly distributed throughout society, with the top 10 percent of the population responsible for 17 percent of the income. This more evenly distributed income would lead you to believe that the overall market in the U.S. is considerably larger as a wider range of the population has access to monetary resources.

7.   Companies typically begin with indirect exporting. Indirect exporting is working through independent international marketing intermediaries. Indirect exporting involves less investment because the firm does not require an overseas marketing organization or network. It involves less risk.

8.   While licensing is the least risky method of entering a foreign market, it is not without risk. The company has less control over the licensee than it would over its own operations. Also, if the licensee is very successful, the firm has given up these profits, and if and when the contract ends, it may find it has created a competitor.

9.   You are looking for a company that basically offers the same products and uses the same marketing strategy everywhere it operates, with only minimal variation. Take a look again at Saab automobiles (www.saab.com) as one example.

10.   The U.K. site contains a bit more partial nudity than is typically acceptable, by U.S. standards. Vaseline would want to tone this down a bit before launching this site in the U.S.

Marketing ADventure Exercises

1.   Ad Interpretation Challenge: Global Firm
       Ad: Auto—Audi

Yes, Audi is a true global firm. Audi manufactures a line of automobiles that are available in many countries throughout the world. Audi makes these products globally available; however, product adaptation does occur due to local custom, preference, or regulation.

2.   Ad Interpretation Challenge: Tariffs
       Ad: Auto—Audi

By placing a tariff—or tax—on the importation of these cars, the U.S. government is effectively raising the price of these products to consumers. Consumers will end up spending more to purchase one of these products, or will have to turn to another product of less expense. Either way, the consumer loses.

3.   Ad Interpretation Challenge: GATT
       Ad: Student Choice

Almost anything you come up with here would work. GATT has worked to reduce tariffs and other barriers to a vast variety of international goods and services—manufactured goods, agricultural goods, intellectual property, and others.

4.   Ad Interpretation Challenge: European Union
       Ad: Auto—Fiat

One of the primary barriers reduced or eliminated by the EU has been on the migration of labor forces. If Fiat was having difficulty with labor shortages in Italy, being a member of the EU makes it much simpler to recruit labor from other EU countries with minimal restrictions.

5.   Ad Interpretation Challenge: FTAA
       Ad: Food and Beverage—Brazilian Fruit

Currently, Brazil is not a member of an economic community with the United States. By both countries belonging to one community whose goal it is to positively impact trade, possible tariffs on the importation of Brazilian fruit would be reduced or eliminated.

6.   Ad Interpretation Challenge: Raw Material Exporting Economies
       Ad: Auto—Jaguar

If a raw material exporting economy has many foreigners or a wealthy upper class, there is a market for luxury items. Saudi Arabia is one such example.

7.   Ad Interpretation Challenge: Industrializing Economies
       Ad: Student Choice

Conspicuous products are in great demand in these emerging classes, as they "announce" to others that their owners have "made it." Such products as Mercedes (Autos—Mercedes) and expensive, showy clothing, such as Levi's New Collection Diamond Jeans (Apparel—Levi's) are example of products that would be successful.

8.   Ad Interpretation Challenge: Cultural Environment
       Ad: Apparel—Levi's New Collection Diamond Jeans

Muslim societies are very conservative, when it comes to the role of women and their dress. An advertisement such as this may be considered unacceptable due to the amount of uncovered female body shown. Companies must be aware and respond accordingly to such cultural variations.

9.   Ad Interpretation Challenge: "Americanizing" the World
       Ad: Student Choice

One product that you may consider here is Levi's. Levi's are viewed in many parts of the world as a "true American product." It probably would not take too much for them to become a true iconic symbol. Also, take a look at the ads for Cadillac (Auto-Cadillac) and MTV (Newspapers & TV-MTV). These ads represent two more products that have such potential.

10.   Ad Interpretation Challenge: Adapted Marketing Mix
       Ad: Apparel—Levi's New Collection Diamond Jeans

The easiest thing you can do is to vary the advertising part of the marketing mix. Alter the ads to place emphasis on the jeans, not on the female form.

Chapter 20

Student Exercises

1.   Advertising does add to the product cost, but it also provides information to the consumer. Branded products may cost more. Typically, unbranded or store brands of products are available at less cost to the consumer. However, branding gives buyers assurance of consistent quality. Many consumers want and are willing to pay more for branded products that also provide psychological benefits – they may make them feel special in some way.

2.   Yes. BCBG (like much of the fashion industry) is engaging in planned obsolescence. However, consumers like style changes. They get tired of the old look and want a new look in fashion. No one has to buy the new look, and if not too many people like it, it will fail (consider ponchos from a couple of fashion seasons back).

3.   By looking up the Better Business Bureau report on some of your favorite merchants you are able to get a better understanding of these businesses and how they treat their customers. Hopefully, you will not be faced with any unwelcome surprises!

4.   The primary benefit from Green Globe certification (or that of a number of other environmental certification programs) is through recognition. As travelers become more educated, their concern form the environment continues to rise. Green Globe certification indicates to these travelers that the property they are considering also shares this concern for the environment.

5.   According to Patagonia's mission statement, they are committed to using business to inspire solutions to the growing environmental crisis. The more you read about the company, the more you realize Patagonia easily fits into all parts of the Environmental Sustainability Grid.

6.   You are looking for a company that has made a practice of staying on the cutting edge of its industry and that has consistently turned that cutting edge position into new innovative products and product improvements. One such company you might take a look at is Apple (www.apple.com).

7.   Starbucks takes very seriously its role as a good corporate citizen. You will find evidence of Starbucks view of social responsibility in all of their stores and on their website. Starbucks wants its customers to know where they stand. They believe it is not only the right thing to do, but good for business.

8.   A societal marketing-oriented company wants to design products that are both pleasing AND beneficial to the consumer. One example of such a company is Herman Miller (www.hermanmiller.com). Herman Miller is a company long dedicated to the creation of office furniture that is ascetically pleasing AND ergonomically sound.

9.   Based strictly on the definitions given, you could easily place alcohol into this category; however, as with many other items, you can not always go simply by the strictest of definitions. In this instance, it become somewhat of a personal decision.

10.   This is an interesting question. While there is no doubt that casinos (and gaming in general) generate millions of dollars in tax revenue, some have questions about the social impacts. While the majority of casino patrons may view an evening out at a casino as just that, an entertaining evening out, there is a small percentage that ends up with a gaming addiction. Thus, whether the Hard Rock Casinos are a desirable product or not, tends to become somewhat of a personal assessment.

Marketing ADventure Exercises

1. Ad Interpretation Challenge: Planned Obsolescence
    Ad: Apparel—Levi's New Collection Diamond Jeans

Levi's Diamond Jeans are a fashion forward product, designed to be on the edge of the fashion front. Such products typically do not stay at the forefront of fashion for long, thus encouraging their owners to move on to the next fashion item.

2. Ad Interpretation Challenge: "Shop Till You Drop"
    Ad: Apparel—Johnsons

This ad is promoting a 50 percent off sale. Such sales are designed to draw consumers in with special pricing enticements to encourage them to shop and spend more than they would under normal circumstances.

3. Ad Interpretation Challenge: "Congestion Toll"
    Ad: Auto—Porsche

Congestion tolls are tolls levied on drivers in some heavily congested areas in an effort to encourage them to ditch the car and utilize public transportation. Likewise, HOV (high-occupancy vehicle) and HOT (high-occupancy toll) lanes are being instituted in some areas to encourage greater carpooling.

4. Ad Interpretation Challenge: Consumerism
    Ad: Food and Beverage—McDonald's

McDonald's (along with other fast-food restaurants) has already begun to take some flake for the food they serve to millions of customers a day. Many critics are saying that fast-food restaurants are partly to blame for America's overweight problem. Many say the foods they serve contain too much fat and too many calories to be healthy.

5. Ad Interpretation Challenge: Environmental Sustainability
    Ad: Apparel—Timberland

Timberland is a big believer in supporting environmental sustainability efforts. For specific examples, take a look at their annual corporate social responsibility report.

6. Ad Interpretation Challenge: Consumer-Oriented Marketing
    Ad: Student Choice

This is the type marketing that all good marketing companies want to practice. In essence, they are practicing the marketing concept. Only by viewing the world through their consumers' eyes can a company build long and lasting customer relationships. Just about any of the companies whose ads appear here would fit into this category.

7.   Ad Interpretation Challenge: Innovative Marketing
        Ad: Apparel—Polartec

Yes. Polartec could easily be viewed as a company that practices innovative marketing. A review of its history (found on its website) details the continuous innovations that have helped to make this company one of the most respected in the outdoor clothing market.

8.   Ad Interpretation Challenge: Sense-of-Mission Marketing
        Ad: Travel and Tourism—Wild Drift

Wild Drift adventures believe in immersing its clients in the environment for the dual purposes of excitement and education. By educating its cliental in a manner that is also stimulating and invigorating, the company is not only making money but also instilling a long-term appreciation for the environment in their guests.

9.   Ad Interpretation Challenge: Pleasing Products
        Ad: Student Choice

Remember that pleasing products are products that consumers like; however, they may not actually be good for them in the long run. Two possible solutions to this exercise are Snickers (Food and Beverage—Snickers) and Burger King (Food and Beverage—Burger King). Both of these ads are promoting products that have high fat content and calorie counts. But they are both tasty.

10.   Ad Interpretation Challenge: Marketing Ethics
        Ad: Auto—Jeep

Jeep should adhere to its corporate marketing ethics policies. This takes away the ambiguity that may exist in different cultural settings. Corporate marketing ethics policies are established for just this type of situation. Because different cultures have different ethical standards, it is important that U.S.–based companies have and adhere to their own established corporate ethics policies.